LENIN'S ECONOMIC WRITINGS

LENIN'S ECONOMIC WRITINGS

edited by
Meghnad Desai

HUMANITIES PRESS INTERNATIONAL, INC.
Atlantic Highlands, NJ

First published in 1989 in the United States of America by
Humanities Press International, Inc.,
Atlantic Highlands, NJ 07716

Library of Congress Cataloging-in-Publication Data

Lenin, Vladimir Il'ich, 1870-1924.
  Lenin's economic writings.

  Bibliography: p.
  1. Marxian economics.   2. Economics.   I. Desai,
Meghnad.   II. Title.
HB97.5.L318   1989   335.4'12   88-22985
ISBN 0-391-03609-2

Printed in Great Britain

Contents

Acknowledgements

I would like to thank the late Professor Khaliq Naqvi of the Delhi School of Economics who first encouraged me to look at Lenin's economic writings during my stay there in 1970-71. Others who helped realise this project are Paul Auerbach, George Catephores, Sukhamoy Chakravarti, Ben Fine, Pandora Geddes and Bob Rowthorn. To them my thanks.

Lenin as an Economist

Introduction

Should one take Lenin seriously as an economist? He is
better known as a political leader, strategist and philosopher. When one thinks of famous Marxists who were also
economists of note in Lenin's time one thinks of Rosa
Luxemburg, Rudolf Hilferding and Nikolai Bukharin. But
though at first one does not readily think of Lenin as an
economist, his influence appears widespread in many
economic debates. *Imperialism, the Highest Stage of
Capitalism* (*Imperialism*, hereafter) is perhaps more widely
read than any other economics book/pamphlet. (During the
Cultural Revolution it was used almost as a catechism in
Chinese Universities. In 1973, when visiting Futan
University in Shanghai, I found out that *The Communist
Manifesto, Anti-Duhring* and *Imperialism* were the three
basic texts in the economics course.) The theory of
monopoly capitalism both in western radical circles and as
the official Soviet view of capitalism stems from *Imperialism*.
On the other hand, in many Third World countries, debates
in pre-revolutionary Russia about the social relations in
agriculture – feudal, capitalist or peculiarly Russian – still
command attention. Thus *The Development of Capitalism in
Russia* is a well-known book much cited in Indian debates
about these problems.

Despite these influential writings, there is no overall study
of Lenin as an economist. His education in law included
economics, as was the central European practice in those
days. His early writings are also on economic issues.
However in the year of the Lenin Centenary when I was
invited to a conference to contribute on Lenin as an
economist, I could only find one available account, that by
Alec Nove in a collection *Lenin, the Man, the Theorist, the*

Leader.[1] In the years since there has been some growth of
awareness about Lenin's work as an economist. A major
step in this was the publication of Neil Harding's *Lenin's
Political Thought*.[2] Harding has shown that Lenin not only
did a lot of economic writing but that his economic theory
was absolutely basic to his political thought and action. In
each of his two volumes, a crucial chapter is devoted to
economic analysis.[3]

This collection is offered therefore to acquaint readers
with a small selection of Lenin's economic writings. There
are 133 writings of various lengths which could be labelled
economic in his collected works.[4] The fourteen writings
chosen here are among the longer pamphlets/articles Lenin
wrote on specifically economic questions. They range, as we
shall see below, from early controversies with Narodniks
about the potential for capitalist development in Russia to
the consideration of co-operatives as suitable institutions for
a socialist country with a 'mixed' economy.

Given the range of choice I have had to leave some things
out while choosing others. I also decided to include any
particular piece in its entirety rather than giving doctored
excerpts from it. So *The Development of Capitalism in
Russia* was out of the question, being a book. But in order to
bring to readers' attention Lenin's lesser known pieces, I
also decided to leave *Imperialism* out. This is because it is a
long pamphlet and it is widely available. My aim was to
exhibit the multifaceted range of Lenin's writings. In this
introduction, my aim is twofold: to introduce the major
facets in Lenin's economic writings over a 30 year period and
to give a brief sketch of the particular pieces chosen and
show how they fit into an overall pattern.

At the risk of simplification, the 32 year period in Lenin's
public life from 1892 to 1924 can be divided into five phases.
(1) 1892–1902: from the early involvement in politics till the
split in the Russian Social Democratic Labour Party; (2)
1902–1907: the formation of Lenin's party, the 1905
revolution and the Czar's response to it; (3) 1908–February
1917: exile and theoretical work; (4) February–October
1917: the fall of the monarchy to the Soviet revolution; (5)
October 1917–1924: Lenin as leader of the Bolshevik Party
in power in Russia, and of the Third International. These

are broad phases of different lengths but equal in terms of the written work of Lenin. For our purposes, his economic writing was most evident in the first phase and the last two phases. There is very little in the second phase. Of the fourteen pieces reproduced here, two are taken from the first phase and nine from the last two phases. The middle phases are represented by three short pieces on strikes, which come from the third phase. The second phase is not represented. As readers will see from the complete list of economic writings, this period does not yield a substantial piece of economics though there are a number of short pieces on the agrarian strategy.

This ebb and flow of economic writings is of course determined by the multiple fronts on which Lenin operated. Now one issue became important, then another, and economics was in some the central issue, in others peripheral. In the first phase, Lenin was engaged in economic controversy with the leading Narodnik economists Danielson (writing as Nikolaion) and Vorontsov.[5] The central problem was whether Russia would grow along capitalist lines or whether it would bypass that phase entirely. The Narodniks argued that capitalism was an artificial, hothouse plant in Russia; the poverty of the peasantry meant that there would never be sufficient domestic markets to sustain industries, while international markets would be closed to Russia due to superior competition from the older industrial countries. This problem is the subject of the first of the pieces chosen (*On the So-Called Market Question*). But along with this Lenin wrote many other pieces: a short and intense attack on Narodnik economic philosophy, *Economic Romanticism*, and the longer classic, *Development of Capitalism in Russia*.

The other theme was the prospect of peasant agriculture as capitalism advanced. There was a debate going on in the German SPD about how the socialists should relate to the peasantry – as allies or as reactionary forces. The Russian debate among the Narodniks and Marxists was also about the likely survival of peasant agriculture in the future.[6] A very influential work in this area was Kautsky's *Die Agrarfrage* (The Agrarian Question). Lenin's long review article on it, along with his treatment of Bulgakov's writings, is our second selection chosen.

The second phase in Lenin's life is much better known. With the split in the Russian Social Democratic Labour Party, his energies were engaged in justifying his decision and his model of the revolutionary strategy in Russia against the rival claimants to the title of a socialist party. The revolution in 1905 and the subsequent concessions on the issue of elections, the debate about whether to participate in the elections to the Bulygin Duma, the manoeuvres of Witte, Stolypin and others – all these topics crop up in the writings of this period. The only topic one can call 'economic' in the writings of this period is Lenin's analysis of the changing agrarian relations in Russia and his exposition of the Bolshevik agrarian policy.

The third phase is a quieter phase in Lenin's political life. Neither intra-party battles nor revolutionary events happened as between 1902–1907. From 1908 up to the outbreak of the First World War, Lenin's writings are devoted to deeper questions of philosophy (*Materialism and Empirio Criticism*) as much as economics and politics. From his exile, Lenin kept an active involvement in Russia as well as European socialist affairs. Only after August 1914 is there an increasing urgency and anger as the various socialist parties adopted a chauvinist stance. It is then that Lenin began his study of Hilferding and Hobson to produce *Imperialism*. However as an example of the care and attention with which Lenin followed the minutest developments in Russian economic life, the three pamphlets on strikes are reproduced here. They show a blend of analysis of economic statistics and revolutionary theory.

The period between the February and the October revolutions is once again a phase of intense activity but the focus has now shifted from distant analysis to immediate tasks. Beginning with a trenchant analysis of the limitations of the bourgeois-democratic revolution, Lenin moves over to a formulation of the alternative programme. This is done in a series of rapid improvisations. The philosophical background is *The State and Revolution*, but the practical tasks take up much of the time in the *April Theses* and in *The Impending Catastrophe and How to Combat It* (which we include in the selection). From debating the nature of the state in Marxist theory and in a future socialist state, Lenin has to move on to talk about concrete matters such as how to secure control over banks and how to solve the food crisis. Given more time, a better blending of theory and policy might have been accomplished, but luckily events moved at a pace which did not permit speculation about revolution. The task of accomplishing the revolution proved to be much more urgent.

The last period from the revolution to his final writing is crowded with policy statements, polemics with opposition parties and with comrades of the Bolshevik Party, reviews of achievement on the occasions of anniversaries and appeals for solidarity. This is a period when Lenin was literally thinking on his feet. Immediate tasks were much more mundane and urgent. But even then there had to be a political/economic analysis of every issue. There are six short selections on these issues (chapters 7–12). It is only when we get to the period of the New Economic Policy (NEP) that Lenin undertakes the task of explaining the new policy in some detail. He puts it into a political perspective. The short-run problems of running the economy and the long-run tasks of building socialism, the search for policies and institutions which would best serve the needs of the time – all these are brought together in the brilliant analysis of *The Tax in Kind* (included in this selection). But even as NEP became established, Lenin continued to search for institutions more appropriate to push the 'mixed' economy into a socialist direction. The last selection *On Co-operation* is one of the last things Lenin wrote. It is another example of his constant search for new solutions starting from a firmly grounded theoretical perspective.

This rapid survey of the five phases should give some idea of the variety of themes Lenin dealt with in his economic writings. Obviously I have only pointed to the themes which are illustrated in the selections but as the complete bibliography shows there is much else. In the remaining parts of the introduction I develop the major themes at a greater length.

Economic Themes in Lenin's Writings:
(a) The Prospect of Capitalist Development in Russia

What is very hard for us to remember today is that in the 40 year period between the death of Marx and the death of Lenin, a living Marxian tradition existed in Germany and in Russia.[7] The central debate about the prospects of capitalism in Russia among the Narodniks and the various schools of Marxists was carried out mainly, if not entirely, in the terms of Marx's analysis. No rival school of economics, such as the neo-classical economics of Walras or Menger, made the slightest impact on this debate. Lenin was one among a number of writers, all of them well-read in Marx though differing sharply in their political perspectives, who participated in this debate. Danielson, writing under the pseudonym of Nikolaion, led the Narodniks in his day, but his perspective was based on a study of Marx. It is important to recall that he was the chief Russian correspondent of Engels until the latter's death. Marxism in this period was not a dead letter and Marx was not the 'underground' economist that Keynes later thought him. Marxism had not turned into a dogma nor a weapon with which to beat one's opponents on the head. The only possible rival school of economics to Marxism would have been the (now forgotten) German Historical School. Friedrich List was perhaps the other major economist – read much more widely, and much more relevant to the problems of economic development, than what are now paraded in economics books as the great names of late 19th century economic theory – Walras, Jevons, Menger.

The Russian debate was carried out in close parallel with the debate among the German Marxists. But the latter were dealing with the problems of a relatively more developed capitalist economy – the question of trade cycles and crises for instance.[8] The Russian perspective was that of 'a less developed country'. This expression had not as yet been invented but Russia was at this time the classic backward country undergoing a process of capitalist development. The theory of development and of underdevelopment, of the many problems of capital formation, surplus mobilisation, the dualism of the traditional and the modern sectors existing side by side, of the impact of foreign capital, of the pattern of industrialisation – all these were discussed at length and in a Marxist theoretical framework by the Russian political economists. And not by the virtue of his fame acquired later on, but on the evidence of writings of this period alone, Lenin was heads above his rival debaters.

This is amply substantiated by his major work *The Development of Capitalism in Russia*. Written in prison and in exile, with materials gathered with the help of friends and in private libraries during stops on the way to Siberia, it is a book that repays reading even today. Lenin shows here not only his firm grasp of Marx's theory and the way it is applicable to a backward but developing economy, but also his ability to combine this with detailed statistical and factual analysis of the many sectors of the Russian economy. Reports on agrarian conditions and factory statistics, the most boring and turgid of government publications, were read, summarised and put into the theoretical context of the growth of capitalist relations in Russia. Nothing on that scale has been accomplished by an economist, Marxist or other, for another underdeveloped country.

What are called radical or even revolutionary critiques of underdevelopment today fall sadly short of this.[9] Current critiques much too readily assert that development through a capitalist path is *impossible* for the Third World, that a socialist upheaval is inevitable if not imminent. The radical critics fault capitalism on grounds of creating extreme poverty, inequalities and exploitation. The authors doubt that development can proceed much further while it is based on the foundations of such misery and exploitation. An indictment of foreign capital and of the whole nexus of neo-colonialism is added to this, and often the blame for underdevelopment is laid at foreign doors. Third World groups or Fourth World groups urge an abandonment of the capitalist path and the fashioning of a new way adapted to the age old ways of the Third World. Intermediate technology, land reform, simple communal life patterns, isolation from western or developed countries – are all mooted as cures.

Contrast this analysis with the Russian debate. The Narodnik critique of capitalism in Russia anticipates much of the modern radical critique. Capitalism *was* causing misery. By breaking up the old communal agriculture and destroying the handicrafts, capitalism *did* lead to poverty. This meant for the Narodniks that the home market, the purchasing power of the Russian population, was shrinking. Capitalists could not hope to sell their products to the people they were making poor. This is what led them to seek foreign markets. The limits of capitalist growth in Russia were defined by the shrinkage of the home market; the search for foreign markets, the Narodniks thought, could in the end only prove illusory. A backward country would find itself shut out of the market of developed countries such as Germany, England or USA. Capitalism was a hothouse plant, an imported artificial growth unsuited to Russian conditions. The need was to reject capitalism and to build a new economy reviving the Russian *mir* – the tradition of communal property. One need only add that, while it is now well known that the Narodniks were a populist group, as far as their contemporaries were concerned Danielson and Vorontsov, the chief exponents of the above analysis, were Marxists.

In a substained polemical debate over nearly ten years, Lenin sought to expose the fallacies in this position. 'Economic Romanticism' was the way he described the analysis of Danielson and Vorontsov. Using Marx's Scheme of Expanded Reproduction he showed firstly that no automatic or absolute limit existed on the growth of capitalism in Russia.[10] Indeed, the cause of Russia's backwardness was the underdevelopment of Russian capitalism. Lenin was by no means an apologist for capitalist growth, nor did he fail to point out its contradictions and costs. But he saw the growth of capitalist relations in Russia as a progressive step. From the feudal and in parts 'Asiatic' conditions, Russia was coming under the growing influence of the capitalist mode of production. Whatever the costs, this was a progressive step. It was also predictable using a Marxist scheme of history (see *Economic Romanticism*, in particular).

Lenin did not just assert his views. He used Marx's Scheme for Expanded Reproduction to illustrate and argue his point. It is well known that Marx's scheme involves a two sector division – Dept I producing machine goods and Dept II producing wage goods. Marx then shows the conditions under which sustained capitalist growth can take place. (There is much disagreement about whether Marx's demonstration shows that such crisis-free growth can occur only by economy-level planning and allocation of surplus value between departments from above, or whether it stands in contradiction to his analysis of dynamics of cyclical growth in capitalism. This debate is well reviewed by Rosa Luxemburg in her *The Accumulation of Capital*, and is still alive.) Lenin's use of Marx's Scheme goes beyond the department framework. In the *So-called Market Question*, he sets up an economy with six producers and three branches of industry. To simplify matters, Lenin assumes that each producer produces the same value of output, and in each branch the rate of surplus value is the same. As a consequence the total value of output in the economy is given and does not change for the periods over which Lenin traces the development of the economy. Let us look briefly at his analysis.

To begin with we have a 'natural' economy. Each of the six producers spends some time in producing output in each of the three branches of industry – agriculture, manufacturing and extractive. We have the ideal self-sufficient village economy. There is no buying and selling among the producers. In the next period, one of them decides to drop out of manufacturing but double his production of the extractive good. This leads to a reshuffling of output among the other five since aggregate output of each producer, each branch and the economy as a whole is constant. This immediately leads to trade between the producers.

As the development of the economy is traced over six periods, there is progressive specialisation and the economy ends up with three producers, one in each branch, with the other three working as labourers. There is buying and selling of goods as well as of labour power. Sales of commodities equal two-thirds of total output and sales of labour power equal one-third of total value of output. The progress of specialisation and of the division of labour has created markets for goods and for labour power, maintaining the stringent but obviously unrealistic assumption of no growth in total output.

It is well known that capitalism emerged in various countries from its origins in a natural economy, in petty commodity production. This is a rich and complex historical process and there is a lively debate on the forces that caused the transition from feudalism to capitalism in Europe. Lenin attempts in this essay on the home market to provide a plausible scenario for a purely internal development. It is not a description of a historical process but gives an analytical scheme for understanding the process in its essentials. Lenin's development of Marx's scheme is quite innovative; it has been ignored for much too long and deserves wider discussion.

It may seem something of a paradox that Lenin is optimistic about the possibility of capitalist development in Russia. But this is very much in line with what we should call the '19th century Marxist' view of capitalism as a progressive phase. The notion that capitalist development was progressive should not be taken to mean that it was harmonious nor that it did not generate poverty and misery. It was the nature of all development to be imbued with contradictions and driven further by them. For Marxists, capitalism was preferable to feudalism and to argue otherwise or to seek escape into alternative national paths to development were romantic fantasies. The idea that capitalism and economic development were incompatible would have astonished Lenin's generation of Marxists. After all, the point of all the development and the contradictions was that capitalism created the preconditions for progress towards socialism.

Lenin's analysis is thus in great contrast to present-day Marxist theories of underdevelopment. These theories set up arguments whereby capitalism generates retardation and underdevelopment rather than their opposite. There is however sufficient empirical evidence that over the 40 years since the end of the Second World War, economic growth *has* taken place in countries of the Third World. The Newly Industrialising Countries (NICs) threaten to penetrate the markets of the developed countries and have to be kept out by quotas, tariffs and other arrangements.[11] It is this empirical evidence that has led to challenges to the 'development of underdevelopment' theme, by Bill Warren as well as others. Lenin's essay should thus be of great interest in sharpening this debate. (Related articles in the list below are 5, 6, 7, 8, 11, 14.)

(b) Agriculture and Agrarian Relations

Russia was in many ways the first 'less developed' country. There were other countries, such as Germany, that in the nineteenth century progressed rapidly from an agricultural/feudal state to an industrialised one, but none of them had the features which Russia had. These features – low urbanisation, predominance of small-scale peasant agriculture, low level of agricultural technology, endemic misery and poverty – are shared by today's less developed countries. But Russia was also undergoing a period of rapid growth between 1890 and 1914, especially in the countryside. Lenin's writings are frequently occupied with the encroachment of developed capitalist relations into agriculture. This is one reason why the debates of nearly a century ago are still relevant today.

The Third World countries are all primarily agricultural. If they ever experienced feudalism, it was in a very different form from European feudalism. The stagnation of traditional agriculture created in different places a variety of social institutions in the countryside. Some had exploitative, big landlords who lived by extracting maximum rent from an impoverished population. There were tribes with some form of monarchical leadership, or in other places a dependent relationship of landlords and tenants, and again between tenants and their farm workers. The course of imperialism and the international development of capitalism has broken the traditional pattern nearly everywhere, but agrarian relations have not until recently taken on a capitalist character. The agricultural labourer is unlike the industrial labourer. Often he is a sharecropper, or a small farmer with inadequate land working for a wage on the side, or he works for the same master on a more or less permanently tied basis. He is not exclusively a seller of labour power in exchange for a wage as is the industrial worker. Frequently, as in some parts of Africa, 'he' is a woman.

The emergence of 'free labour' in agriculture is

accompanied by social upheaval in the countryside. The enclosure movement was such an upheaval. The 'Green Revolution', i.e. the introduction of high-yield variety seeds in rice, wheat and other crops, is another such event.[12] After years of stagnation, there is now a prospect of agriculture being *profitable* – of being productive of large amounts of surplus value. When agriculture becomes profitable, then the old ties of landlord-tenant, farmer-worker begin to break up rapidly. Tenants are dispossessed, sharecroppers denied access to land, the tied labourers are forced to fend for themselves. What one witnesses is the transformation of agriculture into a capitalist activity.

This has not yet happened on a large scale. However, wherever the Green Revolution has had an impact, critics have decried its effects on social relations. Many have feared violent social upheaval in the countryside or predicted it hopefully. It is interesting in this context to read Lenin's writings on the encroachment of capitalist relations in Russian agriculture. This is a question he deals with at length in *The Development of Capitalism in Russia*. I have indicated his other writings on this subject and their contemporary relevance in the complete list of his writings.

The selection I have chosen on agriculture is Lenin's long review article of Kautsky's *Die Agrarfrage* (The Agrarian Question). Kautsky's book is not available in English even 85 years after its publication in German.[13] This is a great loss since there is a common impression that Marxian analysis fails to come to grips with agriculture. It is true that Marx himself wrote very sketchily about agrarian relations, and agriculture is not an important part of his model of capitalist growth. Kautsky's book, however, is the most detailed application of a Marxian framework to the agrarian situation. Lenin's account is available in English and we can get a synopsis of Kautsky's book from it. It is obvious from the beginning how highly Lenin thought of Kautsky's book. Kautsky's analysis concerned agriculture in developed countries, while Lenin's work was mainly with under-developed Russian agriculture. They both, however, successfully and imaginatively used Marxian analysis. This account of Kautsky's work, and much of Lenin's writing in this period, is a useful corrective to the idea that somehow a pure 'agrarianist' approach is necessary to understand problems of the peasant, that both neo-classical economic theory and Marxian economic theory have somehow failed to adapt their models of industrial activity to the agrarian situation.[14] (Related writings in the list are 15, 20, 21, 29, 31.)

(c) Strikes; Economic and Political

One of the constant preoccupations of Marxists is to be able to understand and interpret day to day developments in the economy in a way that is better than mere description. Every day we are inundated by economic news and statistics on exchange rates and balance of payments, on growth of consumer credit, of rises in unemployment along with wages and prices. How is one to take all these facts and say more than merely banal things about exploitation or the evils of capitalism? Can one use Marxism as a tool for concrete analysis of short-term economic events without relapsing into either sheer journalism or empty rhetoric?

This is a challenge met in the three selections on strikes reprinted here. I have included them because they illustrate Lenin's use of theory in analysis of current economic statistics, advancing the political lessons to be gained from statistics without divorcing them from economic analysis. The articles on strikes appeared at a time when strike activity was on the upswing in all the developed capitalist countries. Russia had just been through a business cycle trough and was on the upswing again, which lasted till the outbreak of the war.

The starting point of all these papers is the published statistics on strikes. The distinction between economic and political strikes was embodied in the official Russian statistics, and made by the Czar's ministers with much greater disapproval of political strikes than of economic ones. Lenin looks at their frequency, the data on the percentage of workers involved, the regional spread of strike activity, the size of the establishments whose workers struck most often, etc. Workers in the heavy industries were better organised, more politically conscious than their fellow workers in other industries and formed the vanguard in

1905. The industry employing the largest number of workers was the textile industry and there was a dialectical interplay between the vanguard and the most populous industries. This dialectical relation is reflected in the comparative frequency and timing of economic and political strikes in the two spheres.

This work of analysis and interpretation first undertaken in 1910 (*Strike Statistics in Russia*, reprinted here) is followed through in several writings. Statistics are updated to 1912 and the classification by industry and type of strike carried further. Three more such articles are reproduced here and the complete list of Lenin's writings indicates some more (Nos 53, 57, 62, 69).

(d) Imperialism

As explained above, *Imperialism*, Lenin's best known economic pamphlet, is not included here. But any consideration of Lenin as an economist would be incomplete without looking at the theory of monopoly capitalism. However there is another consideration that makes it imperative that we confront this celebrated work. When we look at Lenin's economic writings as a comprehensive whole, *Imperialism* stands out as an anomaly. In this pamphlet, Lenin takes a dramatically different view of the prospects for capitalist development from that which he took in his debates with the Narodniks. What is also not fully appreciated is that after the October revolution, when it came to the problem of running the Russian economy, Lenin could be said to have abandoned the vision of *Imperialism* at least as far as the domestic economy was concerned. *Imperialism* became a basic text for the Third International's revolutionary strategies for the advanced capitalist countries but at the same time Lenin followed his earlier view of capitalist development in economic policy-making. As this view is bound to be controversial it is necessary to look at *Imperialism* in some detail.

The connection of *Imperialism* with Hobson's work is well known. What is not well known is that Hobson's view on imperialism was different from Lenin's. Hobson thought imperialist expansion was economically unprofitable and a waste of resources. The race for large chunks of empty African territory among the European powers in the last decades of the 19th century struck Hobson as irrational. These African countries could not provide markets for the products of industrialised countries and would cost much more than they would return. Hobson thus goes on to demonstrate with all the data he can command that Britain would be better off concentrating on exports to the growing markets of European countries rather than to the remote bush.

Lenin's analysis is, of course, different but it is worth noting that by imperialism Lenin means not so much the metropolis-colony relation but more the relations of financial and industrial penetration within similarly developed countries. The metropolis-colony relation one may call *vertical* imperialism, while the relation between similarly developed economies can be called *horizontal* imperialism. Political domination was an essential part of vertical imperialism (Britain and India) but in horizontal imperialism penetration was often only by economic means (France and Russia, Britain and Argentina). Lenin's concept of imperialism is thus wider in scope than Hobson's, and comprises all unequal relations between capitalist countries.[15]

The profound shift in Lenin's view of the prospects of capitalism was of course caused by the outbreak of the First World War and the collapse of the Second International in the face of chauvinism on the part of workers. But the shock of the war was very great for a whole generation which had grown up under the optimistic assumptions of 19th century rationalism. For others, such as Bernard Shaw and Bertrand Russell, the irrationalism of the war was a great blow to deeply held beliefs in Reason and Progress. Lenin sought an explanation for this aberration in the changing nature of capitalism.

For this purpose, he used Hilferding's theory of finance capital and integrated those aspects of Marx's theory of accumulation which predicted a growing concentration of capital in large industrial units, with the banks playing the role of providers of money capital, to help the movement towards mergers and integration. The need to export capital

and commodities becomes crucial to the development of
capitalism in this view. The division of world capitalism into
separate countries then provides the link between capitalists
of a particular country and the state which serves to extend
the search for markets beyond its borders. The scramble for
markets thus becomes the focus of inter-country rivalry.

This view of capitalism introduces internal limits to the
size of the market, and the need to seek markets abroad for
the sustained development of capitalism. This is contrary to
the view Lenin argued for in his essay on the home market.
Of course, the subject of *Imperialism* was the developed
capitalist nations of Britain, France and Germany, but there
is an uneasy contradiction here. Rosa Luxemburg, in her
critique of Marx's reproduction schemes, had raised exactly
the same problem of the limits imposed by domestic markets
for the realisation of surplus value. In his use of the
reproduction schemes against the Narodniks in the earlier
period, Lenin accepted uncritically Marx's conclusions that
sustained capitalist growth is possible. Now he shifts to the
view that export markets are essential to capitalist growth.

It is possible to reconcile these two contradictory views by
saying that in *Imperialism* Lenin was speaking of the
monopoly capital phase of capitalism whereas the earlier
work concerns competitive capitalism. This cannot however
be accepted as an adequate answer. Rosa Luxemburg had
pointed out that in Marx's original scheme, competitive
capitalism and all, there was a realisation problem that could
not be wished away by manipulating arithmetical tables:
someone had to be found to purchase all that was produced
before the surplus value extracted from workers could be
realised as profits. In addition the distinction between
competitive and monopoly capitalism is taken to be a
temporal, historical one, with one phase succeeding
another, whereas these schema are both conceptual, with no
necessary historical progression (or retrogression) from one
to the other. Monopolies, backed by state support and
subsidies, were crucial to the development of merchant
capitalism in England, France, Holland, etc. The laissez-
faire phase of industrial capitalism flourished in England,
but even there it was England's monopoly position in
international trade in manufactured products, as a result of

being the first industrialised country, which was crucial. Later industrialising countries had cartels, oligopolies and state corporations throughout their capitalist development.

The economic situation differed in the 1900s from the 1860s in that now the size of the individual firm was bigger. The Second Industrial Revolution was in steel, chemicals and electricity. Economies of scale in this category of industries were much greater than in cotton textiles and so large firms became the norm. Largeness is easily confused with monopoly position, and economic concentration for lack of competition. Capitalism had changed since Marx's days as a result of technological as well as other factors. Change was taken for decay by Lenin, due to the pessimism engendered by the war.

Whatever Lenin's reasons for adopting the term imperialism as synonymous with monopoly capitalism, he still does not provide us with an analytical theory for this concept – analytical in the sense that his argument in the *So-called Market Question* is analytical. This would require linking such a concept to a value theory – Marx's value theory. In *Capital* Marx speaks of competitive capitalism, and it is this that he uses to demonstrate the systematic nature of exploitation by which all surplus value is pooled before being apportioned as equal rate of profit on the various individual capitals. If monopoly capital departs from the competitive case it must involve unequal rates of profit. The transformation of surplus value into profits must then be shown to lead to an outcome of unequal rates of profit in a systematic way. This is a question of theory, an analytical basis for a concept such as monopoly capital. Lenin certainly does not provide this. Perhaps he did not have time to do all this in the midst of the war. What is surprising is the tendency ever since to repeat Lenin's statements as a catechism, with no attempt to provide a Marxian value theoretic basis to it. It would take us far afield to survey the attempts made to do this but suffice it to say they are inadequate. They have employed Keynesian macro-economics or Marshallian static micro-economics concepts of excess capacity, or the degree of monopoly; but they have not been rigorously founded in a value theory that could be linked to Marx's work (or any other school of economics for that matter).

There is however a further aspect to Lenin's writing on this subject. After the February and October revolutions, Lenin seems to revert to his earlier views on capitalism. In debates with the left, he characterises state capitalism, such as existed in wartime Germany, as a progressive phase beyond capitalism. He again reverts to his 1890s view that Russia's problem, after the revolution as before it, was the backwardness of its capitalism.

Neil Harding sees this clearly. In Volume 2 of his book, *The Dictatorship of the Proletariat*, he says,

> In his next major piece of writing, 'Left Wing Childishness and the Petty Bourgeois Mentality' completed in early May 1918 Lenin reverts to elements of his *initial* theoretical analysis (that is his analysis of the development of capitalism in Russia developed in the 1890s) to substantiate his new emphasis on the need for a resolute proletarian dictatorship. (p 206)

This is not to imply that Harding's views would be similar to those expressed here.

> Lenin's economic analysis had become more complex and complicated. In dealing with the peculiarities of the Russian situation he had to graft on to his analysis of international finance capitalism large elements of his original theoretical analysis of the development of capitalism in Russia. (p 207)

In my view, such a grafting can only lead to a muddle because these two analyses imply contradictory views of the possibilities of capitalist growth in a single country. The charge in the political forces at the top had not affected the backwardness of Russia's capitalism as an economic fact.

(e) Economic Policy in an 'Intermediate Regime'[16]

The view that Russia's problem was the backwardness of its capitalism emerges most clearly in *The Tax in Kind*. But before we get to it, we need to look at Lenin's writings in the period between February and October 1917. It is tempting with the hindsight that history affords us to foresee the forthcoming October upheaval in Lenin's writing at this time. But such temptation should be resisted. Lenin discusses the problems of a capitalist economy in a specially troublesome phase – after the overthrow of monarchy but during wartime. The bourgeois democratic revolution had not quite taken shape – there were as yet no elected parliaments. Only Soviets represented elected assemblies. Everywhere there was an economic breakdown and the problem of regaining some control over matters.

Lenin's analysis of economic policy problems in this context has much relevance to many countries today. The best that could be expected was a radicalisation of the bourgeois democratic regime. Old capitalist relations still existed but to some extent they were in a state of shock.· The capacity of the capitalists to resist change and add to the chaos was also considerable. The need therefore was for the government to gain an upper hand in the struggle to restore the economy to normal conditions.

In *The Impending Catastrophe and How to Combat It* Lenin analyses the tasks of the provisional government in the emergency famine conditions as 'control, supervision, accounting, regulation by the State, introduction of a proper distribution of labour power in the production and distribution of goods, husbanding of the people's forces, the elimination of all wasteful effort, economy of effort'. The themes of supervision, accounting and control and economic planning in general were to recur when Lenin had to tackle the problems of civil war and famine. But for the present, Lenin was urging economic planning on an *intermediate* regime. Lenin knew, of course, that while the government professed to being 'revolutionary-democratic', its inactivity and delay were serving the capitalists. Consider the following passage from *The Impending Catastrophe* and its relevance to the many governments today which have a full-scale planning apparatus (e.g. India):

> The present, modern republican-democratic sabotage of every kind of control, accounting and supervision consists in the capitalists 'eagerly' accepting in words the 'principle' of control and the necessity for controls (as, of course, do all Mensheviks and Socialist-Revolutionaries), insisting only that this control be introduced 'gradually', methodically and in a 'state-regulated' way. In practice, however, these specious catchwords serve to conceal the *frustration* of control, its nullification, its reduction to a fiction, the mere playing at control, the delay of

all business-like and practically effective measures, the creation of extraordinarily complicated, cumbersome and bureaucratically lifeless institutions of control which are hopelessly dependent on the capitalists, and which do absolutely nothing and cannot do anything.

Lenin proceeds to list the principal measures which the government could implement. They are: amalgamation of all banks under state control, or their nationalisation; nationalisation of the largest, monopolistic capitalist syndicates, abolition of commercial secrecy and compulsory organisation of all merchants, industrialists and employees on the one hand and of the consumers on the other hand. Lenin is not even advocating confiscation (i.e. nationalisation without compensation) of private property. Nationalisation is an instrument for control and regulation but it falls far short of socialism, as Lenin was aware.

On the question of bank nationalisation, as of rationing, Lenin draws a distinction between the reactionary-bureaucratic way of doing things and the revolutionary-democratic alternative. He shows how partial rationing – i.e. rationing of poor people's food and a 'free' market for the rich – leads to suffering for the poor, when the rich can evade all regulation. He ties up the question of rationing with that of control over consumption, especially control over the consumption of the rich exercised by the poor, i.e. by the majority.

It is well known that Marx himself said little about economic policy under socialism or in the transition stage. We have only the *Critique of the Gotha Programme* on this subject, and even this is a critique of a platform for a party which does not actually wield power. While the Paris Commune was held up as a possible political form for a post-revolutionary government, there was little by way of economic policy in the Commune. Lenin is surely the first Marxist to discuss in detail the practical problems of economic policy from a Marxist theoretical position. And he did this both when in opposition and in power.

As *The Impending Catastrophe* shows, he does not fall for revolutionary slogans. His analysis is always backed up by relevant international background and statistical detail. At this time, he had formed a number of policy measures in his mind but we notice increasingly that the example of a capitalist economy run along the lines of a single organisation as in wartime Germany impressed Lenin very much. He knew that the purpose of such organisation was not to benefit the people, but the techniques of organisation and the logic of interdependence and concentration which it made bare were for Lenin a great source of lessons when the Bolsheviks came to power. Through the next five years, this possibility of organising for control – of effective planning and co-ordination – is reiterated by Lenin again and again. But for those who are over-impressed by planning, nationalisation measures and extensions of the public sector, *The Impending Catastrophe* is indispensable as it points out that there can be a large gap between formal measures and actual economic reality if the political will is lacking to give content to such measures. (Related papers are 80 and 81.)

(f) Policy Making for a Revolutionary Government

The period from October 1917 to late 1923, from which date ill-health prevented Lenin from doing any work, was an extremely busy one. A fledgling socialist country could hardly have been born under worse circumstances. Between October 1917 and March 1918 when the Treaty of Brest Litovsk had to be signed, it seemed that, having won power, the Bolsheviks would be able to implement their vision of a state along the lines laid down by the Paris Commune. But the continuing war, and the humiliating terms on which the Russians had to end it, were only the first taste of the severe problems ahead. In the next three years, Russia faced a civil war and famine. This phase also saw a much more comprehensive nationalisation of all aspects of the economy than the Bolsheviks had originally envisaged. The presence of rationing and shortages led to regulation of consumption as well. This was the phase of war communism. Once the civil war ended successfully for the Bolsheviks they began to pay attention to the tremendous cost that had been imposed on the people by the long period of shortages. There was unrest in many cities and a serious uprising on the Kronstadt, erstwhile bastion of the Bolsheviks. It was in this context that the Party Conference in March 1921 adopted a change of tactics and opened the phase of the New Economic Policy. This allowed much greater freedom of trade, growth of small businesses, a free market in foodgrains, etc. This phase continued after Lenin's death till the late 1920s.

It is this complex period that is represented by the last seven papers in this collection. The first four papers are written in a mood of combat against the White Russian forces, the ostracising of Russia by the Great Powers and the constant threat of famine. Procurement of food and its enhanced production are the immediate problems. Food policy – mobilisation of food supplies for the urban areas and the army, the choice of pricing policy as compared to a policy of compulsory procurement, the political battle for the support of the peasants – is tackled by Lenin again and again up to his very last days. The question of institutional transformation of Russian agriculture so as to build socialism is, in this period, a very vexing one. Lenin was thinking very hard at this time about ways of transforming co-operatives into socialist institutions. (Indeed, the selection *Measures Governing the Transition*, though brief, poses the problem very clearly. The last selection in this book again returns to the question of co-operation.) In the light of Russian experience with collectivisation we can only regret that Lenin's life was cut short before he had obtained an answer to this question. The cost of this was enormous to the Russian economy and the Russian people. The political dilemma is seen to be acute as we read Lenin's writings on this question, and the constant search for a solution is also apparent.

The problem of finding new organisational forms was however wider than the problem of co-operatives. 'Accounting and control' was thought by Lenin to be 'the fundamental problem facing the socialist revolution on the morrow of the overthrow of the bourgeoisie'. The victory of the poor over the rich had been accomplished by lightning assaults, by expropriation. Now, instead of the methods of warfare, the methods of administration had to be used in defeating the bourgeoisie who were still around. Lenin not only had to think out the *theory* of socialist economic policy but also had to convince his followers that the task of *administering* the revolution was important. (The quotations here and in the two paragraphs below are from *Immediate Tasks*.)

'Administering a revolution' is however an assignment full of paradoxes. To begin with it meant 'the positive and constructive work of setting up an extremely intricate and delicate system of new organisational relationships extending to the planned production and distribution of the goods required for the existence of tens of millions of people'. Translated into practical terms, it meant several unpleasant choices. Revolution was not any longer just a 'festival of the oppressed'. Labour discipline had to be learnt, a compromise had to be consciously made regarding the hiring of bourgeois experts. The ultimate goal of establishing socialism had to be firmly kept in mind and the class struggle that was going on had to be grasped to achieve victory. Devoid of this political context, these measures would be no different from that in a bourgeois economy. The distinction was regarding who held political power. Lenin was clear that a workers' state could not behave like a bourgeois state. Thus the policy of hiring experts was a compromise but a compromise fully admitted and explained in terms of the political struggle. There was to be no secrecy (at least then) about the policies. 'To conceal from the people the fact that the enlistment of bourgeois experts by means of extremely high salaries is a retreat from the principles of the Paris Commune would be sinking to the level of bourgeois politicians and deceiving the people.'

Lenin thus had to do the tasks Marx left untouched – construction of socialist economic policy in theoretical and practical terms. To this we have to add the task of leadership. The writings in this period contain exhortations, polemics and frequent calls to battle. The slogans of construction have to replace the slogans of war on the bourgeoisie and the new slogans have to be made meaningful to the people.

> Keep regular and honest accounts of money, manage economically, do not be lazy, do not steal, observe the strictest labour discipline – it is these slogans justly scorned by the

revolutionary proletariat when the bourgeoisie used them to conceal its role as a exploiting class, that are now, since the overthrow of the bourgeoisie, becoming the immediate and the principle slogans of the movement.

In this question of the forms of organisation at an enterprise level as well as at the economy level, Lenin has been seen by some authors as pursuing two contradictory policies. In the earlier days after October 1917, he had a model of the post-revolutionary state as modelled on the Paris Commune, with a great amount of decentralisation, local autonomy and workers' control. It was after the hopes of an international workers' upheaval had been disappointed that Lenin turned to the one man management rule. The Workers' Opposition was thus consistent with Lenin's communard position, but political imperatives forced the abandonment of that model in favour of a centralist and hierarchical position.[17]

This is certainly true and persuasive. There is no need however to freeze the alternatives to the two pursued by Lenin. Thus if he had lived on to witness a restored Soviet economy as a result of NEP, there is no reason to suppose that he would not have explored new ways of tackling the question of forms of organisation. His willingness to overcome a lifelong distrust of co-operatives in the last years of his life was witness to the pragmatic strain in Lenin's thinking on policy issues.

During the 1980s, socialist governments in the Soviet Union, China and in Eastern Europe have begun to ask fundamental questions about the nature of their economy. The questions of incentives and motivation for the ordinary people to work towards a socialist commonwealth, long taken for granted, are being raised again. Is there scope for a bit more of a free market or is any such concession the beginning of a retreat from socialism which can only become a rout? There is similarly a questioning of the notion of property. Are there only two kinds of property rights, private and state ownership, or are there intermediate forms which can combine the incentives of profitability with a collectivistic ethos? Such questions have been raised in China, in Hungary and most recently by Gorbachev in the Soviet Union. There is a growing realisation that planning cannot work merely from the top down. There needs to be a new combination of the plan and the market. In his speech to the Central Committee of the CPSU (June 1987), these were the questions that Gorbachev raised.

There are clear and conscious echoes in the present Soviet debate with that during the NEP phase. There is a need to make a transition from a regulated (in some opinion over-regulated) economy to an economy which is semi-planned/semi-market. There is no ready-made formula for this which can be quickly installed in practice. There are not only issues of relative efficiency of plan versus market in resource allocation, a debate which has gone on for a long time, but on the politically much more sensitive issue of property rights. New forms of ownership are being advocated. This debate has equal relevance for those socialists in capitalist economies, where disenchantment with nationalisation is widespread and social ownership remains as yet a face-saving formula rather than a well reasoned strategy. The issues are complex and there is a need to be both flexible and principled. Lenin's writings on co-operatives as well as other issues throughout this last phase show that he was always willing to be flexible, but also to argue his point in a way that took the existing theory and stretched it a bit further.

Nowhere is the challenge to advance theory and to adapt it as objective conditions change more apparent than in Lenin's many writings on food policy. In the period of war communism, when the very survival of the Russian revolution was in doubt, he opposed a policy of relying on the price mechanism for calling forth higher supplies of food. The *Report on Combating the Famine*, which is reprinted here, is an example of the making of economic policy under severe political compulsions. The adoption of a 'free market policy' was not just a technical choice; it was a political choice that the government in the period of civil war could not afford to make. The survival of the population and of the proletarian state take predominance over objectives such as achieving a high growth rate, or achieving economic efficiency in the ordinary sense. In this context, political means and slogans are adapted to achieve political ends.

There is one further aspect of the period of war

communism which deserves some discussion. The need to ration goods by physical control rather than by market relations, the virtual disappearance of money, which was useless since it could not be used to buy goods, and the central allocation of labour, gave some Bolsheviks, especially Bukharin and Preobrazhensky, the feeling that indeed communism had arrived. But while they and some others were enthusiastic about war communism, Lenin did not record any such positive feelings about what, after all, was a wartime scarcity regime imposed by outside forces. He sees the many steps taken as necessary to meet the emergency, as necessary cuts and not as achievements.

This comes out in the fact that most of the writings of this period concern particular, practical measures. At many crucial junctures in the past when Lenin wished to argue the merits of a policy, his way was to write a long pamphlet explaining the policy in political terms. He did this in 1902 and then again with *The State and Revolution* in 1917. There is no long pamphlet defending or extolling the measures of war communism. The rationing and the by-passing of money in a condition of starvation could not be identified with communism, a stage where scarcity is no longer a dominating theme. War communism remained for Lenin a temporary expediency.[18]

The urban workers especially had suffered severe hardships, and survived on half-rations of food. By the time of NEP, the civil war had been won, the survival of the Soviet regime in face of external threats was no longer in question. But the many years of disruption had meant harsh economic conditions for those who had supported the revolution. Now the problem was one of restoring the economy to a reasonable level of production, and of reactivating the light and heavy industry in the cities, so that once again the urban workers could have adequate food in exchange for the light consumer goods that the peasants wanted. In short it was a problem not of war economy but of reconstruction and development. Different policies were necessary – policies which looked like a complete reversal of earlier principles, policies which looked like opportunism.

This is the main reason why the *The Tax in Kind* is an important paper. The contemporary debate on the role of markets in socialism, on the part played by the Law of Value in an economy in transition to socialism can be illuminated by a careful reading of this pamphlet. Here Lenin puts the policy of free trade in foodgrain in a theoretical perspective. Not the perspective of neo-classical economic theory, or of some rigid purist Marxism, but an extension of Marxian theory to make it applicable to the changing real world situation. It may appear paradoxical that Lenin advocated free trade in grain, but then it may appear equally paradoxical that in his pamphlet *On the So-called Market Question* Lenin appears to be defending the prospects of capitalism in Russia.

In *The Tax in Kind* Lenin re-uses his approach of *Left-wing Childishness* and treats the Russian economy in terms of several overlapping modes of production which survived simultaneously. Lenin begins by recognising that many modes not only can but do exist simultaneously in Russia and that it is in this context that trade is a powerful weapon. To begin with, small peasant cultivation with a low level of technology persisted in Russian agriculture. This in turn implied that the surplus on any farm was small and these small surpluses were scattered. In such a case, trade became a weapon for mobilising these surpluses and for combining the peasantry.

Lenin contrasts trade with procurement by bureaucratic methods. Since the civil war had ended, the suitability of compulsory procurement was questionable. But Lenin goes further and analyses the inefficiency caused by bureaucracy in more general terms. He recognises that bureaucracy in advanced capitalism is a different phenomenon from that in Russia.

> In our country, bureaucratic practices have different economic roots, namely the atomised and scattered state of the small producer with his poverty, illiteracy, lack of culture, the absence of roads and *exchange* between agriculture and industry, the absence of competition and interaction between them.

Bureaucracy in Russia was therefore similar to that in France during the Ancien Regime or the bureaucratic obstacles that Adam Smith denounced. In such cases, trade becomes 'an antidote to bureaucracy'.[19]

It is useful to note that this analysis of bureaucracy makes it possible to have different types of bureaucracy related to the nature of the economy – an economy with scattered, small commodity producers as against a highly integrated corporate economy. It would be tedious to mix up different kinds of bureaucracies and declare that the free market was an answer for every kind of bureaucracy. It also opens up the possibility of a Marxist analysis of bureaucracy by integrating it with economic conditions and forms of organisations for mobilising economic surplus.

Lenin's advocacy of trade was not unconditional. It was a product of the historical conditions then prevailing – the modes of production and the constellation of political forces and military circumstances. At that juncture, trade would have strengthened state capitalism. Lenin makes it abundantly clear that of the various overlapping modes of production then prevailing, state capitalism was the most progressive one. It was not socialism, but a transitionary stage towards it. As such it was superior to petty commodity production or private capitalism. This is exactly similar to the view Lenin took when he debated with the Narodniks. At that time capitalism was a progressive mode compared to feudalism and medievalism (as Lenin terms it). This is why as a Marxist, Lenin defended the prospects for capitalism against romantic attacks on it. Similarly we find him advocating free trade in grain and state capitalism against ultra-left attacks on the compromises of the NEP.

A good illustration of this approach, which we have described already as the 19th-century Marxist view, occurs in Marx's work. Lenin cites Marx's lecture on Free Trade in his debates with the Narodniks in the book *A Characterisation of Economic Romanticism*. Marx delivered the speech in January 1848 when the Corn Law agitation had recently carried the day but the Chartist agitation was also in full swing. Was Free Trade in grain, i.e. Corn Law abolition, in workers' interests, or not? Marx favoured the repeal of the Corn Laws not for the sentimental reason that the workers would be better off thereby (though the price of bread did fall) but because it would lead to the further development of productive forces. The fetters put on the accumulation process by the shortage of food, and the drag due to high land rents that the Corn Laws made possible, would be removed. British capitalism would grow faster. As Lenin points out, Sismondi took the romantic view. He was perplexed by the hopeless dilemma that both free trade and its absence led to the ruination of workers. This was not the way Marx viewed the problem,

> Instead of comparing capitalism with some abstract society as it ought to be (i.e. actually with a utopia), the author (Marx) compared it with the *preceeding stages* of social economy, compared the different and successive stages of capitalism, *and established the fact that the productive forces of society develop thanks to the development of capitalism.* (*Economic Romanticism*, Lenin's emphasis.)

Marx was not unaware of the contradictions of capitalism. He knew that the progressive development of productive forces was accompanied by workers' poverty. But at the same time development opened up the possibilities for further contradictions, e.g. development of workers' combination into trade unions once they were concentrated in large factories. Thus does the growth of productive forces lead to new developments in a dialectical process.

Conclusion

Several of the themes pursued by Lenin in his economic writings are still relevant today. Economic Romanticism of the type represented by Sismondi and the Narodniks is not unknown on the left today. Several questions occur which pose the dilemma that Lenin described as Sismondi's – the Green Revolution in Agriculture, the introduction of computer technology in industry, the attitude that a country should take to foreign, and especially multinational, capital. All these issues present a choice between alternatives in any of which one can see problems for the poor. What one lacks is a framework of analysis. It is in this respect that these economic writings are a help.

What I have called above 'the 19th century Marxist view' is of use today. One could label it 'classical' Marxism. Its crucial character is the time-frame in which it operates. To Marx and Engels, as to the German and Russian Marxists of

those days, the transition from capitalism to socialism was a
long process spread over decades if not generations. It is this
long perspective that informs their discussions. Thus while
they speak of crises in, and breakdown of, capitalism, it is
not as if they expect the breakdown to occur in their
lifetime. (Marx once feared in 1857 that capitalism might
end before he had finished his analysis of the system but that
threat soon passed.) In Lenin's case even after the October
revolution, as the debate on NEP shows, there was no
expectation of an immediate establishment of a socialist
economy. But as hopes of international revolution faded and
life got tougher during the period of the war against the
white armies, it began to be asserted that socialism had been
established in USSR by the Bolshevik Party. Once Lenin
had died, this became the orthodoxy.

But it was precisely because of the success of the
Bolsheviks in holding on to power and consolidating it that
in contemporary discussions the impatience for the
transition to socialism is much greater. Discussions of
economic policy for left-wing governments revolve around
talks of an uncompromising dash towards socialism by an
immediate takeover of all industries, or they reverberate
with charges of betrayal. Left-wing governments which were
elected to power in the early 1980s in France, Spain,
Portugal or Greece (some of which are still in office)
uneasily found themselves without any principles on which
to base a policy for an intermediate regime. They dashed for
'sudden and irreversible change' in economic ownership and
control, or receded, defeated, into a thinly disguised
monetarism. Power involves compromise as Lenin found
when 'administering the revolution'. But a compromise need
not be unprincipled. It can be arrived at in light of a
theoretical perspective and can be politically debated. This
is the clear message from these selections as they touch upon
questions of policy.

This is a small selection from the large body of writing that
is given below. I have interpreted economic as broadly as
possible in compiling the bibliography, as well as in making
the selection, but ultimately, for a Marxist, economic and
political questions are inseparable, and Lenin's works are no
exception. By the same token, the interpretations and views

expressed in this introduction are one particular way among the many possible ways of looking at Lenin's work. If they stimulate further interest in Lenin's economic writings, and in debates about socialist economic policy, the undertaking will have been worthwhile.

Notes

[1] Alec Nove, 'Lenin as an Economist' in P Reddaway and L Schapiro (eds), *Lenin, the Man, the Theorist, the Leader: A Reappraisal*, Pall Mall, London 1967.

[2] Neil Harding, *Lenin's Political Thought: Theory and Practice in the Democratic and Socialist Revolutions*, 2 volumes, Macmillan, London 1977 (vol 1), 1981 (vol 2).

[3] Harding, *op cit*, Vol 1, Chpt 4, Vol 2, Chpt 3.

[4] See below, 'A Complete List of Lenin's Economic Writings', pp 346-353.

[5] For brief biographical notes on the persons mentioned in this introduction and in the selections, see the biographical notes on pp 354-360.

[6] See Jairus Banaji, 'Chayanov, Kautsky, Lenin: Considerations Towards A Synthesis', *Economic and Political Weekly*, Vol XI, No 40 (1976), pp 1594-1607; Athar Hussain and Keith Tribe, *Marxism and the Agrarian Question*, Macmillan, London 1981; A V Chayanov, *The Theory of Peasant Economy*, Daniel Thorner, Basile Kerblay and R E F Smith, (eds), Richard D Irwin for the American Economic Association, Hoewood, Illinois, 1966.

[7] For a description of this tradition, see Harding *op cit*, Vol 1, Chpt 2, 'The Background of Orthodoxy'.

[8] This is the debate surveyed in R Luxemburg, *The Accumulation of Capital*, Routledge and Kegan Paul, London 1951. See also M Desai, *Marxian Economics*, Blackwell, Oxford 1979 for a discussion of Marx's model of expanded reproduction.

[9] The literature is very large here. The '*dependencia*' school and authors such as Paul Baran, Andre Gunder Frank, Samir Amin come under the label of 'radical political economy of underdevelopment'. There has recently been a reaction against this trend in underdevelopment literature. See Bill Warren, *Imperialism, Pioneer of Capitalism*, New Left Books, London 1981, Peter Limqueco and Bruce McFarlane (eds), *Neo-Marxist Theories of Development*, St Martin's Press, New York, 1983.

[10] For further details on Schemes of Simple and Expanded Reproduction, see P M Sweezy, *Theory of Capitalist Development*; M Desai, *Marxian Economics* or any textbooks on Marxian economics.

[11] See UNIDO, *Industry and Development Global Report 1985*, UNIDO, Vienna 1985.

[12] There is a large literature here. See, among others, Ashok Rudra, 'The Green and Greedy Revolution', *South Asian Review*, July 1971; T J

Byers, 'The Dialectic of India's Green Revolution', *South Asian Review*, January 1972, provides an extensive bibliography of the Indian material. Also Francine Frankel, *India's Green Revolution: economic gains and political costs*, Princeton University Press, 1971. For a recent revisionist view on the Green Revolution, see John Harriss, 'What Happened to the Green Revolution in South India? Economic Trends, Household Mobility and the Politics of an "Awkward Class" ', Discussion Paper No 175, University of East Anglia, School of Development Studies, December 1985; Michael Lipton, 'Development Studies: Findings, Frontiers and Fights', in L Brown and M Veitch (eds), *The Relevance of Development Studies to the Study of Change in Contemporary Britain*, ESRC 1986, is a similar revision from a non Marxist perspective (pp 64-68).

[13] See however Jairus Banaji, 'Summary of Selected Parts of Kautsky's The Agrarian Question', *Economy and Society*, Vol V, 1976, pp. 2-49; and also A Hussain and K Tribe (eds), *Paths of Development in Capitalist Agriculture: Readings from German Social Democracy*, Macmillan, London 1984. During the course of the preparation of this collection, an English translation has at last become available. *Karl Kautsky: The Agrarian Question* (2 vols), Pete Burgess transl., Zwan Publications 1988.

[14] This view was put forward, to the best of my knowledge, by N Georgescu-Roegen in 'Economic Theory and Agrarian Economics', Oxford Economic Papers, February 1960, pp 1-40. See also Daniel Thorner's introduction to A V Chayanov, *The Theory of Peasant Economy, op cit*. Since then the literature on agrarianism has become very large indeed.

[15] This distinction between vertical and horizontal imperialism was developed in my review of V Kiernan: *Marxism and Imperialism*, Edward Arnold, London 1975. See M Desai, 'Capital and Colonial', *The Times Literary Supplement*, 27 February 1976.

[16] 'Intermediate regimes' was a phrase used by Michal Kalecki. There has been some discussion in India on this issue. See K N Raj's article on intermediate regimes in *Economic and Political Weekly*, 1973.

[17] See Neil Harding, *op cit*, Vol 2, chpts 9-14.

[18] See L Szamuely, *First Models of the Socialist Economics Systems: Principles and Theories*, Akademiai Kiado, Budapest 1974.

[19] M Desai, 'The Role of Exchange and Market Relationships in the Economics of the Transition Period: Lenin on the Tax in Kind', *Indian Economic Review*, 1972.

Note on the Texts

The texts for these selections are all from Lenin's Collected Works in 45 volumes published by Lawrence and Wishart. Volume number is indicated by Roman numerals and page number by arabic. All references to Marx and Engels are also to the Lawrence and Wishart editions, unless there is no English translation.

Note on Some Russian Terms

dessiatine – area measurement roughly equivalent to 2.7 acres.
gubernia – region.
pood – weight measurement equivalent to 36 lb.
uyezd – province.
zemstvo – local council.

1. On the So-called Market Question

I

Can capitalism develop in Russia and reach full development when the masses of the people are poor and are becoming still poorer? The development of capitalism certainly needs an extensive home market: but the ruin of the peasantry undermines this market, threatens to close it altogether and make the organisation of the capitalist order impossible. True, it is said that, by transforming the natural economy of our direct producers into a commodity economy, capitalism is creating a market for itself; but is it conceivable that the miserable remnants of the natural economy of indigent peasants can form the basis for the development in our country of the mighty capitalist production that we see in the West? Is it not evident that the one fact of the masses being impoverished already makes our capitalism something impotent and without foundation, incapable of embracing the entire production of the country and of becoming the *basis* of our social economy?

Such are the questions that are constantly being advanced in our literature in opposition to the Russian Marxists; the absence of a market is one of the principal arguments invoked against the possibility of applying the theory of Marx to Russia. To refute this argument is the aim, incidentally, of the paper *The Market Question*,[1] which we are about to discuss.

II

The main premise of the author of the paper is the assumption of the 'general and exclusive domination of capitalist

Written in St Petersburg autumn 1893, first published 1937.
CW I 75-125.

production'. Proceeding from that premise he expounds the contents of Chapter XXI of Volume II of *Capital* (Part III – 'The Reproduction and Circulation of the Aggregate Social Capital').

Here Marx sets out to investigate how social production replaces the part of the product which serves to satisfy the personal needs of the workers and the capitalists, and that which goes to form the elements of productive capital. Hence, in Volume I, the investigation of the production and reproduction of an *individual* capital could be limited to an analysis of the component parts of capital and the product according to their value – (as is shown in Volume I of *Capital* the value of the product consists of c (constant capital) $+ v$ (variable capital) $+ s$ (surplus-value)) – but here the product must be divided into its material components, because that part of the product which consists of the elements of capital cannot be used for personal consumption, and vice versa. In view of that, Marx divides aggregate social production – and consequently, the aggregate social product – into two departments: I) the production of means of production, i.e. the elements of productive capital – commodities which can serve only for productive consumption, and II) the production of means of consumption, i.e. commodities that serve for the personal consumption of the working class and the capitalist class.

The investigation is based on the following scheme (Arabic numerals indicate units of value – millions of rubles, for example; Roman numerals indicate the above-mentioned departments of social production. The rate of surplus-value is taken at 100 per cent):

$$\text{I } 4{,}000\,c + 1{,}000\,v + 1{,}000\,s = 6{,}000 \quad \text{Capital} = 7{,}500$$
$$\text{II } 2{,}000\,c + 500\,v + 500\,s = 3{,}000 \quad \text{Product} = 9{,}000$$

Let us begin by supposing that we are dealing with simple reproduction, i.e. let us assume that production does not expand, but remains permanently on its former scale; this means that the capitalists consume the whole surplus-value unproductively, that they expend it for their personal needs and not for accumulation. Under those circumstances it is obvious, firstly, that II 500 v and II 500 s must be consumed by the capitalists and the workers in the same department II, since that product exists in the form of means of consumption intended for the satisfaction of personal needs. Further, I 4,000 c in its natural form must be consumed by the capitalists in the same department I, because the condition that the scale of production remains unchanged demands the retention of the same capital for the next year's production of means of production; consequently, the replacement of this part of capital also presents no difficulty; the corresponding part of the product existing in the natural form of coal, iron, machines, etc, will be exchanged among the capitalists engaged in producing means of production and will serve them, as before, as constant capital. Thus, there remains I (v + s) and II c. I 1,000 v + I 1,000 s are products existing in the form of means of production, and II 2,000 c – in the form of means of consumption. The workers and capitalists in department I (under simple reproduction, i.e. consumption of the entire surplus-value) must consume means of consumption to the value of 2,000 (1,000 (v) + 1,000 (s)). To be able to continue production on the previous scale, the capitalists in department II must acquire means of production to the extent of 2,000 in order to replace their constant capital (2,000 II c). It is evident from this that I v + I s must be exchanged for II c, because, if they are not, production on the previous scale will be impossible. The condition for simple reproduction is that the sum of the variable capital and surplus-value in department I must be equal to the constant capital in department II: I (v + s) = II c. In other words, that law may be formulated as follows: the sum of *all the new* values produced in the course of a year (in both departments) must be equal to the gross value of the product existing in the form of means of consumption: I (v + s) + II (v + s) = II (c + v + s).

Actually, of course, there can be no simple reproduction, both because the production of the whole of society cannot remain on the previous scale every year, and because accumulation is a law of the capitalist system. Let us, therefore, examine how social production on an expanding scale, or accumulation, takes place. Where there is accumulation, only part of the surplus-value is consumed by the capitalists for their personal needs, the other part being consumed productivity, i.e. converted into the elements of productive capital for the expansion of production. Therefore, where there is accumulation, I $(v - s)$ and II c cannot be equal: I $(v + s)$ must be greater than II c in order that part of the surplus-value in department I (I s) may be used for the expansion of production, and not exchanged for means of consumption. Thus we get

A. *Scheme of Simple Reproduction*:
I 4,000 c + 1,0000 v + 1,000 s = 6,000
II 2,000 c +   500 v +   500 s = 3,000
I $(v + s)$ = II c.

B. *Initial Scheme of Accumulation*:
I 4,000 c + 1,000 v + 1,000s = 6,000
II 1,500 c +   750 v +   750 s = 3,000
I $(v + s)$ > II c.

Let us now see how social production must proceed if there is accumulation.

First year.

I 4,000 c + 1,000 v + 1,000 s = 6,000   Capital = 7,260
II 1,500 c +   750 v +   750 s = 3,000   Product = 9,000

I (1,000 v + 500 s) are exchanged for II 1,500 c (as in simple reproduction).

I 500 s are accumulated, i.e. go to expand production, are converted into *capital*. If we take the previous division into constant and variable capital we get

I 500 s = 400 c + 100 v.

The additional constant capital (400 c) is contained in the product I (its natural form is means of production); but the additional variable capital (100 v) must be obtained from the capitalists of department II, who, consequently, also have to accumulate: they exchange part of their surplus-value (II 100 s) for means of production (I 100 v) and convert these means of production into additional constant capital. Consequently, their constant capital grows from 1,500 c to 1,600 c; to process it additional labour-power is needed – 50 *v*, which is also taken out of the surplus-value of the capitalists of department II.

By adding the additional capital from department I and

department II to the original capital we get the following distribution of the product:

$$I\ 4,400\ c + 1,100\ v + (500\ s) = 6,000$$
$$II\ 1,600\ c + \quad 800\ v + (600\ s) = 3,000$$

The surplus-value in parentheses represents the capitalists' consumption fund, i.e. the part of surplus-value that does not go for accumulation, but for the personal needs of the capitalists.

If production proceeds on the previous scale, at the end of the year we shall get:

$$I\ 4,400\ c + 1,100\ v + 1,100\ s = 6,600 \quad \text{Capital} = 7,900$$
$$II\ 1,600\ c + \quad 800\ v + \quad 800\ s = 3,200 \quad \text{Product} = 19,800$$

I $(1,100\ v + 550\ s)$ are exchanged for II $1,650\ c$: the additional 50 c are taken from 800 II s (and the increase of c by 50 causes an increase of v by 25).

Further, 550 I s are accumulated as before:

$$550\ \ I\ s = 440\ c + 110\ v$$
$$165\ II\ s = 110\ c + \ \ 55\ v.$$

If to the original capital we now add the additional (to I 4,400 c − 440 c; to I 1,100 v − 110 v: to II 1,600 c − 50 c and 110 c; and to II 800 v − 25 v − and 55 v), we shall get:

$$I\ 4,840\ c + 1,210\ v + (550\ s) = 6,600$$
$$II\ 1,760\ c + \quad 880\ v + (560\ s) = 3,200$$

With the further progress of production we get

$$I\ 4,840\ c + 1,210\ v + 1,210\ s = 7,260 \left\{ \begin{array}{l} \text{Capital} = 8,690 \\ \text{Product} = 10,780 \end{array} \right\}$$
$$II\ 1,760\ c + \quad 880\ v + \quad 880\ s = 3,520$$

and so forth.

Such, in essence, are the results of Marx's investigations in the reproduction of the aggregate social capital. These investigations (the reservation must be made) are given here in a most concise form; very much that Marx analyses in detail has been omitted – for example, circulation of money, replacement of fixed capital which is gradually worn out, and so forth – because all this has no direct bearing on the question under review.

III

What conclusions does the author of the paper draw from these investigations made by Marx? Unfortunately, he does not formulate his conclusions very precisely and definitely, so that we have to make our own judgement of them from certain remarks which do not fully harmonise with each other. Thus, for example, we read:

'We have seen here,' says the author, 'how accumulation takes place in department I, the production of means of production as means of production: ... this accumulation takes place independently both of the progress of the production of articles of consumption and of the personal consumption itself, no matter whose it is'.

Of course, it is wrong to speak of accumulation being 'independent' of the production of articles of consumption, if only because the expansion of production calls for new variable capital and, consequently, articles of consumption; evidently, by using that term the author merely wanted to stress the specific feature of the scheme, namely, that the reproduction of I c – constant capital in department I – takes place without exchanges with department II, i.e. every year a certain quantity of, say, coal is produced in society for the purpose of producing coal. It goes without saying that this production (of coal for the purpose of producing coal) links up, by a series of subsequent exchanges, with the production of articles of consumption – otherwise, neither the coal-owners nor their workers could exist.

Elsewhere, the author expresses himself much more feebly: 'The *principal* movement of capitalist accumulation', he says, 'takes place, and has taken place (except in very early periods) independently of any direct producers, independently of the personal consumption of any stratum of the population'. Here, reference is made only to the predominance of the production of means of production over the production of articles of consumption in the course of the historical development of capitalism. This reference is repeated in another passage: 'On the one hand, the typical feature of capitalist society is accumulation for accumulation, productive but not personal consumption; on the other hand, *typical* of it is precisely the production of means of production as means of production'. If by these references the author wanted to say that capitalist society is distinguished from the other economic organisations which preceded it precisely by the development of machines and the articles necessary for them (coal, iron, and so forth), then he is quite right. In technical level capitalist society is higher than all others, and technical progress is expressed precisely in the fact that the work of machines pushes human labour more and more into the background.

Instead of engaging in criticism of the author's insufficiently clear statements it will, therefore, be better to turn straight to Marx and see whether it is possible to draw from his theory the conclusion that department I 'predominates' over department II, and in what sense this predominance is to be understood.

From Marx's scheme quoted above the conclusion cannot be drawn that department I predominates over department II: both develop on parallel lines. But that scheme does not take technical progress into consideration. As Marx proved in Volume I of *Capital*, technical progress is expressed by the gradual decrease of the ratio of variable capital to constant capital ($\frac{v}{c}$), whereas in the scheme it is taken as unchanged.

It goes without saying that if this change is made in the scheme there will be a relatively more rapid increase in means of production than in articles of consumption. Nevertheless, it seems to me that it will be worth while making that calculation, firstly, for the sake of clarity, and secondly, to avoid possible wrong conclusions from that premise.

(In the following scheme the rate of accumulation is taken as constant: half of the surplus-value is accumulated and half is consumed personally.)

(The reader may skip the following scheme and pass straight to the conclusions on the next page. The letter *a* stands for additional capital used for the expansion of production, i.e. the accumulated part of surplus-value.)

1st I 4,000 c + 1,000 v + 1,000 s = 6,000 ...   v: (c + v) = 20.0%
year II 1,500 c + 750 v + 750 s = 3,000 ...   v: (c + v) = 33.3%
$$\text{I } (1,000 \, v + 500 \, s) = \text{II } 1,500 \, c$$
a. I 500 s = 450 c + 50 v ...   v: (c + v) = $\frac{1}{10}$

a. II 60 s = 50 c + 10 v ...   v: (c + v) = $\frac{1}{6}$
I 4,450 c + 1,050 v + (500 s) = 6,000
II 1,550 c + 760 v + (690 s) = 3,000

2nd I 4,450 c + 1,050 v + 1,050 s = 6,550 ...   v: (c + v) = 19.2%
year II 1,550 c + 760 v + 760 s = 3,070 ...   v: (c + v) = 32.9%
$$\text{I } (1,050 \, v + 525 \, s) = \text{II } 1,575 \, c$$
$$\text{II } (1,550 \, c + 25 \, s)$$

a. II 28 s = 25 c + 3 v ...   v: (c + v) = ab. $\frac{1}{9}$
a. I 525 s = 500 c + 25 v ...   v: (c + v) = ab. $\frac{1}{21}$

a. II 28 s = 25 c + 3 v ...   v: (c + v) = ab. $\frac{1}{9}$
I 4,950 c + 1,075 v + (525 s) = 6,550
II 1,602 c + 766 v + (702 s) = 3,070

3rd I 4,950 c + 1,075 v + 1,075 s = 7,100 ...   v: (c + v) = 17.8%
year II 1,602 c + 766 v + 766 s = 3,134 ...   v: (c + v) = 32.3%
$$\text{I } (1,075 \, v + 537\tfrac{1}{2} \, s) = \text{II } 1,612\tfrac{1}{2} \, c$$
$$\text{II } (1,602 \, c + 10\tfrac{1}{2} \, s)$$

a. II 11½ s = 10½ c + 1 v ...   v: (c + v) = ab. $\frac{1}{12}$
a. I 537½ s = 517½ c + 20 v ...   v: (c + v) = ab. $\frac{1}{26}$

a. II 22 s = 20 c + 2 v ...   v: (c + v) = ab. $\frac{1}{11}$
I 5,467½ c + 1,095 v + (537½ s) = 7,100
II 1,634½ c + 769 v + (730½ s) = 3,134

4th I 5,467½ c + 1,095 v + 1,095 s = 7,657½ ...   v: (c + v) = 16.7%
year II 1,634½ c + 769 v + 769 s = 3,172½ ...   v: (c + v) = 32.0%
and so forth.

Let us now compare the conclusions drawn from this scheme concerning the growth of the various parts of the social product:[2]

	Means of production as means of		Means of production as means of		Means of consumption		Aggregate social product	
	Production	%	Consumption	%		%		%
1st year	4,000	110	2,000	100	3,000	100	9,000	100
2nd year	4,450	111.25	2,100	105	3,070	102	9,620	107
3rd year	4,950	123.75	2,150	107.5	3,134	104	10,234	114
4th year	5,457½	136.7	2,190	109.5	3,172	106	10,828½	120

We thus see that growth in the production of means of production as means of production is the most rapid, then comes the production of means of production as means of consumption, and the slowest rate of growth is in the production of means of consumption. That conclusion could have been arrived at, without Marx's investigation in Volume II of *Capital*, on the basis of the law that constant capital tends to grow faster than variable: the proposition that means of production grow faster is merely a paraphrase of this law as applied to social production as a whole.

But perhaps we should take another step forward? Since we have accepted that the ratio v to $c + v$ diminishes constantly, why not let v decrease to zero, the same number of workers being sufficient for a larger quantity of means of production? In that case, the accumulated part of surplus-value will be added straight to constant capital in department I, and social production will grow exclusively on account of means of production as means of production, complete stagnation reigning in department II.[3]

That would, of course, be a misuse of the schemes, for such a conclusion is based on improbable assumptions and is therefore wrong. Is it conceivable that technical progress, which reduces the proportion of v to c, will find expression only in department I and leave department II in a state of complete stagnation? Is it in conformity with the laws governing capitalist society, laws which *demand* of every capitalist that he enlarge his enterprise on pain of ruin, that no accumulation at all should take place in department II?

Thus, the only correct conclusion that can be drawn from Marx's investigation, outlined above, is that *in capitalist society, the production of means of production increases faster than the production of means of consumption*. As has been stated already, this conclusion follows directly from the generally known proposition that capitalist production attains an immeasurably higher technical level than production in previous times.[4] On this point specifically Marx expresses himself quite definitely only in one passage, and that passage fully confirms the correctness of the formula given:

'What distinguishes capitalist society in this case from the savage is not, as Senior thinks, the privilege and peculiarity of the savage to expend his labour at times in a way that does not procure him any products resolvable (exchangeable) into revenue, i.e. into articles of consumption. No, the distinction consists in the following:

'a) Capitalist society employs more [Nota bene] of its available annual labour in the production of means of production (ergo, of constant capital), which are not resolvable into revenue in the form of wages or surplus-value, but can function only as capital.' (*Capital* Vol II, p 442)

IV

The question now is, what relation has the theory that has been expounded to 'the notorious market question'? The theory is based on the assumption of the 'general and exclusive domination of the capitalist mode of production', whereas the 'question' is one of whether the full development of capitalism is 'possible' in Russia? True, the theory introduces a correction into the ordinary conception of the development of capitalism, but, evidently, the explanation of how capitalism develops *in general* does not in the least help to clear up the question of the 'possibility' (and necessity) of the development of capitalism in Russia.

The author of the paper, however, does not confine himself to expounding Marx's theory of the process of aggregate social production organised on capitalist lines. He points to the necessity of distinguishing 'two *essentially different* features in the accumulation of capital: 1) the development of capitalist production in breadth, when it takes hold of already existing fields of labour, ousting natural economy and expanding at the latter's expense; and 2) the development of capitalist production in depth, if one may so express it, when it expands independently of natural economy, i.e. under the general and exclusive domination of the capitalist mode of production'. Without, for the time being, stopping to criticise this division, let us proceed directly to find out what the author means by the development of capitalism in breadth: the explanation of that process, which consists in the replacement of natural economy by capitalist economy, should show us how Russian capitalism will 'take hold of the whole country'.

The author illustrates the development of capitalism in breadth by the following diagram:[5]

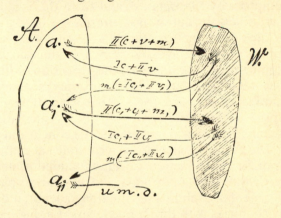

A – capitalists; W – direct producers
a, a_1, a_{11} – capitalist enterprises.
The arrows show the movement of the commodities exchanged.
c, v, m – component parts of the value of commodities.
I, II – commodities in their natural form: I – means of production; II –
means of consumption.

'The essential difference between the spheres A and W', says the author, 'is that in A the producers are capitalists who consume their surplus-value productively, whereas in W they are direct producers, who consume their surplus-value (here I mean the value of the product over and above the value of the means of production and necessary means of subsistence) unproductively.

'If we follow the arrows in the diagram we shall easily see how capitalist production in *A* develops at the expense of consumption in *W*, gradually absorbing it.' The product of the capitalist enterprise *a* goes 'to the direct producers' in the form of articles of consumption; in exchange for it the 'direct producers' return the constant capital (c) in the form of means of production and the variable capital (v) in the form of means of consumption, and the surplus-value (s) in the form of the elements of additional productive capital: $c_1 + v_1$. That capital serves as the basis of the new capitalist enterprise a_1, which in exactly the same way sends its product in the form of articles of consumption to the 'direct producers', and so on. 'From the above diagram of the development of capitalism in breadth it follows that the whole of production is most closely dependent upon consumption in "foreign" markets, upon consumption by the masses (and from the general point of view it makes absolutely no difference where those masses are – alongside the capitalists, or somewhere across the ocean). Obviously, the expansion of production in *A*, i.e. the development of capitalism in this direction, will come to a stop as soon as all the direct producers in *W* turn into commodity producers, for, as we saw above, every new enterprise (or expansion of an old one) is calculated to supply a new circle of consumers in *W*.' In conclusion the author says: 'The current conception of capitalist accumulation, i.e. of capitalist reproduction on an expanded scale, is limited solely to this view of things, and has no suspicion of the development of capitalist production in depth, independently of any countries with direct producers, i.e. independently of so-called foreign markets'.

The only thing we can agree with in this entire exposition is that this conception of the development of capitalism in breadth, and the diagram which illustrates it, is in complete accordance with the current, Narodnik views on the subject.

It would, indeed, be difficult to depict the utter absurdity and vapidity of current views more saliently and strikingly than is done in the diagram given.

The 'current conception' always regarded capitalism in our country as something isolated from the 'people's system', standing apart from it, exactly as it is depicted in the diagram from which it is quite impossible to see what connection there is between the two 'spheres', the capitalist sphere and the people's sphere. Why do commodities sent from A find a market in W? What causes the transformation of natural economy in W into commodity economy? The current view has never answered these questions because it regards exchange as something accidental and not as a certain *system of economy*.

Further, the current view has never *explained* whence and how capitalism arose in our country any more than it is explained by the diagram: the matter is presented as though the capitalists have come from somewhere outside and not from among these very 'direct producers'. Where the capitalists get the 'free workers' who are needed for enterprises, a, a_1, etc. remains a mystery. Everybody knows that in reality those workers are obtained precisely from the 'direct producers', but the diagram does not show at all that when commodity production embraced 'sphere' W, it created there a body of free workers.

In short, the diagram – exactly like the current view – explains absolutely nothing about the phenomena of the capitalist system in our country and is therefore worthless. The object for which it was drawn – to explain how capitalism develops at the expense of natural economy, and embraces the whole country – is not achieved at all, because, as the author himself sees – 'if we adhere consistently to the view under examination, then we must conclude that it is not possible for the development of the capitalist mode of production to become universal'.

After this, one can only express surprise at the fact that the author himself adheres, if only in part, to that view when he says that 'capitalism did indeed (?), in its infancy, develop in this very easy (sic!?) way (very easy because here existing branches of labour are involved) and is partly developing in the same direction even now (??), since there are still remnants of natural economy in the world, and since the population is growing'.

Actually, this is not a 'very easy' way of developing capitalism, but simply a 'very easy' way of understanding the process; so 'very easy' that it would be more correct to call it a total lack of understanding. The Russian Narodniks of all shades make shift to this very day with these 'very easy' tricks: they never dream of *explaining* how capitalism arose in our country, and how it functions, but confine themselves to comparing the 'sore spot' in our system, capitalism, with the 'healthy spot', the direct producers, the 'people'; the former is put on the left, the latter on the right, and all this profound thinking is rounded off with sentimental phrases about what is 'harmful' and what is 'useful' for 'human society'.

V

To correct the diagram given above we must begin by ascertaining the content of the concepts dealt with. By commodity production is meant an organisation of social economy in which goods are produced by separate, isolated producers, each specialising in the making of some one product, so that to satisfy the needs of society it is necessary to buy and sell products (which, therefore, become commodities) in the market. By capitalism is meant that stage of the development of commodity production at which not only the products of human labour, but human labour-power itself becomes a commodity. Thus, in the historical development of capitalism two features are important: 1) the transformation of the natural economy of the direct producers into commodity economy, and 2) the transformation of commodity economy into capitalist economy. The first transformation is due to the appearance of the social division of labour – the specialisation of isolated (NB, this is an essential condition of commodity economy), separate producers in only one branch of industry. The second transformation is due to the fact that separate producers, each producing commodities on his own for the market, enter into competition with one another: each strives to sell at the highest price and to buy at the lowest, a necessary result of which is that the strong become stronger and the weak go under, a minority are enriched and the masses are ruined. This leads to the conversion of independent producers into wage-workers and of numerous small enterprises into a few big ones. The diagram should, therefore, be drawn up to show both these features of the development of capitalism and the changes which this development brings about in the dimensions of the market, i.e. in the quantity of products that are turned into commodities.

The following table (p 58 – *ed*) has been drawn up on these lines: all extraneous circumstances have been abstracted, i.e. taken as constants (for example, size of population, productivity of labour, and much else) in order to analyse the influence on the market of *only those* features of the development of capitalism that are mentioned above.

Let us now examine this table showing the consecutive changes in the system of economy of a community consisting of 6 producers. It shows 6 periods expressing stages in the transformation of natural into capitalist economy.

1st period. We have 6 producers, each of whom expends his labour in all 3 branches of industry (in *a*, in *b* and in *c*). The product obtained (9 from each producer: a + b + c = 9) is spent by each producer on himself in his own household. Hence, we have natural economy in its pure form; no products whatever appear in the market.

2nd period. Producer I changes the productivity of his labour: he leaves industry *b* and spends the time formerly spent in that industry in industry *c*. As a result of this specialisation by one producer, the others cut down production *c*, because producer I has produced more than he consumes himself, and increase production *b* in order to turn out a product for producer I. The division of labour which comes into being inevitably leads to commodity production: producer I sells 1 *c* and buys 1 *b*; the other producers sell 1 *b* (each of the 5 sells ⅕b) and buy 1 *c* (each buying ⅕ c); a quantity of products appears in the market to the value of 6. The dimensions of the market correspond exactly to the degree of specialisation of social labour: specialisation has taken place in the production of one *c* (1 c = d) and of one *b* (1 b = 3); i.e. a ninth part of total social production (18 c (= a = b)), and a ninth part of the total social product has appeared in the market.

3rd period. Division of labour proceeds further, embracing branches of industry *b* and *c* to the full: three producers engage exclusively in industry *b* and three exclusively in industry *c*. Each sells 1 c (or 1 b), i.e. 3 units of value, and also buys 3 – 1 *b* (or 1 c). This increased division of labour leads to an expansion of the market, in which 18 units of value now appear. Again, the dimensions of the market correspond exactly to the degree of specialisation (= division) of social labour: specialisation has taken place in the production of 3 *b* and 3 *c*, i.e. one-third of social production, and one-third of the social product appears in the market.

The 4th period already represents capitalist production: the process of the transformation of commodity into capitalist production did not go into the table and, therefore, must be described separately.

In the preceding period each producer was already a commodity producer (in the spheres of industry *b* and *c*, the only ones we are discussing): each producer separately, on his own, independently of the others, produced for the market, whose dimensions were, of course, not known to any one of them. This relation between isolated producers working for a common market is called competition. It goes without saying that an equilibrium between production and consumption (supply and demand) is, under these circumstances, achieved only by a series of fluctuations. The more skilful, enterprising and strong producer will become still stronger as a result of these fluctuations, and the weak and unskilful one will be crushed by them. The enrichment of a few individuals and the impoverishment of the masses – such are the inevitable consequences of the law of competition. The matter ends by the ruined producers losing economic independence and engaging themselves as wage-workers in the enlarged establishment of their fortunate rival. That is the situation depicted in the table. Branches of industry *b* and *c*, which were formerly divided among all 6 producers, are now concentrated in the hands of 2 producers (I and IV). The rest of the producers are their wage-workers, who no longer receive the whole product of their labour, but the product with the surplus-value deducted, the latter being appropriated by the employer (let me remind you that, by assumption, surplus-value equals one-third of the product, so that the producer of 2 *b* (= 6) will receive from the employer two-thirds – i.e., 4). As a result, we get an increase in division of labour – and a growth of the market, where 22 units now appear, notwithstanding the fact that the 'masses' are 'impoverished': the producers who have become (partly) wage-workers no longer receive the whole product of 9, but only of 7 – they receive 3 from their independent activity (agricultural-industry *a*) and 4 from wage-labour (from the production of 2 *b* or 2 *c*). These producers, now more wage-workers than independent masters, have lost the opportunity of bringing any product of their labour to the market because ruin has deprived them of the means of production necessary for the making of products. They have had to resort to 'outside employments', i.e. to take their labour-power to the market and with the money obtained from the sale of this new commodity to buy the product they need.

The table shows that producers II and III, V and VI each sells labour-power to the extent of 4 units of value and buys articles of consumption to the same amount. As regards the capitalist producers, I and IV, each of them produces products to the extent of 21; of this, he himself consumes 10 (3(=a)+3(=c or b)+4 (surplus-value from 2 *c* or 2 *b*)) and sells 11; but he buys commodities to the extent of 3 (*c* or *b*)+8 (labour-power).

In this case, it must be observed, we do not get complete correspondence between the degree of specialisation of social labour (the production of 5 *b* and 5 *c*, i.e. to the sum of 30, but this error in the table is due to our having taken simple reproduction[6] i.e. with no accumulation; that is why the surplus-value taken from the workers (four units by each capitalist) is all consumed *in kind*. Since absence of accumulation is impossible in capitalist society, the appropriate correction will be made later.

5th period. The differentiation of the commodity producers has spread to the agricultural industry (*a*): the wage-workers could not continue their farming, for they worked mainly in the industrial establishments of others, and were ruined: they retained only miserable remnants of their farming, about a half (which, we assumed, was just enough to cover the needs of their families) – exactly as the present cultivated land of the vast mass of our peasant 'agriculturists' are merely miserable bits of independent farming. The concentration of industry *a* in an insignificant number of big establishments has begun in an exactly similar way. Since the grain grown by the wage-workers is now not enough to cover their needs, wages, which were kept low by

1. and **2.**

Producers	a	b	c	Totals	Natural consumption	Sells	Buys	Producers	a	b	c	Totals	Natural consumption	Sells	Buys
I	a	b	c	9	9	—	—	I	a	—	2c	9	6	3	3
II	a	b	c	9	9	—	—	II	a	6/5b	4/5c	9	8 2/5	3/5	3/5
III	a	b	c	9	9	—	—	III	a	6/5b	4/5c	9	8 2/5	3/5	3/5
IV	a	b	c	9	9	—	—	IV	a	6/5b	4/5c	9	8 2/5	3/5	3/5
V	a	b	c	9	9	—	—	V	a	6/5b	4/5c	9	8 2/5	3/5	3/5
VI	a	b	c	9	9	—	—	VI	a	6/5b	4/5c	9	8 2/5	3/5	3/5
Total	6a	6b	6c	54	54	—	—	Total	6a	6b	6c	54	48	6	6

3. and **4.**

Producers	a	b	c	Totals	Natural consumption	Sells	Buys	Producers	a	b	c	Totals	Natural consumption	Sells	Buys
I	a	—	2c	9	6	3	3	I	a	—	6c	21	10	11	3 (+8 l.p.)
II	a	2b	—	9	6	3	3	II	a	-	—	3	3	(4 l.p.)	4
III	a	—	2c	9	6	3	3	III	a	—	—	3	3	(4 l.p.)	4
IV	a	2b	—	9	6	3	3	IV	a	6b	—	21	10	11	3 (+8 l.p.)
V	a	—	2c	9	6	3	3	V	a	—	—	3	3	(4 l.p.)	4
VI	a	2b	—	9	6	3	3	VI	a	—	—	3	3	(4 l.p.)	4
Total	6a	6b	6c	54	36	18	18	Total	6a	6b	6c	54	32	22 (+16 l.p.)	22 (+16 l.p.)

5. and **6.**

Producers	a	b	c	Totals	Natural consumption	Sells	Buys	Producers	a	b	c	Totals	Natural consumption	Sells	Buys
I	2a	—	6c	24	11	I	3 (+10 l.p.)	I	6a	—	—	18	6	12	6 (+6 l.p.)
II	1/2a	-	-	1 1/2	1 1/2	(5 l.p)	5	II	—	—	—	—	—	(6 l.p.)	6
III	1/2a	—	—	1 1/2	1 1/2	(5 l.p.)	5	III	—	6b	—	18	6	12	6 (+6 l.p.)
IV	2a	6b	—	24	11	13	3 (+10 l.p.)	IV	—	—	—	—	—	(6 l.p.)	6
V	1/2a	—	—	1 1/2	1 1/2	(5 l.p.)	5	V	—	—	6c	18	6	12	6 (+6 l.p.)
VI	1/2a	—	—	1 1/2	1 1/2	(5 l.p.)	5	VI	—	—	—	—	—	(6 l.p.)	6
Total	6a	6b	6c	54	28	26 (+20 l.p.)	26 (+20 l.p.)	Total	6a	6b	6c	54	18	36 (+18 l.p.)	36 (+18 l.p.)

EXPLANATION OF TABLE

I — II . . . — VI are producers.

a, b, c are branches of industry (for example, agriculture, manufacturing and extractive industries)

$a=b=c=3$. The magnitude of value of the products $a=b=c$ equals 3 (three units of value) of which *1* is surplus-value.*

The market column shows the magnitude of value of the *products* sold (and bought); the figures in parentheses show the magnitude of value of the labour-power (= 1. p.) sold (and bought).

The arrows proceeding from one producer to another show that the first is a wage-worker for the second.

Simple reproduction is assumed: the capitalists consume the entire surplus-value unproductively.

---

* The part of value which replaces constant capital is taken as unchanging, and is therefore ignored.

their independent farming, increase and provide the workers with the money to buy grain (although in a smaller quantity than they consumed when they were their own masters): now the worker produces $1\frac{1}{2}(=\frac{1}{2}a)$ and buys 1, getting in all $2\frac{1}{2}$ instead of the former 3 $(=a)$. The capitalist masters, having added expanded farming to their industrial establishments now each produce 2 *a* $(=6)$, of which 2 goes to the workers in the form of wages and $1(\frac{1}{3}a)$ – surplus-value – to themselves. The development of capitalism depicted in this table, is accompanied by the 'impoverishment' of the 'people' (the workers now consume only $6\frac{1}{2}$ each instead of 7, as in the 4th period), and by the growth of the market, in which 26 now appear. The 'decline of farming', in the case of the majority of the producers, did not cause a shrinkage, but an expansion of the market for farm produce.

6th period. The specialisation of occupations, i.e. the division of social labour, is completed. All branches of industry have separated, and have become the speciality of separate producers. The wage-workers have completely lost their independent farms and subsist entirely on wage-labour. We get the same result: the development of capitalism (independent farming on one's own account has been fully eliminated), 'impoverishment of the masses' (although the workers' wages have risen, their consumption has diminished from $6\frac{1}{2}$ to 6: they each produce *9* (3a, 3b, 3c) and give their masters one-third as surplus-value), and a further growth of the market, in which there now appears two-thirds of the social product (36).

VI

Let us now draw the conclusions which follow from the above table.

The first conclusion is that the concept 'market' is quite inseparable from the concept of the social division of labour – that 'general basis of all commodity [and consequently, let us add, of capitalist] production' as Marx calls it. The 'market' arises where, and to the extent that, social division of labour and commodity production appear. The dimensions of the market are inseparably connected with the degree of specialisation of social labour.

'... It [a commodity] cannot acquire the properties of a socially recognised universal equivalent, except by being converted into money. That money, however, is in someone else's pocket. In order to entice the money out of that pocket, our friend's commodity must, above all things, be a use-value to the owner of the money. For this, it is necessary that the labour expended upon it be of a kind that is socially useful, of a kind that constitutes *a branch of the social division of labour*. But division of labour is a system of production which has grown up spontaneously and continues to grow behind the backs of the producers. The commodity to be exchanged may possibly be the product of some new kind of labour that pretends to satisfy newly arisen requirements, or even to give rise itself to new requirements. *A particular operation, though yesterday, perhaps, forming one out of the many operations conducted by one producer in creating a given commodity, may today separate itself from this connection, may establish itself as an independent branch of labour and send its incomplete product to market as an independent commodity*' (*Capital* Vol 1, p 108. My italics).

Thus, the limits of the development of the market, in capitalist society, are set by the limits of the specialisation of social labour. But this specialisation, by its very nature is as infinite as technical developments. To increase the productivity of human labour in, for instance, the making of some part of a whole product, the production of that part must be specialised, must become a special one concerned with mass production and, therefore, permitting (and engendering) the employment of machines, etc. That is on the one hand. On the other hand, technical progress in capitalist socialisation necessarily calls for specialisation in the various functions of the production process, for their transformation from scattered, isolated functions repeated separately in every establishment engaged in this production, into socialised functions concentrated in one, new establishment, and calculated to satisfy the requirements of the whole of society. I shall quote an example:

'Recently, in the United States, the woodworking factories are becoming more and more specialised, "new factories are springing up exclusively for the making of, for instance, axe handles, broom handles, or extensible tables.... Machine building is making constant progress, new machines are being continuously invented to simplify and cheapen some side of production.... Every branch of furniture making, for instance, has become a trade requiring special machines and special workers.... In carriage building, wheel rims are made in special factories (Missouri, Arkansas, Tennessee), wheel spokes are made in Indiana and Ohio, and hubs again are made in special factories in Kentucky and Illinois. All these separate parts are bought by factories which specialise in the making of whole wheels. Thus, quite a dozen factories take part in the building of some cheap kind of vehicle" ' (Mr Tverskoi, 'Ten Years in America', *Vestnik Yevropy*, 1893, 1. I quote from Nik. – on[7] p 91 footnote 1).

This shows how wrong is the assertion that the growth of the market in capitalist society caused by the specialisation of social labour must cease as soon as all natural producers become commodity producers. Russian carriage building has long become commodity production, but wheel rims, say, are still made in every carriage builder's (or wheelwright's) shop; the technical level is low, production is split up among a mass of producers. Technical progress must entail the specialisation of different parts of production, their socialisation, and, consequently, the expansion of the market.

Here the following reservation must be made. All that has been said by no means implies the rejection of the proposition that a capitalist nation cannot exist without foreign markets. Under capitalist production, an equilibrium between production and consumption is achieved only by a series of fluctuations; the larger the scale of production, and the wider the circle of consumers it is calculated to serve, the more violent are the fluctuations. It can be understood, therefore, that when bourgeois production has reached a high degree of development it can no longer keep within the limits of the national state: competition compels the capitalists to keep on expanding production and to seek foreign markets for the mass sale of their products. Obviously, the fact that a capitalist nation must have foreign markets just as little violates the law that the market is a simple expression of the social division of labour under commodity economy and, consequently, that it can grow as infinitely as the division of labour, as crises violate the law of value. Lamentations about markets appeared in Russian literature only when certain branches of our capitalist production (for example, the cotton industry) had reached full development, embraced nearly the entire home market and become concentrated in a few huge enterprises. The best proof that the material basis of the idle talk and 'questions' of markets is precisely the interests of our large-scale capitalist industry, is the fact that nobody in our literature has yet prophesied the ruin of our handicraft industry because of the disappearance of 'markets', although the handicraft industry produces values totalling over a thousand million rubles and supplies the very same impoverished 'people'. The wailing about the ruin of our industry due to the shortage of markets is nothing more than a thinly disguised manoeuvre of our capitalists, who in this way exert pressure on policy, identify (in humble avowal of their own 'impotence') the interests of their pockets with the interests of the 'country' and are capable of making the government pursue a policy of colonial conquest, and even of involving it in war for the sake of protecting such 'state' interests. The bottomless pit of Narodnik utopianism and Narodnik simplicity is needed for the acceptance of this wailing about markets – these crocodile tears of a quite firmly established and already conceited bourgeoisie – as proof of the 'impotence' of Russian capitalism!

The second conclusion is that 'the impoverishment of the masses of the people' (that indispensable point in all the Narodnik arguments about the market) not only does not hinder the development of capitalism, but, on the contrary, is the expression of that development, is a condition of capitalism and strengthens it. Capitalism needs the 'free labourer', and impoverishment consists in the petty producers being converted into wage-workers. The impoverishment of the masses is accompanied by the enrichment of a few exploiters, the ruin and decline of small establishments is accompanied by the strengthening of development of bigger ones; both processes facilitate the growth of the market: the 'impoverished' peasant who formerly lived by his own farming now lives by 'earning', i.e. by the sale of his labour-power; he now has to purchase essential articles of consumption (although in a smaller quantity and of inferior quality). On the other hand, the means of production from which this peasant is freed are concentrated in the hands of a minority, are converted into *capital*, and the product now appears on the market. This is the only explanation of the fact that the mass expropriation of our peasantry in the post-Reform epoch has been accompanied by an increase and not a decrease in the gross productivity of the country[8] and by the growth of the home market: it is a known fact that there has been an enormous increase in the output of the big factories and works and that there has been a considerable extension of the handicraft industries – both work mainly for the home market – and there has been a similar increase in the amount of grain circulating in the home markets (the development of the grain trade within the country).

The third conclusion – about the significance of the production of means of production – calls for a correction to the table. As has already been stated, that table does not at all claim to depict the whole process of development of capitalism, but only to show how the replacement of natural by commodity economy and of the latter by capitalist economy affects the market. That is why accumulation was disregarded in the table. Actually, however, capitalist society cannot exist without accumulating, for competition compels every capitalist on pain of ruin to expand production. Such expansion of production is depicted in the table: producer I, for example, in the interval between the 3rd and 4th periods, expanded his output of *c* threefold: from 2 *c* to 6 *c*; formerly he worked alone in his workshop – now he has two wage-workers. Obviously, that expansion of production could not have taken place without accumulation: he had to build a special workshop for several persons, to acquire implements of production on a larger scale, and to purchase larger quantities of raw materials and much else. The same applies to producer IV, who expanded the production of *b*. This expansion of individual establishments, the concentration of production, must of necessity have entailed (or increased, it makes no difference) the production of means of production for the capitalists: machines, iron, coal, etc. The concentration of production increased the productivity of labour, replaced hand by machine labour and discarded a certain number of workers. On the other hand, there was a development in the production of these machines and other means of production, converted by the capitalist into constant capital which now begins to grow more rapidly than variable capital. If, for example, we compare the 4th period with the 6th, we shall find that the production of means of production has increased 50 per cent (because in the former case there are two capitalist enterprises requiring an increase of constant capital, and in the latter, three): by comparing this increase with the growth in the production of articles of consumption we arrive at the more rapid growth of the production of means of production mentioned above.

The whole meaning and significance of this law of the more rapid growth of means of production lies in the one fact that the replacement of hand by machine labour – in general the technical progress that accompanies machine industry – calls for the intense development of the production of coal and iron, those real 'means of production as means of production'. It is clearly evident from the following statement that the author failed to understand the meaning of this law, and allowed the schemes depicting the process to screen its real nature from him: 'Viewed from the side this production of means of production as means of production seems absolutely absurd, but the accumulation of money for money's sake by Plyushkin[9] was also (?!!)) an absolutely absurd process. Both know not what they do'. That is precisely what the Narodniks try their utmost to prove – the absurdity of Russian capitalism, which, they aver, is ruining the people, but is not providing a higher organisation of production. Of course, that is a fairy-tale. There is nothing 'absurd' in replacing hand by machine labour: on the contrary, the progressive work of human technique consists precisely in this. The higher the level of technical development the more is human hand labour ousted, being replaced by machines of increasing complexity: an ever larger place is taken in the country's total production by machines and the articles needed for their manufacture.[10]

These three conclusions must be supplemented by two further remarks.

Firstly, what has been said does not negate the

'contradiction in the capitalist mode of production' which Marx spoke of in the following words: 'The labourers as buyers of commodities are important for the market. But as sellers of their own commodity – labour-power – capitalist society tends to keep them down to the minimum price' (*Capital*, Vol II, p 320, fn 32). It has been shown above that in capitalist society that part of social production which produces articles of consumption must also grow. The development of the production of means of production merely sets the above-mentioned contradiction aside, but does not abolish it. It can only be eliminated with the elimination of the capitalist mode of production itself. It goes without saying, however, that it is utterly absurd to regard that contradiction as an obstacle to the full development of capitalism in Russia (as the Narodniks are fond of doing); incidentally, that is sufficiently explained by the table.

Secondly, when discussing the relation between the growth of capitalism and of the 'market', we must not lose sight of the indubitable fact that the development of capitalism inevitably entails a rising level of requirements for the entire population, including the industrial proletariat. This rise is created in general by the increasing frequency of exchange of products, which results in more frequent contacts between the inhabitants of town and country, of different geographical localities, and so forth. It is also brought about by the crowding together, the concentration of the industrial proletariat, which enhances their class-consciousness and sense of human dignity and enables them to wage a successful struggle against the predatory tendencies of the capitalist system. This law of increasing requirements has manifested itself with full force in the history of Europe – compare, for example, the French proletariat of the end of the eighteenth and of the end of the nineteenth centuries, or the British worker of the 1840s[11] and of today. This same law operates in Russia, too: the rapid development of commodity economy and capitalism in the post-Reform epoch has caused a rise in the level of requirements of the 'peasantry' too: the peasants have begun to live a 'cleaner' life (as regards clothing, housing, and so forth). That this undoubtedly progressive phenomenon must be placed to the credit of Russian capitalism and of nothing else is proved if only by the generally known fact (noted by all the investigators of our village handicrafts and of peasant economy in general) that the peasants of the industrial localities live a far 'cleaner' life than the peasants engaged exclusively in agriculture and hardly touched by capitalism. Of course, that phenomenon is manifested primarily and most readily in the adoption of the purely outward, ostentatious aspect of 'civilisation', but only arrant reactionaries like Mr V V[12] are capable of bewailing it and seeing nothing in it but 'decline'.

VII

To understand what, in fact, the 'market question' consists of, it is best to compare the Narodnik and Marxist conceptions of the process illustrated by the *diagram* (showing exchanges between the capitalists of sphere *A* and the direct producers of sphere *W*) and by the *table* (showing the conversion of the natural economy of 6 producers into capitalist economy).

If we take the diagram we get no explanation at all. Why does capitalism develop? Where does it come from? It is represented as a sort of 'accident'; its emergence is attributed either to '*we* took the wrong road' ... or to 'implantation' by the authorities. Why do 'the masses become impoverished'? This again is not answered by the diagram, and in place of an answer the Narodniks dispose of the matter with sentimental phrases about a 'time-hallowed system', deviation from the true path, and similar nonsense which the celebrated 'subjective method in sociology' is so good at inventing.

The inability to explain capitalism, and preference for utopias instead of a study and elucidation of reality, lead to a denial of the significance and strength of capitalism. It is like a hopeless invalid who has no source from which to draw strength for development. And we shall introduce into the condition of that invalid an insignificant, almost impalpable improvement if we say that he can develop by producing 'means of production as means of production'.[13] That requires the technical development of capitalism, and we see that precisely this development is lacking. For that capitalism must embrace the whole country, but we see that 'it is not possible for the development of capitalism to become universal'.

If, however, we take the table, neither the development of capitalism nor the impoverishment of the people will appear to be accidental. They are necessary concomitants of the growth of commodity production based on the division of social labour. The question of the market is entirely eliminated, because the market is nothing other than the expression of that division of labour and commodity production. The development of capitalism is now seen not only as a possibility (something the author of the paper could at best[14] have proved), but also as a necessity, because once social economy is based on the division of labour and the commodity form of the product, technical progress must inevitably lead to the strengthening and deepening of capitalism.

The question now arises: why should we accept the second view? By what criterion is it correct?

By the facts of contemporary Russian economic reality.

The pivot of the table is the transition from commodity to capitalist economy, the differentiation of the commodity producers into capitalists and proletarians. And if we turn to the phenomena of the contemporary social economy of Russia we shall see that the foremost of them is precisely the *differentiation* of our small producers. If we take the peasant agriculturists, we shall find that, on the one hand, masses of peasants are giving up the land, losing economic independence, turning into proletarians, and, on the other hand, peasants are continually enlarging their crop areas and adopting improved farming methods. On the one hand, peasants are losing farm property (livestock and implements) and, on the other hand, peasants are acquiring improved implements, are beginning to procure machines, and so forth (*Cf.* V V, *Progressive Trends in Peasant Farming*). On the one hand, peasants are giving up the land, selling or leasing their allotments, and, on the other hand, peasants are renting allotments and are greedily buying privately-owned land. All these are commonly known facts,[15] established long, long ago, the only *explanation* of which lies in the laws of commodity economy, which splits our 'community' peasants, too, into a bourgeoisie and a proletariat. If we take the village handicraftsmen we shall find that in the post-Reform epoch not only have new industries emerged and the old ones developed more rapidly (the result of the differentiation of the agricultural peasantry just mentioned, the result of the progressing social division of labour[16]), but, in addition, the mass of handicraftsmen have been growing poorer and poorer, sinking into dire poverty and losing economic independence, while an insignificant minority have been growing rich at the expense of that mass, accumulating vast amounts of capital, and turning into buyers-up, monopolising the market, and in the overwhelming majority of our handicraft industries, have, in the end, organised a completely capitalist *domestic system of large-scale production*.

The existence of these two polarising trends among our petty producers clearly shows that capitalism and mass impoverishment, far from precluding, actually condition each other, and irrefutably proves that capitalism is already the main background of the economic life of Russia.

That is why it will be no paradox to say that the fact of the break-up of the peasantry provides the answer to the 'question of markets'.

One cannot help noting, also, that the very (current) presentation of the notorious 'market question' harbours a number of absurdities. The usual formula is based on the most incredible assumptions – that the economic system of society can be built or destroyed at the will of some group of persons – 'intellectuals' or the 'government' (otherwise the question could not be raised – 'can' capitalism develop? 'must' Russia pass through capitalism? 'should' the village community be preserved? and so forth) – that capitalism precludes the impoverishment of the people, that the market is something separate from and independent of capitalism, some special condition for its development.

Unless these absurdities are corrected, the question cannot be answered.

Indeed, let us imagine that in answer to the question: 'Can capitalism develop in Russia, when the masses of the people are poor and are becoming still poorer?' somebody would say the following: 'Yes, it can, because capitalism will develop not on account of articles of consumption, but on account of means of production'. Obviously, such an answer is based on the absolutely correct idea that the total productivity of a capitalist nation increases chiefly on account of means of production (i.e. more on account of means of production than of articles of consumption); but it is still more obvious that such an answer cannot advance the solution of the question one iota, just as you cannot draw a correct conclusion from a syllogism with a correct minor premise but an absurd major premise. Such an answer (I repeat) already presupposes that capitalism is developing, is embracing the whole country, passing to a higher technical stage (large-scale machine industry), whereas the question itself is based on the denial of the possibility of capitalism developing and of small-scale production being replaced by large-scale production.

The 'market question' must be removed from the sphere of fruitless speculation about 'possibility' and 'necessity' to the solid ground of reality, that of studying and *explaining* what shape the Russian economic order is taking, and why it is taking that shape and no other.

I shall confine myself to quoting some examples from the material in my possession in order to show concretely on what data this proposition is based.

To illustrate the differentiation of the small producers and the fact that not only a process of impoverishment, but also of the creation of large-scale (relatively) bourgeois economy is taking place among them. I shall quote data for three purely agricultural uyezds in different gubernias of European Russia: Dnieper Uyezd in Taurida Gubernia, Novouzensk Uyezd in Samara Gubernia, and Kamyshin Uyezd in Saratov Gubernia. The data are taken from Zemstvo statistical abstracts. To forestall possible statements that the uyezds chosen are not typical (in our outlying regions, which hardly experienced serfdom and largely became populated only under post-Reform, 'free' conditions, differentiation has, indeed, made more rapid strides than at the centre) let me say the following:

1) Of the three mainland uyezds of Taurida Gubernia I have chosen Dnieper Uyezd because it is wholly Russian (0.6% are colonist farms) and is inhabited by community peasants.

2) For Novouzensk Uyezd the data concern only the

Groups of peasants according to economic strength	Dnieper Uyezd					Nouvouzensk	
	No of house-holds	%	Crop area (dess.)	%	Crop area per house-hold (dess.)	No. of house-holds	%
Poor group	7,880	40	38,439	11	4.8 ⎫	10,504	37
Middle group	8,234	42	137,344	43	16.6 ⎬ 10.9	10,757	38
Prosperous group	3,643	18	150,614	46	41.3 ⎭	7,014	25
Totals	19,757	100	326,397	100	17.8	28,275	100

Russian (community) population (see *Statistical Returns for Novouzensk Uyezd*, pp 432-39, column *a*), and do not include the so-called farmstead peasants, i.e. those community peasants who have left the community and have settled separately on purchased or rented land. The addition of these direct representatives of capitalist farming[17] would show an even greater differentiation.

3) For Kamyshin Uyezd the data concern only the Great-Russian (community) population.

The classification in the abstracts is – for Dnieper Uyezd – according to dessiatines of crop area per household; for the others – according to number of draught animals.

The *poor* group includes households – in Dnieper Uyezd – cultivating no land, or with crop areas of up to 10 dessiatines per household; in Novouzensk and Kamyshin uyezds – households having no draught animals or one. The *middle* group includes households in Dnieper Uyezd having from 10 to 25 dessiatines of crop area; in Novouzensk Uyezd – households having from 2 to 4 draught animals; in Kamyshin Uyezd – households having from 2 to 3 draught animals. The *prosperous* group includes households having over 25 dessiatines (Dnieper Uyezd), or having more than 4 draught animals (Nouvouzensk Uyezd) and more than 3 (Kamyshin Uyezd).

From these data it is quite evident that the process going on among our agricultural and community peasants is not

	Uyezd				Kamyshin Uyezd		
Crop area (dess.)	%	Crop area per house-hold (dess.)	No of house-holds	%	Crop area (dess.)	%	Crop area per house-hold (dess.)
36,007	8	3.4 ⎫	9,313	54	29,194	20	3.1 ⎫
128,986	29	12 ⎬ 7.75	4,980	29	52,735	35	10.6 ⎬ 5.7
284,069	63	40.5 ⎭	2,881	17	67,844	45	23.5 ⎭
449,062	100	15.9	17,174	100	149,703	100	8.7

one of impoverishment and ruin in general, but a process of splitting into a bourgeoisie and a proletariat. A vast mass of peasants (the poor group) – about a half on the average – are losing economic independence. They now have only an insignificant part of the total farming of the local peasants – some 13% (on the average) of the crop area; the area under crops is 3-4 dessiatines per household. To show what such a crop area means, let me say that in Taurida Gubernia, for a peasant household to subsist exclusively by independent farming, without resorting to so-called 'outside employments', it must have 17-18 dessiatines[18] under crops. Obviously, the members of the bottom group already subsist far less by their farming than by outside employments, i.e. the sale of their labour-power. And if we turn to more detailed data characterising the conditions of the peasants in this group we shall see that precisely this group provides the largest contingent of those who give up their farming, lease their allotments, have no working implements and seek employment elsewhere. The peasants in this group represent our rural proletariat.

But, on the other hand, from among these very same community peasants quite another group, of an entirely opposite character, is emerging. The peasants in the top group have crop areas 7 to 10 times larger than those of the peasants in the bottom group. If we compare these crop areas (23-40 dessiatines per household) with the 'normal' number of dessiatines under crops that a family needs in order to live comfortably by its farming alone, we shall find that they are double or treble that amount. Obviously, these peasants already engage in agriculture to obtain an income, to trade in grain. They accumulate considerable savings and use them to improve their farms and farming methods; for example, they buy agricultural machines and improved implements. In Novouzensk Uyezd as a whole, for instance, 14% of the householders have improved agricultural implements; of the peasants in the top group 42% of the householders have improved implements (so that the peasants in the top group account for 75% of the total number of households in the uyezd possessing improved agricultural implements), and concentrate in their hands 82% of the total improved implements owned by the 'peasantry'.[19] The peasants in the top group can no longer manage their crop sowing with their own labour force and therefore resort to the hiring of workers: for example, in Novouzensk Uyezd 35% of the householders in the top group employ regular wage-workers (not counting those hired, for instance, for the harvesting, etc.); it is the same in Dnieper Uyezd. In short, the peasants in the top group undoubtedly constitute a bourgeoisie. Their strength now is not based on plundering other producers (as is the strength of the usurers and 'kulaks'), but on the independent organisation[20] of production: in the hands of this group, which constitutes only one-fifth of the peasantry, is concentrated more than one-half of the total crop area (I take the general average area for all three uyezds). If we bear in mind that the productivity of labour (i.e. the harvests) of these peasants is immeasurably higher than that of the ground-scratching proletarians in the bottom group, we cannot but draw the conclusions that the chief motive force in grain production is the rural bourgeoisie.

What influence was this splitting of the peasantry into a bourgeoisie and a proletariat (the Narodniks see nothing in this process but the 'impoverishment of the masses') bound to have on the size of the 'market', i.e. on the proportion of grain that is converted into a *commodity*? Obviously, that proportion was bound to grow considerably, because the mass of grain possessed by the peasants in the top group far exceeded their own needs and went to the market; on the other hand, the members of the bottom group had to buy extra grain with money earned by outside work.

To quote exact data on this point we must now turn not to Zemstvo statistical abstracts, but to V Y Postnikov's book: *Peasant Farming in South Russia*. Using Zemstvo statistical data, Postnikov describes peasant farming in three mainland uyezds of Taurida Gubernia (Berdyansk, Melitopol and Dnieper) and analyses that farming according to different groups of peasants (divided into 6 categories according to crop area: 1) cultivating no land; 2) cultivating up to 5 dessiatines; 3) from 5 to 10 dessiatines; 4) 10 to 25 dessiatines; 5) 25 to 50 dessiatines; 6) over 50 dessiatines). Investigating the relation of the different groups to the market, the author divides the crop area of each farm into the following 4 parts: 1) the *farm-service area* – as Postnikov calls the part of the crop area which provides the seed necessary for sowing; 2) the *food area* – provides grain for the sustenance of the family and labourers; 3) the *fodder area* – provides fodder for the draught animals, and lastly, 4) the *commercial* or *market area* provides the product which is converted into a commodity and disposed of on the market. It goes without saying that only the last area provides income in *cash*, whereas the others yield it in kind, i.e. provide a product that is consumed on the farm.

Calculating the size of each of these plots in the different crop-area groups of the peasantry, Postnikov presents the following table (p 74 – *ed*).

We see from these data that the bigger the farm, the more it assumes a commodity character and the larger is the proportion of grain grown for sale (12-36-52-61% according to group). The principal grain growers, the peasants in the two top groups (they have more than half the total area under crops), sell more than half of their total agricultural product (52% and 61%).

If the peasantry were not split up into a bourgeoisie and a proletariat, if, in other words, the area under crops were divided among all the 'peasants' 'equally', *all* of them would then belong to the middle group (those cultivating 10 to 25 dessiatines), and only 36% of the total grain, i.e. the product of 518,136 dessiatines of crop area (36% of 1,439,267 = 518,

		Out of 100 dess. under crops			Cash income		In the 3 uyezds of Taurida Gubernia		
		Food area	Fodder area	Commercial area	Per dess. under crops	Per household	Total under crops (dessiatines)	Of which, commercial areas (dessiatines)	Average under crops in each group
					rubles				
Cultivating up to 5 dess.	6	90.7	42.3	−30	—	—	34.070	—	3.5 dess.
Cultivating 5 to 10 dess.	6	44.7	37.5	+11.8	3.77	30	140.426	16.851	8
Cultivating 10 to 25 dess.	6	27.5	30	36.5	11.68	191	540.093	194.433	16.4
Cultivating 25 to 50 dess.	6	17.0	25	52	16.64	574	494.095	256.929	34.5
Cultivating over 50	6	12.0	21	61	19.52	1.500	230.583	140.656	75
Totals	6			42			1.439.267	608.869	17-18 dess.

1) Postnikov does not give the penultimate column: I compiled it myself.

2) Postnikov calculates the cash income on the assumption that the entire commercial area is planted to wheat, and taking the average yield and the average price of grain.

136), would appear on the market. But now, as can be seen from the table, 42% of the total grain, the product of 608,869 dessiatines, goes to the market. Thus, the 'impoverishment of the masses', the complete decline of the farms of 40% of the peasants (the poor group, i.e. those cultivating up to 10 dessiatines), the formation of a rural proletariat have led to the produce of *90,000*[21] dessiatines of land under crops being thrown on to the market.

I do not at all want to say that the growth of the 'market' as a consequence of the differentiation of the peasantry was limited only to this. Far from it. We have seen, for example, that the peasants acquire improved implements, i.e. turn their savings to the 'production of means of production'. We have seen that, in addition to grain, another commodity, human labour-power, has come on to the market. I do not refer to all this only because I have quoted this example for a narrow and specific purpose: to show that here in Russia the impoverishment of the masses is actually leading to the strengthening of commodity and capitalist economy. I deliberately chose a product like grain, which everywhere and always is the last and the slowest to be drawn into commodity circulation. And that is why I took an exclusively agricultural locality.

I shall now take another example, relating to a purely industrial area – Moscow Gubernia. Peasant farming is described by the Zemstvo statisticians in volumes VI and VII of *Statistical Returns for Moscow Gubernia*, which contain a number of excellent essays on the handicraft industries. I shall confine myself to quoting one passage from the essay on 'The Lace Industry'[22] which explains how and why the post-Reform epoch saw a particularly rapid development of peasant handicrafts.

The lace industry arose in the twenties of the present century in two neighbouring villages of Voronovo Volost, Podolsk Uyezd. 'In the 1840s it began to spread slowly to other nearby villages, although it did not yet cover a big area. But beginning with the sixties and especially during the last three or four years, it has spread rapidly to the surrounding countryside.'

Of the 32 villages in which this industry is practised at the present time it began: in 2 villages in 1820; in 4 villages in 1840; in 5 villages in the 1860s; in 7 villages in 1870-1875; in 14 villages in 1876-1879.

'If we investigate the causes of this phenomenon', says the author of the essay, 'i.e. the extremely rapid spread of the industry precisely in the last few years, we shall find that, on the one hand, during that period the peasants' living conditions greatly deteriorated and, on the other hand, that the requirements of the population – that part of it which is in more favourable circumstances – considerably increased.'

In confirmation of this the author borrows from the Moscow Zemstvo statistics the following data, which I give in the form of a table (p 77 – *ed*).[23]

'These figures', continues the author, 'are eloquent proof that the *total* number of horses, cows and small livestock in that volost increased, but this increased prosperity fell to the lot of certain individuals, namely, the category of householders owning 2-3 and more horses....

'... Consequently, we see that, side by side with an increase in the number of peasants who have neither cows nor horses, there is an increase in the number of those who stop cultivating their land: they have no animals, and, therefore, not enough manure; the land becomes exhausted, it is not worth tilling; to get food for themselves and their families, to avert starvation, it is not enough for the males alone to engage in some industry – they did that previously, when they were free from farm work – now, other members of the family must also seek outside employment....

'... The figures we gave in the tables showed us something else; in those villages there was also an *increase* in the number of people having 2-3 horses, or cows. Consequently, the prosperity of those peasants increased, and yet, at the same time, we said that "all the women and children in such and such a village engage in industry". How is this to be explained?... To explain this phenomenon we must see what sort of life is lived in those villages, and become more closely acquainted with their domestic conditions, and then, perhaps, ascertain what accounts for this strong urge to produce goods for the market.

'We shall not, of course, stop here to investigate in detail under what fortunate circumstances there gradually emerge from the peasant population stronger individuals, stronger families, what conditions enable that prosperity, once it has appeared, to grow rapidly and cause it to grow to such an extent as to considerably distinguish one section of the village inhabitants from the other. To follow this process it is sufficient to point to one of the most ordinary occurrences in a peasant village. In a village, a certain peasant is reputed among his fellow villagers to be a healthy, strong, sober working man. He has a large family, mostly sons, also distinguished for their physical strength and good traits. They all live together; there is no dividing up. They get an allotment for 4-5 persons. It does not, of course, require the labour of all the members of the family to cultivate it. And so, two or three of the sons regularly engage in some outside or local industry, and only during the haymaking season do they drop their industry for a short time and help the family with the field work. The individual

VORONOVO VOLOST, PODOLSK UYEZD:

In Voronovo Volost	Number of householders	Number of		Per 100 persons of both sexes			Numbers of householders owning					Number of horses owned by householders having				Number of allotment-holding householders				
		Horses	Cows	Horses	Cows	Small livestock	No horses	1 horse	2 horses	3 horses	More than 3 horses	1 horse	2 horses	3 horses	More than 3 horses	Total	cultivating allotment themselves	with hired labour	Not cultivating land	
In 1869 there were	1,233	1,473	1,472	22	22	30	276 / 22%	567 / 46%	298 / 24%	70 / 6%	22 / 2%	567 / 39%	596 / 40%	210 / 14%	100 / 7%	1,067	900 / 84%	92 / 9%	75 / 7%	
In 1877 there were	1,244	1,607	1,726	25	27	38	319 / 26%	465 / 37%	313 / 25%	95 / 8%	52 / 4%	465 / 29%	626 / 39%	285 / 18%	231 / 14%	1,166	965 / 82.5%	5 / 0.5%	196 / 17%	

members of the family do not keep their earnings, but pool them. Given other favourable circumstances, the combined income considerably exceeds the expenditure necessary to satisfy the family's requirements. Money is saved and, as a consequence, the family is able to engage in industry under better conditions: it can buy raw materials for cash at first hand, it can sell the goods produced when they fetch a good price, and can dispense with the services of all kinds of "hirers-out of labour", men and women dealers, and so forth.

'It becomes possible to hire a worker or two, or give out work to be done at home by poor peasants who have lost the possibility of doing any job quite independently. Due to these and similar circumstances, the strong family we have mentioned is able to obtain profit not only from its own labour. We are not speaking here, of course, of those cases where individuals known as kulaks, sharks, emerge from those families; we are examining the most ordinary occurrences among the peasant population. The tables given in Volume II of the *Abstract* and in Part I of Volume VI clearly show that as the conditions of one section of the peasantry grow worse, in the majority of cases there is an increase in the prosperity of the other, smaller section, or of individual members.

'As industrial occupation spreads, intercourse with the outside world, with the town, in this case with Moscow, becomes more frequent, and some of the Moscow customs gradually penetrate into the village and are met with at first precisely in these more prosperous families. They buy samovars, table crockery and glass, they wear "neater" clothes. Whereas at first this neatness of clothing takes the shape, among men, of boots in place of bast shoes, among the women leather shoes and boots are the crowning glory, so to speak, of neater clothing; they prefer bright, motley calicoes and kerchiefs, figured woollen shawls, and similar charms....

'... In the peasant family it has been the custom "for ages" for the wife to clothe her husband, herself and the children.... As long as they grew their own flax, less money had to be spent on the purchase of cloth and other materials required for clothing, and this money was obtained from the sale of poultry, eggs, mushrooms, berries, a spare skein of yarn, or piece of linen. All the rest was made at home. It was such circumstances, i.e. the domestic production of all those articles which the peasant women were expected to make, and the fact that they spent on it all the time they had free from field work, that explain, in the present case, the extremely slow development of the lace industry in the villages in Voronovo Volost. Lace was made mainly by the young women of the more prosperous or of the larger families, where it was not necessary for all the women to spin flax or weave linen. But cheap calico gradually began to oust linen, and to this other circumstances were added: either the flax crop failed, or the wife wanted to make her husband a red calico shirt and herself a smarter dress, and so the custom of weaving various sorts of linen and kerchiefs at home for peasants' clothing gradually died out, or became very restricted. And the clothing itself underwent a change, partly because homespun cloth was displaced by factory-made cloth....

'... That explains why the majority of the population do all they can to make articles for sale, and even put their children to this work.'

This artless narrative of a careful observer clearly shows how the process of division of social labour takes place among our peasant masses, how it leads to the enhancement of commodity production (and, consequently, of the market), and how this commodity production, of itself, i.e. by virtue of the very relations in which it places the producer to the market, leads to the purchase and sale of labour-power becoming 'a most ordinary occurrence'.

VIII

In conclusion, it will, perhaps, be worth while to illustrate the disputed issue which, I think, is overburdened with abstractions, diagrams and formulae – by an examination of the argument advanced by one of the latest and most prominent representatives of 'current views'.

I am referring to Mr Nikolai – on.[24]

He regards as the greatest 'obstacle' to the development of capitalism in Russia the 'contraction' of the home market and the 'diminution' of the purchasing power of the peasants. The capitalisation of the handicraft industries, he says, ousted the domestic production of goods; the peasants had to buy their clothing. To obtain the money for this, the peasant took to the expansion of his crop area, and as the allotments were inadequate he carried this expansion far beyond the limits of rational farming; he raised the payment for rented land to scandalous heights, and in the end he was ruined. Capitalism dug its own grave, it brought 'people's economy' to the frightful crisis of 1891 and … stopped, having no ground under its feet, unable to 'continue along the same path'. Realising that '*we* have departed from the time-hallowed people's system' Russia is now waiting … for orders from the authorities 'to infuse large-scale production into the village community'.

Wherein lies the absurdity of this 'ever new' (for the Russian Narodniks) theory?

Is it that its author fails to understand the significance of the 'production of means of production as means of production'? Of course, not. Mr Nik. – on knows that law very well and even mentions that it operates in our country, too (pp 186, 203-204). True, in view of his faculty for castigating himself with contradictions, he sometimes (cf. p 123) forgets about that law, but it is obvious that the correction of such contradictions would not in the least correct the author's main (above-quoted) argument.

The absurdity of his theory lies in his inability to explain capitalism in this country and in basing his arguments about it on pure fictions.

The 'peasantry', who were ruined by the ousting of home-made products by factory-made products, are regarded by Mr Nik. – on as something homogeneous, internally cohesive, and reacting to all the events of life as one man.

Nothing of the kind exists in reality. Commodity production could not have arisen in Russia if the productive units (the peasant households) had not existed separately, and everybody knows that actually each of our peasants conducts his farming separately and independently of his fellows; he carries on the production of products, which become his private property, at his own exclusive risk; he enters into relation with the 'market' on his own.

Let us see how matters stand among the 'peasantry'.

'Being in need of money, the peasant enlarges his crop area excessively and is ruined.'

But, only the prosperous peasant can enlarge his crop area, the one who has seed for sowing, and a sufficient quantity of livestock and implements. *Such* peasants (and they, as we know, are the minority) do, indeed, extend their crop areas and expand their farming to such an extent that they cannot cope with it without the aid of hired labourers. The majority of peasants, however, are quite unable to meet their need for money by expanding their farming, for they have no stocks, or sufficient means of production. *Such* a peasant, in order to obtain money, seeks 'outside employments', i.e. takes his labour-power and not his product to the market. Naturally, work away from home entails a further decline in farming, and in the end the peasant leases his allotment to a rich fellow community member, who rounds off his farm and, of course, does not himself consume the product of the rented allotment, but sends it to the *market*. We get the 'impoverishment of the people', the growth of capitalism and the expansion of the market. But that is not all. Our rich peasant, fully occupied by his extended farming, can no longer produce as hitherto for his own needs, let us say footwear: it is more advantageous for him to buy it. As to the impoverished peasant, he, too, has to buy footwear; he cannot produce it on his farm for the simple reason that he no longer has one. There arises a demand for footwear and a supply of grain, produced in abundance by the enterprising peasant, who touches the soul of Mr V V with the progressive trend of his farming. The neighbouring handicraft footwear-makers find themselves in the same position as the agriculturists just described: to buy grain, of which the declining farm yields too little, production must be expanded. Again, of course, production is expanded only by the handicraftsman who has savings, i.e. the representative of the minority; he is able to hire workers, or give work out to poor peasants to be done at home. The members of the majority of handicraftsmen, however, cannot even think of enlarging their workshops: they are glad to 'get work' from the moneyed buyer-up, i.e.

to find a purchaser of their only commodity – their labour-power. Again we get the impoverishment of the people, the growth of capitalism and the expansion of the market; a new impetus is given to the further development and intensification of the social division of labour. Where will that movement end? Nobody can say, just as nobody can say where it began, and after all that is not important. The important thing is that we have before us a single, living organic process, the process of the development of commodity economy and the growth of capitalism. 'Depeasantising' in the countryside shows us the beginning of this process, its genesis, its early stages; large-scale capitalism in the towns shows us the end of the process, its tendency. Try to tear these phenomena apart, try to examine them separately and independently of each other and you will not get your argument to hang together; you will be unable to explain either one phenomenon or the other, either the impoverishment of the people or the growth of capitalism.

Mostly, however, those who advance such arguments, which have neither beginning nor end, being unable to explain the process, break off the investigation with the statement that one of the two phenomena equally unintelligible to them (and, of course, precisely the one that contradicts 'the morally developed sense of the critically thinking individual') is 'absurd', 'accidental', 'hangs in the air'.

In actual fact, what is 'hanging in the air' is of course only their own arguments.

Notes

[1] 'The Market Question' was a lecture given by G B Krasin and discussed in St Petersburg marxist circles – *ed*.

[2] There are two errors in Lenin's manuscript: 3,172 instead of 3,172½, and 10,828½ instead of 10,830, as can be seen from the scheme given in the text – *ed*.

[3] I do not mean to say that such a thing is absolutely impossible as an individual case. Here, however, we are not discussing special cases, but the general law of development of capitalist society. I shall explain this point by the following scheme:

I 4,000c + 1,000v + 1,000s = 6,000
II 1,500c + 750v + 750s = 3,000
I (1,000v + 500s) = II 1,500c
I 500s are accumulated, added to I 4,000c:
I 4,500c + 1,000v + (500s) = 6,000
II 1,500c + 750v + 750s = 3,000

I 4,500c + 1,000v + 1,000s = 6,500
II 1,500c + 750v + 750s = 3,000

I (1,000v + 500s) = 1,500c
I 500s are accumulated as before, and so forth.

[4] That is why the conclusion drawn can be formulated somewhat differently: in capitalist society, production (and, consequently, 'the market') can grow either on account of the growth of articles of consumption, or, and mainly, of technical progress, i.e. the ousting of hand by machine labour, for the change in proportion of v to c expressed precisely the diminution of the role of hand labour.

[5] m stands for 'mehrwert' – surplus value; u.m.d. means 'and so on' – *ed*.

[6] This also applies to the 5th and 6th periods.

[7] Nik. – on or N. – on was the pseudonym of N F Danielson, one of the ideologists of Liberal Narodism of the 1880s and 1890s. The book by Nik. – on quoted here is called *Sketches on our Post-Reform Social Economy*, St Petersburg 1893 – *ed*.

[8] This may be a debatable point only in relation to the agricultural industry. 'Grain production is in a state of absolute stagnation', says Mr N. – on, for example. He bases his conclusion on the data for only eight years (1871-1878). Let us examine the data for a longer period; an eight year period is, of course, too short. Let us compare the statistics for the 1860s (*Military Statistical Abstract*, 1871), the 1870s (N. – on's data) and the 1880s (*Returns for Russia*, 1890). The data cover 50 gubernias of European Russia and all crops, including potatoes.

Annual average for	Sown (thousands of chetverts)		Harvested (thousands of chetverts)		Yield (times)	Population (thousands)
1864-1866 (3)	71,696	100	151,840	100	3.12	61,421,100 (1867)
1871-1878 (8)	71,378	99.5	195,024	128.4	3.73	76,594,124.7 (1876)
1883-1887 (5)	80,293	111.9	254,914	167.8	4.17	85,395,139 (1886)

[9] Plyushkin is a character in Gogol's *Dead Souls*. The name Plyushkin, a tight-fisted landlord, has come to typify extreme avarice – *ed*.

[10] Naturally, therefore, it is wrong to divide the development of

capitalism into development in breadth and in depth: the entire development proceeds on account of division of labour; there is no 'essential' difference between the two features. Actually, however, the difference between them boils down to different stages of technical progress. In the lower stages of the development of capitalist technique – simple co-operation and manufacture – the production of means of production as means of production does not yet exist: it emerges and attains enormous development only at the higher stage – larger-scale machine history.

[11] Cf Frederick Engels, *The Condition of The Working Class in England in 1844*. That was a state of most horrible and sordid poverty (in the literal sense of the word) and of utter loss of the sense of human dignity.

[12] V V is the abbreviation for Vorontsov, another Narodnik economist – *ed*.

[13] That is, the replacement of small industrial units by big ones, the ousting of hand by machine labour.

[14] That is, if he correctly appraised and properly understood the significance of the production of means of production.

[15] The peasants themselves very aptly call this process 'depeasantising'. (See *Agricultural Survey of Nizhni-Novgorod Gubernia for 1892*, Nizhni-Novgorod, 1893, Vol III pp 186-87).

[16] One of Mr Nikolai – on's biggest theoretical mistakes is that he ignores this phenomenon.

[17] Indeed 2,294 farmstead peasants have 123,252 dessiatines under crops (i.e. an average of 53 dessiatines per farmer). They employ 2,662 male labourers (and 234 women). They have over 40,000 horses and oxen. Very many improved implements: see p 453 of *Statistical Returns for Novouzensk Uyezd*.

[18] In Samara and Saratov gubernias the amount will be about a third lower, as the local population is less prosperous.

[19] Altogether, the peasants in the uyezd have 5,724 improved implements.

[20] Which, of course, is also based on plunder, only not the plunder of independent producers, but of workers.

[21] 90,733 dessiatines = 6.3% of the total crop area.

[22] *Statistical Returns for Moscow Gubernia*. Section of Economic Statistics Vol VI, Issue 2, Handicraft Industries of Moscow Gubernia, Moscow 1880.

[23] I have omitted data on the distribution of cows (the conclusion is the same) and added the percentages.

[24] It goes without sasying that there can be no question here of examining his entire work, a separate book would be required for that. We can only examine *one* of his favourite arguments.

2. Capitalism in Agriculture – Kautsky's Book and Mr Bulgakov's Article

First Article

Nachalo, No. 1-2 (Section II, pp 1-21), contains an article by Mr S Bulgakov entitled: 'A Contribution to the Question of the Capitalist Evolution of Agriculture', which is a criticism of Kautsky's work on the agrarian question. Mr Bulgakov rightly says that 'Kautsky's book represents a whole world outlook', that it is of great theoretical and practical importance. It is, perhaps, the first systematic and scientific investigation of a question that has stimulated a heated controversy in all countries, and still continues to do so, even among writers who are agreed on general views and who regard themselves as Marxists. Mr Bulgakov 'confines himself to negative criticism', to criticism of 'individual postulates in Kautsky's book' (which he 'briefly' – too briefly and very inexactly, as we shall see – reviews for the readers of *Nachalo*). 'Later on', Mr Bulgakov hopes 'to give a systematic exposition of the question of the capitalist evolution of agriculture' and thus 'also present a whole world outlook' in opposition to Kautsky's.

We have no doubt that Kautsky's book will give rise to no little controversy among Marxists in Russia, and that in Russia, too, some will oppose Kautsky, while others will support him. At all events, the writer of these lines disagrees most emphatically with Mr Bulgakov's opinion, with his appraisal of Kautsky's book. Notwithstanding Mr Bulgakov's admission that *Die Agrarfrage* [The Agrarian

---

Written in 1899. First published in the magazine *Zhizn* in 1900.
CW IV 109-159.

Question – *ed*] is a remarkable work', his appraisal is astonishingly sharp, and is written in a tone unusual in a controversy between authors of related tendencies. Here are samples of the expressions Mr Bulgakov uses: 'extremely superficial' ... 'equally little of both real agronomics and real economics' ... 'Kautsky employs *empty phrases* to evade serious scientific problems' (Mr Bulgakov's italics!!), etc, etc. We shall therefore carefully examine the expressions used by the stern critic and at the same time introduce the reader to Kautsky's book.

I

Even before Mr Bulgakov gets to Kautsky, he, in passing, takes a shot at Marx. It goes without saying that Mr Bulgakov emphasises the enormous services rendered by the great economist, but observes that in Marx's works one 'sometimes' comes across even 'erroneous views ... which have been sufficiently refuted by history'. 'Among such views is, for example, the one that in agriculture variable capital diminishes in relation to constant capital just as it does in manufacturing industry, so that the organic composition of agricultural capital continuously rises.' Who is mistaken here, Marx or Mr Bulgakov? Mr Bulgakov has in mind the fact that in agriculture the progress of technique and the growing intensity of farming often leads *to an increase* in the amount of labour necessary to cultivate a given plot of land. This is indisputable; but it is very far from being a refutation of the theory of the diminution of variable capital *relatively* to constant capital, *in proportion* to constant capital. Marx's theory merely asserts that the ratio $\frac{v}{c}$ (v = variable capital, c = constant capital) in general has a tendency to diminish, even when v increases per unit of area. Is Marx's theory refuted if, simultaneously, c increases still more rapidly? Agriculture in capitalist countries, taken by and large, shows a diminution of v and an increase of c. The rural population and the number of workers employed in agriculture are diminishing in Germany, in France, and in England, whereas the number of machines employed in agriculture is increasing. In Germany, for example, from 1882 to 1895, the rural population diminished from

19,200,000 to 18,500,000 (the number of wage-workers in agriculture diminished from 5,900,000 to 5,600,000), whereas the number of machines employed in agriculture increased from 458,369 to 913,391[1]; the number of steam-driven machines employed in agriculture increased from 2,731 (in 1879) to 12,856 (in 1897), while the total horse power of the steam-driven machinery employed increased still more. The number of cattle increased from 15,800,000 to 17,500,000 and the number of pigs from 9,200,000 to 12,200,000 (in 1883 and 1892 respectively). In France, the rural population diminished from 6,900,000 ('independent') in 1882 to 6,600,000 in 1892; and the number of agricultural machines increased as follows: 1862 – 132,784; 1882 – 278,896; 1892 – 355,795. The number of cattle was as follows: 12,000,000; 13,000,000; 13,700,000 respectively; the number of horses: 2,910,000; 2,840,000; 2,790,000 respectively (the reduction in the number of horses in the period 1882-92 was less significant than the reduction in the rural population). Thus, by and large, the history of modern capitalist countries has certainly not refuted, but has *confirmed* the applicability of Marx's law to agriculture. The mistake Mr Bulgakov made was that he too hastily raised certain facts in agronomics, without examining their significance, to the level of *general* economic laws. We emphasise 'general', because neither Marx nor his disciples ever regarded this law otherwise than as the law of the general tendencies of capitalism, and not as a law for all individual cases. Even in regard to industry Marx himself pointed out that periods of technical change (when the ratio $\frac{v}{c}$ diminishes) are followed by periods of progress on the given technical basis (when the ratio $\frac{v}{c}$ remains constant, and in certain cases may even increase). We know of cases in the industrial history of capitalist countries in which this law is contravened by entire branches of industry, as when large capitalist workshops (incorrectly termed factories) are broken up and supplanted by capitalist domestic industry. There cannot be any doubt that in agriculture the process of development of capitalism is immeasurably more complex and assumes incomparably more diverse forms.

Let us now pass to Kautsky. The outline of agriculture in the feudal epoch with which Kautsky begins is said to be 'very superficially compiled and superfluous'. It is difficult to understand the motive for such a verdict. We are sure that if Mr Bulgakov succeeds in realising his plan to give a systematic exposition of the capitalist evolution of agriculture, he will have to outline the main features of the *pre-capitalist* economics of agriculture. Without this the character of *capitalist* economics and the transitional forms which connect it with feudal economics cannot be understood. Mr Bulgakov himself admits the enormous importance of 'the form which agriculture assumed *at the beginning* [Mr Bulgakov's italics] of its capitalist course'. It is precisely with 'the beginning of the capitalist course' of European agriculture that Kautsky begins. In our opinion, Kautsky's outline of feudal agriculture is excellent; it reveals that remarkable distinctness and ability to select what is most important and essential without becoming submerged in details of secondary importance which, in general, are characteristic of this author. In his introduction Kautsky first of all gives an extremely precise and correct presentation of the question. In most emphatic terms he declares: 'There is not the slightest doubt – we are prepared to accept this *a priori (von vornherein)* – that agriculture does not develop according to the same pattern as industry: it is subject to special laws (pp 5-6). The task is 'to investigate whether capital is bringing agriculture under its domination and how it is dominating it, how it transforms it, how it invalidates old forms of production and forms of property and creates the need for new forms' (p 6). Such, and only such, a presentation of the question can result in a satisfactory explanation of 'the development of agriculture in capitalist society' (the title of the first, theoretical, part of Kautsky's book).

At the beginning of the 'capitalist course', agriculture was in the hands of the *peasantry*, which, as a general rule, was subordinated to the feudal regime of social economy. Kautsky first of all characterises the *system* of peasant farming, the combining of agriculture with domestic industry, and further the elements of decay in this paradise of petty-bourgeois and conservative writers (*à la* Sismondi), the significance of usury and the gradual 'penetration into the countryside, deep into the peasant household itself, of the class antagonism which destroys the ancient harmony and community of interests' (p 13). This process, which began as far back as the Middle Ages, has not completely come to an end to this day. We emphasise this statement because it shows immediately the utter incorrectness of Mr Bulgakov's assertion that Kautsky did not even raise the question of who was the carrier of technical progress in agriculture. Kautsky raised and answered that question quite definitely; anyone who reads his book carefully will grasp the truth (often forgotten by the Narodniks, agronomists, and many others) that the carrier of technical progress in modern agriculture is the *rural bourgeoisie*, both petty and big; and (as Kautsky has shown) the big bourgeoisie plays a more important role in this respect than the petty bourgeoisie.

II

After describing (in Chapter III) the main features of feudal agriculture: the predominance of the three-field system, the most conservative system in agriculture; the oppression and expropriation of the peasantry by the big landed aristocracy; the organisation of feudal-capitalist farming by the latter; the transformation of the peasantry into starving paupers (*Hungerleider*) in the seventeenth and eighteenth centuries; the development of bourgeois peasants (*Grossbauern*, who cannot manage without regular farm labourers and day labourers), for whom the old forms of rural relations and land tenure were unsuitable; the abolition of these forms and the paving of the way for 'capitalist, intensive farming' (p 26) by the forces of the bourgeois class which had developed in the womb of industry and the towns – after describing all this, Kautsky goes on to characterise 'modern agriculture' (Chapter IV).

This chapter contains a remarkably exact, concise, and lucid outline of the gigantic revolution which capitalism brought about in agriculture by transforming the routine craft of peasants crushed by poverty and ignorance into the scientific application of agronomics, by disturbing the age-long stagnation of agriculture, and by giving (and

continuing to give) an impetus to the rapid development of
the productive forces of social labour. The three-field system
gave way to the crop rotation system, the maintenance of
cattle and the cultivation of the soil were improved, the yield
increased and specialisation in agriculture and the division of
labour among individual farms greatly developed. Pre-
capitalist uniformity was replaced by increasing diversity,
accompanied by technical progress in all branches of
agriculture. Both the use of machinery in agriculture and the
application of steam power were introduced and underwent
rapid development; the employment of electric power,
which, as specialists point out, is destined to play an even
greater role in this branch of production than steam power,
has begun. The use of access roads, land improvement
schemes, and the application of artificial fertilisers adapted
to the physiology of plants have been developed; the
application of bacteriology to agriculture has begun. Mr
Bulgakov's assertion that 'Kautsky's data[2] are not
accompanied by an *economic* analysis' is completely
groundless. Kautsky shows precisely the connection
between this revolution and the growth of the *market*
(especially the growth of the towns), and the subordination
of agriculture to *competition* which *forced* the changes and
specialisation. This revolution, which has its origin in urban
capital, increases the dependence of the farmer on the
market and, moreover, constantly changes market conditions of importance to him. A branch of production that was
profitable while the local market's only connection with the
world market was a high road becomes unprofitable and
must necessarily be superseded by another branch of
production when a railway is run through the locality. If, for
example, the railway brings cheaper grain, grain production
becomes unprofitable; but at the same time a market for
milk is created. The growth of commodity circulation makes
it possible to introduce new, improved varieties of crops into
the country', etc. (pp 37-38). 'In the feudal epoch', says
Kautsky, 'the only agriculture was small-scale agriculture,
for the landlord cultivated his fields with the peasant's
implements. Capitalism first created the possibility for
large-scale production in agriculture, which is technically
more rational than small-scale production'. In discussing

agricultural machinery, Kautsky (who, it should be said in passing, points precisely to the specific features of agriculture in this respect) explains the *capitalist* nature of its employment; he explains the influence of agricultural machinery upon the workers, the significance of machinery as a factor of progress, and the 'reactionary utopianism' of schemes for restricting the employment of agricultural machinery. 'Agricultural machines will continue their transformative activity: they will drive the rural workers into the towns and in this way serve as a powerful instrument for raising wages in the rural districts, on the one hand, and for the further development of the employment of machinery in agriculture, on the other' (p 41). Let is be added that in special chapters Kautsky explains in detail the capitalist character of modern agriculture, the relation between large- and small-scale production, and the proletarianisation of the peasantry. As we see, Mr Bulgakov's assertion that Kautsky 'does not raise the question of knowing why all these wonder-working changes were necessary' is entirely untrue.

In Chapter V ('The Capitalist Character of Modern Agriculture') Kautsky expounds Marx's theory of value, profit, and rent. 'Without money, modern agricultural production is impossible', says Kautsky, 'or, what is the same thing, it is impossible *without capital*. Indeed, under the present mode of production any sum of money which does not serve the purpose of individual consumption can be transformed into capital, i.e. into a value begetting surplus-value and, as a general rule, actually is transformed into capital. Hence, modern agricultural production is capitalist production' (p 56). This passage, incidentally, enables us to appraise the following statement made by Mr Bulgakov: 'I employ this term (capitalist agriculture) in the ordinary sense (Kautsky also employs it in the same sense), i.e. in the sense of large-scale production in agriculture. Actually, however (*sic*!), when the *whole* of the national economy is organised on capitalist lines, there is no *non*-capitalist agriculture, the *whole* of it being determined by the general conditions of the organisation of production, and only within these limits should the distinction be made between large-scale, entrepreneur farming and small-scale farming. For the sake of clarity a new term is required here

also.' And so it seems, Mr Bulgakov *is correcting* Kautsky....
'Actually, however', as the reader sees, Kautsky *does not
employ* the term 'capitalist agriculture' in the 'ordinary',
inexact sense in which Mr Bulgakov employs it. Kautsky
understands perfectly well, and says so very precisely and
clearly, that under the capitalist mode of production all
agricultural production is 'as a general rule' capitalist
production. In support of this opinion he adduces the simple
fact that in order to carry on modern agriculture money is
needed, and that in modern society money which does not
serve the purpose of individual consumption becomes
capital. It seems to us that this is somewhat clearer than Mr
Bulgakov's 'correction', and that Kautsky has fully proved
that it is possible to dispense with a 'new term'.

In Chapter V of his book Kautsky asserts, *inter alia*, that
both the tenant farmer system, which has developed so fully
in England, and the mortgage system, which is developing
with astonishing rapidity in continental Europe, express, in
essence, one and the same process, viz. *the separation of the
land from the farmer*.[3] Under the capitalist tenant farmer
system this separation is as clear as daylight. Under the
mortgage system it is 'less clear, and things are not so
simple; but in essence it amounts to the same thing' (p 86).
Indeed, it is obvious that the mortgaging of land is the
mortgaging, or sale, of ground rent. Consequently, under
the mortgage system, as well as under the tenant farmer
system, the recipients of rent (= the landowners) are
separated from the recipients of the profit of enterprise (=
farmers, rural entrepreneurs). 'In general, the significance
of this assertion of Kautsky is unclear' to Mr Bulgakov. 'It
can hardly be considered as proved that the mortgage system
expresses the separation of the land from the farmer.'
'Firstly, it cannot be proved that debt absorbs the *whole*
rent; this is possible only by way of exception....' To this we
reply: There is no need to prove that interest on mortgage
debts absorbs the *whole* rent, just as there is no need to
prove that the *actual amount* paid for land leased coincides
with rent. It is sufficient to prove that mortgage debts are
growing with enormous rapidity; that the landowners strive
to mortgage all their land, to sell the whole of the rent. The
existence of this tendency – a theoretical economic analysis
can, in general, deal only with tendencies – cannot be

doubted. Consequently, there can be no doubt about the process of separation of the land from the farmer. The combination of the recipient of rent and the recipient of the profit of enterprise in one person is, 'from the historical point of view, an exception' (*ist historisch eine Ausnahme*, p 91....) 'Secondly, the causes and sources of the debt must be analysed in each separate case for its significance to be understood'. Probably this is either a misprint or a slip. Mr Bulgakov cannot demand that an economist (who, moreover, is dealing with the 'development of agriculture in capitalist society' *in general*) should investigate the causes of the debt '*in each separate case*' or even expect that he would be able to do so. If Mr Bulgakov wanted to say that it is necessary to analyse the causes of debt in different countries at different periods, we cannot agree with him. Kautsky is perfectly right in saying that too many monographs on the agrarian question have accumulated, and that the urgent task of modern theory is not to add new monographs but to 'investigate the main trends of the capitalist evolution of agriculture as a whole' (Foreword p VI). Among these main trends is undoubtedly the separation of the land from the farmer in the form of an increase in mortgage debts. Kautsky precisely and clearly defined the real significance of mortgages, their progressive historical character (the separation of the land from the farmer being one of the conditions for the socialisation of agriculture, p 88), and the essential role they play in the capitalist evolution of agriculture.[4] All Kautsky's arguments on this question are extremely valuable theoretically and provide a powerful weapon against the widespread bourgeois talk (particularly in 'any handbook of the economics of agriculture') about the 'misfortune' of debts and about 'measures of assistance'.... 'Thirdly', concludes Mr Bulgakov, 'land leased out may, in its turn, be mortgaged; and in this sense it may assume the same position as land not leased out'. A strange argument! Let Mr Bulgakov point to at least one economic phenomenon, to at least one economic category, that is not interwoven with others. The fact that there are cases of combined leasing and mortgaging does not refute, does not even weaken, the theoretical proposition that the separation of the land from the farmer is expressed in two forms: in the tenant farmer system and in mortgage debts.

Mr Bulgakov also declares that Kautsky's statement that 'countries in which the tenant farmer system is developed are also countries in which large land ownership predominates' (p 88) is 'still more unexpected' and 'altogether untrue'. Kautsky speaks here of the concentration of land ownership (under the tenant farmer system) and the concentration of mortgages (under the system in which the landowners manage their own farms) as conditions that facilitate the abolition of the private ownership of land. On the question of concentration of land ownership, continues Kautsky, there are no statistics 'which would enable one to trace the amalgamation of several properties in single hands'; but 'in general it may be taken' that the increase in the number of leases and in the area of the leased land proceeds side by side with the concentration of land ownership. 'Countries in which the tenant farmer system is developed are also countries in which large land ownership predominates.' It is clear that Kautsky's entire argument applies only to countries in which the tenant farmer system is developed; but Mr Bulgakov refers to East Prussia, where he 'hopes to show' an increase in the number of leases side by side with the break-up of large landed properties – and he thinks that by means of this single example he is refuting Kautsky! It is a pity, however, that Mr Bulgakov forgets to inform his readers that Kautsky himself points to the break-up of large estates and the growth of peasant tenant farming in the East Elbe province and, in doing so, explains, as we shall see later, the real significance of these processes.

Kautsky points to the concentration of mortgage institutions as proof that the concentration of land ownership is taking place in countries in which mortgage debts exist. Mr Bulgakov thinks that this is no proof. In his opinion, 'It might easily be the case that the deconcentration of capital (by the issue of shares) is proceeding side by side with the concentration of credit institutions'. Well, we shall not argue with Mr Bulgakov on this point.

III

After examining the main features of feudal and capitalist agriculture, Kautsky passes on to the question of 'large-and small-scale production' in agriculture (Chapter VI). This chapter is one of the best in Kautsky's book. In it he first examines the 'technical superiority of large-scale production'. In deciding the question in favour of large-scale production, Kautsky does not give an abstract formula that ignores the enormous variety of agricultural relations (as Mr Bulgakov, altogether groundlessly, supposes); on the contrary, he clearly and precisely points to the necessity of taking this variety into account in the practical applications of the theoretical law. In the first place, *it goes without saying* that the superiority of large-scale over small-scale production in agriculture is inevitable only when *'all other conditions are equal'* (p 100. My italics). In industry, also, the law of the superiority of large-scale production is not as absolute and as simple as is sometimes thought; there, too, it is the equality of *'other conditions'* (not always existing in reality) that ensures the full applicability of the law. In agriculture, however, which is distinguished for the incomparably greater complexity and variety of its relations, the full applicability of the law of the superiority of large-scale production is hampered by considerably stricter conditions. For instance, Kautsky very aptly observes that on the borderline between the peasant and the small landlord estates 'quantity is transformed into quality': the big peasant farm may be 'economically, if not technically, superior' to the small landlord farm. The employment of a scientifically educated manager (one of the important advantages of large scale production) is too costly for a small estate; and the management by the owner himself is very often merely 'Junker', and by no means scientific, management. Secondly, large-scale production in agriculture is superior to small production only up to a certain limit. Kautsky closely investigates this limit further on. It also goes without saying that this limit differs in different branches of agriculture and under different social-economic conditions. Thirdly, Kautsky does not in the least ignore the fact that, *'so far'*, there are branches of agriculture in which, as experts admit, small-scale production can compete with large-scale production; for example, vegetable gardening, grape growing, industrial crops, etc. (p 115). But these branches occupy a position quite subordinate to the decisive (*entscheidenden*) branches of agriculture, viz the production of grain and animal husbandry. Moreover, even in vegetable gardening and grape growing there are already fairly successful large-scale enterprises' (p 115). Hence, 'taking agriculture as a whole (*in Allgemeinen*), those branches in which small-scale production is superior to large-scale production need not be taken into account, and it is quite permissible to say that large-scale production is decidedly superior to small-scale production' (p 116).

After demonstrating the technical superiority of large-scale production in agriculture (we shall present Kautsky's arguments in greater detail later on in examining Mr Bulgakov's objections), Kautsky asks: 'What can small production offer against the advantages of large-scale production?' And he replies: 'The greater diligence and greater care of the worker, who, unlike the hired labourer, works for himself, and the low level of requirements of the small independent farmer, which is even lower than that of the agricultural labourer' (p 106); and, by adducing a number of striking facts concerning the position of the peasants in France, England, and Germany, Kautsky leaves no doubt whatever about 'overwork and under-consumption in small-scale production'. Finally, he points out that the superiority of large-scale production also finds expression in the striving of farmers to form *associations*: 'Associated production is large-scale production'. The fuss made by the ideologists of the petty bourgeoisie in general, and the Russian Narodniks in particular (e.g. the above-mentioned book by Mr Kablukov), over the small farmers' associations is well known. The more significant, therefore, is Kasutsky's excellent analysis of the role of these associations. Of course, the small farmers' associations are a link in economic progress; but they express *a transition to capitalism (Fortschritt zum Kapitalismus) and not toward collectivism*, as is often thought and asserted (p 118). Associations do not diminish but enhance the superiority (*Vorsprung*) of large-scale over small-scale production in agriculture, because the big farmers enjoy greater opportunities of forming associations and take greater advantage of these opportunities. It goes without saying that Kautsky very emphatically maintains that communal, collective large-scale production is superior to capitalist large-scale production. He deals with the experiments in collective farming made in England by the followers of Robert Owen[5] and with analogous communes in the United States of North America. All these experiments, says Kautsky, *irrefutably prove* that it is quite possible for workers to carry on large-scale modern farming collectively, but that for this possibility to become a reality 'a number of definite economic, political, and intellectual conditions' are necessary. The transition of the small producer (both artisan and peasant) to collective production is hindered by the extremely low development of solidarity and discipline, the isolation, and the 'property-owner fanaticism', noted not only among West-European peasants, but, let us add, also among the Russian 'commune' peasants (recall A N Engelhardt and G Uspensky). Kautsky categorically declares that 'it is absurd to expect that the peasant in *modern society* will go over to communal production' (p 129).

Such is the extremely rich content of Chapter VI of Kautsky's book. Mr Bulgakov is particularly displeased with this chapter. Kautsky, we are told, is guilty of the 'fundamental sin' of confusing various concepts; 'technical advantages are confused with economic advantages'. Kautsky 'proceeds from the false assumption that the *technically* more perfect mode of production is also *economically* more perfect, i.e. more viable'. Mr Bulgakov's emphatic statement is altogether groundless, of which, we hope, the reader has been convinced by our exposition of Kautsky's line of argument. Without in the least confusing technique with economics,[6] Kautsky rightly investigates the question of the relation of large-scale to small-scale production in agriculture, *other conditions being equal*, under the capitalist system of production. *In the opening sentence of the first section of Chapter VI Kautsky points precisely to this connection between the level of development of capitalism and the degree of the general applicability of the law of the superiority of large-scale agriculture*: 'The more capitalist agriculture becomes, the more it develops the qualitative difference between the techniques of small- and large-scale production' (p 92). This qualitative difference did not exist in pre-capitalist agriculture. What then can be

said of this stern admonition to which Mr Bulgakov treats
Kautsky: 'In point of fact, the question should have been put
as follows: what significance in the competition between
large- and small-scale production can any of the specific
features of either of these forms of production have *under
the present social-economic conditions*?' This 'correction'
bears the same character as the one we examined above.

Let us see now how Mr Bulgakov refutes Kautsky's
arguments in favour of the technical superiority of
large-scale production in agriculture. Kautsky says: 'One of
the most important features distinguishing agriculture from
industry is that in agriculture production in the proper sense
of the word [*Wirtschaftsbetrieb*, an economic enterprise] is
usually connected with the household (*Haushalt*), which is
not the case in industry'. That the larger household has the
advantage over the small household in the saving of labour
and materials hardly needs proof.... The former purchases
(note this! V I) 'kerosene, chicory, and margarine
wholesale; the latter purchases these articles retail, etc'
(p 93). Mr Bulgakov 'corrects': 'Kautsky did not mean to
say that this was technically more advantageous, but that it
cost less'!... Is it not clear that in this case (as in all the
others) Mr Bulgakov's attempt to 'correct' Kautsky was
more than unfortunate? 'This argument', continues the stern
critic, 'is also very questionable in itself, because under
certain conditions the value of the product may not include
the value of the scattered huts, whereas the value of a
common house is included, even with the interest added.
This, too, depends upon social-economic conditions, which
– and not the alleged technical advantages of large-scale
over small-scale production – should have been investigated.' ... In the first place, Mr Bulgakov forgets the trifle
that Kautsky, after comparing the significance of large-scale
production with that of small-scale production, *all other
conditions being equal*, proceeds to examine these
conditions in detail. Consequently, Mr Bulgakov wants to
throw different questions together. Secondly, how is it that
the value of the peasants' huts does not enter into the value
of the product? Only because the peasant 'does not count'
the value of the timber he uses or the labour he expends in
building and repairing his hut. Insofar as the peasant still

conducts a natural economy, he, of course, may 'not count' his labour; there is no justification for Mr Bulgakov's not telling his readers that *Kautsky very clearly and precisely points this out on pp 165-67 of his book* (Chapter VIII, 'The Proletarisation of the Peasant'). But we are now discussing the 'social-economic condition' of capitalism and not of natural economy or of simple commodity production. Under capitalist social conditions 'not to count' one's labour means to work for nothing (for the merchant or another capitalist); it means to work for incomplete remuneration for the labour-power expended; it means to lower the level of consumption below the standard. As we have seen, Kautsky fully recognised and correctly appraised *this* distinguishing feature of small production. In his objection to Kautsky, Mr Bulgakov repeats the usual trick and the usual mistake of the bourgeois and petty-bourgeois economists. These economists have deafened us with their praises of the 'viability' of the small peasant, who, they say, need not count his own labour, or chase after profit and rent, etc. These good people merely forget that such arguments confuse the 'social-economic conditions' of natural economy, simple commodity production, and capitalism. Kautsky excellently explains all these mistakes and *draws a strict distinction* between the various systems of social-economic relations. He says: 'If the agricultural production of the small peasant is not drawn into the sphere of commodity production, if it is merely a part of household economy, it also remains outside the sphere of the centralising tendencies of the modern mode of production. However irrational his parcellised economy may be, no matter what waste of effort it may lead to, he clings to it tightly, just as his wife clings to her wretched household economy, which likewise produces infinitely miserable results with an enormous expenditure of labour-power, but which represents the only sphere in which she is not subject to another's rule and is free from exploitation' (p 165). The situation changes when natural economy is supplanted by commodity economy. The peasant then has to sell his produce, purchase implements, and *purchase land*. As long as the peasant remains *a simple commodity producer*, he can be satisfied with the standard of living of the wage-worker; he needs neither profit nor rent;

he can pay a higher price for land than the capitalist entrepreneur (p 166). But simple commodity production is supplanted by *capitalist production*. If, for instance, the peasant has mortgaged his land, he must also obtain the rent which he has sold to the creditor. At this stage of development the peasant can only formally be regarded as a simple commodity producer. *De facto*, he usually has to deal with the *capitalist* – the creditor, the merchant, the industrial entrepreneur – from whom he must seek 'auxiliary employment', i.e. to whom he must sell his labour-power. At this stage – and Kautsky, we repeat, compares large-scale with small-scale farming in capitalist society – the possibility for the peasant 'not to count his labour' means only one thing to him, namely, to work himself to death and continually to cut down his consumption.

Equally unsound are the other objections raised by Mr Bulgakov. Small-scale production permits of the employ-ment of machinery within narrower limits; the small proprietor finds credit more difficult to obtain and more expensive, says Kautsky. Mr Bulgakov considers these arguments false and refers to – peasant associations! He completely ignores the evidence brought forward by Kautsky, whose appraisal of these associations and their significance we quoted above. On the question of machinery, Mr Bulgakov again reproaches Kautsky for not raising the 'more general economic question: What, upon the whole, is the economic role of machinery in agriculture [Mr Bulgakov has forgotten Chapter IV of Kautsky's book!] and is it as inevitable an instrument in agriculture as in manufacturing industry?' Kautsky clearly pointed to the capitalist nature of the use of machinery in modern agriculture (p 39, 40, et seq); noted the specific features of agriculture which create 'technical and economic difficulties' for the employment of machinery in agriculture (p 38, et seq); and adduced data on the growing employment of machinery (p 40), on its technical significance (p 42, et seq), and on the role of steam and electricity. Kautsky indicated the size of farm necessary, according to agronomic data, for making the fullest use of various machines (p 94), and pointed out that according to the German census of 1895 the employment of machinery steadily and rapidly increases from the small farms to the big ones (2 per cent in farms up to two hectares, 13.8 per cent in farms of 2 to 5 hectares, 45.8 per cent in farms of 5 to 20 hectares, 78.8 per cent in farms of 20 to 100 hectares, and 94.2 per cent in farms of 100 and more hectares). Instead of these figures, Mr Bulgakov would have preferred 'general' arguments about the 'invincibility' or non-invincibility of machines!...

'The argument that a larger number of draught animals per hectare is employed in small-scale production is unconvincing ... because the relative intensity of animal maintenance per farm ... is not investigated' – says Mr Bulgakov. We open Kautsky's book at the page that contains this argument and read the following: 'The large number of cows in small-scale farming [per 1,000 hectares] is to no small extent also determined by the fact that the peasant engages more in animal husbandry and less in the production of grain than the big farmer; but this does not explain the difference in the number of horses maintained' (page 96, on which are quoted figures for Saxony for 1860, for the whole of Germany for 1883, and for England for 1880). We remind the reader of the fact that in Russia the Zemstvo statistics reveal the same law expressing the superiority of large-scale over small-scale farming: the big peasant farms manage with a smaller number of cattle and implements per unit of land.[7]

Mr Bulgakov gives a far from complete exposition of Kautsky's arguments on the superiority of large-scale over small-scale production in capitalist agriculture. The superiority of large-scale farming does not only lie in the fact that there is less waste of cultivated area, a saving in livestock and implements, fuller utilisation of implements, wider possibilities of employing machinery, and more opportunities for obtaining credit; it also lies in the commercial superiority of large-scale production, the employment in the latter of scientifically trained managers (Kautsky, p 104). Large-scale farming utilises the co-operation of workers and division of labour to a larger extent. Kautsky attaches particular importance to the scientific, agronomic education of the farmer. 'A scientifically well-educated farmer can be employed only by a farm sufficiently large for the work of management and supervision to engage fully the person's labour-power' (p 98: 'The size of such farms varies, according to the type of production', from three hectares of vineyards to 500 hectares of extensive farming). In this connection Kautsky mentions the interesting and extremely characteristic fact that the establishment of primary and secondary agricultural schools benefits the big farmer and not the peasant by providing the former with employees (the same thing is observed in Russia). 'The higher education that is required for fully rationalised production is hardly compatible with the peasants' present conditions of existence. This, of course, is a condemnation, not of higher education, but of the peasants' conditions of life. It merely means that peasant production is able to exist side by side with large-scale production, not because of its higher productivity, but because of its lower requirements' (p 99). Large-scale production must employ, not only peasant labourers, but also urban workers, whose requirements are on an incomparably higher level.

Mr Bulgakov calls the highly interesting and important data which Kautsky adduces to prove 'overwork and under-consumption in small-scale production' 'a few (!) casual(??) quotations'. Mr Bulgakov 'undertakes' to cite as many 'quotations of an opposite character'. He merely forgets to say whether he also undertakes to make *an opposite assertion* which he would prove by 'quotations of an opposite character'. This is the whole point! Does Mr Bulgakov undertake to assert that large-scale production in capitalist society differs from peasant production in the prevalence of overwork and the lower consumption of its workers? Mr Bulgakov is too cautious to make such a ludicrous assertion. He considers it possible to avoid the fact of the peasants' overwork and lower consumption by remarking that 'in some places peasants are prosperous and in other places they are poor'!! What would be said of an economist who, instead of generalising the data on the position of small- and large-scale production, began to investigate the difference in the 'prosperity' of the population of various 'places'? What would be said of an economist who evaded the overwork and lower consumption of handicraftsmen, as compared with factory workers, with the remark that 'in some places handicraftsmen are prosperous and in other places they are poor'? Incidentally, a word about handicraftsmen. Mr Bulgakov writes: 'Apparently Kautsky was mentally drawing a parallel with *Hausindustrie*, [domestic industry – *ed*] where there are no technical limits to overwork [as in agriculture], but this parallel is unsuitable here'. Apparently, we say in reply, Mr Bulgakov was astonishingly inattentive to the book he was criticising, for Kautsky did not 'mentally draw a parallel' with *Hausindustrie*, but *pointed to it directly and precisely on the very first page of that part of the chapter* which deals with the question of overwork (Chapter VI, p 106): 'As in domestic industry (*Hausindustrie*), the work of the children of the family in small peasant farming is even more harmful than wage-labour for others'. However emphatically Mr Bulgakov decrees that this parallel is unsuitable here, his opinion is nevertheless entirely erroneous. In industry, overwork has no technical limits; but for the peasantry it is 'limited by the technical conditions of agriculture', argues Mr Bulgakov. The question arises: who, indeed, confuses technique with economics, Kautsky or Mr Bulgakov? What has the technique of agriculture, or of domestic industry, to do with the case when facts prove that the small producer in agriculture and in industry drives his children to work at an earlier age, works more hours per day, lives 'more frugally' and cuts down his requirements to such a level that he stands out in a civilised country as a real 'barbarian' (Marx's expression)? Can the economic similarity of such phenomena in agriculture and in industry be denied on the grounds that agriculture has a large number of specific features (which Kautsky does not forget in the least)? 'The small peasant could not put in more work than his field requires even if he wanted to', says Mr Bulgakov. But the small peasant can and does work fourteen, and not twelve, hours a day; he can and does work with that super-normal intensity which wears out his nerves and muscles much more quickly than the normal intensity. Moreover, what an incorrect and extreme abstraction it is to reduce all the peasant's work to field work! You will find nothing of the kind in Kautsky's book. Kautsky knows perfectly well that the peasant also works in the household, works on building and repairing his hut, his cowshed, his implements, etc, '*not counting*' all this additional work, for which a wage-worker on a big farm would demand payment at the usual rate. Is it not clear to every unprejudiced person that overwork has *incomparably wider limits* for the peasant – for the small farmer – than for the small industrial producer if he is *only* such? The overwork of the small farmer is strikingly demonstrated as a universal phenomenon by the fact that all bourgeois writers unanimously testify to the 'diligence' and 'frugality' of the peasant and accuse the workers of 'indolence' and 'extravagance'.

The small peasants, says an investigator of the life of the rural population in Westphalia quoted by Kautsky, overwork their children to such an extent that their physical development is retarded; working for wages has not such bad sides. A small Lincolnshire farmer stated the following to the parliamentary commission which investigated agrarian conditions in England (1897): 'I have brought up a family and nearly worked them to death'. Another said: 'I and my children have been working eighteen hours a day for several days and average ten to twelve during the year.' A third: 'We work much harder than labourers, in fact, like slaves'. Mr Read described to the same commission the conditions of the small farmer, in the districts where agriculture in the strict sense of the word predominates, in the following manner: 'The only way in which he can possibly succeed is this, in doing the work of two agricultural labourers and living at the expense of one … as regards his family, they are worse educated and harder worked than the children of the agricultural labourers' (Royal Commission on Agriculture, 'Final Report, pp 34, 358, Quoted by Kautsky, p 109). Will Mr Bulgakov assert that not less frequently a day labourer does the work of two peasants? Particularly characteristic is the following fact cited by Kautsky showing that 'the peasant art of starvation (*Hungerkunst*) may lead to the economic superiority of small production': a comparison of the profitableness of two peasant farms in Baden shows a deficit of 933 marks in one, *the large one*, and a surplus of 191 marks in the other, which was *only half the size* of the first. But the first farm, which was conducted exclusively with the aid of hired labourers, had to feed the latter properly, at a cost of nearly one mark (about 45 kopeks) per person per day; whereas the smaller farm was conducted exclusively with the aid of the members of the family (the wife and six grown-up children), whose maintenance *cost only half the amount* spent on the day labourers: 48 pfennigs per person per day. If the family of the small peasant had been fed as well as the labourers hired by the big farmer, the small farmer would have suffered a deficit of 1,250 marks! 'His surplus came, not from his full corn bins, but from his empty stomach.' What a huge number of similar examples would be discovered, were the comparison of the 'profitableness' of large and small farms accompanied by calculation of the consumption and work of peasants and of wage-workers.[8] Here is another calculation of the higher profit of a small farm (4.6 hectares) as compared with a big farm (26.5 hectares), a calculation made in one of the special magazines. But how is this higher profit obtained? – asks Kautsky. It turns out that the small farmer is assisted by his children, assisted from the time they begin to walk; whereas the big farmer has to spend money on his children (school, *gymnasium*). In the small farm even the old people, over 70 years of age, 'take the place of a full worker'. 'An ordinary day labourer, particularly on a big farm, goes about his work and thinks to himself: "I wish it was knocking-off time". The small peasant, however, at all events in all the busy seasons, thinks to himself: "Oh, if only the day were an hour or two longer".' The small producers, the author of this article in the agricultural magazine says didactically, make better use of their time in the busy seasons: 'They rise earlier, retire later and work more quickly, whereas the labourers, employed by the big farmer do not want to get up earlier, go to bed later or work harder than at other times'. The peasant is able to obtain a net income thanks to the 'simple' life he leads: he lives in a mud hut built mainly by the labour of his family; his wife has been married for 17 years and has worn out only one pair of shoes; usually she goes barefoot, or in wooden sabots; and she makes all the clothes for her family. Their food consists of potatoes, milk, and on rare occasions, herring. Only on Sundays does the husband smoke a pipe of tobacco. 'These people did not realise that they were leading a particularly simple life and did not express dissatisfaction with their position.... Following this simple way of life, they obtained nearly every year a small surplus from their farm.'

IV

After completing his analysis of the interrelations between large- and small-scale production in capitalist agriculture, Kautsky proceeds to make a special investigation of the 'limits of capitalist agriculture' (Chapter VII). Kautsky says that objection to the theory that large-scale farming is superior to small-scale is raised mainly by the 'friends of humanity' (we almost said, friends of the people ...) among the bourgeoisie, the pure Free Traders, and the agrarians. Many economists have recently been advocating small-scale farming. The statistics usually cited are those showing that big farms are not eliminating small farms. And Kautsky quotes these statistics: in Germany, from 1882 to 1895, it was the area of the medium-sized farms that increased most; in France, from 1882 to 1892, it was the area of the smallest and biggest farms that increased most; the area of the medium-sized farms diminished. In England, from 1885 to 1895, the area of the smallest and the biggest farms diminished; it was the area of the farms ranging from 40 to 120 hectares (100 to 300 acres), i.e. farms that cannot be put in the category of small farms, which increased most. In America, the average area of farms is diminishing: in 1850 it was 203 acres; in 1860 – 199 acres; in 1870 – 153 acres; in 1880 – 134 acres; and in 1890 – 137 acres. Kautsky makes a closer examination of the American statistics and, Mr Bulgakov's opinion notwithstanding, his analysis is extremely important from the standpoint of *principle*. The main reason for the diminution in the average farm area is the break-up of the large plantations in the South after the emancipation of the Negroes; in the Southern States the average farm area diminished by more than one-half. 'Not a single person who understands the subject will regard these figures as evidence of the victory of small-scale over *modern* [= capitalist] large-scale production.' In general, an analysis of American statistics *by regions* shows a large variety of relations. In the principal 'wheat states', in the northern part of the Middle West, the average farm area *increased* from 122 to 133 acres. 'Small-scale production becomes predominant only in those places where agriculture is in a state of decline, or where pre-capitalist, large-scale production enters into competition with peasant production' (p 35). This conclusion of Kautsky is very important, for it shows that if certain conditions are not adhered to, the handling of statistics may become merely *mishandling*: a distinction must be drawn between capitalist and pre-capitalist large-scale production. A *detailed* analysis must be made for separate districts that differ materially from one another in the forms of farming and in the historical conditions of its development. It is said, 'Figures prove!' But one must analyse the figures to see what they prove. They only prove *what they directly say*. The figures do not speak directly of the scale on which production is carried on, but of the *area* of the farms. It is possible, and in fact it so happens, that 'with intensive farming, production can be carried on upon a larger scale on a small estate than on a large estate extensively farmed'. 'Statistics that tell us only about the area of farms tell us nothing as to whether the diminution of their area is due to the actual diminution of the scale of farming, or to its intensification' (p 46). Forestry and pastoral farming, these first forms of capitalist large-scale farming, permit of the largest area of estates. Field cultivation requires a smaller area. But the various systems of field cultivation differ from one another in this respect: the exhaustive, extensive system of farming (which has prevailed in America up to now) permits of huge farms (up to 10,000 hectares, such as the *bonanza farms* [these words are in English in the original – *ed*] of Dalrymple, Glenn, and others. In our steppes, too, peasant farms, and particularly merchants, farms, attain such dimensions). The introduction of fertilisers, etc. necessarily leads to a diminution in the area of farms, which in Europe, for instance, are smaller than in America. The transition from field farming to animal husbandry again causes a diminution in the area of farms: in England, in 1880, the average size of livestock farms was 52.3 acres, whereas that of field farms was 74.2 acres. That is why the transition from field farming to animal husbandry which is taking place in England *must* give rise to a tendency for the area of farms to diminish. 'But it would be judging very superficially if the conclusion were drawn from this that there has been a decline in production' (p 149). In East Elbe (by the investigation of which Mr Bulgakov hopes some time to refute Kautsky), it is precisely the introduction of intensive farming that is taking place: the big farmers, says Sering, whom Kautsky quotes, are increasing the productivity of their soil and are selling or leasing to peasants the remote parts of their estates, since with intensive farming it is difficult to utilise these remote parts. 'Thus, large estates in East Elbe are being reduced in size and in their vicinity small peasant farms are being established; this, however, is not because small-scale production is superior to large-scale, but because the former dimensions of the estates were adapted to the needs of extensive farming' (p 150). The diminution in farm area in all these cases usually leads to an increase in the quantity of products (per unit of land) and frequently to an increase in the number of workers employed, i.e. to an actual *increase* in the scale of production.

From this it is clear how little is proved by general agricultural statistics on the *area* of farms, and how cautiously one must handle them. In industrial statistics we have *direct* indices of the scale of production (quantity of goods, total value of the output, and number of workers employed), and, besides, it is easy to distinguish the different branches. Agricultural statistics hardly ever satisfy these necessary conditions of evidence.

Furthermore, the monopoly in landed property limits agricultural capitalism: in industry, capital grows as a result of *accumulation*, as a result of the conversion of surplus-value into capital; *centralisation*, i.e. the amalgamation of several small units of capital into a large unit, plays a lesser role. In agriculture, the situation is different. The whole of the land is occupied (in civilised countries), and it is possible to enlarge the area of a farm only by *centralising* several lots; this must be done in such a way as to form *one continuous area*. Clearly, enlarging an estate by purchasing the surrounding lots is a very difficult matter, particularly in view of the fact that the small lots are partly occupied by agricultural labourers (whom the big farmer needs), and partly by small peasants who are masters of the art of maintaining their hold by reducing consumption to an unbelievable minimum. For some reason or other the statement of this simple and very clear fact, which indicates the limits of agricultural capitalism, seemed to Mr Bulgakov to be a mere 'phrase' (??!!) and provided a pretext for the most groundless rejoicing: 'And so [!], the superiority of large-scale production comes to grief [!] at the very first obstacle'. First, Mr Bulgakov misunderstands the law of the superiority of large-scale production, ascribing to it excessive abstractness, from which Kautsky is very remote, and then turns his misunderstanding into an argument against Kautsky! Truly strange is Mr Bulgakov's belief that he can refute Kautsky by referring to Ireland (large landed property, but without large-scale production). The fact that large landed property is one of the conditions of large-scale production does not in the least signify that it is a sufficient condition. Of course, Kautsky could not examine the historical and other causes of the specific features of Ireland, or of any other country, in a general work on capitalism in agriculture. It would not occur to anyone to demand that Marx, in analysing the general laws of capitalism in industry, should have explained why small industry continued longer in France, why industry was developing slowly in Italy, etc. Equally groundless is Mr Bulgakov's assertion that concentration 'could' proceed gradually: it is not as easy to enlarge estates by purchasing neighbouring lots as it is to add new premises to a factory for an additional number of machines, etc.

In referring to this purely fictitious possibility of the gradual concentration, or renting, of land for the purpose of forming large farms. Mr Bulgakov paid little attention to the really specific feature of agriculture in the process of concentration – a feature which Kautsky indicated. This is the latifundia, the concentration of several estates in the hands of a single owner. Statistics usually register the number of individual estates and tell us nothing about the process of concentration of various estates in the hands of big landowners. Kautsky cites very striking instances, in Germany and Austria, of such concentration which leads to a special and higher form of large-scale capitalist farming in

which several large estates are combined to form a single
economic unit managed by a single central body. Such
gigantic agricultural enterprises make possible the combination of the most varied branches of agriculture and the most
extensive use of the advantages of large-scale production.

The reader will see how remote Kautsky is from
abstractness and from a stereotyped understanding of
'Marx's theory', to which he remains true. Kautsky warned
against this stereotyped understanding, even inserting a
special section on the doom of small-scale production in
industry in the chapter under discussion. He rightly points
out that even in industry the victory of large-scale
production is not so easy of achievement, and is not so
uniform, as those who talk about Marx's theory being
inapplicable to agriculture are in the habit of thinking. It is
sufficient to point to capitalist domestic industry; it is
sufficient to recall the remark Marx made about the extreme
variety of transitional and mixed forms which obscure the
victory of the factory system. How much more complicated
this is in agriculture! The increase in wealth and luxury
leads, for example, to millionaires purchasing huge estates
which they turn into forests for their pleasure. In Salzburg,
in Austria, the number of cattle has been declining since
1869. The reason is the sale of the Alps to rich lovers of the
hunt. Kautsky says very aptly that if agricultural statistics are
taken in general, and uncritically, it is quite easy to discover
in the capitalist mode of production a tendency to transform
modern nations into hunting tribes!

Finally, among the conditions setting the limits to
capitalist agriculture, Kautsky also points to the fact that the
shortage of workers – due to the migration of the rural
population – compels the big landowners to allot land to
labourers, to create a small peasantry to provide
labour-power for the landlord. An absolutely propertyless
agricultural labourer is a rarity, because in agriculture rural
economy, in the strict sense, is connected with household
economy. Whole categories of agricultural wage-workers
own or have the use of land. When small production is
eliminated too greatly, *the big landowners try to strengthen
or revive it* by the sale or lease of land. Sering, whom
Kautsky quotes, says: 'In all European countries, a

movement has recently been observed towards ... settling rural labourers by allotting plots of land to them.' Thus, within the limits of the capitalist mode of production it is impossible to count on small-scale production being entirely eliminated from agriculture, for the capitalists and agrarians themselves strive to revive it when the ruination of the peasantry has gone too far. Marx pointed to this rotation of concentration and parcellisation of the land in capitalist society as far back as 1850, in the *Neue Rheinische Zeitung*.

Mr Bulgakov is of the opinion that these arguments of Kautsky contain 'an element of truth, but still more of error'. Like all Mr Bulgakov's other verdicts, this one has also extremely weak and nebulous grounds. Mr Bulgakov thinks that Kautsky has 'constructed a theory of proletarian small-scale production', and that this theory is true for a very limited region. We hold a different opinion. The agricultural wage-labour of small cultivators (or what is the same thing, the agricultural labourer and day labourer with an allotment) is *a phenomenon characteristic, more or less, of all capitalist countries*. No writer who desires to describe capitalism in agriculture can, without violating the truth, leave this phenomenon in the background.[9] Kautsky, in Chapter VIII of his book, viz 'The Proletarianisation of the Peasant', adduces extensive evidence to prove that in Germany, in particular, proletarian small-scale production is general. Mr Bulgakov's statement that other writers, including Mr Kablukov, have pointed to the 'shortage of workers' *leaves the most important thing in the background* the enormous difference in principle between Mr Kablukov's theory and Kautsky's theory. Because of his characteristically *Kleinbürger* [petty-bourgeois –ed] point of view, Mr Kablukov 'constructs' out of the shortage of workers the theory that large-scale production is unsound and that small-scale production is sound. Kautsky gives an accurate description of the facts and indicates their true significance in modern class society: the class interests of the landowners compel them to strive to allot land to the workers. As far as class position is concerned, the agricultural wage-workers with allotments are situated between the petty bourgeoisie and the proletariat, but closer to the latter. In other words, Mr Kablukov develops one side of a complicated process into a theory of the unsoundness of large-scale production, whereas Kautsky analyses the special forms of social-economic relations created by the interests of large-scale production at a certain stage of its development and under certain historical conditions.

V

We shall now pass to the next chapter of Kautsky's book, the title of which we have just quoted. In this chapter Kautsky investigates, firstly, the 'tendency toward the parcellisation of landholdings', and, secondly, the 'forms of peasant auxiliary employments'. Thus, here are depicted those extremely important trends of capitalism in agriculture that are typical of the overwhelming majority of capitalist countries. Kautsky says that the break-up of landholdings leads to an increased demand for small plots on the part of small peasants, who pay a higher price for the land than the big farmers. Several writers have adduced this fact to prove that small-scale farming is superior to large-scale farming. Kautsky very appropriately replies to this by comparing the price of land with the price of houses: it is well known that small and cheap houses are *dearer* per unit of capacity (per cubic foot, etc.) than large and costly houses. The higher price of small plots of land is not due to the superiority of small-scale farming, but to the particularly oppressed condition of the peasant. The enormous number of dwarf farms that capitalism has called into being is seen from the following figures: in Germany (1895), out of 5,500,000 farms, 4,250,000, i.e. more than three-fourths, are of an area of less than five hectares (58 per cent are less than two hectares). In Belgium, 78 per cent (709,500 out of 909,000) are less than two hectares. In England (1895), 118,000 out of 520,000 are less than two hectares. In France (1892), 2,200,000 (out of 5,700,000) are less than one hectare; 4,000,000 are less than five hectares. Mr Bulgakov thinks that he can refute Kautsky's argument that these dwarf farms are very irrational (insufficient cattle, implements, money, and labour-power which is diverted to auxiliary occupations) by arguing that 'very often' (??) the land is spade-tilled 'with an incredible degree of intensity', although

... with 'an extremely irrational expenditure of labour-power'. It goes without saying that this objection is totally groundless, that individual examples of excellent cultivation of the soil by small peasants are as little able to refute Kautsky's general characterisation of this type of farming as the above-quoted example of the greater profitableness of a small farm is able to refute the thesis of the superiority of large-scale production. That Kautsky is quite right in placing these farms, *taken as a whole*,[10] in the proletarian category is seen from the fact, revealed by the German census of 1895, that very many of the small farmers cannot dispense with subsidiary earnings. Of a total of 4,700,000 persons obtaining an independent livelihood in agriculture, 2,700,000, or *57 per cent*, have subsidiary earnings. Of 3,200,000 farms of less than two hectares each, only 400,000, or *13 per cent*, have no subsidiary incomes! In the whole of Germany, out of 5,500,000 farms, *1,500,000* belong to agricultural and industrial wage-workers (+ 704,000 to artisans). And after this Mr Bulgakov presumes to assert that the theory of proletarian small landholdings was 'constructed' by Kautsky![11] Kautsky thoroughly investigated the forms assumed by the proletarisation of the peasantry (the forms of peasant auxiliary employment) (p 174-93). Unfortunately, space does not permit us to deal in detail with his description of these forms (agricultural work for wages, domestic industry – *Hausindustrie*, 'the vilest system of capitalist exploitation' – work in factories and mines, etc). Our only observation is that Kautsky makes the same appraisal of *auxiliary employment* as that made by Russian economists. Migratory workers are less developed and have a lower level of requirements than urban workers; not infrequently, they have a harmful effect on the living conditions of the urban workers. 'But for those places from which they come and to which they return they are pioneers of progress.... They acquire new wants and new ideas' (p 192), they awaken among the backwoods peasants consciousness, a sense of human dignity, and confidence in their own strength.

In conclusion we shall deal with the last and particularly sharp attack Mr Bulgakov makes upon Kautsky. Kautsky says that in Germany, from 1882 to 1895, it was the smallest (in area) and the largest farms that grew most in number (so that the parcellisation of the land proceeded at the expense of the medium farms). Indeed, the number of farms under one hectare increased by 8.8 per cent; those of 5 to 20 hectares increased by 7.8 per cent; while those of over 1,000 hectares increased by 11 per cent (the number of those in the intervening categories hardly increased at all, while the total number of farms increased by 5.3 per cent). Mr Bulgakov is extremely indignant because the percentage is taken of the biggest farms, the number of which is insignificant (515 and 572 for the respective years). Mr Bulgakov's indignation is quite groundless. He forgets that these farms, insignificant in number, are the largest in size and that they *occupy nearly as much land* as 2,300,000 to 2,500,000 dwarf farms (up to one hectare). If I were to say that the number of very big factories in a country, those employing 1,000 and more workers, increased, say, from 51 to 57, by 11 per cent, while the total number of factories increased 5.3 per cent, would not that show an increase in large-scale production, notwithstanding the fact that the *number* of very large factories may be insignificant as compared with the total number of factories? Kautsky is fully aware of the fact that it was the peasant farms of from 5 to 20 hectares which grew most in total area (Mr Bulgakov, p 18), and he deals with it in the ensuing chapter.

Kautsky then takes the changes in area in the various categories in 1882 and 1895. It appears that the largest increase (+ 563,477 hectares) occurred among the peasant farms of from 5 to 20 hectares, and the next largest among the biggest farms, those of more than 1,000 hectares (+ 94,014), whereas the area of farms of from 20 to 1,000 hectares *diminished* by 86,809 hectares. Farms up to one hectare increased their area by 32,683 hectares, and those from 1 to 5 hectares, by 45,604 hectares.

And Kautsky draws the following conclusion: the diminution in the area of farms of from 20 to 1,000 hectares (more than balanced by an increase in the area of farms of 1,000 hectares and over) is due, not to the decline of large-scale production, but to its intensification. We have already seen that intensive farming is making progress in Germany and that it frequently requires a diminution in the area of farms. That there is intensification of large-scale production can be seen from the growing utilisation of steam-driven machinery, as well as from the enormous increase in the number of agricultural non-manual employees, who in Germany are employed only on large farms. The number of estate managers (inspectors), overseers, bookkeepers, etc. increased from 47,465 in 1882 to 76,978 in 1895, i.e. by 62 per cent; the percentage of women among these employees increased from 12 to 23.4.

'All this shows clearly how much more intensive and more capitalist large-scale farming has become since the beginning of the eighties. The next chapter will explain why simultaneously there has been such a big increase in the area of middle-peasant farms' (p 174).

Mr Bulgakov regards this description as being 'in crying contradiction to reality', but the arguments he falls back on again fail to justify such an emphatic and bold verdict, and not by one iota do they shake Kautsky's conclusion. 'In the first place, the intensification of farming, if it took place, would not in itself explain the relative and absolute diminution of the cultivated area, the diminution of the total proportion of farms in the 20- to 1,000-hectare group. The cultivated area could have increased simultaneously with the increase in the number of farms. The latter need merely (*sic*!) have increased somewhat faster, so that the area of each farm would have diminished.'[12]

We have deliberately quoted in full this argument, from which Mr Bulgakov draws the conclusion that 'the diminution in the size of farms owing to the growth of intensive farming is pure fantasy' (*sic*!), because it strikingly reveals the very mistake of mishandling 'statistics' against which Kautsky seriously warned. Mr Bulgakov puts ridiculously strict demands upon the statistics of the *area* of farms and ascribes to these statistics a significance which they never can have. Why, indeed, should the cultivated area have increased 'somewhat'? Why 'should not' the intensification of farming (which, as we have seen, sometimes leads to the sale and renting to peasants of parts of estates remote from the centre) have shifted a certain number of farms from a higher category to a lower? Why 'should it not' have diminished the cultivated area of farms of from 20 to 1,000 hectares?[13] In industrial statistics a reduction in the *output* of the very big factories would have indicated a decline in large-scale production. But the diminution in *area* of large estates by 1.2 per cent does not and *cannot indicate* the volume of production, which very often increases with a decrease in the area of the farm. We know that the process of livestock breeding replacing grain farming, particularly marked in England, is going on in Europe as a whole. We know that sometimes this change causes a decrease in the farm area; but would it not be strange to draw from this the conclusion that the smaller farm area implied a decline in large-scale production? That is why, incidentally, the 'eloquent table' given by Mr Bulgakov on page 20, showing the reduction in the number of large and small farms and the increase in the number of medium farms (5 to 20 hectares) possessing animals for field work, proves nothing at all. This may have been due to a change in the system of farming.

That large-scale agricultural production in Germany has become more intensive and more capitalist is evident, firstly, from the increase in the number of *steam-driven* machines employed: from 1879 to 1897 their number increased fivefold. It is quite useless for Mr Bulgakov to argue in his objection that the number of *all* machines *in general* (and not steam-driven machines only) owned by small farms (up to 20 hectares) is much larger than that owned by the large farms; and also that in America machines are employed in extensive farming. We are not discussing America now, but Germany, where there are no *bonanza farms*. The following table gives the percentage of farms in Germany (1895) employing steam ploughs and steam threshing machines:

Farms	Per cent of farms employing	
	steam ploughs	steam threshing machines
Under 2 hectares	0.00	1.08
2 to 5 hectares	0.00	5.20
5 to 20 hectares	0.01	10.95
20 to 100 hectares	0.10	16.60
100 hectares and over	5.29	61.22

And now, if the total number of steam-driven machines employed in agriculture in Germany has increased fivefold, does it not prove that large-scale farming has become more intensive? Only it must not be forgotten, as Mr Bulgakov forgets on page 21, that an increase in the size of enterprises in agriculture is not always identical with an increase in the area of farms.

Secondly, the fact that large-scale production has become more capitalist is evident from the increase in the number of agricultural non-manual employees. It is useless for Bulgakov to call this argument of Kautsky a 'curiosity': 'an increase in the number of officers, side by side with a reduction of the army' – with a reduction in the number of agricultural wage-workers. Again we say: *Rira bien qui rira le dernier*![14] Kautsky not only does not forget the reduction in the number of agricultural labourers, but shows it in detail in regard to a number of countries; only this fact has absolutely nothing to do with the matter in hand, because the rural population as a whole is diminishing, while the number of proletarian small farmers is increasing. Let us assume that the big farmer abandons the production of grain and takes up the production of sugar-beet and the manufacture of sugar (in Germany in 1871-72, 2,200,000 tons of beets were converted into sugar: in 1881-82, 6,300,000 tons: in 1891-92, 9,500,000 tons, and in 1896-97, 13,700,000 tons). He might even sell, or rent, the remote parts of his estate to small peasants, particularly if he needs the wives and children of the peasants as day labourers on the beet plantations. Let us assume that he introduces a steam plough which eliminates the former ploughmen (on the beet plantations in Saxony – 'models of intensive farming'[15] – steam ploughs have now come into common use). The number of wage-workers diminishes. The number of higher grade employees (bookkeepers, managers, technicians, etc) necessarily increases. Will Mr Bulgakov deny that we see here an increase in intensive farming and capitalism in large-scale production? Will he assert that nothing of the kind is taking place in Germany?

To conclude the exposition of Chapter VIII of Kautsky's book, viz. on the proletarianisation of the peasants, we need to quote the following passage. 'What interests us here', says Kautsky, after the passage we have cited above, quoted also by Mr Bulgakov, 'is the fact that the proletarianisation of the rural population is proceeding in Germany, as in other places, notwithstanding the fact that the tendency to parcellise medium estates has ceased to operate there. From 1882 to 1895 the total number of farms increased by 281,000. By far the greater part of this increase was due to the greater number of proletarian farms up to one hectare in area. The number of these farms increased by 206,000.

'As we see, the development of agriculture is quite a special one, quite different from the development of industrial and trading capital. In the preceding chapter we pointed out that in agriculture the tendency to centralise farms does not lead to the complete elimination of small-scale production. When this tendency goes too far it gives rise to an opposite tendency, so that the tendency to centralise and the tendency to parcellise alternate with each other. Now we see that both tendencies can operate side by side. There is an increase in the number of farms whose owners come into the commodity market as proletarians, as sellers of labour-power.... All the material interests of these small farmers as sellers of the commodity labour-power are identical with the interests of the industrial proletariat, and their land ownership does not give rise to antagonism between them and the proletariat. His land more or less emancipates the peasant small holder from the dealer in food products; but it does not emancipate him from the exploitation of the capitalist entrepreneur, whether industrial or agricultural' (p 174).

In the following article we shall deal with the remaining part of Kautsky's book and give the work a general appraisal; in passing, we shall examine the objections Mr Bulgakov raises in a later article.

Second Article

I

In Chapter IX of his book ('The Growing Difficulties of Commercial Agriculture') Kautsky proceeds to analyse the *contradictions* inherent in capitalist agriculture. From the objections which Mr Bulgakov raises against this chapter, which we shall examine later, it is evident that the critic has not quite properly understood the general significance of these 'difficulties'. There are 'difficulties' which, while being an 'obstacle' to the full development of rational agriculture, at the same time *stimulate the development* of capitalist agriculture. Among the 'difficulties' Kautsky points, for example, to the depopulation of the countryside. Undoubtedly, the migration from the countryside of the best and most intelligent workers is an 'obstacle' to the full development of rational agriculture; but it is equally indubitable that the farmers combat this obstacle by *developing technique*, e.g. by introducing machinery.

Kautsky investigates the following 'difficulties': a) ground rent; b) right of inheritance; c) limitation of right of inheritance, entailment (*fideicommissum, Anerbenrecht*); d) the exploitation of the countryside by the town; e) depopulation of the countryside.

Ground rent is that part of surplus-value which remains after the average profit on invested capital is deducted. The monopoly of landed property enables the landowner to appropriate this surplus, and the price of land (= capitalised rent) *keeps* rent at the level it has once reached. Clearly, rent 'hinders' the complete rationalisation of agriculture: under the tenant farmer system the incentive to improvements, etc, becomes weaker, and under the mortgage system the major part of the capital has to be invested, not in production, but in the purchase of land. In his objection Mr Bulgakov points out, first, that there is 'nothing terrible' in the growth of mortgage debts. He forgets, however, that Kautsky, not 'in another sense', but precisely in this sense, has pointed to the necessary increase in mortgages even when agriculture is prospering (see above, First Article, II). Here, Kautsky does not raise the question as to whether an increase in mortgages is 'terrible' or not, but asks what difficulties prevent capitalism from accomplishing its mission. Secondly, in Mr Bulgakov's opinion, 'it is hardly correct to regard increased rent only as an obstacle.... The rise in rent, the possibility of raising it, serves as an independent incentive to agriculture, stimulating progress of technique and every other form' of progress ('process' is obviously a misprint). Stimuli to progress in capitalist agriculture are: population growth, growth of competition, and growth of industry; rent, however, is a tribute exacted by the landowner from social development, from the growth of technique. It is, therefore, incorrect to state that the rise in rent is an *'independent* incentive' to progress. Theoretically, it is possible for capitalist production to exist in the absence of private property in land, i.e. with the land nationalised (Kautsky, p 207), when absolute rent would not exist at all, and differential rent would be appropriated by the state. This would not weaken the incentive to agronomic progress; on the contrary, it would greatly increase it.

'There can be nothing more erroneous than to think that it is in the interest of agriculture to force up (*in die Höhe treiben*) the prices of estates or artificially to keep them at a high level', says Kautsky. 'This is in the interest of the present (*augenblicklichen*) landowners, of the mortgage banks and the real estate speculators, but not in the interest of agriculture, and least of all in the interest of its future, of the future generation of farmers' (p 199). As to the price of land, it is capitalised rent.

The second difficulty confronting commercial agriculture is that it necessarily requires private property in land. This leads to the situation in which the land is either split up on passing to heirs (such parcellisation even leading in *some places* to technical retrogression) or is burdened by mortgages (when the heir who receives the land pays the co-heirs money capital which he obtains by a mortgage on the land). Mr Bulgakov reproaches Kautsky for 'overlooking, in his exposition, the positive side' of the mobilisation of the land. This reproach is absolutely groundless; for in the historical part of his book (in particular Chapter III of Part I, which deals with feudal agriculture and the reasons for its supersession by capitalist agriculture) as well as in the practical part,[16] Kautsky clearly pointed out to his readers the positive side and the historical necessity of private property in land, of the subjection of agriculture to competition, and, consequently, of the mobilisation of the land. The other reproach that Mr Bulgakov directs at Kautsky, namely, that he does not investigate the problem of 'the different degrees of growth of the population in different places', is one that we simply cannot understand.

Did Mr Bulgakov really expect to find studies in demography in Kautsky's book?

Without dwelling on the question of entailment, which, after what has been said above, represents nothing new, we shall proceed to examine the question of the exploitation of the countryside by the town. Mr Bulgakov's assertion that Kautsky 'does not contrapose the positive to the negative sides and, primarily, the importance of the town as a market for agricultural produce', is in direct contradiction to the facts. Kautsky deals very definitely with the importance of the town as a market for agriculture *on the very first page* of the chapter which investigates 'modern agriculture' (p 30, et seq). It is precisely to 'urban industry' (p 292) that Kautsky ascribes the principal role in the transformation of agriculture, in its rationalisation, etc.[17]

That is why we cannot possibly understand how Mr Bulgakov could repeat in his article (page 32, *Nachalo*, No. 3) these very ideas *as if in opposition to Kautsky*! This is a particularly striking example of this stern critic's false exposition of the book he is subjecting to criticism. 'It must not be forgotten', Mr Bulgakov says to Kautsky admonishingly, that 'part of the values [which flow to the towns] returns to the countryside'. Anyone would think that Kautsky forgets this elementary truth. As a matter of fact Kautsky distinguishes between the flow of values (from the countryside to the town) with or without an equivalent return much more clearly than Mr Bulgakov attempts to do. In the first place, Kautsky examines the 'flow of commodity values from the country to the town without equivalent return (*Gegenleistung*)' (p 210) (rent which is spent in the towns, taxes, interest on loans obtained in city banks) and justly regards this as the economic exploitation of the countryside by the town. Kautsky further discusses the question of the efflux of values with an equivalent return, i.e. the exchange of agricultural produce for manufactured goods. He says: 'From the point of view of the law of value, this efflux does not signify the exploitation of agriculture[18]; actually, however, in the same way as the above-mentioned factors, it leads to its agronomic (*stofflichen*) exploitation, to the impoverishment of the land in nutritive substances' (p 211).

As for the agronomic exploitation of the countryside by the town, here too Kautsky adheres to one of the fundamental propositions of the theory of Marx and Engels, i.e. that the antithesis between town and country destroys the necessary correspondence and interdependence between agriculture and industry, and that with the transition of capitalism to a higher form this antithesis must disappear.[19] Mr Bulgakov thinks that Kautsky's opinion on the agronomic exploitation of the country by the town is a 'strange' one; that, 'at all events, Kautsky has here stepped on the soil of absolute fantasy' (*sic*!!!). What surprises us is that Mr Bulgakov ignores the fact that Kautsky's opinion, which he criticises, is identical with one of the fundamental ideas of Marx and Engels. The reader would be right in concluding that Mr Bulgakov considers the idea of the 'absolute fantasy'. If such indeed is the critic's opinion, then we emphatically disagree with him and go over to the side of 'fantasy' (actually, not to the side of fantasy, of course, but to that of a more profound criticism of capitalism). The view that the idea of abolishing the antithesis between town and country is a fantasy is not new by any means. It is the ordinary view of the bourgeois economists. It has even been borrowed by several writers with a more profound outlook. For example, Dühring was of the opinion that antagonism between town and country 'is inevitable by the very nature of things'.

Further, Mr Bulgakov is 'astonished' (!) at the fact that Kautsky refers to the growing incidence of epidemics among plants and animals as one of the difficulties confronting commercial agriculture and capitalism. 'What has this to do with capitalism …?' asks Mr Bulgakov. 'Could any higher social organisation abolish the necessity of improving the breeds of cattle?' We in our turn are astonished at Mr Bulgakov's failure to understand Kautsky's perfectly clear idea. The old breeds of plants and animals created by natural selection are being superseded by 'improved' breeds created by artificial selection. Plants and animals are becoming more susceptible and more demanding; with the present means of communication epidemics spread with astonishing rapidity. Meanwhile, farming remains individual, scattered, frequently small (peasant) farming, lacking knowledge and resources. Urban capitalism strives to provide all the resources of modern science for the development of the technique of agriculture, but it leaves the social position of the producers at the old miserable level; it does not systematically and methodically transplant urban culture to the rural districts. No higher social organisation will abolish the necessity of improving the breeds of cattle (and Kautsky, of course, did not think of saying anything so absurd); but the more technique develops, the more susceptible the breeds of cattle and plants[20] become, the more the present capitalist social organisation suffers from lack of social control and from the degraded state of the peasants and workers.

The last 'difficulty' confronting commercial agriculture that Kautsky mentions is the 'depopulation of the countryside', the absorption by the towns of the best, the most energetic and most intelligent labour forces. Mr Bulgakov is of the opinion that in its general form this proposition 'is at all events incorrect', that 'the present development of the urban at the expense of the rural population in no sense expresses a law of development of capitalist agriculture', but the migration of the agricultural population of industrial, exporting countries overseas, to the colonies. I think that Mr Bulgakov is mistaken. The growth of the urban (more generally: industrial) population *at the expense of* the rural population is not only a present-day phenomenon but a general phenomenon which expresses *precisely the law* of capitalism. The theoretical grounds of this law are, as I have pointed out elsewhere,[21] first, that the growth of social division of labour wrests from primitive agriculture an increasing number of branches of industry,[22] and, secondly, that the variable capital required to work a given plot of land, on the whole, diminishes (cf. *Capital* Vol 3, p 526, Russian translation, which I quote in my book, *The Development of Capitalism*, pp 4 and 444[23]). We have indicated above that in certain cases and certain periods we observed an increase in the variable capital required for the cultivation of a given plot of land; but this does not affect the correctness of the general law. Kautsky, of course, would not think of denying that not in every case does the relative diminution of the agricultural population become absolute diminution; that the degree of this absolute diminution is also determined by the growth of capitalist colonies. In relevant places in his book Kautsky very clearly points to this growth of capitalist colonies which flood Europe with cheap grain. ('The flight from the land of the rural population (*Landflucht*) which leads to the depopulation of the European countryside, constantly brings, not only to the towns, but also to the colonies, fresh crowds of robust country dwellers ...' p 242.) The phenomenon of industry depriving agriculture of its strongest, most energetic, and most intelligent workers is general, not only in industrial, but also in agricultural, countries; not only in Western Europe, but also in America and in Russia. The contradiction between the culture of the towns and the barbarism of the countryside which capitalism creates inevitably leads to this. The 'argument' that 'a decrease in the agricultural population side by side with a general increase in the population is inconceivable without the importation of large quantities of grain' is, in Mr Bulgakov's opinion, 'obvious'. But in my opinion this argument is not only not obvious, but wrong. A decrease in the agricultural population side by side with a general increase in the population (growth of the towns) is quite conceivable without grain imports (the productivity of agricultural labour increases and this enables a smaller number of workers to produce as much as and even more than was formerly produced). A general increase in the population parallel with a decrease in the agricultural population and a decrease (or a disproportionate increase) in the quantity of agricultural products is also conceivable – 'conceivable' because the nourishment of the people has deteriorated under capitalism.

Mr Bulgakov asserts that the increase of the medium-sized peasant farms in Germany in the period 1882-95, a fact established by Kautsky, which he connected with the other fact that these farms suffer least from a shortage of labour, 'is capable of shaking the whole structure' of Kautsky's argument. Let us examine Kautsky's statements more closely.

According to agricultural statistics, the largest increase in area in the period 1882-95 occurred in the farms of from 5 to

20 hectares. In 1882 these farms occupied 28.8 per cent of the total area of all farms and in 1895, 29.9 per cent. This increase in the total area of medium-sized peasant farms was accompanied by a decrease in the area of big peasant farms (20 to 100 hectares; 1882 – 31.1 per cent, 1895 – 30.3 per cent). 'These figures', says Kautsky, 'gladden the hearts of all good citizens who regard the peasantry as the strongest bulwark of the present system. "And so, it does not move, this agriculture", they exclaim in triumph; "Marx's dogma does not apply to it".' This increase in the medium-sized peasant farms is interpreted as the beginning of a new era of prosperity for peasant farming.

'But this prosperity is rooted in a bog', Kautsky replies to these good citizens. 'It arises, not out of the *well-being* of the peasantry, but out of the *depression* of agriculture as a whole' (p 230). Shortly before this Kautsky said that, 'notwithstanding all the technical progress which has been made, *in some places* [Kautsky's italics] there is a decline in agriculture; there can be no doubt of that' (p 228). This decline is leading, for example, to the revival of feudalism – to attempts to tie the workers to the land and impose certain duties upon them. Is it surprising that backward forms of agriculture should revive on the soil of this 'depression'? That the peasantry, which in general is distinguished from workers employed in large-scale production by its lower level of requirements, greater ability to starve, and greater exertion while at work, can hold out longer during a crisis?[24] 'The agrarian crisis effects all agricultural classes that produce commodities; it does not stop at the middle peasant' (p 231).

One would think that all these propositions of Kautsky are so clear that it is impossible not to understand them. Nevertheless, the critic has evidently failed to understand them. Mr Bulgakov does not come forward with an opinion: he does not tell us how he explains this increase in the medium-sized peasant farms, but he ascribes to Kautsky the opinion that 'the development of the capitalist mode of production is ruining agriculture'. And Mr Bulgakov exclaims angrily: 'Kautsky's assertion that agriculture is being destroyed is wrong, arbitrary, unproved, and contradicts all the main facts of reality', etc, etc.

To this we can only say that Mr Bulgakov *conveys Kautsky's ideas altogether incorrectly*. Kautsky does not state that the development of capitalism is ruining agriculture; he says the opposite. Only by being very inattentive in reading Kautsky's book can one deduce from his words on the depression (= crisis) in agriculture and on the technical retrogression to be observed *in some places (nota bene)* that he speaks of the 'destruction', the 'doom' of agriculture. In Chapter X, which deals especially with the question of overseas competition (i.e. the main reason for the agrarian crisis), Kautsky says: 'The impending crisis, of course (*natürlich*), need not necessarily (*braucht nicht*) ruin the industry which it affects. It does so only in very rare cases. As a general rule, a crisis merely causes a change in the existing property relations in the capitalist sense' (pp 273-74). This observation made in connection with the crisis in the agricultural industries clearly reveals Kautsky's general view of the significance of a crisis. In the same chapter Kautsky again expresses the view in relation to the whole of agriculture: 'What has been said above does not give one the least right to speak about the doom of agriculture (*Man braucht deswegen noch lange nicht von einem Untergang der Landwirtschaft zu sprechen*), but where the modern mode of production has taken a firm hold its conservative character has disappeared for ever. The continuation of the old routine (*das Verharren beim Alten*) means certain ruin for the farmer; he must constantly watch the development of technique and continuously adapt his methods of production to the new conditions.... Even in the rural districts economic life, which hitherto has with strict uniformity moved in an eternal rut, has dropped into a state of constant revolutionisation, a state that is characteristic of the capitalist mode of production' (p 289).

Mr Bulgakov 'does not understand' how trends toward the development of productive forces in agriculture can be combined with trends that increase the difficulties of commercial agriculture. What is there unintelligible in this? Capitalism in both agriculture and industry gives an enormous impetus to the development of productive forces; but it is precisely this development which, the more it proceeds, causes the contradictions of capitalism to become more acute and creates new 'difficulties' for the system. Kautsky develops one of the fundamental ideas of Marx, who categorically emphasised the progressive historical role of agricultural capitalism (the rationalisation of agriculture, the separation of the land from the farmer, the emancipation of the rural population from the relations of master and slave, etc), at the same time no less categorically pointing to the impoverishment and oppression of the direct producers and to the fact that capitalism is incompatible with the requirements of rational agriculture. It is very strange indeed that Mr Bulgakov, who admits that his 'general social-philosophic world outlook is the same as Kautsky's',[25] should fail to note that Kautsky here develops a fundamental idea of Marx. The readers of *Nachalo* must inevitably remain in perplexity over Mr Bulgakov's attitude towards these fundamental ideas and wonder how, in view of the identity of their general world outlook, he can say: '*De principiis non est disputandum*'!!?[26] We permit ourselves not to believe Mr Bulgakov's statement; we consider that an argument between him and other Marxists is possible precisely because of the community of these '*principia*'. In saying that capitalism rationalises agriculture, etc. Mr Bulgakov merely repeats one of these '*principia*'. Only he should not have said 'quite the opposite' in this connection. Readers might think that Kautsky holds a different opinion, whereas he very emphatically and definitely develops these fundamental ideas of Marx in his book. He says: 'It is precisely industry which has created the technical and scientific conditions for new, rational agriculture. It is precisely industry which has revolutionised agriculture by means of machines and artificial fertilisers, by means of the microscope and the chemical laboratory, giving rise in this way to the technical superiority of large-scale capitalist production over small-scale, peasant production' (p 292). Thus, Kautsky does not fall into the contradiction in which we find Mr Bulgakov bogged: on the one hand, Mr Bulgakov admits that 'capitalism (i.e. production carried on with the aid of wage-labour, i.e. not peasant, but large-scale production) rationalises agriculture', while on the other, he argues that 'it is not large-scale production which is the vehicle of this technical progress'!

II

Chapter X of Kautsky's book deals with the question of overseas competition and the industrialisation of agriculture. Mr Bulgakov treats this chapter in a very offhand manner: 'Nothing particularly new or original, more or less well-known main facts', etc, he says, leaving in the background the fundamental question of the conception of the agrarian crisis, its essence and significance. And yet this question is of enormous theoretical importance.

The conception of the agrarian crisis inevitably follows from the general conception of agrarian evolution which Marx presented and on which Kautsky enlarges in detail. Kautsky sees the essence of the agrarian crisis in the fact that, owing to the competition of countries which produce very cheap grain, agriculture in Europe has lost the opportunity of shifting to the masses of consumers the burdens imposed on it by the private ownership of land and capitalist commodity production. From now on agriculture in Europe *'must itself bear them* [these burdens], *and this is what the present agrarian crisis amounts to'* (p 239, Kautsky's italics). Ground rent is the main burden. In Europe, ground rent has been raised by preceding historical development to an extremely high level (both differential and *absolute* rent) and is fixed in the price of land.[27] On the other hand, in the colonies (America, Argentina, and others), insofar as they remain colonies, we see *free* land occupied by new settlers, either entirely gratis or for an insignificant price; moreover, the virginal fertility of this land reduces production costs to a minimum. Up to now, capitalist agriculture in Europe has quite naturally transferred the burden of excessively high rents to the consumer (in the form of high grain prices); now, however, the burden of these rents falls upon the farmers and the landowners themselves and ruins them.[28] Thus, the agrarian crisis has upset, and continues to upset the prosperity which capitalist landed property and capitalist agriculture formerly enjoyed. Hitherto capitalist landed property has exacted an ever-increasing tribute from social development; and it fixed the level of this tribute in the price of land. Now it has to forego this tribute.[29] Capitalist agriculture has now been reduced to the state of instability that is characteristic of capitalist industry and is compelled to adapt itself to new market conditions. Like every crisis, the agrarian crisis is ruining a large number of farmers, is bringing about important changes in the established property relations, and *in some places* is leading to technical retrogression, to the revival of medieval relations and forms of economy. Taken as a whole, however, it is *accelerating* social evolution, ejecting patriarchal stagnation from its last refuge, and making necessary the further specialisation of agriculture (a principal factor of agricultural progress in capitalist society), the further application of machinery, etc. On the whole, as Kautsky shows by data for several countries, in Chapter IV of his book, *even* in Western Europe, instead of the stagnation in agriculture in the period 1880-90, we see technical progress. We say *even* in Western Europe, because in America, for example, this progress is still more marked.

In short, there are no grounds for regarding the agrarian crisis as an obstacle to capitalism and capitalist development.

Notes

[1] Machines of various types are combined. Unless otherwise stated, all figures are taken from Kautsky's book.

[2] 'All these data', thinks Mr Bulgakov, 'can be obtained from any (sic) handbook of the economics of agriculture'. We do not share Mr Bulgakov's roseate views on 'handbooks'. Let us take from 'any' of the Russian books those of Messrs Skvortsov (*Steam Transport*) and N Kablukov (*Lectures*, half of them reprinted in a 'new' book *The Conditions of Development of Peasant Economy in Russia*). Neither from the one nor the other would the reader be able to obtain a picture of that transformation which was brought about by *capitalism* in agriculture, because neither even sets out to give a general picture of the transition from feudal to capitalist economy.

[3] Marx pointed to this process in Volume III of *Capital* (without examining its various *forms* in different countries) and observed that this separation of 'land as an instrument of production from landed property and landowner' is one of the major results of the capitalist mode of production (*Capital* Vol III, p 617-618).

[4] The increase in mortgage debts does not always imply that agriculture is in a depressed state ... The progress and prosperity of agriculture (as well as its decline) 'should find expression in an increase in mortgage debts – firstly, because of the growing need of capital on the part of progressing agriculture, and, secondly, because of the increase in ground rent, which facilitates the expansion of agricultural credit' (p 87).

[5] On pages 124-26 Kautsky describes the agricultural commune in Ralahine, of which, incidentally, Mr Dioneo tells his Russian readers in *Russkoye Bogatstvo*, No 2 for this year (1899 – *ed*).

[6] The only thing Mr Bulgakov could quote in support of his claim is the *title* Kasutsky gave to the first section of his Chapter VI: '(a) The *Technical* Superiority of Large-Scale Production', although this section deals with both the technical and the economic advantages of large-scale production. But does this prove that Kautsky *confuses* technique with economics? And, strictly speaking, it is still an open question as to whether Kautsky's title is inexact. The point is that Kautsky's object was to contrast the content of the first and second sections of Chapter VI: in the first section (a) he deals with the technical superiority of large-scale production in capitalist agriculture, and here, in addition to machinery, etc, he mentions, for instance, credit. 'A peculiar sort of technical superiority', says Mr Bulgakov ironically. But *Rira bien qui rira le dernier*! (He who laughs last laughs best – *ed*.) Glance into Kautsky's book and you will see that he has in mind, principally, the progress made in the *technique* of credit business (and further on in the technique of trading), which is accessible *only* to the big farmer. On the other hand, in the second section of this chapter (b) he compares the quantity of labour expended and the rate of consumption by the workers in large-scale production with those in small-scale production. Consequently, in this part Kautsky examines *the purely economic difference* between small- and large-scale production. The *economics* of credit and commerce is the same for both; but the *technique* is different.

[7] See V Y Postnikov, *Peasant Farming in South Russia*. CF V Ilyin, *The Development of Capitalism in Russia*, Chapter II, Section 1 (CW Vol 3 – *ed*).

[8] Cf V Ilyin, *The Development of Capitalism in Russia*, pp 112, 175, 201 (CW Vol 3 pp 168-70, 244-46, 273-75 – *ed*).

[9] Cf *The Development of Capitalism in Russia*, Chapter II Section 12, p 120 (CW Vol 3 p 178 – *ed*). It is estimated that in France about 75 per cent of the rural labourers own land. Other examples are also given.

[10] We emphasise 'taken as a whole', because it cannot, of course, be denied that in certain cases even these farms having an insignificant area of land can provide a large quantity of products and a large income (vineyards, vegetable gardens, etc). But what would we say of an economist who tried to refute the reference to the lack of horses among Russian peasants by pointing, for instance, to the vegetable growers in the suburbs of Moscow who may sometimes carry on rational and profitable farming without horses?

[11] In a footnote to page 15, Mr Bulgakov says that Kautsky, believing that grain duties were not in the interest of the overwhelming majority of the rural population, repeats the mistake committed by authors of the book on grain prices*. We cannot agree with this opinion either. The authors of the book on grain prices made a large number of mistakes (which I indicated repeatedly in the above mentioned book); but there is no mistake whatever in admitting that high grain prices are not in the interests of the mass of the population. What is a mistake is the *direct* deduction that the interests of the masses coincide with the interests of the whole social

development. Messrs Tugan-Baranovsky and Struve have rightly pointed out that the *criterion* in appraising grain prices must be whether, more or less rapidly, through capitalism, they eliminate labour-service, whether they stimulate social development. This is a question of fact which I answer differently from the way Struve does. I do not at all regard it as proved that the development of capitalism in agriculture is retarded by low prices. On the contrary, the particularly rapid growth of the agricultural machinery industry and the stimulus to specialisation in agriculture which was given by the reduction of grain prices show that low prices *stimulate* the development of capitalism in Russian agriculture (cf *The Development of Capitalism in Russia*, Chapter III, Section V, p 147, footnote 2). CW Vol 3 pp 212-13 – ed) The reduction of grain prices has a profound transforming effect upon all other relations in agriculture.

Mr Bulgakov says: 'One of the important conditions for the intensification of farming is the raising of grain prices'. (The same opinion is expressed by Mr P S in the 'Review of Home Affairs' column, p 299 in the same issue of *Nachalo*.) This is inexact. Marx showed in Part VI of Volume III of *Capital* that the productivity of additional capital invested in land may diminish, *but may also increase*; with a reduction in the price of grain, rent may fall, *but it may also rise*. Consequently, intensification may be due – in different historical periods and in different countries – to altogether different conditions, irrespective of the level of grain prices.

* This is a reference to *The Influence of Harvests and Grain Prices on Certain Aspects of Russian Economy*, edited by A I Chuprov and A S Posnikov, published in 1897 – *ed*.

[12] Mr Bulgakov adduces data, in still greater detail, but they add nothing whatever to Kautsky's data, since they show the same increase in the number of farms in one group of big proprietors and a reduction in the land area.

[13] There was a reduction in this category from 16,986,101 hectares to 16,802,115 hectares, i.e. by a whole … 1.2 per cent! Does this speak in favour of the 'death agony' of large-scale production seen by Mr Bulgakov?

[14] What is indeed a curiosity is Mr Bulgakov's remark that the increase in the number of non-manual employees testifies, perhaps, to the growth of agricultural industry, *but not* (!) to the growth of intensive large-scale farming. Until now we have thought one of the most important forms of increased intensification to be the growth of industry in agriculture (*described in detail and appraised by Kautsky in Chapter X*).

[15] Kärger, quoted by Kautsky, p 45.

[16] Kautsky emphatically expressed his opposition to every medieval restriction upon the mobilisation of the land, to entailment (*fidei-commissum, Anerbenrecht*), and to the preservation of the medieval peasant commune (p 332), etc.

[17] Cf also p 214, where Kautsky discusses the role urban capital plays in the rationalisation of agriculture.

[18] Let the reader compare Kautsky's clear statement as quoted above with the following 'critical' remark by Mr Bulgakov: 'If Kautsky regards the giving of grain to the non-agricultural population by direct grain producers as exploitation', etc. One cannot believe that a critic who has read

Kautsky's book at all attentively could have written that 'if'!

[19] It goes without saying that the opinion that it is necessary to abolish the antithesis between town and country in a society of associated producers does not in the least contradict the admission that the attraction of the population to industry from agriculture plays a *historically* progressive role. I had occasion to discuss this elsewhere (*Studies*, p 81, footnote 69) (CW Vol 2, p 229 – *ed*).

[20] That is why in the practical part of his book Kautsky recommends the sanitary inspection of cattle and of the conditions of their maintenance (p 397).

[21] *The Development of Capitalism in Russia*, Chapter I, Section II, and Chapter VIII, Section II (CW Vol 3 – *ed*).

[22] Pointing to this circumstance, Mr Bulgakov says that 'the agricultural population may diminish *relatively* [his italics] even when agriculture is flourishing.' Not only 'may', but *necessarily must* in capitalist society.... 'The relative diminution [of the agricultural population] merely (*sic!*) indicates here a growth of new branches of people's labour', concludes Mr Bulgakov. That 'merely' is very strange. New branches of industry do actually withdraw 'the most energetic and most intelligent labour forces' from agriculture. Thus, this simple reason is sufficient to enable one to accept Kautsky's general thesis as being *fully correct*: the *relative* diminution of the rural population sufficiently confirms the correctness of the general thesis (that capitalism withdraws the most energetic and most intelligent labour forces from agriculture).

[23] CW Vol III pp 40, 561 – *ed*.

[24] Kautsky says elsewhere: 'The small farmers hold out longer in a hopeless position. We have every reason to doubt that this is an advantage of small-scale production' (p 134).

In passing, let us mention data fully confirming Kautsky's view that are given by Koenig in his book, in which he describes in detail the condition of English agriculture in a number of typical counties (*Die Lage der englischen Landwirtschaft, etc* [*The Condition of English Agriculture, etc*], Jena 1896, Dr F Koenig). In this book we find *any amount* of evidence of overwork and under-consumption on the part of the small farmers, as compared with hired labourers, but no evidence of the opposite. We read, for instance, that the small farms pay 'because of immense (*ungeheuer*) diligence and frugality' (p 88); the farm buildings of the small farmers are inferior (p 107); the small landowners (*yeoman farmers* [these words are in English in the original – *ed*) are worse off than the tenant farmers (p 149); their conditions are very miserable (in Lincolnshire), their cottages being worse than those of the labourers employed on the big farms, and some are in a very bad state. The small landowners work harder and for longer hours than ordinary labourers, but they earn less. They live more poorly and eat less meat ... their sons and daughters work without pay and are badly clothed (p 157). 'The small farmers work like slaves; in the summer they often work from 3 a m to 9 p m' (a report of the Chamber of Agriculture in Boston, p 158). 'Without a doubt', says a big farmer, 'the small man (*der kleine Mann*), who has little capital and on whose farm all the work is done by members of his family, finds it easier to cut down housekeeping expenses, while the big farmer must feed his labourers equally well in bad years and good' (p 218). The small farmers (in Ayrshire) 'are extraordinarily (*ungeheuer*) diligent; their wives and children do no less, and often more, work than the day labourers; it is said that two of them will do as much work in a day as three hired labourers' (p 231). 'The life of the small tenant farmer, who must work with his whole family, is the life of a slave' (p 253). 'Taken as a whole ... the small farmers have evidently withstood the crisis better than the big farmers; but this does not imply that the small farm is more profitable. The reason, in our opinion, is that the small man (*der kleine Mann*) utilises the unpaid assistance of his family.... Usually ... the whole family of the small farmer works on the farm.... The children are fed and clothed, and only rarely do they get a definite daily wage' (p 277-78), etc, etc.

[25] As for the philosophic world outlook, we do not know whether what Mr Bulgakov says is true. Kautsky does not seem to be an adherent of the critical philosophy, as Mr Bulgakov is.

[26] There can be no argument when it comes to a matter of principle – *ed*.

[27] For the process of inflating and fixing rent see the apt remarks of Parvus in *The World Market and the Agricultural Crisis*. Parvus shares Kautsky's main views on the crisis and on the agrarian question generally.

[28] Parvus, *op cit* p 141, quoted in a review of Parvus' book in *Nachalo*, No 3, p 117 (CW p 66 – *ed*). We should add that the other 'difficulties' of commercial agriculture confronting Europe affect the colonies to an incomparably smaller degree.

[29] Absolute rent is the result of monopoly. 'Fortunately, there is a limit to the raising of absolute rent.... Until recent times it rose steadily in Europe in the same way as differential rent. But overseas competition has undermined this monopoly to a very considerable extent. We have no grounds for thinking that differential rent in Europe has suffered as a result of overseas competition, except for a few counties in England.... But absolute rent has dropped, and this has benefited (*zu gute gekommen*) primarily the working classes' (p 80; cf also p 328).

3. Strike Statistics in Russia

I

The well-known publications of the Ministry of Trade and Industry, *Statistics of Workers' Strikes in Factories and Mills* for the decade 1895-1904 and for 1905-08, have been commented on in our press on a number of occasions. There is such a wealth of valuable material collected in these publications that a complete study and thorough analysis of it will require a great deal of time. The analysis made in them is but a first, and very far from adequate, approach to the subject. In the present article we intend to acquaint the readers with the preliminary results of an attempt at a more detailed analysis, deferring a full exposition of the subject for publication elsewhere.

To begin with, the fact has been fully established that the strike movement in Russia in the years 1905-07 represented a phenomenon unparalleled anywhere else in the world. Here are the figures showing the number of strikers (in thousands) by years and countries:

Average	Russia	U.S.A.	Germany	France
for 1895-1904	431			
for 1905	2,863	660	527	438
for 1906	1,108	Maximum number during		
for 1907	740	the fifteen years		
for 1908	176	1894-1908		
for 1909	64			

The three-year period 1905-07 is particularly remarkable. The minimum number of strikers in Russia during these three years is greater than the maximum ever attained in any of the most developed capitalist countries. This does not

Published in December 1910 and January 1911 in the magazine *Mysl*.
CW XVI 393-421.

mean, of course, that the Russian workers are more highly developed or stronger than the workers in the West. But it does mean that mankind had never known before what energy the industrial proletariat is *capable* of displaying in this sphere. The specific feature of the historical course of events was expressed in the fact that the approximate dimensions of this capability were first revealed in a backward country which is still passing through a bourgeois revolution.

In order to be clear on the question as to how it happened that, with the rather small number of factory workers in Russia compared with Western Europe, the number of strikers was so large, we must bear in mind the *repeated* strikes. Here are figures showing the percentage of repeated strikes by years and the ratio between the number of strikers and the number of workers:

Years	The number of strikers as a percentage of the total number of workers	The number of repeated strikes as a percentage of the total number of strikes
1895-1904	1.46-5.10	36.2
1905	163.8	85.5
1906	65.8	74.5
1907	41.9	51.8
1908	9.7	25.4

Hence we see that the triennium 1905-07, which is conspicuous for the number of strikers, is also distinguished for the frequency of repeated strikes and for the high percentage of strikers in relation to the total number of workers.

The statistical data cover also the number of establishments in which strikes occurred and the number of workers who took part in those strikes. Here are the figures for the various years:

	Percentage of strikers in establishments affected by strikes, in relation to the total number of workers
Aggregate for ten years (1895-1904)	27.0
1905	60.0
1906	37.9
1907	32.1
1908	11.9

This table, like the preceding one, shows that the decline in the number of strikers in 1907 compared with 1906 was, in general, *considerably less* than the decline in 1906 compared with 1905. We shall see further on that some industries and some districts registered not a decline, but an intensification of the strike movement in 1907 compared with 1906. For the time being we shall note that the figures by gubernias of the number of workers who actually participated in strikes reveal the following interesting phenomena. Compared with 1905 the percentage of workers who took part in strikes in 1906 declined in the overwhelming majority of industrially developed gubernias. On the other hand, there were a number of gubernias in which this percentage *increased* in 1906. They were those least developed industrially, and most out-of-the-way, as it were. They include, for instance, the gubernias of the Far North: Archangel (11,000 factory workers; in 1905, 0.4 per cent of the workers took part in strikes, in 1906 – 78.6 per cent), Vologda (6,000 factory workers; 26.8 and 40.2 per cent for the years mentioned), Olonets (1,000 factory workers; 0 and 2.6 per cent); then there is Chornoye Morye (Black Sea) Gubernia (1,000 factory workers; 42.4 and 93.5 per cent); of Volga Region – Simbirsk (14,000 factory workers; 10 and 33.9 per cent); of the central agricultural gubernias – Kursk (18,000 factory workers; 14.4 and 16.9 per cent); in the Eastern border area, Orenburg (3,000 factory workers; 3.4 and 29.4 per cent).

The significance of the increase in the percentage of workers who took part in strikes in these provinces in 1906 compared with 1905 is clear: the wave had not reached them in 1905; they began to be drawn into the movement only after a year of unparalleled struggle on the part of the more advanced workers. We shall come across this phenomenon – one very important for an understanding of the historical course of events – more than once in our further exposition.

On the other hand, in 1907 compared with 1906 the percentage of workers who took part in strikes increased in some gubernias that are very highly developed industrially: for instance, St Petersburg (68 per cent in 1906 and 85.7 per cent in 1907 – almost as high as in 1905, when 85.9 per cent of the workers took part in strikes), Vladimir (37.1 and 49.6 per cent), Baku (32.9 and 85.5 per cent), Kiev (10.9 and 11.4

per cent), and several others. Consequently, while the increased percentage of strikers in 1906 compared with 1905 in a number of gubernias reveals the rearguard of the working class, which had lagged behind at the moment of the highest development of the struggle, the increase of this percentage in 1907 as compared with 1906 in a number of other gubernias shows us the vanguard of the working class striving to raise the struggle again, to halt the retreat that had begun.

In order to make this correct conclusion even more precise, we shall quote the absolute figures of the number of workers and the number of actual strikers in the gubernias of the first and of the second category.

Gubernias in which the percentage of workers who took part in strikes increased in 1906 compared with 1905:

Number of such gubernias	Number of factory workers in them	Number of workers who actually took part in strikes	
		in 1905	in 1906
10	61,800	6,564	21,484

The average number of factory workers per gubernia is 6,000. The increase in the number of workers who actually took part in strikes totalled 15,000.

Gubernias in which the percentage of workers who took part in strikes increased in 1907 compared with 1906:

Number of such gubernias	Number of factory workers in them	Number of workers who actually took part in strikes	
		in 1906	in 1907
19	572,132	186,926	285,673

The average number of factory workers per gubernia is 30,000. The increase in the number of workers who actually took part in strikes amounted to 100,000, or, if we exclude the Baku oil workers who were not included in the figures for 1906 (probably not more than 20-30,000), to about 70,000.

The role of the rearguard in 1906 and of the vanguard in 1907 is clearly seen from these figures.

For a still more exact idea of the extent of the movement we must take the figures for the various areas of Russia and compare the number of strikers with the number of factory workers. Here is a summary of these figures:

Factory areas	Number of factory workers in 1905 (thousands)	Number of strikers (in thousands) per year				
		1895-1904 total	1905	1906	1907	1908
I. St. Petersburg	298	137	1,033	307	325	44
II. Moscow	567	123	540	170	154	28
III. Warsaw	252	69	887	525	104	35
IV-VI: Kiev, Volga and Kharkov	543	102	403	106	157*	69*
Total	1,660	431	2,863	1,108	740	176

* These figures are not strictly comparable with the figures for the preceding years, since the oil workers were not included in the data prior to 1907. The resulting increase is probably not more than 20-30,000.

The extent to which the workers took part in the movement varied in the different districts. Altogether there were 2,863,000 strikers in 1905 to a total of 1,660,000 workers, or 164 strikers for every 100 workers; in other words, on the average more than half of all the workers struck twice in that year. But this average glosses over the fundamental distinction between the St Petersburg and Warsaw areas, on the one hand, and all the other areas, on the other. The St Petersburg and Warsaw areas together comprise one-third of all the factory workers (550,000 out of 1,660,000), but they accounted for two-thirds of all the strikers (1,920,000 out of 2,863,000). In these areas every worker struck, on the average, nearly four times in 1905. In the other areas there were 943,000 strikers to 1,110,000 workers, i.e. the proportion of strikers was only a quarter of that in the two above-mentioned areas. This by itself shows how wrong are the assertions of the liberals, which are repeated by our liquidators,[1] that the workers overestimated their strength. On the contrary, the facts prove that they underestimated their strength, for they did not make full use of it. Had the energy and persistence displayed in the strike struggle (we refer here only to this one form of struggle) been the same throughout Russia as they were in the St Petersburg and Warsaw areas, the total number of strikers would have been *twice as many*. This conclusion can also be expressed in the following way: the workers were able to estimate only one-half of their strength in this sphere of the movement, for they had not yet brought the other half into play. In geographical terms, this may be stated as follows: the West and Northwest had woken up, but the Centre, the East and the South were still half asleep. The development of capitalism contributes something every day to awakening the tardy.

Another important conclusion from the figures by areas is that in 1906 compared with 1905 the movement declined everywhere, although unevenly; in 1907 compared with 1906 there was a very large decline in the Warsaw area and a rather slight decline in the Moscow, Kiev and Volga areas, whereas in the St Petersburg and Kharkov areas there was an *increase* in the number of strikers. This means that, with the level of political consciousness and preparedness of the population as it was at the time, this particular form of the movement had exhausted itself in 1905; inasmuch as the objective contradictions in social and political life had not disappeared, the movement was bound to pass to a higher form. But after a year of recuperation, as it were, or of the mustering of forces during 1906, there were signs of a new upsurge, which actually began in part of the country. In appraising this period the liberals, echoed by the liquidators, speak contemptuously about 'the expectations of the romanticists'; a Marxist, however, must state that by refusing to support this partial upsurge the liberals frustrated the last opportunity of upholding the democratic gains.

As regards the territorial distribution of the strikers, it should be noted that the vast majority of them is accounted for by *six* gubernias with highly developed industries, and with big cities in five of them. The six gubernias are: St Petersburg, Moscow, Vladimir, Warsaw, Petrokov and Livonia. In 1905 there were 827,000 factory workers in these gubernias, out of a total of 1,661,000; thus they accounted for nearly half of the total. As for the number of strikers in these gubernias, there were 246,000 in all during the decade 1895-1904, out of 431,000, or about 60 per cent of the total number of strikers; in 1905 there were 2,072,000 out of a total of 2,863,000, or about 70 per cent; in 1906 – 852,000 out of a total of 1,108,000, i.e. approximately 75 per cent; in

1907 – 517,000 out of a total of 740,000, or approximately 70 per cent; in 1908 – 85,000 out of total of 176,000, i.e. less than a half.[2]

Consequently, the role of these six gubernias was *greater* during the three-year period 1905-07 than in the period before or after it. It is therefore clear that the big urban centres, including the capitals, displayed a considerably greater energy than all the other localities during these three years. The workers scattered in villages and in relatively small industrial centres and towns, comprising half of the total number of workers, accounted for 40 per cent of the total number of strikers in the decade 1895-1904, and for only 25-30 per cent during the period 1905-07. Supplementing the conclusion we arrived at above, we may say that the big cities had woken up, while the small towns and villages were largely still asleep.

As regards the countryside in general, i.e. as regards the factory workers living in villages, we have additional statistical data covering the *number of strikes* (but not that of strikers) in towns and non-urban localities. Here are the figures:

Total for the ten years	In cities	Number of strikes In non-urban localities	Total
1895-1904	1,326	439	1,765
1905	11,891	2,104	13,995
1906	5,328	786	6,114
1907	3,258	315	3,573
1908	767	125	892

In citing these data, the compilers of the official statistics point out that, according to the well-known investigations of Mr Pogozhev, 40 per cent of all the factories in Russia are located in towns, and 60 per cent in non-urban localities.[3] Consequently, in the normal period (1895-1904), while the number of strikes in the towns was three times as high as in the rural districts, the number of strikes as a per centage of the number of establishments was *4½ times* as great in the towns as in the rural districts. In 1905 this ratio was approximately 8:1; in 1906 it was 9:1; in 1907 – 15:1 and in 1908[4] – 6:1. In other words, compared with the part played by the factory workers in the villages, the *part played* by the urban factory workers in the strike movement was considerably greater in 1905 than in the previous years; moreover, their role became greater and greater in 1906 and 1907, i.e. proportionately the part played in the movement by the village workers became less and less. The factory workers in the villages, less prepared for the struggle by the preceding decade (1895-1904), showed the least firmness and were the quickest to retreat after 1905. The vanguard, i.e. the urban factory workers, made a special effort in 1906, and a *still greater* effort in 1907, to halt this retreat.

Let us now examine the distribution of the strikers according to industries. For this purpose we single out four main groups of industries: A) metal-workers; B) textile-workers; C) printers, wood-workers, leather-workers, and workers in chemical industries; D) workers in the mineral products industries and food industries. Here are the figures for the different years:

Groups of industries	Total number of factory workers in 1904 (thousands)	Number of strikers (in thousands) for the years				
		1895-1904 total	1905	1906	1907	1908
A	252	117	811	213	193	41
B	708	237	1,296	640	302	56
C	277	38	471	170	179	24
D	454	39	285	85	66	55
Total	1,691	431	2,863	1,108	740	176

The metal-workers were best prepared by the decade preceding 1905. During that decade nearly half of them took part in strikes (117,000 out of 252,000). Since they were the best prepared, they made the best showing in 1905 as well. The number of strikers among them was *more than three times* the total number of workers (811,000 as against 252,000). Their role as vanguard stands out even more clearly when we examine the monthly figures for 1905 (it is impossible to give a detailed analysis of these figures in a short article, and we shall do so elsewhere). In 1905 the month with the maximum number of strikers among the metal-workers was not October, as was the case in *all* the other groups of industries, but January. The vanguard displayed the maximum energy in inaugurating the movement, 'stirring up' the entire mass. In January 1905 alone 155,000 metal-workers went on strike, i.e. two-thirds of their total number (252,000). In that month alone more metal-workers were on strike than in all the preceding ten years (155,000 as against 117,000). But this, almost superhuman, energy exhausted the strength of the vanguard towards the end of 1905; in 1906 the metal-workers account for the biggest decline in the movement. The maximum drop in the number of strikers is among them: from 811,000 to 213,000, i.e. by nearly three-fourths. In 1907 the vanguard had again gathered strength: the total decline in the number of strikers was very slight (from 213,000 to 193,000), and in the three most important branches – namely, engineering, shipbuilding and foundries – the number of strikers actually *increased* from 104,000 in 1906 to 125,000 in 1907.

The textile-workers constitute the main mass of the Russian factory workers – a little less than half the total (708,000 out of 1,691,000). As regards their preparatory experience in the ten years prior to 1905 they occupy the second place: one-third of their number (237,000 out of 708,000) took part in strikes. They also occupy the second place for the intensity of the movement among them in 1905: about 180 strikers to every 100 workers. They entered the struggle later than the metal-workers: in January the number of strikers among them was slightly greater than among the metal-workers (164,000 as against 155,000), but in October they had more than twice as many strikers (256,000 as against 117,000). Having entered the struggle later, this main mass proved to be the most firm of all in 1906: in that year the decline was general, but it was *smallest of all* among the textile-workers, the number of strikers among them dropping by a half (640,000 as against 1,296,000), compared with a decrease of nearly three-quarters among the metal-workers (from 811,000 to 213,000) and of from three-fifths to five-sevenths among the other groups. Only by 1907 was the force of the main mass also exhausted: in 1907 it was this group which showed the *greatest* drop, by more than a half compared with 1906 (302,000 as against 640,000).

Without making a detailed analysis of the figures for the other industries, we shall only note that group D lags behind all of them. It was the least prepared, and its part in the movement was the smallest. If we take the metal-workers as the standard, it may be said that group D 'defaulted' to the extent of over a million strikers in 1905 alone.

The relation between the metal-workers and the textile-workers is characteristic as reflecting the relation between the advanced section and the broad mass of the workers. Owing to the absence of free organisations, a free press, a parliamentary platform, etc, during the period 1895-1904, the masses could rally in 1905 only spontaneously, in the course of the struggle itself. This process took the form of successive waves of strikers; but in order to 'stir up' the broad mass, the vanguard was obliged to spend such a tremendous amount of energy at the beginning of the movement that it proved relatively weakened when the movement reached its apogee. In January 1905, there were 444,000 strikers, including 155,000 metal-workers, i.e. 34 per cent of the total; in October, however, when the number of strikers reached 519,000, the number of metal-workers among them was 117,000, i.e. 22 per cent. It is obvious that this unevenness of the movement was tantamount to a certain dissipation of forces owing to the fact that they were scattered, insufficiently concentrated. This means, firstly, that the effect might have been heightened if the forces had been better concentrated, and, secondly, that owing to the objective conditions characteristic of the period under discussion at the beginning of each wave a number of groping actions, as it were, reconnaissances, trial moves, etc, were inevitable and were necessary for the success of the movement. Therefore, when the liberals, echoed by liquidators like Martov, proceeding from their theory that 'the proletariat had overestimated its forces', accuse us of having 'followed in the wake of the spontaneous class struggle', these gentlemen are condemning themselves and are paying us, against their will, the greatest compliment.

In conclusion our review of the strike figures for each year, we shall deal also with the figures showing the size and the duration of the strikes, and the losses incurred as a result of the strikes.

The average number of strikers per establishment was as follows:

In the ten years 1895-1904	244
In 1905	205
In 1906	181
In 1907	207
In 1908	197

The decrease in the size of strikes (as regards the number of workers involved) in 1905 is explained by the fact that a great number of small establishments joined the struggle, thus lowering the average number of strikers per establishment. The further decrease in 1906 apparently reflects the waning energy of the struggle. 1907 shows a certain advance.

If we take the average number of workers who took part in purely political strikes, we get the following figures for the various years: 1905 – 180; 1906 – 174; 1907 – 203; 1908 – 197. These figures indicate even more strikingly the waning energy of the struggle in 1906 and its new growth in 1907, or (and, perhaps, at the same time) the fact that it was mostly the biggest establishments that took part in the movement in 1907.

The number of days on strike per striker was as follows:

In the ten years 1895-1904	4.8
In 1905	8.7
In 1906	4.9
In 1907	3.2
In 1908	4.9

The persistence of the struggle, as characterised by the above figures, was greatest in 1905; then it diminished rapidly until 1907, showing a new increase only in 1908. It should be pointed out that, as regards the persistence of the struggle, strikes in Western Europe are on an incomparably higher level. In the five-year period 1894-98 the number of days on strike per striker was 10.3 in Italy, 12.1 in Austria, 14.3 in France, and 34.2 in Britain.

Taking separately the purely political strikes, the figures are as follows: 1905 – 7 days per striker, 1906 – 1.5 days, 1907 – 1 day. Economic strikes are always more protracted.

If we bear in mind the difference in the persistence of the strike struggles in the different years, we arrive at the conclusion that the figures of the number of strikers are not sufficient to give a proper idea of the relative sizes of the movement in these years. An accurate index is provided by figures of striker-days, which were as follows:

		Of which in purely political strikes
In the ten years 1894-1904 a total of	2,079,408	—
In 1905 a total of	23,609,387	7,569,708
In 1906 a total of	5,512,749	763,605
In 1907 a total of	2,433,123	521,647
In 1908 a total of	864,666	89,021

Thus we see that the accurate figures representing the size of the movement in the year 1905 alone are *more than 11 times* as great as those for all the preceding ten years taken together. In other words, the size of the movement in 1905 was *115 times* as great as the *average per year* for the preceding decade.

This ratio shows us how purblind are those people, whom we encounter only too often among the representatives of official science (and not only among them), who consider the tempo of social-political development in the so-called 'peaceful', 'organic', 'evolutionary' periods as the standard for all times, as the index of the highest possible pace of development modern humanity can achieve. Actually, the tempo of 'development' in the so-called 'organic' periods is an index of the greatest stagnation, of the greatest obstacles placed in the way of development.

The compiler of the official statistics uses the figures of the number of striker-days to determine the losses incurred by industry. These losses (representing the drop in output) amounted to 10,400,000 rubles in the ten years 1895-1904, to 127,300,000 rubles in 1905, to 31,200,000 rubles in 1906, to 15,000,000 rubles in 1907, and to 5,800,000 rubles in 1908. In the three years 1905-07, therefore, the drop in output amounted to 173,500,000 rubles.

The losses of the workers in unpaid wages for strike days (determined in accordance with the average daily wages in the various industries) were as follows:

Group of industries (see above p 141)	Number of factory workers in 1905 (thousands)	Losses incurred by workers as a result of strikes (in thousands of rubles)				
		1895-1904 total	1905	1906	1907	1908
A	252	650	7,654	891	450	132
B	708	715	6,794	1,968	659	228
C	277	137	1,997	610	576	69
D	454	95	1,096	351	130	22
Total	1,691	1,597	17,541	3,820	1,815	451

In the three years 1905-07 the losses of the workers amounted to 23,200,000 rubles, or over 14 times more than in the entire preceding decade.[5] According to the calculation of the compiler of the official statistics, the average loss per worker employed in factories (and not per striker) amounted to about ten kopeks a year during the first decade, about ten rubles in 1905, about two rubles in 1906, and about one ruble in 1907. But this calculation leaves out of account the enormous differences in this respect between the workers of the various industries. Here is a more detailed calculation made on the basis of the figures quoted in the above table:

Groups of industries	Average loss (in rubles) caused by strikes, per factory worker				
	total for 10 years 1895-1904	1905	1906	1907	1908
A	2.6	29.9	3.5	1.8	0.5
B	1.0	9.7	2.8	0.9	0.3
C	0.5	7.2	2.2	2.1	0.2
D	0.2	2.4	0.7	0.3	0.05
Total	0.9	10.4	2.3	1.1	0.3

Hence, we see that the losses per metal-worker (Group A) amounted to nearly 30 rubles in 1905, or three times more than the average, and over ten times more than the average loss per worker in the mineral products industries and in the food industries (Group D). The conclusion we arrived at above, namely, that by the end of 1905 the metal-workers had spent their strength in this particular form of the movement, is even more strikingly confirmed by this table: in Group A the amount of the losses dropped to less than one-eighth in the period from 1905 to 1906; whereas in the other groups it dropped to one-third or one-fourth.

This concludes the analysis of the strike statistics by years. In the next section we shall deal with the monthly figures.

II

A year is too long a period to enable us to investigate the wave-like character of the strike movement. The statistics now give us the right to say that during the three years 1905-07 every month counted for a year. In those three years the working-class movement advanced a full thirty years. In 1905 there was not a single month when the number of strikers dropped below the minimum *per year* during the decade 1895-1904; there were but two such months in 1906 and two in 1907.

It is to be regretted that the treatment of the monthly data, as well as of the data for the separate gubernias, is very unsatisfactory in the official statistics. Many summaries need to be worked out anew. For this reason, and also for considerations of space, we shall confine ourselves for the time being to the *quarterly* data. With regard to the breakdown into economic and political strikes, it should be noted that the official statistics for 1905 and for 1906-07 are not quite comparable. Strikes of a mixed nature – in the official statistics Group 12 with economic demands and Group 12b with economic demands – were classified as political in 1905 and as economic in the subsequent years. We shall classify them as economic strikes in 1905 too.

				Number of strikers (in thousands)									
	Year		1905				1906				1907		
	Quarter	I	II	III	IV	I	II	III	IV	I	II	III	IV
	Total	810	481	294	1.277	269	479	296	63	146	323	77	193
Of which	Econ.	604	239	165	430	73	222	125	37	52	52	66	30
	Polit.	206	242	129	847	196	257	171	26	94	271	11	163

The boxes indicate the periods during which the wave rose highest. It is obvious from even a cursory glance at the table that these periods coincide with political events of cardinal importance that are characteristic of the entire triennium. 1905, first quarter – January 9 and its consequences; 1905, fourth quarter – the October and December events; 1906, second quarter – the First Duma; 1907, second quarter – the Second Duma; the last quarter of 1907 shows the least rise occasioned by the November political strike (134,000 strikers) in connection with the trial of the workers' deputies of the Second Duma. Hence this period, which completes the triennium and represents a transition to a new stage in Russian history, is just that exception which proves the rule: the rise of the strike wave in this case does not imply a general social-political upsurge, but on closer examination we see that there was really no strike *wave* – but only an isolated demonstration strike.

The rule applying to the triennium that we are studying is that the rise of the strike wave indicates crucial turning-points in the entire social and political evolution of the country. The strike statistics show us graphically what was the principal driving force of this evolution. This does not mean, of course, that the form of the movement we are examining was the sole or the highest form – we know that this was not the case; nor does it mean that we can draw direct conclusions from this form of the movement with regard to particular questions of social and political evolution. But it does mean that what we have before us is a statistical picture (far from complete, of course) of the movement of the class which was the mainspring responsible for the general direction taken by events. The movements of the other classes are grouped around this centre; they follow it, their direction is determined (in a favourable or unfavourable way) by it, they depend on it.

One has only to recall the principal movements in the political history of Russia during the triennium under review to realise that this conclusion is correct. Let us take the first quarter of 1905. What did we see on the eve of this period? The well-known Zemstvo banquet campaign.[6] Was it right to regard the actions of the workers in that campaign as 'the highest type of demonstration'? Was the talk about refraining from causing 'panic' among the liberals justified? Consider these questions in conjunction with the strike statistics (1903 – 87,000 strikers; 1904 – 25,000; January 1905 – 444,000, including 123,000 political strikers), and the answer will be obvious. The above-mentioned controversy over the question of the tactics in the Zemstvo campaign only reflected the antagonism between the liberal and working-class movements, an antagonism rooted in objective conditions.

What do we see after the January upsurge?[7] The well-known February edicts, which marked the inauguration of a certain amount of change in the organisation of the state.

Take the third quarter of 1905. The principal event in the political history was the law of August 6 (the so-called Bulygin Duma)[8]. Was the law destined to be put into effect? The liberals thought that it was and decided to act accordingly. In the camp of the Marxists a contrary view prevailed, which was not shared by those who objectively supported the views of the liberals. The events of the last quarter of 1905 decided the controversy.

The figures referring to whole quarters make it appear that there was one upsurge at the end of 1905. Actually there were two, separated by an interval during which there was a slight abatement of the movement. The number of strikers in October was 519,000, including 328,000 involved in purely political strikes; in November 325,000 (including 147,000 in political strikes); in November 325,000 (including 147,000 in political strikes); and in December 433,000 (including 372,000 in political strikes). Publications dealing with the history of the period express the view of the liberals and our liquidators (*Cherevanin and Co*) according to which there was an element of 'artificiality' in the December upsurge. The statistical data refute this view, for they show that it was precisely this month that accounted for the *highest* number of workers involved in purely political strikes – 372,000. The tendencies that impelled the liberals to arrive at their particular appraisal are obvious, but from a purely scientific standpoint it is absurd to regard a movement of such dimensions as at all 'artificial', when in one month the number of workers involved in purely political strikes was almost nine-tenths of the total number of strikers during a whole decade.

Finally, let us consider the last two waves – in the spring of 1906 and in the spring of 1907.[9] What distinguishes both of them from the January and May waves in 1905 (of which the first was also stronger than the second) is that they came during the ebb of the movement, whereas the first two waves took place during the rising tide of the movement. This distinction is generally characteristic of the two last years compared with the first year of the triennium. Hence, the correct explanation of the increase registered during these periods of 1906 and 1907 is that they denote a halt in the retreat and an attempt on the part of the retreating forces to resume the offensive. Such is the objective meaning of these upsurges, which is now clear to us in the light of the final results of the whole 'three-year period of storm and stress'. The First and the Second Dumas represented nothing else than political negotiations and political demonstrations on top, prompted by the half in the retreat below.

This clearly shows how short-sighted are the liberals who see in these negotiations something self-sufficient and independent, unrelated to whether a particular halt in the retreat is going to be of long duration, or what its outcome will be. This also shows clearly the objective dependence on the liberals of those liquidators who, like Martov, now speak with scorn of the 'expectations of the romanticists' during the period of retreat. The statistical data show that it was not a question of the 'expectations of the romanticists', but of actual interruptions, halts of the retreat. Had it not been for these halts, the coup d'état of June 3, 1907, which was historically absolutely inevitable since the retreat was a fact, would have taken place sooner, perhaps a year or even more than a year earlier.

Now that we have examined the history of the strike movement in its relation to the principal moments of the political history of the period, let us pass on to an investigation of the interrelation between the economic and the political strikes. The official statistics provide very interesting data touching on this subject. Let us first deal with the general total for each of the three years under review (see p 151 – *ed*).

The first conclusion to be drawn from these figures is that there is a very close connection between the economic and

		Number of strikers (in thousands)		
		1905	1906	1907
Economic strikes		1,439	458	200
Political strikes		1,424	650	540
Total		2,863	1,108	740

the political strikes. They rise simultaneously and drop simultaneously. The force of the movements in the period of the offensive (1905) results from the fact that the political strikes are built, as it were, on the broad basis of the no less powerful economic strikes which, even taken by themselves, far exceed the figures for the entire decade of 1895-1904.

During the decline of the movement the number of those engaged in economic strkes drops faster than the number of those engaged in political strikes. The weakness of the movement in 1906, and particularly in 1907, is undoubtedly the result of the fact that the broad and firm base of the economic struggle was absent. On the other hand, the slower drop in the number of workers involved in political strikes, in general, and the particularly insignificant decrease in that number in 1907 compared with 1906, apparently testify to the phenomenon with which we are already familiar: namely, that the advanced sections were exercising their utmost energy to halt the retreat and to turn it into an offensive.

This conclusion is fully corroborated by the data showing the interrelation between economic and political strikes in the various groups of industries. In order to avoid overburdening the article with figures we shall confine ourselves to a comparison of the quarterly data for the year

		Number of strikers (in thousands)			
	1905, Quarters	I	II	III	IV
Group A	Economic	120	42	37	31
(metal workers)	Political	159	76	63	283
	Total	279	118	100	314
Group B	Economic	196	109	72	182
(textile workers)	Political	111	154	53	418
	Total	307	263	125	600

1905 with reference to the metal-workers and the textile-workers, using in this instance the summary of the official statistics,[10] which, as mentioned before, classified the mixed strikes that took place that year as political strikes.

Here we see clearly the distinction between the advanced section and the mass of the workers. Among the advanced section those involved in purely economic strikes were a minority from the very beginning, and this holds good for the whole year. Even in this group, however, in the first quarter of the year the number of workers involved in purely economic strikes was very high (120,000). Clearly, among the metal-workers too there were considerable sections which had to be 'stirred up', and which started off by presenting purely economic demands. Among the textile workers we see a very great preponderance of those taking part in purely economic strikes in the initial stage of the movement (in the first quarter of the year). These became a minority during the second quarter, only to become a majority again in the third quarter. In the fourth quarter, when the movement reached its zenith, the number of metal-workers involved in purely economic strikes was 10 per cent of the total number of strikers and 12 per cent of the total number of metal-workers; while among the textile-workers the number of those involved in purely economic strikes represented 30 per cent of the total number of strikers and 25 per cent of the total number of textile-workers.

The interdependence between the economic and political strike is thus quite obvious: no really broad, no really mass movement is possible without a close connection between the two; the concrete expression of this connection consists, on the one hand, in the fact that at the beginning of the movement, and when new sections are just entering it, the purely economic strike is the prevalent form, and, on the other, in the fact that the political strike rouses and stirs the backward sections, generalises and extends the movement, and raises it to a higher level.

It would be extremely interesting to trace in detail precisely how new recruits were drawn into the movement during the whole three-year period. The main material contains data relating to this subject, for the information obtained was entered on cards dealing with each strike separately. But the analysis of this information in the official statistics is very unsatisfactory, and a wealth of material contained in the cards has been lost, since it was not included in the analysis. An approximate idea is given by the following table showing the number of strikes as a percentage of the number of establishments of different sizes:

| | Number of strikes as a percentage of the number of establishments | | | | |
Groups of establishments	Total for 10 years 1895-1904	1905	1906	1907	1908
20 workers or less	2.7	47.0	18.5	6.0	1.0
21 to 50 workers	7.5	89.4	38.8	19.0	4.1
51 to 100 workers	9.4	108.9	56.1	37.7	8.0
101 to 500 workers	21.5	160.2	79.2	57.5	16.9
501 to 1,000 workers	49.9	163.8	95.1	61.5	13.0
Over 1,000 workers	89.7	231.9	108.8	83.7	23.0

The advanced section, which we have so far observed from the data dealing with the different districts and different groups of industries, now stands out from the data dealing with the various groups of establishments. The general rule throughout these years is that as the size of the establishments increases there is an increase in the percentage of establishments in which strikes occurred. The characteristic features of the year 1905 are, firstly, that the bigger the establishment the larger the number of repeated strikes, and, secondly, that compared with the decade 1895-1904 the rise in the percentage is the steeper the *smaller* the establishments. This clearly indicates the especial rapidity with which new recruits were drawn into the movement, and with which sections that had never before taken part in strikes were enlisted. Rapidly drawn into the movement in the period of the greatest upsurge, these new recruits proved the least stable: the drop in the percentage of establishments in which strikes occurred in 1907 as compared with 1906 was greatest in the small establishments, and least in the big establishments. It was the vanguard which worked the longest and the most persistently to halt the retreat.

But to return to the interrelation between the economic and the political strike. The quarterly data for the entire triennium, quoted above,[11] show, in the first place, that all the great advances in the movement were accompanied by a rise not only in the number of workers involved in political strikes, but also of those involved in economic strikes. The only exception was the upsurge in the spring of 1907; in that year the largest number of workers involved in economic strikes was not in the second but in the third quarter.

At the beginning of the movement (first quarter of 1905) we see an overwhelming prevalence of workers involved in economic strikes over those involved in political strikes (604,000 as against 206,000). The zenith of the movement (fourth quarter of 1905) brings with it a new wave of economic strikes, not as high as in January, however, and with political strikes strongly predominating. The third advance, in the spring of 1906, again shows a very large increase in the number of participants both in economic and in political strikes. These data alone are sufficient to refute the opinion according to which the combination of the economic with the political strike represented a 'weak aspect of the movement'. This opinion has been often expressed by the liberals; it has been repeated by the liquidator Cherevanin in relation to November 1905; recently it has been repeated by Martov too in relation to the same period. The failure of the struggle for an eight-hour day is especially often referred to as confirming this opinion.

This failure is an undeniable fact; it is also undeniable that any failure implies that the movement is weak. But the view of the liberals is that it is the combination of the economic with the political struggle that is the 'weak aspect of the movement'; the Marxist view, on the other hand, is that the weakness lay in the insufficiency of this combination, in the insufficient number of workers involved in economic strikes. The statistical data furnish graphic confirmation of the correctness of the Marxist view, for they reveal the 'general law' of the three-year period – namely, that the movement becomes intensified as a result of the intensification of the economic struggle. And there is a logical connection between this 'general law' and the basic features of every capitalist society, in which there always exist backward sections which can be aroused only by the most extraordinary accentuation of the movement, and it is only by means of economic demands that the backward sections can be drawn into the struggle.

If we compare the upsurge in the last quarter of 1905 with the one before it and the one after it, i.e. with the first quarter of 1905 and the second quarter of 1906, we see clearly that the upsurge in October-December had a *narrower* economic base than either the one before or the one after, i.e. as regards the number of workers involved in economic strikes as a percentage of the total number of strikers. Undoubtedly, the demand for an eight-hour day antagonised many elements among the bourgeoisie who might have sympathised with the other aspirations of the workers. But there is also no doubt that this demand attracted many elements, not of the bourgeoisie, who had not so far been drawn into the movement. These elements were responsible for 430,000 workers taking part in economic strikes in the last quarter of 1905, their number dropping to 73,000 in the first quarter of 1906, and increasing again to 222,000 in the second quarter of 1906. Consequently, the weakness lay not in the absence of sympathy on the part of the bourgeoisie, but in the insufficient, or insufficiently timely, support on the part of non-bourgeois elements.

It is in the nature of liberals to be dismayed by the fact that a movement of the kind we are discussing always antagonises certain elements of the bourgeoisie. It is in the nature of Marxists to note the fact that this kind of movement always attracts large sections outside the ranks of the bourgeoisie. *Suum cuique* – to each his own.

The official statistics dealing with the results of the strikes are highly instructive as regards the vicissitudes of the struggle between the workers and the employers. The following is a summary of these statistics:

Percentage of workers involved in strikes
with the results indicated

Results of strikes	10 years 1895-1904	1905	1906	1907	1908
In favour of the workers	27.1	23.7	35.4	16.2	14.1
Mutual concessions (compromise)	19.5	46.9	31.1	26.1	17.0
In favour of the employers (against the workers)	51.6	29.4	33.5	57.6	68.8

The general conclusion to be drawn from this is that the maximum force of the movement signifies also the maximum success for the workers. The year 1905 was the most favourable for the workers, because in that year the force of the strike struggle was greatest. That year was also distinguished by the unusual frequency of compromises: the parties had not yet adapted themselves to the new unusual conditions, the employers were bewildered by the frequency of the strikes, which more often than ever before ended in a compromise. In 1906 the struggle became more stubborn: cases of compromise were incomparably rarer; but on the whole the workers were still victorious: the percentage of strikers who won a victory was greater than the percentage of those who lost. Beginning with 1907 defeats for the workers continually increased, and cases of compromise became rarer.

From the absolute figures it will be seen that in the ten years 1895-1904 the total number of workers who won their strikes was 117,000, whereas in 1905 alone more than three times as many workers won their strikes (369,000), and in 1906, one-and-a-half times as many (163,000).

A year, however, is too long a period for a proper study of the wave-like progress of the strike struggle in 1905-07. Since the monthly data would take up too much space, we shall cite the quarterly data for 1905 and 1906. We can omit the data for 1907, since, judging by the results of the strikes, there were no breaks in that year, no declines and rises, but a continuous retreat on the part of the workers and an offensive on the part of the capitalists, as has been fully brought out in the yearly data already cited.

The conclusions that follow from these data are highly interesting and require a detailed examination. On the whole, as we have seen, the success of the struggle, as far as the workers are concerned, depends on the force of their onslaught. Do the data cited above confirm this conclusion? The first quarter of 1905 appears to have been less favourable for the workers than the second quarter, although in the latter the movement was weaker. This inference would be wrong, however, since the quarterly data combine the upsurge in January (321,000 workers involved in economic strikes) and the decline in February (228,000) and in March (56,000). If we single out January, the month of upsurge, we find that in this month the workers were victorious: 87,000 won their strikes, 81,000 lost, and 152,000 concluded a compromise. The two months of decline (February and March) brought the workers defeat.

Years		1905				1906		
Quarters	I	II	III	IV	I	II	III	IV
Results of strikes								
In favour of the workers	158	71	45	95	34	86	37	6
Compromise	267	109	61	235	28	58	46	8
In favour of the employers	179	59	59	100	11	78	42	23
*Total**	604	239	165	430	73	222	125	37

* The official statistics provide no monthly totals relating to this question; they had to be obtained by adding up the figures for the various industries.

The next period (the second quarter of 1905) was one of an advance, which reached its climax in May. The rise of the struggle signified victory for the workers: 71,000 won their strikes, 59,000 lost, and 109,000 compromised.

The third period (third quarter of 1905) was one of decline. The number of strikers was much less than in the second quarter. The decline in the force of the onslaught signified victory for the employers: 59,000 workers lost their strikes, and only 45,000 won. The workers who lost their strikes represented 35.6 per cent of the total, *i.e. more than in 1906.* This means that the 'general atmosphere of sympathy' with the workers in 1905, which the liberals talk so much of as being the main cause of the workers' victories (recently Martov, too, wrote of the sympathy of the bourgeoisie as 'the main cause'), in no way prevented the defeat of the workers *when the force of their onslaught diminished.* 'You are strong when society sympathises with you', the liberals say to the workers. 'Society sympathises with you when you are strong', the Marxists say to the workers.

The last quarter of 1905 seems to be an exception: although it was the period of the greatest advance, the workers suffered defeat. But this is only a seeming exception, for this period again combines the month of upsurge in October, when the workers were victorious in the economic sphere as well (+ 57,000, − 22,000 strikers won and lost respectively) with the two months of November (+ 25,000, − 47,000) and December (+ 12,000, − 31,000), when the economic struggle was on the decline and the workers were defeated. Furthermore, November − a month that was a turning-point, a month of the greatest wavering, of the greatest uncertainty as regards total results and the general trend of the further history of Russia as a whole and of the history of the relations between employers and workers in particular − was a month that shows a *larger* percentage of strikes ending in compromise than any other month in 1905: of 179,000 workers involved in economic strikes in that month, 106,000, or 59.2 per cent, ended by compromising.[12]

The first quarter of 1906 again seems to be an exception: the greatest decline in the economic struggle coupled with, proportionately, the largest number of workers winning their strikes (+ 34,000, − 11,000). But here, too, we have the combination of a month in which the workers suffered defeat − namely, January (+ 4,000, − 6,000) − with months in which the workers scored victories: February (+ 14,000, − 2,000) and March (+ 16,000, − 2,500). The number of workers involved in economic strikes is on the decline throughout this period (January, 26,600; February, 23,300; March, 23,200); but there were already clear indications of an upward trend in the movement as a whole (the total number of strikers amounted to 190,000 in January, 27,000 in February, and 52,000 in March).

The second quarter of 1906 marked a big advance in the movement, which brought with it victories for the workers (+ 86,000, − 78,000); the greatest victories were scored in May and June, the total number of workers involved in economic strikes in June reaching 90,000 – the maximum for the whole year; whereas April represents an exception: a defeat for the workers, despite the growth of the movement as compared with March.

Beginning with the third quarter of 1906, we see, on the whole, an uninterrupted decline of the economic struggle lasting to the end of the year, and, correspondingly, defeats of the workers (with a slight exception in August 1906, when the workers were victorious for the last time in the economic struggle: + 11,300, – 10,300).

Summed up briefly, the vicissitudes of the economic struggle in the years 1905 and 1906 may be formulated as follows: in 1905 there can be clearly distinguished three main advances in the strike struggle in general and in the economic struggle in particular – January, May and October. The number of workers involved in economic strikes in these three months amounted to 667,000, out of a total of 1,439,000 for the whole year; that is to say, not a quarter of the total, but nearly a half. And in all these three months the workers scored victories in the economic struggle, that is to say, the number of workers who won their strikes exceeded the number of those who lost.

In 1906, there is on the whole a clear distinction between the first and the second half of the year. The first half is marked by a halt in the retreat and a considerable advance; the second is marked by a serious decline. In the first half of the year 295,000 workers took part in economic strikes; in the second half, 162,000. The first half brought the workers victories in the economic struggle, the second half brought them defeat.

This general summary fully confirms the conclusion that it was not the 'atmosphere of sympathy', not the sympathy of the bourgeoisie, but the force of the onslaught that played the decisive part in the economic struggle as well.

Notes

[1] 'Liquidators' was the title commonly given to those Mensheviks who from 1906 onwards advocated giving up any 'underground' Social Democratic organisation and instead sought to form a 'broad Labour party' after the British model.

[2] In 1908, Baku Gubernia topped the list with 47,000 strikers. The last of the Mohicans of the mass political strike!

[3] A V Pogozhev, Report on the Number and Composition of Workers in Russia, Labour Statistics Data, St Petersburg, published by the Imperial Academy of Sciences, 1906 – *ed*.

[4] The figures for 1908 include 228 strikes, and the figures for 1907 include 230 strikes, in the oilfields, which for the first time came under the Inspectorate in 1906.

[5] It should be borne in mind that in the period when the movement was at its height the workers compelled the employers to cover *part* of these losses. Beginning with 1905, the statistics had to deal with a special cause of strikes (Cause Group *3 b*, according to the official nomenclature): *demand of pay for the time of the strike*. In 1905 there were 632 cases when this demand was presented; in 1906 – 256 cases, in 1907 – 48 cases, and in 1908 – 9 cases (prior to 1905 this demand was never presented). The results of the struggle of the workers for this demand are known only for the years 1906 and 1907, and only two or three cases when this was the *main* demand: in 1906, out of 10,966 workers who struck primarily for this demand, 2,171 won the strike, 2,626 lost, and 6,169 concluded a compromise. In 1907, out of 93 workers who struck primarily for this demand, not one won the strike, 52 lost, and 41 compromised. From what we know of the strikes in 1905 we may surmise that in that year the strikes for this demand were more successful than in 1906.

[6] In November 1904 constitutionalists and liberals in the zemstvos initiated a series of public banquets from which to launch calls for varying degrees, usually quite limited, of democratisation and enfranchisement. This was a middle class campaign, and the Social Democrats, though not actively opposed to it, were highly critical of its limited aims and class nature – *ed*.

[7] The quarterly data would make it appear that there was only one upsurge. Actually, there were two: in January, with 444,000 strikers, and in May, with 220,000 strikers. In the interval between these two months, March accounted for the minimum number of strikers – 73,000.

[8] In February 1905 the Tzar ordered Bulygin, the minister of the interior, to draw up a plan to convene a duma. On August 6, Bulygin published the law setting out the basis on which this should be done – which was very narrowly restricted. However, the events of October meant that the law was never put into effect. Thus the 'Bulygin Duma' never took place – *ed*.

[9] It should be noted that the history of the strike movement in Russia from 1895 to 1904 shows that there is usually an increase in economic strikes in the second quarter of the year. The average number of strikers per year during the entire decade was 43,000, divided as follows: first quarter, 10,000; second quarter, 15,000; third quarter, 12,000; and fourth quarter, 6,000. A mere comparison of the figures makes it quite obvious that the rise in the strike wave in the spring of 1906 and in the spring of 1907 cannot be explained by the 'general' causes of the summer increase in the number of strikes in Russia. One has only to glance at the figures showing the numbers of workers engaged in political strikes.

[10] According to this summary, 1,021,000 workers took part in economic strikes and 1,842,000 in political strikes in 1905. The proportion of the workers who took part in economic strikes thus appears to be less than in 1906. We have already explained that this is wrong.

[11] See page 147 – *ed*.

[12] The total number of workers involved in economic strikes was as follows: October, 190,000; November, 179,000; December, 61,000.

4. Economic and Political Strikes

Ever since 1905 the official strike statistics kept by the Ministry of Commerce and Industry have subdivided strikes into economic and political. This subdivision was necessitated by reality, which has evolved *distinctive* forms of the strike movement. The combination of economic and political strike is one of the main features of these forms. And now that there is a revival of the strike movement, it is in the interest of a scientific analysis, of an intelligent attitude to events, that the workers should look closely into this distinctive feature of the strike movement in Russia.

To begin with, we shall cite several basic figures taken from the government strike statistics. For three years, 1905-07, the strike movement in Russia kept at a height *unprecedented in the world*. Government statistics cover only factories, so that mining, railways, building and numerous other branches of wage-labour are left out. But even in factories alone, the number of strikers was 2,863,000, or a little less than 3 million, in 1905, 1,108,000 in 1906, and 740,000 in 1907. In the fifteen years from 1894 to 1908, during which strike statistics began to be systematically studied in Europe, the greatest number of strikers for one year – 660,000 – was registered in America.

Consequently, the Russian workers were *the first in the world* to develop the strike struggle on the mass scale that we witnessed in 1905-07. Now it is the British workers who have lent a new great impetus to the strike movement with regard to economic strikes. The Russian workers owe their leading role, not to greater strength, better organisation or higher development compared with the workers in Western Europe, but to the fact that so far Europe has not gone

First published in *Nevskaya Zvezda* May 1912.
CW XVIII 83-90.

through great national crises with the proletarian masses taking an independent part in them. When such crises do set in, mass strikes in Europe will be even more powerful than they were in Russia in 1905.

What was the ratio of economic to political strikes in that period? Government statistics give the following answer:

	Number of strikers (thousands)		
	1905	1906	1907
Economic strikes	1,439	458	200
Political strikes	1,424	650	240
Total	2,863	1,108	740

This shows the close and inseparable connection between the two kinds of strike. When the movement was at its highest (1905), the *economic* basis of the struggle was the broadest; in that year the political strike rested on the firm and solid basis of economic strikes. The number of economic strikers was *greater* than that of political strikers.

We see that as the movement declined, in 1906 and 1907, the economic basis *contracted*: the number of economic strikers dropped to 0.4 of the total number of strikers in 1906 and to 0.3 in 1907. Consequently, the economic and the political strike support each other, each being a source of strength for the other. Unless these forms of strike are closely interlinked, a really wide mass movement – moreover, a movement of *national* significance – is impossible. When the movement is in its early stage, the economic strike often has the effect of awakening and stirring up the backward, of making the movement a general one, of raising it to a higher plane.

In the first quarter of 1905, for instance, economic strikes noticeably predominated over political strikes, the number of strikers being 604,000 in the former case and only 206,000 in the latter. In the last quarter of 1905, however, the ratio was reversed: 430,000 workers took part in economic strikes, and 847,000 in political strikes. This means that in the early stage of the movement many workers put the economic struggle first, while at the height of the movement it was the other way round. But *all the time* there was a *connection* between the economic and the political strike.

Without such a connection, we repeat, it is impossible to have a really great movement, one that achieves great aims.

In a political strike, the working class comes forward as the advanced class of the whole people. In such cases, the proletariat plays not merely the role of one of the classes of bourgeois society, but the role of guide, vanguard, leader. The political ideas manifested in the movement involve the whole people, i.e. they concern the basic, most profound conditions of the political life of the whole country. This character of the political strike, as has been noted by all scientific investigators of the period 1905-07, brought into the movement all the classes, and particularly, of course, the widest, most numerous and most democratic sections of the population, the peasantry, and so forth.

On the other hand, the mass of the working people will never agree to conceive of a general 'progress' of the country without economic demands, without an immediate and direct improvement in their condition. The masses are drawn into the movement, participate vigorously in it, value it highly and display heroism, self-sacrifice, perseverance and devotion to the great cause only if it makes for improving the economic condition of those who work. Nor can it be otherwise, for the living conditions of the workers in 'ordinary' times are incredibly hard. As it strives to improve its living conditions, the working class also progresses morally, intellectually and politically, becomes more capable of achieving its great emancipatory aims.

The strike statistics published by the Ministry of Commerce and Industry fully bear out this tremendous significance of the economic struggle of the workers in the period of a general revival. The stronger the onslaught of the workers, the greater their achievements in improving their standard of living. The 'sympathy of society' and better conditions of life are both results of a high degree of development of the struggle. Whereas the liberals (and the liquidators) tell the workers: 'You are strong when you have the sympathy of "society",' the Marxist tells the workers something different, namely: 'You have the sympathy of "society" when you are strong.' What we mean by society in this case is all the various democratic sections of the population, the petty bourgeoisie, the peasants, and the intellectuals, who are in close touch with the life of the workers, office employees, etc.

The strike movement was strongest in 1905. And what was the result? We see that in that year the workers achieved the greatest improvements in their condition. Government statistics show that in 1905 *only* 29 out of every 100 strikers stopped their fight without having gained *anything*, i.e. were completely defeated. In the previous ten years (1895-1904), as many as 52 strikers out of 100 stopped fighting without having gained anything! It follows that the large scale of the struggle contributed immensely to its *success*, almost doubling it.

When the movement began to decline, the success of the struggle began to diminish accordingly. In 1906, 33 strikers out of 100 stopped fighting without having gained anything, or having been defeated, to be exact; in 1907 the figure was 58, and in 1908, as high as 69 out of 100!!

Thus the scientific statistical data over a number of years fully confirm the personal experience and observations of every class-conscious worker as regards the necessity of combining the economic and the political strike, and the inevitability of this combination in a really broad movement of the whole people.

The present strike wave likewise fully confirms this conclusion. In 1911 the number of strikers was double that in 1910 (100,000 against 50,000), but even so their number was extremely small; purely economic strikes remained a relatively 'narrow' cause, they did not assume national significance. On the other hand, today it is obvious to one and all that the strike movement following the well-known events of last April had *precisely this* significance.[1]

It is therefore highly important to rebuff from the outset the attempts of the liberals and liberal labour politicians (liquidators) to *distort* the character of the movement. Mr Severyanin, a liberal, contributed to *Russkiye Vedomosti*[2] an article *against* 'admixing' economic or 'any other (aha!) demands' to the May Day strike, and the Cadet *Rech* sympathetically reprinted the main passages of the article.

'More often than not,' writes the liberal gentleman, 'it is unreasonable to link such strikes with May Day.... Indeed, it would be rather strange to do so: we are celebrating the international workers' holiday, and we use the occasion to demand a ten per cent rise for calico of such-and-such grades.' (*Rech* No. 132.)

What is quite clear to the workers seems 'strange' to the liberal. Only the defenders of the bourgeoisie and its excessive profits can sneer at the demand for a 'rise'. But the workers know that it is the *widespread* character of the demand for a rise, it is the *comprehensive* character of a strike, that has the greatest power to attract a multitude of new participants, to ensure the strength of the onslaught and the sympathy of society, and to guarantee both the success of the workers and the national significance of their movement. That is why it is necessary to fight with determination against the liberal distortion preached by Mr Severyanin, *Russkiye Vedomosti* and *Rech*, and to warn the workers in every way against this kind of sorry advisers.

Mr V Yezhov, a liquidator, writing in the very first issue of the liquidationist *Nevsky Golos*,[3] offers a similar purely liberal distortion, although he approaches the question from a somewhat different angle. He dwells in particular on the strikes provoked by the May Day fines. Correctly pointing out that the workers are not sufficiently organised, the author draws from his correct statement conclusions that are quite wrong and most harmful to the workers. Mr Yezhov sees a lack of organisation in the fact that while in one factory the workers struck merely in protest, in another they added economic demands, etc. Actually, however, this *variety* of forms of strike does not in itself indicate any lack of organisation at all; it is ridiculous to imagine that organisation necessarily means uniformity! Lack of organisation is not at all to be found where Mr Yezhov looks for it. But his *conclusion* is still worse:

'Owing to this [i.e., owing to the variety of the strikes and to the different forms of the combination of economics and politics], the principle involved in the protest (after all, it was not over a few kopeks that the strike was called) became obscured in a considerable number of cases, being complicated by economic demands....'

This is a truly outrageous, thoroughly false and

thoroughly liberal argument! To think that the demand 'for a few kopeks' is *capable* of 'obscuring' the principle involved in the protest means sinking to the level of a Cadet. On the contrary, Mr Yezhov, the demand for 'a few kopeks' deserves full recognition and not a sneer! On the contrary, Mr Yezhov, that demand, *far from* 'obscuring' 'the principle involved in the protest', *emphasises* it! Firstly, the question of a higher standard of living is *also* a question of principle, and a most important one; secondly, whoever protests, not against one, but against two, three, etc, manifestations of oppression, does not thereby weaken his protest but strengthens it.

Every worker will indignantly reject Mr Yezhov's outrageous liberal distortion of the matter.

In the case of Mr Yezhov, it is by no means a slip of the pen. He goes on to say even more outrageous things:

> 'Their own experience should have suggested to the workers that it was advisable to complicate their protest by economic demands, just as it is inadvisable to complicate an ordinary strike by a demand involving a principle.'

This is untrue, a thousand times untrue! The *Nevsky Golos* has disgraced itself by printing such stuff. What Mr Yezhov thinks inadvisable is perfectly advisable. Both each worker's *own experience* and the experience of a very large number of Russian workers in the recent past testify to *the reverse* of what Mr Yezhov preaches.

Only liberals can object to 'complicating' even the most 'ordinary' strike by 'demands involving principles'. That is the first point. Secondly, our liquidator is sorely mistaken in measuring the present movement with the yardstick of an 'ordinary' strike.

And Mr Yezhov is wasting his time in trying to cover up his liberal contraband with someone else's flag, in confusing the question of *combining* the economic and the political strike with the question of *preparations* for the one or the other! Of course, it is most desirable to make preparations and to be prepared, and to do this as thoroughly, concertedly, unitedly, intelligently and firmly as possible. That is beyond dispute. But, contrary to what Mr Yezhov says, it is necessary to make preparations precisely for a *combination* of the two kinds of strike.

> 'A period of economic strikes is ahead of us,' writes Mr Yezhov. 'It would be an irreparable mistake to allow them to become intertwined with political actions of the workers. Such combination would have a harmful effect on both the economic and the political struggle of the workers.'

One could hardly go to greater lengths! These words show in the clearest possible way that the liquidator has sunk to the level of an ordinary liberal. Every sentence contains an error! We must convert every sentence into its *direct* opposite to get at the truth!

It is not true that a period of economic strikes is ahead of us. Quite the reverse. What we have ahead of us is a period of something more than just economic strikes. We are facing a period of political strikes. The facts, Mr Yezhov, are stronger than your liberal distortions; and if you could look at the statistical cards dealing with strikes, which are filed in the Ministry of Commerce and Industry, you would see that *even* these government statistics fully refute you.

It is not true that 'intertwining' would be a mistake. Quite the reverse. It would be an irreparable mistake if the workers failed to understand the great singularity, the great significance, the great necessity, and the great fundamental importance of precisely such 'intertwining'. Fortunately, however, the workers understand this perfectly, and they brush aside with contempt the preaching of liberal labour politicians.

Lastly, it is not true that such intertwining 'would have a harmful effect' on both forms. Quite the reverse. It *benefits* both. It strengthens both.

Mr Yezhov lectures some 'hotheads' whom he seems to have discovered. Listen to this:

'It is necessary to give organisational form to the sentiments of the workers....' This is gospel truth! 'It is necessary to increase propaganda for trade unions, to recruit new members for them....'

Quite true, *but* – but, Mr Yezhov, it is impermissible to *reduce* 'organisational form' to the trade unions alone! Remember this, Mr Liquidator!

'This is all the more necessary since there are many hotheads among the workers nowadays who are carried away by the mass movement and speak at meetings *against unions*, alleging them to be useless and unnecessary.'

This is a liberal slur on the workers. It is not 'against unions' that the workers – who have been, and always will be, a thorn in the side of the liquidators – have been coming out. No, the workers have been coming out against the attempt to *reduce* the organisational form to 'trade unions' alone, an attempt which is so evident from Mr Yezhov's preceding sentence.

The workers have been coming out, not 'against unions', but against the liberal distortion of the nature of the struggle they are waging, a distortion which pervades the whole of Mr Yezhov's article.

The Russian workers have become sufficiently mature politically to realise the great significance of their movement for the whole people. They are sufficiently mature to see how very false and paltry liberal labour policy is and they will always brush it aside with contempt.

Notes

[1] In April 1912, during a strike at Lena goldfields in Siberia, 270 workers were shot and killed. The shootings led to widespread protest strikes in other parts of Russia – *ed*.

[2] *Russkiye Vedomosti* (Russian Recorder) was described by Lenin as 'a unique combination of Right Cadetism and Narodnik overtones' (CW XIX, p 135) – *ed*.

[3] *Nevsky Golos* (Neva Voice) was a St Petersburg Menshevik newspaper published from May to August 1912 – *ed*.

5. Factory Owners on Workers' Strikes

I

P P Ryabushinsky's press in Moscow has published an interesting book entitled *The Association of Factory Owners in the Moscow Industrial Area in 1912* (Moscow, 1913). The price is not given. The factory owners do not wish their publications to be put on sale.

Yuli Petrovich Guzhon, the president of the association, when opening this year's annual meeting on March 30, congratulated the industrialists 'on the beginning of the seventh operative year' of their organisation and declared that the industrialists had, 'by their unity created for themselves a conception of the might of the industrial corporation that could not be ignored'. 'The present main task of new members of the association must be the strengthening of the prestige of that might', said Mr Guzhon.

As you see, the speech was not what one might call literate, it was reminiscent of the speech of some army clerk; nevertheless it was full of arrogance.

Let us look at the sections of the book dealing with facts. More than one-third of it (pp 19-69) is taken up by the section devoted to *strikes*. The industrialists give us the following picture of the total number of workers taking part in strikes in 1912.

It is easy to see that the industrialists' figures are *an understatement*. But for the time being we shall not deal with that (the Lena strike of 6,000 workers has been omitted

Published in *Pravda*, 1913, on May 30, June 2, 5 and 9.
CW XIX, 125-131.

Category of strike	Number of striking workers	
	1912	1911
Economic	*207,720*	*96,730*
Metal goods industry	64,200	17,920
Textiles goods industry	90,930	51,670
Other branches	52,590	27,140
Political	*855,000*	*8,380*
Over Lena events	215,000	
May Day celebrations	300,000	
Autumn political strikes	340,000	
Totals	*1,062,720*	*105,110*

because the Lena Goldfields do not come under the Factory Inspectorate), but we shall examine the factory owners' statistics.

The number of workers who took part in strikes in 1912 was *more than a half* of the total number of industrial workers in Russia, to be exact, 51.7 per cent. Economic strikes, furthermore, accounted for only *one-tenth* of the workers (10.1 per cent) and political strikes for more than *four-tenths* (41.6 per cent).

'Typical of the past year,' write the factory owners, 'was the extraordinary growth in the number of political strikes that time and again interrupted the normal course of work and kept the entire industry in a state of tension.' This is followed by a list of the most important strikes in the second half of the year – August, in Riga, against the disenfranchisement of workers; September, in Warsaw, over the events at the Kutomary Penal Colony; October, in St Petersburg, over the annulment of the elections of representatives, in Revel, in memory of the events of 1905, and in St Petersburg, over the well-known verdict in the case of naval ratings; November, in St Petersburg, over the Sevastopol verdict and on the day of the opening of the Duma, and then a strike on the occasion of the second anniversary of Leo Tolstoy's death; December, in St Petersburg, over the appointment of workers in insurance institutions. From this the factory owners draw the conclusion:

'The frequency of the demonstration strikes, which occur one after another, and the unusual variety and difference in the importance of the motives for which the workers considered it necessary to interrupt work, are evidence, not only of a considerable thickening of the political atmosphere, but also of the decline of factory discipline.' Then follow the usual threats of 'severe measures' – fines, stopping of bonuses, lock-outs. 'The interests of the country's production,' declare the factory owners, 'urgently demand the raising of factory discipline to the high level at which it stands in the West-European countries.'

The factory owners wish to raise 'discipline' to the 'Western' level but do not think of raising the 'political atmosphere' to the same level....

We shall leave for subsequent articles the data concerning strike distribution over various areas, and in various branches of industry and according to the degree of success achieved.

II

The 1912 data of the Moscow Factory Owners Association on the incidence of strikes in various areas and branches of industry are very badly compiled. It would do no harm if our millionaires were to hire, say, some high-school boy to help them compile their books and check the tables. Mistakes and absurdities leap to the eye when we compare, for example, the data given on pages 23, 26 and 48. Oh yes, we love talking about culture and 'the prestige of the might' of the merchants, but we can't do even the simplest job half-way decently.

Below we give the factory owners' strike statistics – *for economic strikes only* – by areas for 1912 as a whole and for the last seven months of that year:

Areas	For all 1912		For the last 7 months of 1912	
	Number of strikers	Number of days lost (000)	Number of strikers	Number of days lost (000)
Moscow	60,070	799.2	48,140	730.6
St. Petersburg	56,890	704.8	35,390	545.7
Baltic	18,950	193.5	13,210	153.6
South	23,350	430.3	22,195	427.6
Kingdom of Poland	21,120	295.7	12,690	249.9
Total	180,380	2,423.5	131,625	2,107.4

A glance at the figures for the South is enough to show how useless, i.e. extremely incomplete, the factory owners' statistics are. The figures for the last seven months of 1912 seem to be more reliable, because here, and only here, the distribution of strikers is given in detail according to areas, major industries and the results achieved.

The area data show us that the St Petersburg workers are in advance of all the workers of Russia in the economic struggle as well (to say nothing of the political struggle). The number of strikers in the St Petersburg area (35,000 for the last seven months of 1912) is about three-quarters of the number of strikers in the Moscow area (48,000) although the number of factory workers there is *about four times* that of the number in the St Petersburg area. In the Kingdom of Poland there are slightly more workers than in the St Petersburg area but the number of strikers there was little more than a third of the St Petersburg figure.

As far as Moscow is concerned, there is, of course, the need to consider the worsening marketing conditions in the textile industry, although in Poland two-thirds of those participating in economic strikes were textile workers and we shall see later that these textile strikes in Poland were particularly successful.

In 1912, therefore, the St Petersburg workers to a certain extent drew the workers of other parts of Russia into the economic strike movement.

In respect of *determination*, on the other hand, the strikes in the South and in Poland take first place; in these areas nineteen days per striker were lost, whereas in St Petersburg and Moscow the figure was fifteen days (in the Baltic area 12 days per striker). The average for all Russia was sixteen days on strike per striker. The gentlemen who compile the factory owners' statistics give the figure for the whole of 1912 as 13.4 days. It follows from this that the persistence of the workers and their determination in struggle were greater in the second half of the year.

Statistics show, furthermore, the *increased persistence* of the workers in the strike struggle. From 1895 to 1904 the average number of days lost per striker was 4.8, in 1909 it was 6.5 days, in 1911 it was 7.5 days (8.2 days if political strikes are excluded) and in 1912, 13.4 days.

The year 1912, therefore, showed that there is a *growing persistence* among workers in the economic struggle and that the number of strikers – compared with the number of workers – is greatest in St Petersburg.

In our next article we shall examine data on the degree of success achieved by strikes.

III

The factory owners' statistics give the following figures for strikers (in economic strikes) for 1912 according to branches of industry:

Branch of industry	For all 1912		For the last 7 months of 1912	
	Number of strikers	Number of days lost (000)	Number of strikers	Number of days lost (000)
Metalworkers	57,000	807.2	40,475	763.3
Textile workers	85,550	1,025.8	66,590	930.6
Others	37,830	590.5	24,560	413.5
Total	180,380	2,423.5	131,625	2,107.4

Here, the extreme insufficiency of the factory owners' statistics and the extreme carelessness with which they have been compiled are still more apparent – the number of strikers for the first five months (which was 79,970) added to that for the last seven months gives a total of 211,595, and not 180,000, and not 207,000!

The factory owners themselves prove that they *underestimate* the number of strikers.

The metalworkers are in the lead both in the ratio of number of strikers to the total number of workers and in the duration of the strikes; 18 days were lost per metalworker on strike, 14 days per textile worker and 16 days per worker in other industries. The better marketing conditions in the iron and steel industry do not, as we see, relieve the workers of the necessity of striking for a tiny wage increase!

As far as the results of the strikes are concerned, the factory owners' statistics declare that 1912 was a *less favourable* year for the workers than 1911 had been. In 1911, they say, 49 per cent of the strikers suffered a defeat and in

1912 52 per cent were defeated. These data, however, are not convincing, because the figures compared are for *the whole* of 1911 and for *seven months* of 1912.

The strikes of 1912 were offensive and not defensive in character. The workers were fighting *for improved* working conditions and not *against worse conditions*. This means that 52 per cent of the workers did not gain any improvement, 36 per cent were fully or partially *successful* and for 12 per cent the results are unclear. It is very likely that the factory owners concealed their defeat in this 12 per cent of all cases because every success of capital over labour arouses their special attention and jubilation.

If we compare the outcome of strikes for the last seven months of 1912 by areas and by branches of industry, we get the following picture.

The least successful of all were the strikes in the Moscow area – 75 per cent of the strikers failed (i.e. did not gain any improvement); then follow the St Petersburg area with 63 per cent, the South with 33 per cent, the Baltic area with 20 per cent and Poland with 11 per cent of failures. In the last-named *three* areas, therefore, the workers achieved *tremendous* victories. Out of the 48,000 strikers in these three areas, *27,000* achieved improvements, *they were victorious*: 11,000 suffered defeats; the results achieved by 10,000 are uncertain.

In the first two areas (Moscow and St Petersburg), on the contrary, out of the 83,000 strikers only *20,000* were successful; 59,000 were defeated (i.e. did not achieve any improvement) and the results achieved by 4,000 are uncertain.

Taken by branches of industry, the numbers of strikers who were defeated was: textile workers, 66 per cent, metalworkers, 47 per cent, and others, 30 per cent.

Marketing conditions were worst of all for the textile workers. In the Moscow area only *6,000* of the 38,000 strikers in the textile industry were successful, 32,000 were defeated; in St Petersburg there were 4,000 successful and 9,000 defeated. Textile workers in Poland, however, had *8,000* successful strikers and 400 defeated.

The financial results of the strikes (economic strikes) for the last two years are shown as follows by the factory owners' statistics:

	Industrialists' direct losses	Losses of wages	Losses in output for the country
		(thousand rubles)	
Iron and steel industry	558	1,145	4,959
Textile industry	479	807	6,010
Other branches	328	529	3,818
Totals for 1912	1,365	2,481	14,787
Totals for 1911	402	716	4,563

Thus the factory owners' total losses for two years amount to 1,800,000 rubles, workers' losses in wages to *3,000,000 rubles*, and losses in output to 19,000,000 rubles.

Here the factory owners place a period. How wise they are! What did the workers *gain*?

In two years *125,000 workers* gained a victory. Their wages for the year amount to 30,000,000 rubles. They demanded pay increases of 10 per cent, 25 per cent and even 40 per cent, as the factory owners themselves admit. Ten per cent of 30,000,000 rubles is *3,000,000 rubles*. And the reduction in the working day?

And what of the '*new*' (the factory owners' expression) demands, such as the demand '*not* to discharge workers without the consent of their fellow-workers'?

You are wrong, you gentlemen who own factories! Even in the economic sense (to say nothing of the political strikes) the workers' gains are *terrifying*. The bourgeoisie does not understand either workers' solidarity or the conditions of proletarian struggle.

About 300,000 workers have sacrificed 3,000,000 rubles to the economic struggle in two years. A direct gain was *immediately* achieved by 125,000 workers. And the whole working class made a step forward.

6. The Impending Catastrophe and How to Combat it

Famine is Approaching

Unavoidable catastrophe is threatening Russia. The railways are incredibly disorganised and the disorganisation is progressing. The railways will come to a standstill. The delivery of raw materials and coal to the factories will cease. The delivery of grain will cease. The capitalists are deliberately and unremittingly sabotaging (damaging, stopping, disrupting, hampering) production, hoping that an unparalleled catastrophe will mean the collapse of the republic and democracy, and of the Soviets and proletarian and peasant associations generally, thus facilitating the return to a monarchy and the restoration of the unlimited power of the bourgeoisie and the landowners.

The danger of a great catastrophe and of famine is imminent. All the newspapers have written about this time and again. A tremendous number of resolutions have been adopted by the parties and by the Soviets of Workers', Soldiers' and Peasants' Deputies – resolutions which admit that a catastrophe is unavoidable, that it is very close, that extreme measures are necessary to combat it, that 'heroic efforts' by the people are necessary to avert ruin, and so on.

Everybody says this. Everybody admits it. Everybody has decided it is so.

Yet nothing is being done.

Six months of revolution have elapsed. The catastrophe is even closer. Unemployment has assumed a mass scale. To think that there is a shortage of goods in the country, the

Published as a pamphlet in 1917.
CW XXV 319-365.

country is perishing from a shortage of food and labour, although there is a sufficient quantity of grain and raw materials, and yet in such a country, at so critical a moment, there is mass unemployment! What better evidence is needed to show that after six months of revolution (which some call a great revolution, but which so far it would perhaps be fairer to call a rotten revolution), in a democratic republic, with an abundance of unions, organs and institutions which proudly call themselves 'revolutionary-democratic', absolutely *nothing* of any importance has actually been done to avert catastrophe, to avert famine? We are nearing ruin with increasing speed. The war will not wait and is causing increasing dislocation in every sphere of national life.

Yet the slightest attention and thought will suffice to satisfy anyone that the ways of combating catastrophe and famine are available, that the measures required to combat them are quite clear, simple, perfectly feasible, and fully within reach of the people's forces, and that these measures are *not* being adopted *only* because, *exclusively* because, their realisation would affect the fabulous profits of a handful of landowners and capitalists.

And, indeed, it is safe to say that every single speech, every single article in a newspaper of any trend, every single resolution passed by any meeting or institution quite clearly and explicitly recognises the chief and principal measure of combating, of averting, catastrophe and famine. This measure is control, supervision, accounting, regulation by the state, introduction of a proper distribution of labour-power in the production and distribution of goods, husbanding of the people's forces, the elimination of all wasteful effort, economy of effort. Control, supervision and accounting are the prime requisites for combating catastrophe and famine. This is indisputable and universally recognised. And it is just what *is not being done* from fear of encroaching on the supremacy of the landowners and capitalists, on their immense, fantastic and scandalous profits, profits derived from high prices and war contracts (and, directly or indirectly, nearly everybody is now 'working' for the war), profits about which everybody knows and which everybody sees, and over which everybody is sighing and groaning.

And absolutely nothing is being done to introduce such control, accounting and supervision by the state as would be in the least effective.

Complete Government Inactivity

There is a universal, systematic and persistent sabotage of every kind of control, supervision and accounting and of all state attempts to institute them. And one must be incredibly naïve not to understand where this sabotage comes from and by what means it is being carried on. For this sabotage by the bankers and capitalists, their *frustration* of every kind of control, supervision and accounting, is being adapted to the state forms of a democratic republic, to the existence of 'revolutionary-democratic' institutions. The capitalist gentlemen have learnt very well a fact which all supporters of scientific socialism profess to recognise but which the Mensheviks and Socialist-Revolutionaries tried to forget as soon as their friends had secured cushy jobs as ministers, deputy ministers, etc. The fact is that the economic substance of capitalist exploitation is in no wise affected by the substitution of republican-democratic forms of government for monarchist forms, and that, consequently, the reverse is also true – only the *form* of the struggle for the inviolability and sanctity of capitalist profits need be changed in order to uphold them under a democratic republic as effectively as under an absolute monarchy.

The present, modern republican-democratic sabotage of every kind of control, accounting and supervision consists in the capitalists 'eagerly' accepting in words the 'principle' of control and the necessity for controls (as, of course, do all Mensheviks and Socialist-Revolutionaries), insisting only that this control be introduced 'gradually', methodically and in a 'state-regulated' way. In practice, however, these specious catchwords serve to conceal the *frustration* of control, its nullification, its reduction to a fiction, the mere playing at control, the delay of all business-like and practically effective measures, the creation of extraordinarily complicated, cumbersome and bureaucratically lifeless institutions of control which are hopelessly dependent on the capitalists, and which do absolutely nothing and cannot do anything.

So as not to trot out bald statements, let us cite witnesses from among the Mensheviks and Socialist-Revolutionaries, i.e. the very people who had the majority in the Soviets during the first six months of revolution, who took part in the 'coalition government' and who are therefore politically responsible to the Russian workers and peasants for winking at the capitalists and allowing them to frustrate all control.

Izvestia TsIK (i.e. the newspaper of the Central Executive Committee of the All-Russia Congress of Soviets of Workers', Soldiers' and Peasants' Deputies), the official organ of the highest of the so-called 'fully authorised' (no joke!) bodies of 'revolutionary' democracy, in issue No. 164, of September 7, 1917, printed a *resolution* by a special control organisation created and run by these very Mensheviks and Socialist-Revolutionaries. This special institution is the Economic Department of the Central Executive Committee. Its resolution officially records as a fact *'the complete inactivity of the central bodies set up under the government for the regulation of economic life'*.

Now, how could one imagine any more eloquent testimony to the collapse of the Menshevik and Socialist-Revolutionary policy than this statement signed by the Mensheviks and Socialist-Revolutionaries themselves?

The need for the regulation of economic life was already recognised under tsarism, and certain institutions were set up for the purpose. But under tsarism economic chaos steadily grew and reached monstrous proportions. It was at once recognised that it was the task of the republican, revolutionary government to adopt effective and resolute measures to put an end to the economic chaos. When the 'coalition' government was formed with the Mensheviks and Socialist-Revolutionaries participating, it promised and undertook, in its most solemn public declaration of May 6, to introduce state control and regulation. The Tseretelis and Chernovs, like all the Menshevik and Socialist-Revolutionary leaders, vowed and swore that not only were they responsible for the government, but that the 'authorised bodies of revolutionary democracy' under their control actually kept an eye on the work of the government and verified its activities.

Four months have passed since May 6, four long months, in which Russia has sacrificed the lives of hundreds of thousands of soldiers for the sake of the absurd imperialist 'offensive', in which chaos and disaster have been advancing in seven-league strides, in which the summer season afforded an exceptional opportunity to do a great deal in the matter of water transport, agriculture, prospecting for minerals, and so on and so forth – and after four months the Mensheviks and Socialist-Revolutionaries have been obliged officially to admit the 'complete inactivity' of the control institutions set up under the government!!

And these Mensheviks and Socialist-Revolutionaries, with the serious mien of statesmen, now prate (I am writing this on the very eve of the Democratic Conference of September 12[1]) that matters can be furthered by replacing the coalition with the Cadets by a coalition with commercial and industrial Kit Kityches,[2] the Ryabushinskys, Bublikovs, Tereshchenkos and Co.

How, one may ask, are we to explain this astonishing blindness of the Mensheviks and Socialist-Revolutionaries? Are we to regard them as political babes in the wood who in their extreme foolishness and naïveté do not realise what they are doing and err in good faith? Or does the abundance of posts they occupy as ministers, deputy ministers, governors-general, commissars and the like have the property of engendering a special kind of 'political' blindness?

Control Measures are Known to All and Easy to Take

One may ask: aren't methods and measures of control extremely complex, difficult, untried and even unknown? Isn't the delay due to the fact that although the statesmen of the Cadet Party, the merchant and industrial class, and the Menshevik and Socialist-Revolutionary parties have for six months been toiling in the sweat of their brow, investigating, studying and discovering measures and methods of control, still the problem is incredibly difficult and has not yet been solved?

Unfortunately, this is how they are trying to present

matters to hoodwink the ignorant, illiterate and downtrodden muzhiks and the Simple Simons who believe everything
and never look into things. In reality, however, even
tsarism, even the 'old regime', when it set up the War
Industries Committees,[3] *knew* the principal measure, the
chief method and way to introduce control, namely, by
uniting the population according to profession, purpose of
work, branch of labour, etc. But tsarism *feared* the union of
the population and therefore did its best to restrict and
artificially hinder this generally known, very easy and quite
practical method and way of control.

All the belligerent countries, suffering as they are from
the extreme burdens and hardships of the war, suffering – in
one degree or another – from economic chaos and famine,
have long ago outlined, determined, applied and tested a
whole series of control measures, which consist almost
invariably in uniting the population and in setting up or
encouraging unions of various kinds, in which state
representatives participate, which are under the supervision
of the state, etc. All these measures of control are known to
all, much has been said and written about them, and the laws
passed by the advanced belligerent powers relating to
control have been translated into Russian or expounded in
detail in the Russian press.

If our state really *wanted* to exercise control in a
businesslike and earnest fashion, if its institutions had not
condemned themselves to 'complete inactivity' by their
servility to the capitalists, all the state would have to do
would be to draw freely on the rich store of control measures
which are already known and have been used in the past.
The only obstacle to this – an obstacle concealed from the
eyes of the people by the Cadets, Socialist-Revolutionaries
and Mensheviks – was, and still is, that control would bring
to light the fabulous profits of the capitalists and would cut
the ground from under these profits.

To explain this most important question more clearly (a
question which is essentially equivalent to that of the
programme of *any* truly revolutionary government that
would wish to save Russia from war and famine), let us
enumerate these principal measures of control and examine
each of them.

We shall see that all a government would have had to do, if its name of revolutionary-democratic government were not merely a joke, would have been to decree, in the very first week of its existence, the adoption of the principal measures of control, to provide for strict and severe punishment to be meted out to capitalists who fraudulently evaded control, and to call upon the population itself to exercise supervision over the capitalists and see to it that they scrupulously observed the regulations on control – and control would have been introduced in Russia long ago.

These principal measures are:

(1) Amalgamation of all banks into a single bank, and state control over its operations, or nationalisation of the banks.

(2) Nationalisation of the syndicates, i.e. the largest, monopolistic capitalist associations (sugar, oil, coal, iron and steel, and other syndicates).

(3) Abolition of commercial secrecy.

(4) Compulsory syndication (i.e. compulsoɪy amalgamation into associations) of industrialists, merchants and employers generally.

(5) Compulsory organisation of the population into consumers' societies, or encouragement of such organisation, and the exercise of control over it.

Let us see what the significance of each of these measures would be if carried out in a revolutionary-democratic way.

Nationalisation of the Banks

The banks, as we know, are centres of modern economic life, the principal nerve centres of the whole capitalist economic system. To talk about 'regulating economic life' and yet evade the question of the nationalisation of the banks means either betraying the most profound ignorance or deceiving the 'common people' by florid words and grandiloquent promises with the deliberate intention of not fulfilling these promises.

It is absurd to control and regulate deliveries of grain, or the production and distribution of goods generally, without controlling and regulating bank operations. It is like trying to snatch at odd kopeks and closing one's eyes to millions of rubles. Banks nowadays are so closely and intimately bound up with trade (in grain and everything else) and with industry that without 'laying hands' on the banks nothing of any value, nothing 'revolutionary-democratic', can be accomplished.

But perhaps for the state to 'lay hands' on the banks is a very difficult and complicated operation? They usually try to scare philistines with this very idea – that is, the capitalists and their defenders try it, because it is to their advantage to do so.

In reality, however, nationalisation of the banks, which would not deprive any 'owner' of a single kopek, presents absolutely no technical or cultural difficulties, and is being delayed *exclusively* because of the vile greed of an insignificant handful of rich people. If nationalisation of the banks is so often confused with the confiscation of private property, it is the bourgeois press, which has an interest in deceiving the public, that is to blame for this widespread confusion.

The ownership of the capital wielded by and concentrated in the banks is certified by printed and written certificates called shares, bonds, bills, receipts, etc. Not a single one of these certificates would be invalidated or altered if the banks were nationalised, i.e. if all the banks were amalgamated into a single state bank. Whoever owned fifteen rubles on a savings account would continue to be the owner of fifteen rubles after the nationalisation of the banks; and whoever had fifteen million rubles would continue after the nationalisation of the banks to have fifteen million rubles in the form of shares, bonds, bills, commercial certificates and so on.

What, then, is the significance of nationalisation of the banks?

It is that no effective control of any kind over the individual banks and their operations is possible (even if commercial secrecy, etc, were abolished) because it is impossible to keep track of the extremely complex, involved and wily tricks that are used in drawing up balance sheets, founding fictitious enterprises and subsidiaries, enlisting the services of figureheads, and so on, and so forth. Only the amalgamation of all banks into one, which in itself would imply no change whatever in respect of ownership, and which, we repeat, would not deprive any owner of a single kopek, would make it *possible* to exercise real control – provided, of course, all the other measures indicated above were carried out. Only by nationalising the banks *can* the state *put itself in a position* to know where and how, whence and when, millions and billions of rubles flow. And only control over the banks, over the centre, over the pivot and chief mechanism of capitalist circulation, would make it possible to organise real and not fictitious control over all economic life, over the production and distribution of staple goods, and organise that 'regulation of economic life' which otherwise is inevitably doomed to remain a ministerial phrase designed to fool the common people. Only control over banking operations, provided they were concentrated in a single state bank, would make it possible, if certain other easily-practicable measures were adopted, to organise the effective collection of income tax in such a way as to prevent the concealment of property and incomes; for at present the income tax is very largely a fiction.

Nationalisation of the banks has only to be decreed and it would be carried out by the directors and employees themselves. No special machinery, no special preparatory steps on the part of the state would be required, for this is a measure that can be effected by a single decree, 'at a single stroke'. It was made economically feasible by capitalism itself once it had developed to the stage of bills, shares, bonds and so on. *All* that is required is to *unify accountancy*. And if the revolutionary-democratic government were to decide that immediately, by telegraph, meetings of managers and employees should be called in every city, and conferences in every region and in the country as a whole, for the immediate amalgamation of all banks into a single state bank, this reform would be carried out in a few weeks. Of course, it would be the managers and the higher bank officials who would offer resistance, who would try to deceive the state, delay matters, and so on, for these gentlemen would lose their highly remunerative posts and the opportunity of performing highly profitable fraudulent operations. *That is the heart of the matter*. But there is not the slightest technical difficulty in the way of the amalgamation of the banks; and if the state power were revolutionary not only in word (i.e. if it did not fear to do away with inertia and routine), if it were democratic not only in word (i.e. if it acted in the interests of the majority of the people and not of a handful of rich men), it would be enough to decree confiscation of property and imprisonment as the penalty for managers, board members and big shareholders for the slightest delay or for attempting to conceal documents and accounts. It would be enough, for example, to organise the poorer employees *separately* and to reward them for detecting fraud and delay on the part of the rich for nationalisation of the banks to be effected as smoothly and rapidly as can be.

The advantages accruing to the whole people from nationalisation of the banks – *not* to the workers especially (for the workers have little to do with banks) but to the mass of peasants and small industrialists – would be enormous. The saving in labour would be gigantic, and, assuming that the state would retain the former number of bank employees, nationalisation would be a highly important step towards making the use of the banks universal, towards increasing the number of their branches, putting their operations within easier reach, etc, etc. The availability of credit on easy terms for the *small* owners, for the peasants, would increase immensely. As to the state, it would for the first time be in a position first to *review* all the chief monetary operations, which would be unconcealed, then to *control* them, then to *regulate* economic life, and finally to *obtain* millions and billions for major state transactions, without paying the capitalist gentlemen sky-high 'commissions' for their 'services'. That is the reason – and the only reason – why all the capitalists, all the bourgeois professors, all the bourgeoisie, and all the Plekhanovs, Potresovs and Co., who serve them, are prepared to fight tooth and nail against nationalisation of the banks and invent thousands of excuses to prevent the adoption of this very easy and very pressing measure, although *even* from the standpoint of the 'defence' of the country, i.e. from the military standpoint, this measure would provide a gigantic advantage and would tremendously enhance the 'military might' of the country.

The following objection might be raised: why do such

advanced states as Germany and the USA 'regulate economic life' so magnificently without even thinking of nationalising the banks?

Because, we reply, *both* these states are not merely capitalist, but also imperialist states, although one of them is a monarchy and the other a republic. As such, they carry out the reforms they need by reactionary-bureaucratic methods, whereas we are speaking here of revolutionary-democratic methods.

This 'little difference' is of major importance. In most cases it is 'not the custom' to think of it. The term 'revolutionary democracy' has become with us (especially among the Socialist-Revolutionaries and Mensheviks) almost a conventional phrase, like the expression 'thank God', which is also used by people who are not so ignorant as to believe in God or like the expression 'honourable citizen', which is sometimes used even in addressing staff members of *Dyen* or *Yedinstvo*, although nearly everybody guesses that these newspapers have been founded and are maintained by the capitalists in the interests of the capitalists, and that there is therefore very little 'honourable' about the pseudo-socialists contributing to these newspapers.

If we do not employ the phrase 'revolutionary democracy' as a stereotyped ceremonial phrase, as a conventional epithet, but *reflect* on its meaning, we find that to be a democrat means reckoning in reality with the interests of the majority of the people and not the minority, and that to be a revolutionary means destroying everything harmful and obsolete in the most resolute and ruthless manner.

Neither in America nor in Germany, as far as we know, is any claim laid by either the government or the ruling classes to the name 'revolutionary democrats', to which our Socialist-Revolutionaries and Mensheviks lay claim (and which they prostitute).

In Germany there are only *four* very large private banks of national importance. In America there are only *two*. It is easier, more convenient, more profitable for the financial magnates of those banks to unite privately, surreptitiously, in a reactionary and not a revolutionary way, in a bureaucratic and not a democratic way, bribing government officials (this is the general rule both in America *and in Germany*), and preserving the private character of the banks in order to preserve secrecy of operations, to milk the state of millions upon millions in 'super-profits', and to make financial frauds possible.

Both America and Germany 'regulate economic life' in such a way as to create conditions of *war-time penal servitude* for the workers (and partly for the peasants) and a *paradise* for the bankers and capitalists. Their regulation consists in 'squeezing' the workers to the point of starvation, while the capitalists are guaranteed (surreptitiously, in a reactionary-bureaucratic fashion) profits *higher* than before the war.

Such a course is quite possible in republican-imperialist Russia too. Indeed, it is the course being followed not only by the Milyukovs and Shingaryovs, but also by Kerensky in partnership with Tereshchenko, Nekrasov, Bernatsky, Prokopovich and Co, who *also uphold*, in a reactionary-bureaucratic manner, the 'inviolability' of the banks and their sacred right to fabulous profits. So let us better tell the *truth*, namely, that in republican Russia they want to regulate economic life in a reactionary-bureaucratic manner, but 'often' find it difficult to do so owing to the existence of the 'Soviets', which Kornilov No. 1 did not manage to disband, but which Kornilov No. 2 will try to disband.

That would be the truth. And this simple if bitter truth is more useful for the enlightenment of the people than the honeyed lies about 'our', 'great', 'revolutionary' democracy.

Nationalisation of the banks would greatly facilitate the simultaneous nationalisation of the insurance business, i.e. the amalgamation of all the insurance companies into one, the centralisation of their operations, and state control over them. Here, too, congresses of insurance company employees could carry out this amalgamation immediately and without any great effort, provided a revolutionary-democratic government decreed this and ordered directors and big shareholders to effect the amalgamation without the slightest delay and held every one of them strictly accountable for it. The capitalists have invested hundreds of millions of rubles in the insurance business; the work is all done by the employees. The amalgamation of this business would lead to lower insurance premiums, would provide a host of facilities and conveniences for the insured and would make it possible to increase their number without increasing expenditure of effort and funds. Absolutely nothing but the inertia, routine and self-interest of a handful of holders of remunerative jobs are delaying this reform, which, among other things, would enhance the country's defence potential by economising national labour and creating a number of highly important opportunities to 'regulate economic life' not in word, but in deed.

Nationalisation of the Syndicates

Capitalism differs from the old, pre-capitalist systems of economy in having created the closest interconnection and interdependence of the various branches of the economy. Were this not so, incidentally, no steps towards socialism would be technically feasible. Modern capitalism, under which the banks dominate production, has carried this interdependence of the various branches of the economy to the utmost. The banks and the more important branches of industry and commerce have become inseparably merged. This means, on the one hand, that it is impossible to nationalise the banks alone, without proceeding to create a state monopoly of commercial and industrial syndicates (sugar, coal, iron, oil, etc), and without nationalising them. It means, on the other hand, that if carried out in earnest, the regulation of economic activity would demand the simultaneous nationalisation of the banks and the syndicates.

Let us take the sugar syndicate as an example. It came into being under tsarism, and at that time developed into a huge capitalist combine of splendidly equipped refineries. And, of course, this combine, thoroughly imbued with the most reactionary and bureaucratic spirit, secured scandalously high profits for the capitalists and reduced its employees to the status of humiliated and downtrodden slaves lacking any rights. Even at that time the state controlled and regulated production – in the interests of the rich, the magnates.

All that remains to be done here is to transform reactionary-bureaucratic regulation into revolutionary-democratic regulation by simple decrees providing for the summoning of a congress of employees, engineers, directors and shareholders, for the introduction of uniform accountancy, for control by the workers' unions, etc. This is an exceedingly simple thing, yet it has not been done! Under what is a democratic republic, the regulation of the sugar industry *actually* remains reactionary-bureaucratic; everything remains as of old – the dissipation of national labour, routine and stagnation, and the enrichment of the Bobrinsky's and Tereschchenkos. Democrats and not bureaucrats, the workers and other employees and not the 'sugar barons', should be called upon to exercise independent initiative – and this could and should be done in a few days, at a single stroke, if only the Socialist-Revolutionaries and Mensheviks did not befog the minds of the people by plans for 'association' with these very sugar barons, for the very association with the wealthy from which the 'complete inaction' of the government in the matter of regulating economic life follows with absolute inevitability, and of which it is a consequence.[4]

Take the oil business. It was to a vast extent 'socialised' by the earlier development of capitalism. Just a couple of oil barons wield millions and hundreds of millions of rubles, clipping coupons and raking in fabulous profits from a 'business' which is *already* actually, technically and socially organised on a national scale and is *already* being conducted by hundreds and thousands of employees, engineers, etc. Nationalisation of the oil industry could be effected *at once* by, and is imperative for, a revolutionary-democratic state, especially when the latter suffers from an acute crisis and when it is essential to economise national labour and to increase the output of fuel at all costs. It is clear that here bureaucratic control can achieve nothing, can change nothing, for the 'oil barons' can cope with the Tereshchenkos, the Kerenskys, the Avksentyevs and the Skobelevs as easily as they coped with the tsar's ministers – by means of delays, excuses and promises, and by bribing the bourgeois press directly or indirectly (this is called 'public opinion', and the Kerenskys and Avksentyevs 'reckon' with it), by bribing officials (left by the Kerenskys and Avksentyevs in their old jobs in the old state machinery which means intact).

If anything real is to be done bureaucracy must be abandoned for democracy, and in a truly revolutionary way, i.e. war must be declared on the oil barons and shareholders, the confiscation of their property and punishment by imprisonment must be decreed for delaying nationalisation of the oil business, for concealing incomes or accounts, for sabotaging production, and for failing to take steps to increase production. The initiative of the workers and other employees must be drawn on; *they* must be immediately summoned to conferences and congresses; a certain proportion of the profits must be assigned to *them*, provided they institute overall control and increase production. Had these revolutionary-democratic steps been taken at once, immediately, in April 1917, Russia, which is one of the richest countries in the world in deposits of liquid fuel, could, using water transport, have done a very great deal during this summer to supply the people with the necessary quantities of fuel.

Neither the bourgeois nor the coalition Socialist-Revolutionary-Menshevik-Cadet government has done anything at all. Both have confined themselves to a bureaucratic playing at reforms. They have not dared to take a single revolutionary-democratic step. Everything has remained as it was under the tsars – the oil barons, the stagnation, the hatred of the workers and other employees for their exploiters, the resulting chaos, and the dissipation of national labour – only the *letterheads* on the incoming and outgoing papers in the 'republican' offices have been changed!

Take the coal industry. It is technically and culturally no less 'ripe' for nationalisation, and is being no less shamelessly managed by the robbers of the people, the coal barons, and there are a number of most striking *facts* of direct sabotage, direct *damage* to and stoppage of production by the industrialists. Even the ministerial *Rabochaya Gazeta* of the Mensheviks has admitted these facts. And what do we find? Absolutely nothing has been done, except to call the old, reactionary-bureaucratic meetings 'on a half-and-half basis' – an equal number of workers and bandits from the coal syndicate! Not a single revolutionary-democratic step has been taken, not a shadow of an attempt has been made to establish the only control which is real – control from *below*, through the employees' union, through the workers, and by using terror against the coal industrialists who are ruining the country and bringing production to a standstill! How can this be done when we are 'all' in favour of the 'coalition' – if not with the Cadets, then with commercial and industrial circles. And coalition means leaving power in the hands of the capitalists, letting them go unpunished, allowing them to hamper affairs, to blame everything on the workers, to intensify the chaos and *thus* pave the way for a new Kornilov revolt!

Abolition of Commercial Secrecy

Unless commercial secrecy is abolished, either control over production and distribution will remain an empty promise, only needed by the Cadets to fool the Socialist-Revolutionaries and Mensheviks, and by the Socialist-Revolutionaries and Mensheviks to fool the working classes, or control can be exercised only by reactionary-bureaucratic methods and means. Although this is obvious to every unprejudiced person, and although *Pravda* persistently demanded the abolition of commercial secrecy (and was suppressed largely for this reason by the Kerensky government which is subservient to capital), neither our republican government nor the 'authorised bodies of revolutionary democracy' have even thought of this *first step* to real control.

This is the very key to all control. Here we have the most sensitive spot of capital, which is robbing the people and sabotaging production. And this is exactly why the Socialist-Revolutionaries and Mensheviks are afraid to do anything about it.

The usual argument of the capitalists, one reiterated by the petty bourgeoisie without reflection, is that in a capitalist economy the abolition of commercial secrecy is in general absolutely impossible, for private ownership of the means of production, and the dependence of the individual undertakings on the market render essential the 'sanctity' of commercial books and commercial operations, including, of course, banking operations.

Those who in one form or another repeat this or similar arguments allow themselves to be deceived and themselves deceive the people by shutting their eyes to two fundamental, highly important and generally known facts of modern economic activity. The first fact is the existence of large-scale capitalism, i.e. the peculiar features of the economic system of banks, syndicates, large factories, etc. The second fact is the war.

It is modern large-scale capitalism, which is everywhere becoming monopoly capitalism, that deprives commercial secrecy of every shadow of reasonableness, turns it into hypocrisy and into an instrument exclusively for concealing financial swindles and the fantastically high profits of big capital. Large-scale capitalist economy, by its very technical nature, is socialised economy, that is, it both operates for millions of people and, directly or indirectly, unites by its operations hundreds, thousands and tens of thousands of families. It is not like the economy of the small handicraftsman or the middle peasant who keep no commercial books at all and who would therefore not be affected by the abolition of commercial secrecy!

As it is, the operations conducted in large-scale business are known to hundreds or more persons. Here the law protecting commercial secrecy does not serve the interests of production or exchange, but those of speculation and profit-seeking in their crudest form, and of direct fraud, which, as we know, in the case of joint-stock companies is particularly widespread and very skilfully concealed by reports and balance-sheets, so compiled as to deceive the public.

While commercial secrecy is unavoidable in small commodity production, i.e. among the small peasants and handicraftsmen, where production itself is not socialised but scattered and disunited, in large-scale capitalist production, the protection of commercial secrecy means protection of the privileges and profits of literally a handful of people *against* the interest of the whole people. This has already been recognised by the law, inasmuch as provision is made for the publication of the accounts of joint-stock companies. But *this* control, which has already been introduced in all advanced countries, as well as in Russia, is a reactionary-bureaucratic control which does not open the eyes of the *people* and which *does not allow the whole truth* about the operations of joint-stock companies to become known.

To act in a revolutionary-democratic way, it would be necessary to immediately pass another law abolishing commmercial secrecy, compelling the big undertakings and the wealthy to render the fullest possible accounts, and investing every group of citizens of substantial democratic numerical strength (1,000 or 10,000 voters, let us say) with the right to examine *all* the records of any large undertaking. Such a measure could be fully and easily effected by a simple decree. It *alone* would allow full scope for *popular* initiative in control, through the office employees' unions, the workers' unions and all the political parties, and it alone would make control effective and democratic.

Add to this the war. The vast majority of commercial and industrial establishments are now working not for the 'free market', but *for the government*, for the war. This is why I have already stated in *Pravda* that people who counter us with the argument that socialism cannot be introduced are liars, and barefaced liars at that, because it is not a question of introducing socialism now, directly, overnight, but of *exposing plunder of the state*.[5]

Capitalist 'war' economy (i.e. economy directly or indirectly connected with war contracts) is systematic and legalised *plunder*, and the Cadet gentry, who, together with the Mensheviks and Socialist-Revolutionaries, are opposing the abolition of commercial secrecy, are nothing but *aiders and abettors of plunder*.

The war is now costing Russia fifty million rubles *a day*. These fifty million go mostly to army contractors. Of these fifty, at least five million *daily*, and probably ten million or more, constitute the 'honest income' of the capitalists, and of the officials who are in one way or another in collusion with them. The very large firms and banks which lend money for war contracts transactions thereby make fantastic profits, and do so by plundering the state, for no other epithet can be applied to this defrauding and plundering of the people 'on the occasion of' the hardships of war, 'on the occasion of' the deaths of hundreds of thousands and millions of people.

'Everybody' knows about these scandalous profits made on war contracts, about the 'letters of guarantee' which are concealed by the banks, about who benefits by the rising cost of living. It is smiled on in 'society'. Quite a number of precise references are made to it *even* in the bourgeois press, which as a general rule keeps silent about 'unpleasant' facts and avoids 'ticklish' questions. Everybody knows about it, yet everybody keeps silent, everybody tolerates it, everybody puts up with the government, which prates eloquently about 'control' and 'regulation'!!

The revolutionary democrats, were they real revolutionaries and democrats, would immediately pass a law abolishing commercial secrecy, compelling contractors and merchants to render accounts public, forbidding them to abandon their field of activity without the permission of the authorities, imposing the penalty of confiscation of property and shooting[6] for concealment and for deceiving the people, organising verification and control *from below*, democratically, by the people themselves, by unions of workers and other employees, consumers, etc.

Our Socialist-Revolutionaries and Mensheviks fully deserve to be called scared democrats, for on this question they repeat what is said by all the scared philistines, namely, that the capitalists will 'run away' if 'too severe' measures are adopted, that 'we' shall be unable to get along without the capitalists, that the British and French millionaires, who are, of course, 'supporting' us, will most likely be 'offended' in their turn, and so on. It might be thought that the Bolsheviks were proposing something unknown to history, something that has never been tried before, something 'utopian', while, as a matter of fact, even 125 years ago, in France, people who were real 'revolutionary democrats', who were really convinced of the just and defensive character of the war they were waging, who really had popular support and were sincerely convinced of this, were able to establish *revolutionary* control over the rich and to achieve results which earned the admiration of the world. And in the century and a quarter that have since elapsed, the development of capitalism, which resulted in the creation of banks, syndicates, railways and so forth, has greatly facilitated and simplified the adoption of measures of really democratic control by the workers and peasants over the exploiters, the landowners and capitalists.

In point of fact, the whole question of control boils down to' who controls whom, i.e. which class is in control and which is being controlled. In our country, in republican Russia, with the help of the 'authorised bodies' of supposedly revolutionary democracy, it is the landowners and capitalists who are still recognised to be, and still are, the controllers. The inevitable result is the capitalist robbery that arouses universal indignation among the people, and the economic chaos that is being artificially kept up by the capitalists. We must resolutely and irrevocably, not fearing to break with the old, not fearing boldly to build the new, pass to control *over* the landowners and capitalists *by* the workers and peasants. And this is what our Socialist-Revolutionaries and Mensheviks fear worse than the plague.

Compulsory Association

Compulsory syndication, i.e. compulsory association, of the industrialists, for example, is already being practised in Germany. Nor is there anything new in it. Here, too, through the fault of the Socialist-Revolutionaries and Mensheviks, we see the utter stagnation of republican Russia, whom these none-too-respectable parties 'entertain' by dancing a quadrille with the Cadets, or with the Bublikovs, or with Tereshchenko and Kerensky.

Compulsory syndication is, on the one hand, a means whereby the state, as it were, expedites capitalist development, which everywhere leads to the organisation of the class struggle and to a growth in the number, variety and importance of unions. On the other hand, compulsory 'unionisation' is an indispensable precondition for any kind of effective control and for all economy of national labour.

The German law, for instance, binds the leather manufacturers of a given locality or of the whole country to form an association, on the board of which there is a representative of the state for the purpose of control. A law of this kind does not directly, i.e. in itself, affect property relations in any way; it does not deprive any owner of a single kopek and does not predetermine whether the control is to be exercised in a reactionary-bureaucratic or a revolutionary-democratic form, direction or spirit.

Such laws can and should be passed in our country immediately, without wasting a single week of precious time; it should be left to *social conditions themselves* to determine the more specific forms of enforcing the law, the speed with which it is to be enforced, the methods of supervision over its enforcement, etc. In this case, the state requires no special machinery, no special investigation, nor preliminary enquiries for the passing of such a law. All that is required is the determination to break with certain private interests of the capitalists, who are 'not accustomed' to such interference and have no desire to forfeit the super-profits which are ensured by the old methods of management and the absence of control.

No machinery and no 'statistics' (which Chernov wanted to substitute for the revolutionary initiative of the peasants) are required to *pass* such a law, inasmuch as its implementation must be made the duty of the manufacturers or industrialists themselves, of the *available* public forces, under the control of the available public (i.e. non-government, non-bureaucratic) forces too, which, however, must consist by all means of the so-called 'lower estates', i.e. of the oppressed and exploited classes, which in history have always proved to be immensely *superior* to the exploiters in their capacity for heroism, self-sacrifice and comradely discipline.

Let us assume that we have a really revolutionary-democratic government and that it decides that the manufacturers and industrialists in every branch of production who employ, let us say, not less than two workers shall immediately amalgamate into uyezd and gubernia associations. Responsibility for the strict observance of the law is laid in the first place on the manufacturers, directors, board members, and big share-holders (for they are the real leaders of modern industry, its real masters). They shall be regarded as deserters from military service, and punished as such, if they do not work for the immediate implementation of the law, and shall bear mutual responsibility, one answering for all, and all for one, with the whole of their property. Responsibility shall next be laid on all office employees, who shall also form *one* union, and on all workers and their trade union. The purpose of 'unionisation' is to institute the fullest, strictest and most detailed accountancy, but chiefly to *combine operations* in the purchase of raw materials, the scale of products, and the *economy* of national funds and forces. When the separate establishments are amalgamated into a single syndicate, this economy can attain tremendous proportions, as economic science teaches us and as is shown by the example of all syndicates, cartels and trusts. And it must be repeated that this unionisation will not in itself alter property relations one iota and will not deprive any owner of a single kopek. This circumstance must be strongly stressed, for the bourgeois press constantly 'frightens' small and medium proprietors by asserting that socialists in general, and the Bolsheviks in particular, want to 'expropriate' them – a deliberately false assertion, as socialists do not intend to, cannot and will not expropriate the small peasant *even if there is a fully socialist* revolution. All the time we are speaking *only* of the immediate and urgent measures, which have already been introduced in Western Europe and which a democracy that is at all consistent ought to introduce immediately in our country to combat the impending and inevitable catastrophe.

Serious difficulties, both technical and cultural, would be encountered in amalgamating the small and very small proprietors into associations, owing to the extremely small proportions and technical primitiveness of their enterprises and the illiteracy or lack of education of the owners. But precisely such enterprises could be exempted from the law (as was pointed out above in our hypothetical example). Their non-amalgamation, let alone their belated amalgamation, could create no serious obstacle, for the part played by the huge number of small enterprises in the sum total of production and their importance to the economy as a whole are *negligible*, and, moreover, they are often in one way or another dependent on the big enterprises.

Only the big enterprises are of decisive importance; and here the technical and cultural means and forces for 'unionisation' *do exist*; what is lacking is the firm, determined initiative of a *revolutionary* government which should be ruthlessly severe towards the exploiters to set these forces and means in motion.

The poorer a country is in technically trained forces, and in intellectual forces generally, the more *urgent* it is to decree compulsory association as early and as resolutely as possible and to begin with the bigger and biggest enterprises when putting the decree into effect, for it is association that will *economise* intellectual forces and make it possible to use them *to the full* and to distribute them more correctly. If, after 1905, even the Russian peasants in their out-of-the-way districts, under the tsarist government, in face of the thousands of obstacles raised by that government, were able to make a tremendous forward stride in the creation of all kinds of associations, it is clear that the amalgamation of large- and medium-scale industry and trade could be effected in several months, if not earlier, provided compulsion to this end were exercised by a really revolutionary-democratic government relying on the support, participation, interest and advantage of the 'lower ranks', the democracy, the workers and other employees, and calling upon *them* to exercise control.

Regulation of Consumption

The war has compelled all the belligerent and many of the neutral countries to resort to the regulation of consumption. Bread cards have been issued and have become customary, and this has led to the appearance of other ration cards. Russia is no exception and has also introduced bread cards.

Using this as an example, we can draw, perhaps, the most striking comparison of all between reactionary-bureaucratic methods of combating a catastrophe, which are confined to minimum reforms, and revolutionary-democratic methods, which, to justify their name, must directly aim at a violent rupture with the old, obsolete system and at the achievement of the speediest possible progress.

The bread card – this typical example of how consumption is regulated in modern capitalist countries – aims at, and achieves (at best), one thing only, namely, distributing available supplies of grain to give everybody his share. A maximum limit to consumption is established, not for all foodstuffs by far, but only for principal foodstuffs, those of 'popular' consumption. And that is all. There is no intention of doing anything else. Available supplies of grain are calculated in a bureaucratic way, then divided on a per capita basis, a ration is fixed and introduced, and there the matter ends. Luxury articles are not affected, for they are 'anyway' scarce and 'anyway' so dear as to be beyond the reach of the 'people'. And so, in *all* the belligerent countries without exception, *even* in Germany, which evidently, without fear of contradiction, may be said to be a model of the most careful, pedantic and strict regulation of consumption – *even* in Germany we find that the rich constantly *get around* all 'rationing'. This, too, 'everybody' knows and 'everybody' talks about with a smile; and in the German socialist papers, and sometimes even in the bourgeois papers, despite the fierce military stringency of the German censorship, we constantly find items and reports about the 'menus' of the rich, saying how the wealthy can obtain white bread in any quantity at a certain health resort (visited, on the plea of illness, by everybody who has plenty of money), and how the wealthy substitute choice and rare articles of luxury for articles of popular consumption.

A reactionary capitalist state which *fears* to undermine the pillars of capitalism, of wage slavery, of the economic supremacy of the rich, which *fears* to encourage the initiative of the workers and the working people generally, which *fears* to provoke them to a more exacting attitude – *such* a state will be quite content with bread cards. Such a state does not for a moment, in any measure it adopts, lose sight of the *reactionary* aim of strengthening capitalism, preventing its being undermined, and confining the 'regulation of economic life' in general, and the regulation of consumption in particular, to such measures as are absolutely essential to feed the people, *and makes no attempt* whatsoever at real regulation of consumption by exercising *control over the rich* and laying the *greater part* of the burden in war-time on those who are better off, who are privileged, well fed and overfed in peace-time.

The reactionary-bureaucratic solution to the problem with which the war has confronted the peoples confines itself to bread cards, to the equal distribution of 'popular' foodstuffs, of those absolutely essential to feed the people, without retreating one little bit from bureaucratic and reactionary ideas, that is, from the aim of *not* encouraging the initiative of the poor, the proletariat, the mass of the people ('demos'), of *not* allowing *them* to exercise control over the rich, and of leaving *as many* loopholes *as possible* for the rich to compensate themselves with articles of luxury. And a great number of loopholes are left in *all* countries, we repeat, even in Germany – not to speak of Russia; the 'common people' starve while the rich visit health resorts, supplement the meagre official ration by all sorts of 'extras' obtained on the side, and do *not* allow *themselves* to be controlled.

In Russia, which has only just made a revolution against the tsarist regime in the name of liberty and equality, in Russia, which, as far as its actual political institutions are concerned, has at once become a democratic republic, what particularly strikes the people, what particularly arouses popular discontent, irritation, anger and indignation is that *everybody* sees the easy way in which the wealthy get around the bread cards. They do it very easily indeed. 'From under the counter', and for a very high price, especially if one has '*pull*' (which only the rich have), one can obtain anything, and in large quantities, too. It is the people who are starving. The regulation of consumption is confined within the narrowest bureaucratic-reactionary limits. The government has not the slightest intention of putting regulation on a really revolutionary-democratic footing, is not in the least concerned about doing so.

'Everybody' is suffering from the queues – but the rich send their servants to stand in the queues, and even engage special servants for the purpose! And that is 'democracy'!

At a time when the country is suffering untold calamities, a revolutionary-democratic policy would not confine itself to bread cards to combat the impending catastrophe but would add, firstly, the compulsory organisation of the whole population in consumers' societies, for otherwise control over consumption cannot be fully exercised; secondly, labour service for the rich, making them perform without pay secretarial and similar duties for these consumers' societies; thirdly, the equal distribution among the population of absolutely all consumer goods, so as really to distribute the burdens of the war equitably; fourthly, the organisation of control in such a way as to have the poorer classes of the population exercise control over the consumption of the rich.

The establishment of real democracy in this sphere and the display of a real revolutionary spirit in the organisation of control by the most needy classes of the people would be a very great stimulus to the employment of all available intellectual forces and to the development of the truly revolutionary energies of the entire people. Yet now the ministers of republican and revolutionary-democratic Russia, exactly like their colleagues in all other imperialist countries, make pompous speeches about 'working in common for the good of the people' and about 'exerting every effort', but the people see, feel and sense the hypocrisy of this talk.

The result is that no progress is being made, chaos is spreading irresistibly, and a catastrophe is approaching, for our government cannot introduce war-time penal servitude for the workers in the Kornilov, Hindenburg, general imperialist way – the traditions, memories, vestiges, habits and institutions of the *revolution* are still too much alive among the people; our government does not want to take any really serious steps in a revolutionary-democratic direction, for it is thoroughly infected and thoroughly enmeshed by its dependence on the bourgeoisie, its 'coalition' with the bourgeoisie, and its fear to encroach on their real privileges.

Government Disruption of the Work of the Democratic Organisations

We have examined various ways and means of combating catastrophe and famine. We have seen everywhere that the contradictions between the democrats, on the one hand, and the government and the bloc of the Socialist-Revolutionaries and Mensheviks which is supporting it, on the other, are irreconcilable. To prove that these contradictions exist in reality, and not merely in our exposition, and that their irreconcilability is *actually* borne out by conflicts affecting the people as a whole, we have only to recall two very typical 'results' and lessons of the six months' history of our revolution.

The history of the 'reign' of *Palchinsky* is one lesson. The history of the 'reign' and fall of *Peshekhonov* is the other.

The measures to combat catastrophe and hunger described above boil down to the all-round encouragement (even to the extent of compulsion) of 'unionisation' of the population, and primarily the democrats, i.e. the majority of the population, or, above all, the oppressed classes, the workers and peasants, especially the poor peasants. And this is the path which the population itself spontaneously began to adopt in order to cope with the unparalleled difficulties, burdens and hardships of the war.

Tsarism did everything to hamper the free and independent 'unionisation' of the population. But after the fall of the tsarist monarchy, democratic organisations began to spring up and grow rapidly all over Russia. The struggle against the catastrophe began to be waged by spontaneously arising democratic organisations – by all sorts of committees of supply, food committees, fuel councils, and so on and so forth.

And the most remarkable thing in the whole six months' history of our revolution, as far as the question we are examining is concerned, is that a *government* which calls itself republican and revolutionary, and which is *supported* by the Mensheviks and Socialist-Revolutionaries in the name of the 'authorised bodies of revolutionary democracy', *fought* the democratic organisations and *defeated them*!!

By this fight, Palchinsky earned extremely wide and very sad notoriety all over Russia. He acted behind the government's back, without coming out publicly (just as the Cadets generally preferred to act, willingly pushing forward Tsereteli 'for the people', while they themselves arranged all the important business on the quiet). Palchinsky hampered and thwarted every serious measure taken by the spontaneously created democratic organisations, for no serious measure could be taken without 'injuring' the excessive profits and wilfulness of the Kit Kityches. And Palchinsky was in fact a loyal defender and servant of the Kit Kityches. Palchinsky went so far – and this fact was reported in the newspapers – as simply to *annul* the orders of the spontaneously created democratic organisations!

The whole history of Palchinsky's 'reign' – and he 'reigned' for many months, and just when Tsereteli, Skobelev and Chernov were 'ministers' – was a monstrous scandal from beginning to end; the will of the people and the decisions of the democrats were frustrated to *please* the capitalists and meet their filthy greed. Of course, only a negligible part of Palchinsky's 'feats' could find its way into the press, and a full investigation of the manner in which he *hindered* the struggle against famine can be made only by a truly democratic government of the proletariat when it gains power and submits all the actions of Palchinsky and his like, without concealing anything, *to the judgement* of the people.

It will perhaps be argued that Palchinsky was an exception, and that after all he was removed. But the fact is that Palchinsky was not the exception but the *rule*, that the situation has in no way improved with his removal, that his place has been taken by the same kind of Palchinskys with different names, and that all the 'influence' of the capitalists, and the entire policy of *frustrating the struggle against hunger to please the capitalists*, has remained intact. For Kerensky and Co, are only a screen for defence of the interests of the capitalists.

The most striking proof of this is the resignation of Peshekhonov, the Food Minister. As we know, Peshekhonov is a very, very moderate Narodnik. But in the organisation of food supply he wanted to work honestly, in contact with and supported by the democratic organisations. The *experience* of Peshekhonov's work and his *resignation* are all the more interesting because this extremely moderate Narodnik, this member of the Popular Socialist Party, who was ready to accept any compromise with the bourgeoisie, was nevertheless compelled to resign! For the Kerensky government, to please the capitalists, landowners and kulaks, had *raised* the fixed prices of grain!

This is how M Smith describes this 'step' and its significance in the newspaper *Svobodnaya Zhizn*[7] No. 1, of September 2:

'Several days before the government decided to raise the fixed prices, the following scene was enacted in the national Food Committee: Rolovich, a Right-winger, a stubborn defender of the interests of private trade and a ruthless opponent of the grain monopoly and state interference in economic affairs, publicly announced with a smug smile that he understood the fixed grain prices would shortly be raised.

'The representative of the Soviet of Workers' and Soldiers' Deputies replied by declaring that he knew nothing of the kind, that as long as the revolution in Russia lasted such an act could not take place, and that at any rate the government could not take such a step without first consulting the authorised democratic bodies – the Economic Council and the national Food Committee. This statement was supported by the representative of the Soviet of Peasants' Deputies.

'But, alas, reality introduced a very harsh amendment to this counter-version! It was the representative of the wealthy elements and not the representatives of the democrats who turned out to be right. He proved to be excellently informed of the preparations for an attack on democratic rights, although the democratic representatives indignantly denied the very possibility of such an attack.'

And so, both the representative of the workers and the representative of the peasants explicitly state their opinion in the name of the vast majority of the people, yet the Kerensky government acts contrary to that opinion, in the interests of the capitalists!

Rolovich, a representative of the capitalists, turned out to be excellently informed behind the backs of the democrats – just as we have always observed, and now observe, that the bourgeois newspapers, *Rech* and *Birzhevka*, are best informed of the doings in the Kerensky government.

What does this possession of excellent information show? Obviously, that the capitalists have their 'channels' and *virtually* hold power in their own hands. Kerensky is a figurehead which they use as and when they find necessary. The interests of tens of millions of workers and peasants turn out to have been sacrificed to the profits of a handful of the rich.

And how do our Socialist-Revolutionaries and Mensheviks react to this outrage to the people? Did they address an appeal to the workers and peasants, saying that after this, prison was the only place for Kerensky and his colleagues?

God forbid! The Socialist-Revolutionaries and Mensheviks, through their Economic Department, confined themselves to adopting the impressive resolution to which we have already referred! In this resolution they declare that the raising of grain prices by the Kerensky government is 'a *ruinous* measure which deals a *severe blow* both at the food supply and at the whole economic life of the country', and that these ruinous measures have been taken in direct '*violation*' of the law!!

Such are the results of the policy of compromise, of flirting with Kerensky and desiring to 'spare' him!

The government violates the law by adopting, in the interests of the rich, the landowners and capitalists, a measure which *ruins* the whole business of control, food supply and the stabilisation of the extremely shaky finances, yet the Socialist-Revolutionaries and Mensheviks continue to talk about an understanding with commercial and industrial circles, continue to attend conferences with Tereshchenko and to spare Kerensky, and confine themselves to a paper resolution of protest, which the government very calmly pigeonholes!!

This reveals with great clarity the fact that the Socialist-Revolutionaries and Mensheviks have betrayed the people and the revolution, and that the Bolsheviks are becoming the real leaders of the masses, *even* of the Socialist-Revolutionary and Menshevik masses.

For only the winning of power by the proletariat, headed by the Bolshevik Party, can put an end to the outrageous actions of Kerensky and Co and *restore* the work of democratic food distribution, supply and other organisations, which Kerensky and his government are *frustrating*.

The Bolsheviks are acting – and this can be very clearly seen from the above example – as the representatives of the interests of the *whole* people, which are to ensure food distribution and supply and meet the most urgent needs of the workers *and peasants*, despite the vacillating, irresolute and truly treacherous policy of the Socialist-Revolutionaries and Mensheviks, a policy which has brought the country to an act as shameful as this raising of grain prices!

Financial Collapse and Measures to Combat It

There is another side to the problem of raising the fixed grain prices. This raising of prices involves a new chaotic increase in the issuing of paper money, a further increase in the cost of living, increased financial disorganisation and the approach of financial collapse. Everybody admits that the issuing of paper money constitutes the worst form of compulsory loan, that it most of all affects the conditions of the workers, of the poorest section of the population, and that it is the chief evil engendered by financial disorder.

And it is to this measure that the Kerensky government, supported by the Socialist-Revolutionaries and Mensheviks, is resorting!

There is no way of effectively combating financial disorganisation and inevitable financial collapse except that of revolutionary rupture with the interests of capital and that of the organisation of really democratic control, i.e. control from 'below', control by the workers and the poor peasants *over* the capitalists, a way to which we referred throughout the earlier part of this exposition.

Large issues of paper money encourage profiteering, enable the capitalists to make millions of rubles, and place tremendous difficulties in the way of a very necessary expansion of production, for the already high cost of materials, machinery, etc, is rising further by leaps and bounds. What can be done about it when the wealth acquired by the rich through profiteering is being concealed?

An income tax with progressive and very high rates for larger and very large incomes might be introduced. Our government has introduced one, following the example of other imperialist governments. But it is largely a fiction, a dead letter, for, firstly, the value of money is falling faster and faster, and, secondly, the more incomes are derived from profiteering and the more securely commercial secrecy is maintained, the greater their concealment.

Real and not nominal control is required to make the tax real and not fictitious. But control over the capitalists is impossible if it remains bureaucratic, for the bureaucracy is itself bound to and interwoven with the bourgeoisie by thousands of threads. That is why in the West-European imperialist states, monarchies and republics alike, financial order is obtained solely by the introduction of 'labour service', which creates *war-time penal servitude* or *war-time slavery* for the workers.

Reactionary-bureaucratic control is the only method known to imperialist states – not excluding the democratic republics of France and America – of foisting the burdens of the war on to the proletariat and the working people.

The basic contradiction in the policy of our government is that, in order not to quarrel with the bourgeoisie, not to destroy the 'coalition' with them, the government has to introduce reactionary-bureaucratic control, which it calls 'revolutionary-democratic' control, deceiving the people at every step and irritating and angering the masses who have just overthrown tsarism.

Yet only revolutionary-democratic measures, only the organisation of the oppressed classes, the workers and peasants, the masses, into unions would make it possible to establish a most effective control *over the rich* and wage a most successful fight against the concealment of incomes.

An attempt is being made to encourage the use of cheques as a means of avoiding excessive issue of paper money. This measure is of no significance as far as the poor are concerned, for anyway they live from hand to mouth, complete their 'economic cycle' in one week and return to the capitalists the few meagre coppers they manage to earn. The use of cheques might have great significance as far as the rich are concerned. It would enable the state, especially in conjunction with such measures as nationalisation of the banks and abolition of commercial secrecy, *really to control* the incomes of the capitalists, really to impose taxation on them, and really to 'democratise' (and at the same time bring order into) the financial system.

But this is hampered by the fear of infringing the privileges of the bourgeoisie and destroying the 'coalition' with them. For unless truly revolutionary measures are adopted and compulsion is very seriously resorted to, the capitalists will not submit to any control, will not make known their budgets, and will not surrender their stocks of paper money for the democratic state to 'keep account' of.

The workers and peasants, organised in unions, by

nationalising the banks, making the use of cheques legally compulsory for all rich persons, abolishing commercial secrecy, imposing confiscation of property as a penalty for concealment of incomes, etc, might with extreme ease make control both effective and universal – control, that is, over the rich, and such control as would *secure the return* of paper money *from those* who have it, *from those* who conceal it, *to the treasury*, which issues it.

This requires a revolutionary dictatorship of the democracy, headed by the revolutionary proletariat; that is, it requires that the democracy should become revolutionary *in fact*. That is the crux of the matter. But that is just what is not wanted by our Socialist-Revolutionaries and Mensheviks, who are deceiving the people by displaying the *flag* of 'revolutionary democracy' while they are in fact supporting the reactionary-bureaucratic policy of the bourgeoisie, who, as always, are guided by the rule: '*Après nous le déluge*' – after us the deluge!

We usually do not even notice how thoroughly we are permeated by anti-democratic habits and prejudices regarding the 'sanctity' of bourgeois property. When an engineer or banker publishes the income and expenditure of a worker, information about his wages and the productivity of his labour, this is regarded as absolutely legitimate and fair. Nobody thinks of seeing it as an intrusion into the 'private life' of the worker, as 'spying or informing' on the part of the engineer. Bourgeois society regards the labour and earnings of a wage-worker as *its* open book, any bourgeois being entitled to peer into it at any moment, and at any moment to expose the 'luxurious living' of the worker, his supposed 'laziness', etc.

Well, and what about reverse control? What if the unions of employees, clerks and *domestic servants* were invited by a *democratic* state to verify the income and expenditure of capitalists, to publish information on the subject and to assist the government in combating concealment of incomes?

What a furious howl against 'spying' and 'informing' would be raised by the bourgeoisie! When 'masters' control servants, or when capitalists control workers, this is considered to be in the nature of things; the private life of the working and exploited people is *not* considered inviolable. The bourgeoisie are entiled to call to account any 'wage slave' and at any time to make public his income and expenditure. But if the oppressed attempt to control the oppressor, to show up *his* income and expenditure, to expose *his* luxurious living even in war-time, when his luxurious living is directly responsible for armies at the front starving and perishing – oh, no, the bourgeoisie will not tolerate 'spying' and 'informing'!

It all boils down to the same thing: the rule of the bourgeoisie *is irreconcilable* with truly-revolutionary true democracy. We cannot be revolutionary democrats in the twentieth century and in a capitalist country *if we fear* to advance towards socialism.

Can We Go Forward If We Fear To Advance Towards Socialism?

What has been said so far may easily arouse the following objection on the part of a reader who has been brought up on the current opportunist ideas of the Socialist-Revolutionaries and Mensheviks. Most measures described here, he may say, are *already* in effect socialist and not democratic measures!

This current objection, one that is usually raised (in one form or another) in the bourgeois, Socialist-Revolutionary and Menshevik press, is a reactionary defence of backward capitalism, a defence decked out in a Struvean garb. It seems to say that we are not ripe for socialism, that it is too early to 'introduce' socialism, that our revolution is a bourgeois revolution and therefore we must be the menials of the bourgeoisie (although the great bourgeois revolutionaries in France 125 years ago made their revolution a great revolution by exercising *terror* against all oppressors, landowners and capitalists alike!).

The pseudo-Marxist lackeys of the bourgeoisie, who have been joined by the Socialist-Revolutionaries and who argue in this way, do not understand (as an examination of the theoretical basis of their opinion shows) what imperialism is, what capitalist monopoly is, what the state is, and what revolutionary democracy is. For anyone who understands this is bound to admit that there can be no advance except towards socialism.

Everybody talks about imperialism. But imperialism is merely monopoly capitalism.

That capitalism in Russia has also become monopoly capitalism is sufficiently attested by the examples of the Produgol, the Prodamet, the Sugar Syndicate, etc. This Sugar Syndicate is an object-lesson in the way monopoly capitalism develops into state-monopoly capitalism.

And what is the state? It is an organisation of the ruling class – in Germany, for instance, of the Junkers and capitalists. And therefore what the German Plekhanovs (Scheidemann, Lensch, and others) call 'war-time socialism' is in fact war-time state-monopoly capitalism, or, to put it more simply and clearly, war-time penal servitude for the workers and war-time protection for capitalist profits.

Now try to *substitute* for the Junker-capitalist state, for the landowner-capitalist state, a *revolutionary-democratic* state, i.e. a state which in a revolutionary way abolishes *all* privileges and does not fear to introduce the fullest democracy in a revolutionary way. You will find that, given a really revolutionary-democratic state, state-monopoly capitalism inevitably and unavoidably implies a step, and more than one step, towards socialism!

For if a huge capitalist undertaking becomes a monopoly, it means that it serves the whole nation. If it has become a state monopoly, it means that the state (i.e. the armed organisation of the population, the workers and peasants above all, provided there is *revolutionary* democracy) directs the whole undertaking. In whose interest?

Either in the interest of the landowners and capitalists, in which case we have not a revolutionary-democratic, but a reactionary-bureaucratic state, an imperialist republic.

Or in the interest of revolutionary democracy – and then *it is a step towards socialism*.

For socialism is merely the next step forward from state-capitalist monopoly. Or, in other words, socialism is merely state-capitalist monopoly *which is made to serve the interests of the whole people* and has to that extent *ceased* to be capitalist monopoly.

There is no middle course here. The objective process of development is such that it is *impossible* to advance from *monopolies* (and the war has magnified their number, role and importance tenfold) without advancing towards socialism.

Either we have to be revolutionary democrats in fact, in which case we must not fear to take steps towards socialism. Or we fear to take steps towards socialism, condemn them in the Plekhanov, Dan or Chernov way, by arguing that our revolution is a bourgeois revolution, that socialism cannot be 'introduced', etc, in which case we inevitably sink to the level of Kerensky, Milyukov and Kornilov, i.e. we in a *reactionary-bureaucratic* way suppress the 'revolutionary-democratic' aspirations of the workers and peasants.

There is no middle course.

And therein lies the fundamental contradiction of our revolution.

It is impossible to stand still in history in general, and in war-time in particular. We must either advance or retreat. It is *impossible* in twentieth-century Russia, which has won a republic and democracy in a revolutionary way, to go forward without *advancing* towards socialism, without taking *steps* towards it (steps conditioned and determined by the level of technology and culture: large-scale machine production cannot be 'introduced' in peasant agriculture nor abolished in the sugar industry).

But to fear to advance *means* retreating – which the Kerenskys, to the delight of the Milyukovs and Plekhanovs, and with the foolish assistance of the Tseretelis and Chernovs, are actually doing.

The dialectics of history is such that the war, by extraordinarily expediting the transformation of monopoly capitalism into state-monopoly capitalism, has *thereby* extraordinarily advanced mankind towards socialism.

Imperialist war is the eve of socialist revolution. And this not only because the horrors of the war give rise to proletarian revolt – no revolt can bring about socialism unless the economic conditions for socialism are ripe – but because state-monopoly capitalism is a complete *material* preparation for socialism, the *threshold* of socialism, a rung on the ladder of history between which and the rung called socialism *there are no intermediate rungs*.

Our Socialist-Revolutionaries and Mensheviks approach the question of socialism in a doctrinaire way, from the standpoint of a doctrine learnt by heart but poorly understood. They picture socialism as some remote, unknown and dim future.

But socialism is now gazing at us from all the windows of modern capitalism; socialism is outlined directly, *practically* by every important measure that constitutes a forward step on the basis of this modern capitalism.

What is universal labour conscription?

It is a step forward on the basis of modern monopoly capitalism, a step towards the regulation of economic life as a whole, in accordance with a certain general plan, a step towards the economy of national labour and towards the prevention of its senseless wastage by capitalism.

In Germany it is the Junkers (landowners) and capitalists who are introducing universal labour conscription, and therefore it inevitably becomes war-time penal servitude for the workers.

But take the same institution and think over its significance in a revolutionary-democratic state. Universal labour conscription, introduced, regulated and directed by the Soviets of Workers', Soldiers' and Peasants' Deputies, will *still not* be socialism, but it will *no longer* be capitalism. It will be a tremendous *step towards* socialism, a step from which, if complete democracy is preserved, there can no longer be any retreat back to capitalism, without unparalleled violence being committed against the masses.

The Struggle Against Economic Chaos – And the War

A consideration of the measures to avert the impending catastrophe brings us to another supremely important question, namely, the connection between home and foreign policy, or, in other words, the relation between a war of conquest, an imperialist war, and a revolutionary, proletarian war, between a criminal predatory war and a just democratic war.

All the measures to avert catastrophe we have described would, as we have already stated, greatly enhance the defence potential, or, in other words, the military might of the country. That, on the one hand. On the other hand, these measures cannot be put into effect without turning the war of conquest into a just war, turning the war waged by the capitalists in the interests of the capitalists into a war waged by the proletariat in the interests of all the working and exploited people.

And, indeed, nationalisation of the banks and syndicates, taken in conjunction with the abolition of commercial secrecy and the establishment of workers' control over the capitalists, would not only imply a tremendous saving of national labour, the possibility of economising forces and means, but would also imply an improvement in the conditions of the working *masses*, of the majority of the population. As everybody knows, economic organisation is of decisive importance in modern warfare. Russia has enough grain, coal, oil and iron; in this respect, we are in a better position than any of the belligerent European countries. And given a struggle against economic chaos by the measures indicated above, enlisting popular initiative in this struggle, improving the people's conditions, and nationalising the banks and syndicates, Russia could use her revolution and her democracy to raise the whole country to an incomparably higher level of economic organisation.

If instead of the 'coalition' with the bourgeoisie, which is hampering every measure of control and sabotaging production, the Socialist-Revolutionaries and Mensheviks had in April effected the transfer of power to the Soviets and had directed their efforts not to playing at 'ministerial leapfrog', not to bureaucratically occupying, side by side with the Cadets, ministerial, deputy-ministerial and similar posts, but to guiding the workers and peasants in *their* control *over* the capitalists, in their *war against* the capitalists, Russia would now be a country completely transformed economically, with the land in the hands of the peasants, and with the banks nationalised, i.e. would *to that extent* (and these are extremely important economic bases of modern life) be *superior* to all other capitalist countries.

The defence potential, the military might, of a country whose banks have been nationalised is *superior* to that of a country whose banks remain in private hands. The military might of a peasant country whose land is in the hands of peasant committees is *superior* to that of a country whose land is in the hands of landowners.

Reference is constantly being made to the heroic patriotism and the miracles of military valour performed by the French in 1792-93. But the material, historical economic conditions which alone made such miracles possible are forgotten. The suppression of obsolete feudalism in a really revolutionary way, and the introduction throughout the country of a superior mode of production and free peasant land tenure, effected, moreover, with truly revolutionary-democratic speed, determination, energy and devotion – such were the material, economic conditions which with 'miraculous' speed saved France by *regenerating* and *renovating* her economic foundation.

The example of France shows one thing, and one thing only, namely, that to render Russia capable of self-defence, to obtain in Russia, too, 'miracles' of mass heroism, all that is obsolete must be swept away with 'Jacobin' ruthlessness and Russia renovated and regenerated *economically*. And in the twentieth century this cannot be done merely by sweeping tsarism away (France did not confine herself to this 125 years ago). It cannot be done even by the mere revolutionary abolition of the landed estates (we have not even done that, for the Socialist-Revolutionaries and Mensheviks have betrayed the peasants), by the mere transfer of the land to the peasants. For we are living in the twentieth century, and mastery over the land *without mastery over the banks* cannot regenerate and renovate the life of the people.

The material, industrial renovation of France at the end of the eighteenth century was associated with a political and spiritual renovation, with the dictatorship of revolutionary democrats and the revolutionary proletariat (from which the democrats had not dissociated themselves and with which they were still almost fused), and with a ruthless war declared on everything reactionary. The whole people, and especially the masses, i.e. the *oppressed* classes, were swept up by boundless revolutionary enthusiasm; *everybody* considered the war a just war of defence, as it *actually was*. Revolutionary France was defending herself against reactionary monarchist Europe. It was not in 1792-93, but many years later, *after* the victory of reaction within the country, that the counter-revolutionary dictatorship of Napoleon turned France's wars from defensive wars into wars of conquest.

And what about Russia? We continue to wage an imperialist war in the interests of the capitalists, in alliance with the imperialists and in accordance with the secret treaties the *tsar* concluded with the capitalists of Britain and other countries, promising the Russian capitalists in these treaties the spoliation of foreign lands, of Constantinople, Lvov, Armenia, etc.

The war will remain an unjust, reactionary and predatory war on Russia's part as long as she does not propose a just peace and does not break with imperialism. The social character of the war, its true meaning, is not determined by the position of the enemy troops (as the Socialist-Revolutionaries and Mensheviks think, stooping to the vulgarity of an ignorant yokel). What determines this character is the *policy* of which the war is a continuation ('war is the continuation of politics'), the *class* that is waging the war, and the aims for which it is waging this war.

You cannot lead the people into a predatory war in accordance with secret treaties and expect them to be enthusiastic. The foremost class in revolutionary Russia, the proletariat, is becoming increasingly aware of the criminal character of the war, and not only have the bourgeoisie been unable to shatter this popular conviction, but, on the contrary, awareness of the criminal character of the war is growing. The proletariat *of both metropolitan cities* of Russia has definitely become internationalist!

How, then, can you expect mass enthusiasm for the war!

One is inseparable from the other – home policy is inseparable from foreign policy. The country cannot be made capable of self-defence without the supreme heroism of the people in boldly and resolutely carrying out great economic transformations. And it is impossible to arouse popular heroism without breaking with imperialism, without proposing a democratic peace to all nations, and without thus turning the war from a criminal war of conquest and plunder into a just, revolutionary war of defence.

Only a thorough and consistent break with the capitalists

in both home and foreign policy can save our revolution and our country, which is gripped in the iron vice of imperialism.

The Revolutionary Democrats and the Revolutionary Proletariat

To be really revolutionary, the democrats of Russia today must march in very close alliance with the proletariat, supporting it in its struggle as the only thoroughly revolutionary class.

Such is the conclusion prompted by an analysis of the means of combating an impending catastrophe of unparalleled dimensions.

The war has created such an immense crisis, has so strained the material and moral forces of the people, has dealt such blows at the entire modern social organisation that humanity must now choose between perishing or entrusting its fate to the most revolutionary class for the swiftest and most radical transition to a superior mode of production.

Owing to a number of historical causes – the greater backwardness of Russia, the unusual hardships brought upon her by the war, the utter rottenness of tsarism and the extreme tenacity of the traditions of 1905 – the revolution broke out in Russia earlier than in other countries. The revolution has resulted in Russia, catching up with the advanced countries in a few months, as far as her *political* system is concerned.

But that is not enough. The war is inexorable; it puts the alternative with ruthless severity: either perish or overtake and outstrip the advanced countries *economically as well*.

That is possible, for we have before us the experience of a large number of advanced countries, the fruits of their technology and culture. We are receiving moral support from the war protest that is growing in Europe, from the atmosphere of the mounting world-wide workers' revolution. We are being inspired and encouraged by a revolutionary-democratic freedom which is extremely rare in time of imperialist war.

Perish or forge full steam ahead. That is the alternative put by history.

And the attitude of the proletariat to the peasants in such a situation confirms the old Bolshevik concept, correspondingly modifying it, that the peasants must be wrested from the influence of the bourgeoisie. That is the sole guarantee of salvation for the revolution.

And the peasants are the most numerous section of the entire petty-bourgeois mass.

Our Socialist-Revolutionaries and Mensheviks have assumed the reactionary function of keeping the peasants under the influence of the bourgeoisie and leading them to a coalition with the bourgeoisie, and not with the proletariat.

The masses are learning rapidly from the experience of the revolution. And the reactionary policy of the Socialist-Revolutionaries and Mensheviks is meeting with failure: they have been beaten in the Soviets of both Petrograd and Moscow.[8] A 'Left' opposition is growing in both petty-bourgeois-democratic parties. On September 10, 1917, a city conference of the Socialist-Revolutionaries held in Petrograd gave a two-thirds majority to the *Left* Socialist-Revolutionaries, who incline towards an alliance with the proletariat and reject an alliance (coalition) with the bourgeoisie.

The Socialist-Revolutionaries and Mensheviks repeat a favourite bourgeois comparison – bourgeoisie and democracy. But, in essence, such a comparison is as meaningless as comparing pounds with yards.

There is such a thing as a democratic bourgeoisie, and there is such a thing as bourgeois democracy; one would have to be completely ignorant of both history and political economy to deny this.

The Socialist-Revolutionaries and Mensheviks needed a false comparison to *conceal* the indisputable fact that between the bourgeoisie and the proletariat stand the *petty bourgeoisie*. By virtue of their economic class status, the latter inevitably vacillate between the bourgeoisie and the proletariat.

The Socialist-Revolutionaries and Mensheviks are trying to draw the petty bourgeoisie into an alliance with the bourgeoisie. That is the whole meaning of their 'coalition', of the coalition cabinet, and of the whole policy of Kerensky, a typical semi-Cadet. In the six months of the revolution this policy has suffered a complete fiasco.

The Cadets are full of malicious glee. The revolution, they say, has suffered a fiasco; the revolution has been *unable* to cope either with the war or with economic dislocation.

That is not true. It is the *Cadets*, and the *Socialist-Revolutionaries and Mensheviks* who have suffered a fiasco, for this alliance has ruled Russia for six months, only to increase economic dislocation and confuse and aggravate the military situation.

The more complete the fiasco of the *alliance* of the bourgeoisie and the *Socialist-Revolutionaries and Mensheviks*, the sooner the people will *learn their lesson* and the more easily they will find the *correct* way out, namely, the alliance of the peasant poor, i.e. the majority of the peasants, and the proletariat.

Notes

[1] The All-Russia Democratic Conference was held in Petrograd between September 14 (27) and September 22 (October 5), 1917. It was called by Mensheviks and Socialist-Revolutionaries to promote a parliamentary, non-revolutionary strategy – *ed*.

[2] Kit Kitych (literally, Whale Whaleseon) was the nickname for Tit Titych, a rich merchant in Alexander Ostrovsky's comedy *Shouldering Another's Troubles* – hence Lenin's use to indicate a tycoon – *ed*.

[3] The War Industries Committees were set up in 1915 by Russian businessmen to help in the war effort. The Committee of Businessmen attempted to recruit, under its leadership, 'workers' groups', so that there could be 'class peace' in a time of war – *ed*.

[4] These lines had been written when I learnt from the newspapers that the Kerensky government is introducing a sugar monopoly, and, of course, is introducing it in a reactionary-bureaucratic way, without congresses of the workers and other employees, without publicity, and without curbing the capitalists!

[5] See CW XXV, pp 68-9 – *ed*.

[6] I have already had occasion to point out in the Bolshevik press that it is right to argue against the death penalty only when it is applied by the exploiters against the *mass* of the working people with the purpose of maintaining exploitation (See CWXXV pp 261-4 – *ed*). It is hardly likely that any revolutionary government whatever could do without applying the death penalty to the *exploiters* (i.e. the landowners and capitalists).

[7] *Svobodnaya Zhizn* (Free Life) was a Menshevik paper published in Petrograd from September 2-8 (15-21), 1917, instead of the suspended *Novaya Zhizn* – *ed*.

[8] On August 31 (September 13) 1917, the Petrograd Soviet, for the first

time, gave majority support to a Bolshevik resolution calling for the transfer of all power to the Soviets, and supporting revolutionary changes. On September 5 (18) the Moscow Soviet of Workers' and Soldiers' Deputies supported a similar resolution – *ed*.

7. The Immediate Tasks of the Soviet Government

The International Position of the Russian Soviet Republic and the Fundamental Tasks of the Socialist Revolution

Thanks to the peace which has been achieved – despite its extremely onerous character and extreme instability – the Russian Soviet Republic has gained an opportunity to concentrate its efforts for a while on the most important and most difficult aspect of the socialist revolution, namely, the task of organisation.

This task was clearly and definitely set before all the working and oppressed people in the fourth paragraph (Part 4) of the resolution adopted at the Extraordinary Congress of Soviets in Moscow on March 15, 1918, in that paragraph (or part) which speaks of the self-discipline of the working people and of the ruthless struggle against chaos and disorganisation.[1]

Of course, the peace achieved by the Russian Soviet Republic is unstable not because she is now thinking of resuming military operations; apart from bourgeois counter-revolutionaries and their henchmen (the Mensheviks and others), no sane politician thinks of doing that. The instability of the peace is due to the fact that in the imperialist states bordering on Russia to the West and the East, which command enormous military forces, the military party, tempted by Russia's momentary weakness and egged on by capitalists, who hate socialism and are eager for plunder, may gain the upper hand at any moment.

Under these circumstances the only real, not paper, guarantee of peace we have is the antagonism among the

Published in *Pravda* and *Izvestia*, April 1918.
CW XXVII, 237-277.

imperialist powers, which has reached extreme limits, and which is apparent on the one hand in the resumption of the imperialist butchery of the peoples in the West, and on the other hand in the extreme intensification of imperialist rivalry between Japan and America for supremacy in the Pacific and on the Pacific coast.

It goes without saying that with such an unreliable guard for protection, our Soviet Socialist Republic is in an extremely unstable and certainly critical international position. All our efforts must be exerted to the very utmost to make use of the respite given us by the combination of circumstances so that we can heal the very severe wounds inflicted by the war upon the entire social organism of Russia and bring about an economic revival, without which a real increase in our country's defence potential is inconceivable.

It also goes without saying that we shall be able to render effective assistance to the socialist revolution in the West, which has been delayed for a number of reasons, only to the extent that we are able to fulfil the task of organisation confronting us.

A fundamental condition for the successful accomplishment of the primary task of organisation confronting us is that the people's political leaders, i.e. the members of the Russian Communist Party (Bolsheviks), and following them all the class-conscious representatives of the mass of the working people, shall fully appreciate the radical distinction in this respect between previous bourgeois revolutions and the present socialist revolution.

In bourgeois revolutions, the principal task of the mass of working people was to fulfil the negative or destructive work of abolishing feudalism, monarchy and medievalism. The positive or constructive work of organising the new society was carried out by the property-owning bourgeois minority of the population. And the latter carried out this task with relative ease, despite the resistance of the workers and the poor peasants, not only because the resistance of the people exploited by capital was then extremely weak, since they were scattered and uneducated, but also because the chief organising force of anarchically built capitalist society is the spontaneously growing and expanding national and international market.

In every socialist revolution, however – and consequently in the socialist revolution in Russia which we began on October 25, 1917 – the principal task of the proletariat, and of the poor peasants which it leads, is the positive or constructive work of setting up an extremely intricate and delicate system of new organisational relationships extending to the planned production and distribution of the goods required for the existence of tens of millions of people. Such a revolution can be successfully carried out only if the majority of the population, and primarily the majority of the working people, engage in independent creative work as makers of history. Only if the proletariat and the poor peasants display sufficient class-consciousness, devotion to principle, self-sacrifice and perseverance, will the victory of the socialist revolution be assured. By creating a new, Soviet type of state, which gives the working and oppressed people the chance to take an active part in the independent building up of a new society, we solved only a small part of this difficult problem. The principal difficulty lies in the economic sphere, namely, the introduction of the strictest and universal accounting and control of the production and distribution of goods, raising the productivity of labour and *socialising* production *in practice*.

The development of the Bolshevik Party, which today is the governing party in Russia, very strikingly indicates the nature of the turning-point in history we have now reached, which is the peculiar feature of the present political situation, and which calls for a new orientation of Soviet power, i.e. for a new presentation of new tasks.

The first task of every party of the future is to convince the majority of the people that its programme and tactics are correct. This task stood in the forefront both in tsarist times and in the period of the Chernovs' and Tseretelis' policy of compromise with the Kerenskys and Kishkins. This task has now been fulfilled in the main, for, as the recent Congress of Soviets in Moscow incontrovertibly proved, the majority of the workers and peasants of Russia are obviously on the side of the Bolsheviks; but of course it is far from being completely fulfilled (and it can never be completely fulfilled).

The second task that confronted our Party was to capture political power and to suppress the resistance of the exploiters. This task has not been completely fulfilled either, and it cannot be ignored because the monarchists and Constitutional-Democrats on the one hand, and their hench-men and hangers-on, the Mensheviks and Right Socialist-Revolutionaries, on the other, are continuing their efforts to unite for the purpose of overthrowing Soviet power. In the main, however, the task of suppressing the resistance of the exploiters was fulfilled in the period from October 25, 1917, to (approximately) February 1918, or to the surrender of Bogayevsky.[2]

A third task is now coming to the fore as the immediate task and one which constitutes the peculiar feature of the present situation, namely, the task of organising *administration* of Russia. Of course, we advanced and tackled this task on the very day following October 25, 1917. Up to now, however, since the resistance of the exploiters still took the form of open civil war, up to now the task of administration *could not* become the *main*, the *central* task.

Now it has become the main and central task. We, the Bolshevik Party, have *convinced* Russia. We have *won* Russia from the rich for the poor, from the exploiters for the working people. Now we must *administer* Russia. And the whole peculiarity of the present situation, the whole diffi-culty, lies in understanding *the specific features of the transition* from the principal task of convincing the people and of suppressing the exploiters by armed force to the principal task of *administration*.

For the first time in human history a socialist party has managed to complete in the main the conquest of power and the suppression of the exploiters, and has managed to *approach directly* the task of *administration*. We must prove worthy executors of this most difficult (and most gratifying) task of the socialist revolution. We must *fully realise* that in order to administer successfully, *besides being able to con-vince people, besides being able to win a civil war, we must be able to do practical organisational work*. This is the most difficult task, because it is a matter of organising in a new way the most deep-rooted, the economic, foundations of life of scores of millions of people. And it is the most gratifying task, because only *after* it has been fulfilled (in the principal and main outlines) will it be possible to say that Russia *has become* not only a Soviet, but also a socialist, republic.

The General Slogan of the Moment

The objective situation reviewed above, which has been created by the extremely onerous and unstable peace, the terrible state of ruin, the unemployment and famine we inherited from the war and the rule of the bourgeoisie (represented by Kerensky and the Mensheviks and Right Socialist-Revolutionaries who supported him), all this has inevitably caused extreme weariness and even exhaustion of wide sections of the working people. These people insistently demand – and cannot but demand – a respite. The task of the day is to restore the productive forces destroyed by the war and by bourgeois rule; to heal the wounds inflicted by the war, by the defeat in the war, by profiteering and the attempts of the bourgeoisie to restore the overthrown rule of the exploiters; to achieve economic revival; to provide reliable protection of elementary order. It may sound paradoxical, but in fact, considering the objective conditions indicated above, it is absolutely certain that at the present moment the Soviet system can secure Russia's transition to socialism only if these very elementary, extremely elementary problems of maintaining public life are practically solved in spite of the resistance of the bourgeoisie, the Mensheviks and the Right Socialist-Revolutionaries. In view of the specific features of the present situation, and in view of the existence of Soviet power with its land socialisation law, workers' control law, etc, the practical solution of these extremely elementary problems and the overcoming of the organisational difficulties of the first stages of progress toward socialism are now two aspects of the same picture.

Keep regular and honest accounts of money, manage economically, do not be lazy, do not steal, observe the strictest labour discipline – it is these slogans, justly scorned by the revolutionary proletariat when the bourgeoisie used them to conceal its rule as an exploiting class, that are now, since the overthrow of the bourgeoisie, becoming the immediate and the principal slogans of the moment. On the one hand, the practical application of these slogans by *the mass* of working people is the *sole* condition for the salvation of a country which has been tortured almost to death by the imperialist war and by the imperialist robbers (headed by Kerensky); on the other hand, the practical application of these slogans by the *Soviet* state, by *its* methods, on the basis of *its* laws, is a necessary and *sufficient* condition for the final victory of socialism. This is precisely what those who contemptuously brush aside the ' idea of putting such 'hackneyed' and 'trivial' slogans in the forefront fail to understand. In a small-peasant country, which overthrew tsarism only a year ago, and which liberated itself from the Kerenskys less than six months ago, there has naturally remained not a little of spontaneous anarchy, intensified by the brutality and savagery that accompany every protracted and reactionary war, and there has arisen a good deal of despair and aimless bitterness. And if we add to this the provocative policy of the lackeys of the bourgeoisie (the Mensheviks, the Right Socialist-Revolutionaries, etc) it will become perfectly clear what prolonged and persistent efforts must be exerted by the best and the most class-conscious workers and peasants in order to bring about a complete change in the mood of the people and to bring them on to the proper path of steady and disciplined labour. Only such a transition brought about by the mass of the poor (the proletarians and semi-proletarians) can consummate the victory over the bourgeoisie and particularly over the peasant bourgeoisie, more stubborn and numerous.

The New Phase of the Struggle Against the Bourgeoisie

The bourgeoisie in our country has been conquered, but it has not yet been uprooted, not yet destroyed, and not even utterly broken. That is why we are faced with a new and higher form of struggle against the bourgeoisie, the transition from the very simple task of further expropriating the capitalists to the much more complicated and difficult task of creating conditions in which it will be impossible for the bourgeoisie to exist, or for a new bourgeoisie to arise. Clearly, this task is immeasurably more significant than the previous one; and until it is fulfilled there will be no socialism.

If we measure our revolution by the scale of West-European revolutions we shall find that at the present moment we are approximately at the level reached in 1793 and 1871. We can be legitimately proud of having risen to this level, and of having certainly, in one respect, advanced somewhat further, namely: we have decreed and introduced throughout Russia the highest *type* of state – Soviet power. Under no circumstances, however, can we rest content with what we have achieved, because we have only just started the transition to socialism, we have *not yet* done the decisive thing in *this* respect.

The decisive thing is the organisation of the strictest and country-wide accounting and control of production and distribution of goods. And yet, we have *not yet* introduced branches and fields of economy which we have taken away from the bourgeoisie; and without this there can be no thought of achieving the second and equally essential material condition for introducing socialism, namely, raising the productivity of labour on a national scale.

That is why the present task could not be defined by the simple formula: continue the offensive against capital. Although we have certainly not finished off capital and although it is certainly necessary to continue the offensive against this enemy of the working people, such a formula would be inexact, would not be concrete, would not take into account the *peculiarity* of the present situation in which, in order to go on advancing successfully *in the future*, we must 'suspend' our offensive *now*.

This can be explained by comparing our position in the war against capital with the position of a victorious army that has captured, say, a half or two-thirds of the enemy's territory and is compelled to halt in order to muster its forces, to replenish its supplies of munitions, repair and reinforce the lines of communication, build new storehouses, bring up new reserves, etc. To suspend the offensive of a victorious army under such conditions is necessary precisely in order to gain the rest of the enemy's territory, i.e. in order to achieve complete victory. Those who have failed to understand that the objective state of affairs at the present moment dictates to us precisely such a 'suspension' of the offensive against capital have failed to understand anything at all about the present political situation.

It goes without saying that we can speak about the 'suspension' of the offensive against capital only in quotation marks, i.e. only metaphorically. In ordinary war, a general order can be issued to stop the offensive, the advance can actually be stopped. In the war against capital, however, the advance cannot be stopped, and there can be no thought of our abandoning the further expropriation of capital. What we are discussing is the shifting of the *centre of gravity* of our economic and political work. Up to now measures for the direct expropriation of the expropriators were *in the forefront*. Now the organisation of accounting and control in those enterprises, and in all other enterprises, advances *to the forefront*.

If we decided to continue to expropriate capital at the same rate at which we have been doing it up to now, we should certainly suffer defeat, because our work of organising proletarian accounting and control has obviously – obviously to every thinking person – *fallen behind* the work of *directly* 'expropriating the expropriators'. If we now concentrate all our efforts on the organisation of accounting and control, we shall be able to solve this problem, we shall be able to make up for lost time, we shall *completely* win our 'campaign' against capital.

But is not the admission that we must make up for lost time tantamount to admission of some kind of error? Not in the least. Take another military example. If it is possible to defeat and push back the enemy merely with detachments of light cavalry, it should be done. But if this can be done successfully only up to a certain point, then it is quite conceivable that when this point has been reached, it will be necessary to bring up heavy artillery. By admitting that it is now necessary to make up for lost time in bringing up heavy artillery, we do not admit that the successful cavalry attack was a mistake.

Frequently, the lackeys of the bourgeoisie reproached us for having launched a 'Red Guard' attack on capital. The reproach is absurd and is worthy only of the lackeys of the money-bags, because *at one time* the 'Red Guard' attack on capital was absolutely dictated by circumstances. Firstly, *at that time* capital put up military resistance through the medium of Kerensky and Krasnov, Savinkov and Gotz (Gegechkori is putting up such resistance even now), Dutov and Bogayevsky. Military resistance cannot be broken except by military means, and the Red Guards fought in the noble and supreme historical cause of liberating the working and exploited people from the yoke of the exploiters.

Secondly, we could not at that time put methods of administration in the forefront in place of methods of suppression, because the art of administration is not innate, but is acquired by experience. At that time we lacked this experience; now we have it. Thirdly, at that time we could not have specialists in the various fields of knowledge and technology at our disposal because those specialists were either fighting in the ranks of the Bogayevskys, or were still able to put up systematic and stubborn passive resistance by way of *sabotage*. Now we have broken the sabotage. The 'Red Guard' attack on capital was successful, was victorious, because we broke capital's military resistance and its resistance by sabotage.

Does that mean that a 'Red Guard' attack on capital is *always* appropriate, under *all* circumstances, that we have *no* other means of fighting capital? It would be childish to think so. We achieved victory with the aid of light cavalry, but we also have heavy artillery. We achieved victory by methods of suppression; we shall be able to achieve victory also by methods of administration. We must know how to change our methods of fighting the enemy to suit changes in the situation. We shall not for a moment renounce 'Red Guard' suppression of the Savinkovs and Gegechkoris and all other landowner and bourgeois counter-revolutionaries. We shall not be so foolish, however, as to put 'Red Guard' methods in the forefront at a time when the period in which Red Guard attacks were necessary has, in the main, drawn to a close (and to a victorious close), and when the period of utilising bourgeois specialists by the proletarian state power for the purpose of reploughing the soil in order to prevent the growth of any bourgeoisie whatever is knocking at the door.

This is a peculiar epoch, or rather stage of development, and in order to defeat capital completely, we must be able to adapt the forms of our struggle to the peculiar conditions of this stage.

Without the guidance of experts in the various fields of knowledge, technology and experience, the transition to socialism will be impossible, because socialism calls for a conscious mass advance to greater productivity of labour compared with capitalism, and on the basis achieved by capitalism. Socialism must achieve this advance *in its own way*, by its own methods – or, to put it more concretely, by *Soviet* methods. And the specialists, because of the whole social environment which made them specialists, are, in the main, inevitably bourgeois. Had our proletariat, after capturing power, quickly solved the problem of accounting, control and organisation on a national scale (which was impossible owing to the war and Russia's backwardness), then we, after breaking the sabotage, would also have completely subordinated these bourgeois experts to our-selves by means of universal accounting and control. Owing to the considerable 'delay' in introducing accounting and control generally, we, although we have managed to conquer sabotage, have *not yet* created the conditions which would place the bourgeois specialists at our disposal. The mass of saboteurs are 'going to work', but the best organisers and the top experts can be utilised by the state either in the old way, in the bourgeois way (i.e. for high salaries), or in the new way, in the proletarian way (i.e. creating the conditions of national accounting and control from below, which would inevitably and of itself subordinate the experts and enlist them for our work).

Now we have to resort to the old bourgeois method and to agree to pay a very high price for the 'services' of the top bourgeois experts. All those who are familiar with the subject appreciate this, but not all ponder over the significance of this measure being adopted by the proletarian state. Clearly, this measure is a compromise, a departure from the principles of the Paris Commune and of every proletarian power, which call for the reduction of all salaries to the level of the wages of the average worker, which urge that careerism be fought not merely in words, but in deeds.

Moreover, it is clear that this measure not only implies the cessation – in a certain field and to a certain degree – of the offensive against capital (for capital is not a sum of money, but a definite social relation); it is also *a step backward* on the part of our socialist Soviet state power, which from the very outset proclaimed and pursued the policy of reducing high salaries to the level of the wages of the average worker.

Of course, the lackeys of the bourgeoisie, particularly the small fry, such as the Mensheviks, the *Novaya Zhizn* people and the Right Socialist-Revolutionaries, will giggle over our confession that we are taking a step backward. But we need not mind their giggling. We must study the specific features of the extremely difficult and new path to socialism without concealing our mistakes and weaknesses, and try to be prompt in doing what has been left undone. To conceal from the people the fact that the enlistment of bourgeois experts by means of extremely high salaries is a retreat from the principles of the Paris Commune would be sinking to the level of bourgeois politicians and deceiving the people. Frankly explaining how and why we took this step backward, and then publicly discussing what means are available for making up for lost time, means educating the people and learning from experience, learning together with the people how to build socialism. There is hardly a single victorious military campaign in history in which the victor did not commit certain mistakes, suffer partial reverses, temporarily yield something and in some places retreat. The 'campaign' which we have undertaken against capitalism is a million times more difficult than the most difficult military campaign, and it would be silly and disgraceful to give way to despondency because of a particular and partial retreat.

We shall now discuss the question from the practical point of view. Let us assume that the Russian Soviet Republic requires one thousand first-class scientists and experts in various fields of knowledge, technology and practical experience to direct the labour of the people towards securing the speediest possible economic revival. Let us assume also that we shall have to pay these 'stars of the first magnitude' – of course the majority of those who shout loudest about the corruption of the workers are themselves utterly corrupted by bourgeois morals – 25,000 rubles per annum each. Let us assume that this sum (25,000,000 rubles) will have to be doubled (assuming that we have to pay bonuses for particularly successful and rapid fulfilment of the most important organisational and technical tasks), or even quadrupled (assuming that we have to enlist several hundred foreign specialists, who are more demanding). The question is, would the annual expenditure of fifty or a hundred million rubles by the Soviet Republic for the purpose of reorganising the labour of the people on modern scientific and technological lines be excessive or too heavy? Of course not. The overwhelming majority of the class-conscious workers and peasants will approve of this expenditure because they know from practical experience that our backwardness causes us to lose thousands of millions, and that we have *not yet* reached the degree of organisation, accounting and control which would induce all the 'stars' of the bourgeois intelligentsia to participate voluntarily in *our* work.

It goes without saying that this question has another side to it. The corrupting influence of high salaries – both upon the Soviet authorities (especially since the revolution occurred so rapidly that it was impossible to prevent a certain number of adventurers and rogues from getting into positions of authority, and they, together with a number of inept or dishonest commissars, would not be averse to becoming 'star' embezzlers of state funds) and upon the mass of the workers – is indisputable. Every thinking and honest worker and poor peasant, however, will agree with us, will admit, that we cannot immediately rid ourselves of the evil legacy of capitalism, and that we can liberate the Soviet Republic from the duty of paying an annual 'tribute' of fifty million or one hundred million rubles (a tribute for our own backwardness in organising *country-wide* accounting and control *from below*) only by organising ourselves, by tightening up discipline in our own ranks, by purging our ranks of all those who are 'preserving the legacy of capitalism', who 'follow the traditions of capitalism', i.e. of idlers, parasites and embezzlers of state funds (now all the land, all the factories and all the railways are the 'state funds' of the Soviet Republic). If the class-conscious advanced workers and poor peasants manage with the aid of the Soviet institutions to organise, become disciplined, pull themselves together, create powerful labour discipline in the course of one year, then in a year's time we shall throw off this 'tribute', which can be reduced even before that ... in exact proportion to the successes we achieve in our workers' and peasants' labour discipline and organisation. The sooner we ourselves, workers and peasants, learn the best labour discipline and the most modern technique of labour, using the bourgeois experts to teach us, the sooner we shall liberate ourselves from any 'tribute' to these specialists.

Our work of organising country-wide accounting and control of production and distribution under the supervision of the proletariat has lagged very much behind our work of directly expropriating the expropriators. This proposition is of fundamental importance for understanding the specific features of the present situation and the tasks of the Soviet government that follow from it. The centre of gravity of our struggle against the bourgeoisie is shifting to the organisation of such accounting and control. Only with this as our starting-point will it be possible to determine correctly the immediate tasks of economic and financial policy in the sphere of nationalisation of the banks, monopolisation of foreign trade, the state control of money circulation, the introduction of a property and income tax satisfactory from the proletarian point of view, and the introduction of compulsory labour service.

We have been lagging very far behind in introducing socialist reforms in these spheres (very, very important spheres), and this is because accounting and control are insufficiently organised in general. It goes without saying that this is one of the most difficult tasks, and in view of the ruin caused by the war, it can be fulfilled only over a long period of time; but we must not forget that it is precisely here that the bourgeoisie – and particularly the numerous petty and peasant bourgeoisie – are putting up the most serious fight, disrupting the control that is already being organised, disrupting the grain monopoly, for example, and gaining positions for profiteering and speculative trade. We have far from adequately carried out the things we have decreed, and the principal task of the moment is to concentrate all efforts on the businesslike, practical realisation of the principles of the reforms which have already become law (but not yet reality).

In order to proceed with the nationalisation of the banks and to go on steadfastly towards transforming the banks into nodal points of public accounting under socialism, we must first of all, and above all, achieve real success in increasing the number of branches of the People's Bank, in attracting deposits, in simplifying the paying in and withdrawal of deposits by the public, in abolishing queues, in catching and *shooting* bribe-takers and rogues, etc. At first we must really carry out the simplest things, properly organise what is available, and then prepare for the more intricate things.

Consolidate and improve the state monopolies (in grain, leather, etc) which have already been introduced, and by doing so prepare for the state monopoly of foreign trade. Without this monopoly we shall not be able to 'free ourselves' from foreign capital by paying 'tribute'.[3] And the possibility of building up socialism depends entirely upon whether we shall be able, by paying a certain tribute to foreign capital during a certain transitional period, to safeguard our internal economic independence.

We are also lagging very far behind in regard to the collection of taxes generally, and of the property and income tax in particular. The imposing of indemnities upon the bourgeoisie – a measure which in principle is absolutely permissible and deserves proletarian approval – shows that in this respect we are still nearer to the methods of warfare (to win Russia from the rich for the poor) than to the methods of administration. In order to become stronger, however, and in order to be able to stand firmer on our feet, we must adopt the latter methods, we must substitute for the indemnities imposed upon the bourgeoisie the constant and regular collection of a property and income tax, which will bring a *greater* return to the proletarian state, and which calls for better organisation on our part and better accounting and control.[4]

The fact that we are late in introducing compulsory labour service also shows that the work that is coming to the fore at the present time is precisely the preparatory organisational work that, on the one hand, will finally consolidate our gains and that, on the other, is necessary in order to prepare for the operation of 'surrounding' capital and compelling it to 'surrender'. We ought to begin introducing compulsory labour service immediately, but we must do so very gradually and circumspectly, testing every step by practical experience, and, of course, taking the first step by introducing compulsory labour service *for the rich*. The introduction of work and consumers' budget books for every bourgeois, including every rural bourgeois, would be an important step towards completely 'surrounding' the enemy and towards the creation of a truly popular accounting and control of the production and distribution of goods.

The Significance of the Struggle for Country-Wide Accounting and Control

The state, which for centuries has been an organ for oppression and robbery of the people, has left us a legacy of the people's supreme hatred and suspicion of everything that is connected with the state. It is very difficult to overcome this, and only a Soviet government can do it. Even a Soviet government, however, will require plenty of time and enormous perseverance to accomplish it. This 'legacy' is especially apparent in the problem of accounting and control – the fundamental problem facing the socialist revolution on the morrow of the overthrow of the bourgeoisie. A certain amount of time will inevitably pass before the people, who feel free for the first time now that the landowners and the bourgeoisie have been overthrown, will understand – not from books, but from their own, *Soviet* experience – will understand and *feel* that without comprehensive state accounting and control of the production and distribution of goods, the power of the working people, the freedom of the working people, *cannot* be maintained, and that a return to the yoke of capitalism is *inevitable*.

All the habits and traditions of the bourgeoisie, and of the petty bourgeoisie in particular, also oppose *state* control, and uphold the inviolability of 'sacred private property', of 'sacred' private enterprise. It is now particularly clear to us how correct is the Marxist thesis that anarchism and anarcho-syndicalism are *bourgeois* trends, how irreconcilably opposed they are to socialism, proletarian dictatorship and communism. The fight to instil into the people's minds the idea of *Soviet* state control and accounting, and to carry out this idea in practice; the fight to break with the rotten past, which taught the people to regard the procurement of bread and clothes as a 'private' affair, and buying and selling as a transaction 'which concerns only myself' – is a great fight of world-historic significance, a fight between socialist consciousness and bourgeois-anarchist spontaneity.

We have introduced workers' control as a law, but this law is only just beginning to operate and is only just beginning to penetrate the minds of broad sections of the proletariat. In our agitation we do not sufficiently explain that lack of accounting and control in the production and distribution of goods means the death of the rudiments of socialism, means the embezzlement of state funds (for all property belongs to the state and the state is the Soviet state in which power belongs to the majority of the working people). We do not sufficiently explain that carelessness in accounting and control is downright aiding and abetting the German and the Russian Kornilovs, who can overthrow the power of the working people *only* if we fail to cope with the task of accounting and control, and who, with the aid of the whole of the rural bourgeoisie, with the aid of the Constitutional-Democrats, the Mensheviks and the Right Socialist-Revolutionaries, are 'watching' us and waiting for an opportune moment to attack us. And the advanced workers and peasants do not think and speak about this sufficiently. Until workers' control has become a fact, until the advanced workers have organised and carried out a victorious and ruthless crusade against the violators of this control, or against those who are careless in matters of control, it will be impossible to pass from the first step (from workers' control) to the second step towards socialism, i.e. to pass on to workers' regulation of production.

The socialist state can arise only as a network of producers' and consumers' communes, which conscientiously keep account of their production and consumption, economise on labour, and steadily raise the productivity of labour, thus making it possible to reduce the working day to seven, six and even fewer hours. Nothing will be achieved unless the strictest, country-wide, comprehensive accounting and control of *grain* and the *production of grain* (and later of all other essential goods) are set going. Capitalism left us a legacy of mass organisations which can facilitate our transition to the mass accounting and control of the distribution of goods, namely, the consumers' co-operative societies. In Russia these societies are not so well developed as in the advanced countries, nevertheless, they have over ten million members. The Decree on Consumers' Co-operative Societies, issued the other day, is an extremely significant phenomenon, which strikingly illustrates the peculiar position and the specific tasks of the Soviet Socialist Republic at the present moment.

The decree is an agreement with the bourgeois co-operative societies and the workers' co-operative societies which still adhere to the bourgeois point of view. It is an agreement, or compromise, firstly because the representatives of the above-mentioned institutions not only took part in discussing the decree, but actually had a decisive say in the matter, for the parts of the decree which were strongly opposed by these institutions were dropped. Secondly, the essence of the compromise is that the Soviet government has abandoned the principle of admission of new members to co-operative societies without entrance fees (which is the only consistently proletarian principle); it has also abandoned the idea of uniting the whole population of a given locality in a *single* co-operative society. Contrary to this principle, which is the only socialist principle and which corresponds to the task of abolishing classes, the 'working-class co-operative societies' (which in this case call themselves 'class' societies only because they subordinate themselves to the class interests of the bourgeoisie) were given the right to continue to exist. Finally, the Soviet government's proposal to expel the bourgeoisie entirely from the boards of the co-operative societies was also considerably modified, and only owners of private capitalist trading and industrial enterprises were forbidden to serve on the boards.

Had the proletariat, acting through the Soviet government, managed to organise accounting and control on a national scale, or at least laid the foundation for such control, it would not have been necessary to make such compromises. Through the food departments of the Soviets, through the supply organisations under the Soviets we should have organised the population into a single co-operative society under proletarian management. We should have done this without the assistance of the bourgeois co-operative societies, without making any concession to the purely bourgeois principle which prompts the workers' co-operative societies to remain workers' societies *side by side* with bourgeois societies, *instead of* subordinating these bourgeois co-operative societies entirely to themselves, merging the two together and taking the *entire* management of the society and the supervision of the consumption of the rich *in their own* hands.

In concluding such an agreement with the bourgeois co-operative societies, the Soviet government concretely defined its tactical aims and its peculiar methods of action in the present stage of development as follows: by directing the bourgeois elements, utilising them, making certain partial concessions to them, we create the conditions for further progress that will be slower than we at first anticipated, but surer, with the base and lines of communication better secured and with the positions which have been won better consolidated. The Soviets can (*and should*) now gauge their successes in the field of socialist construction, among other things, by extremely clear, simple and practical standards, namely, in how many communities (communes or villages, or blocks of houses, etc) co-operative societies have been organised, and to what extent their development has reached the point of embracing the whole population.

Raising the Productivity of Labour

In every socialist revolution, after the proletariat has solved the problem of capturing power, and to the extent that the task of expropriating the expropriators and suppressing their resistance has been carried out in the main, there necessarily comes to the forefront the fundamental task of creating a social system superior to capitalism, namely, raising the productivity of labour, and in this connection (and for this purpose) securing better organisation of labour. Our Soviet state is precisely in the position where, thanks to the victories over the exploiters – from Kerensky to Kornilov – it is able to approach this task directly, to tackle it in earnest. And here it becomes immediately clear that while it is possible to take over the central government in a few days, while it is possible to suppress the military resistance (and sabotage) of the exploiters even in different parts of a great country in a few weeks, the capital solution of the problem of raising the productivity of labour requires, at all events (particularly after a most terrible and devastating war), several years. The protracted nature of the work is certainly dictated by objective circumstances.

The raising of the productivity of labour first of all requires that the material basis of large-scale industry shall be assured, namely, the development of the production of fuel, iron, the engineering and chemical industries. The Russian Soviet Republic enjoys the favourable position of having at its command, even after the Brest peace, enormous reserves of ore (in the Urals), fuel in Western Siberia (coal), in the Caucasus and the South-East (oil), in Central Russia (peat), enormous timber reserves, water power, raw materials for the chemical industry (Karabugaz), etc. The development of these natural resources by methods of modern technology will provide the basis for the unprecedented progress of the productive forces.

Another condition for raising the productivity of labour is, firstly, the raising of the educational and cultural level of the mass of the population. This is now taking place extremely rapidly, a fact which those who are blinded by bourgeois routine are unable to see; they are unable to understand what an urge towards enlightenment and initiative is now developing among the 'lower ranks' of the people thanks to the Soviet form of organisation. Secondly, a condition for economic revival is the raising of the working people's discipline, their skill, the effectiveness, the intensity of labour and its better organisation.

In this respect the situation is particularly bad and even hopeless if we are to believe those who have allowed themselves to be intimidated by the bourgeoisie or by those who are serving the bourgeoisie for their own ends. These people do not understand that there has not been, nor could there be, a revolution in which the supporters of the old system did not raise a howl about chaos, anarchy, etc. Naturally, among the people who have only just thrown off an unprecedentedly savage yoke there is deep and widespread seething and ferment; the working out of new principles of labour discipline by the people is a very protracted process, and this process could not even start until complete victory had been achieved over the landowners and the bourgeoisie.

We, however, without in the least yielding to the despair (it is often false despair) which is spread by the bourgeoisie and the bourgeois intellectuals (who have despaired of retaining their old privileges), must under no circumstances conceal an obvious evil. On the contrary, we shall expose it and intensify the Soviet methods of combating it, because the victory of socialism is inconceivable without the victory of proletarian conscious discipline over spontaneous petty-bourgeois anarchy, this real guarantee of a possible restoration of Kerenskyism and Kornilovism.

The more class-conscious vanguard of the Russian proletariat has already set itself the task of raising labour discipline. For example, both the Central Committee of the Metalworkers' Union and the Central Council of Trade Unions have begun to draft the necessary measures and decrees.[5] This work must be supported and pushed ahead with all speed. We must raise the question of piece-work[6] and apply and test it in practice; we must raise the question of applying much of what is scientific and progressive in the Taylor system; we must make wages correspond to the total amount of goods turned out, or to the amount of work done by the railways, the water transport system, etc, etc.

The Russian is a bad worker compared with people in advanced countries. It could not be otherwise under the tsarist regime and in view of the persistence of the hangover from serfdom. The task that the Soviet government must set the people in all its scope is – learn to work. The Taylor system, the last word of capitalism in this respect, like all capitalist progress, is a combination of the refined brutality of bourgeois exploitation and a number of the greatest scientific achievements in the field of analysing mechanical motions during work, the elimination of superfluous and awkward motions, the elaboration of correct methods of work, the introduction of the best system of accounting and control, etc. The Soviet Republic must at all costs adopt all that is valuable in the achievements of science and technology in this field. The possibility of building socialism depends exactly upon our success in combining the Soviet power and the Soviet organisation of administration with the up-to-date achievements of capitalism. We must organise in Russia the study and teaching of the Taylor system and systematically try it out and adapt it to our own ends. At the same time, in working to raise the productivity of labour, we must take into account the specific features of the transition period from capitalism to socialism, which, on the one hand, require that the foundations be laid of the socialist organisation of competition, and, on the other hand, require the use of compulsion, so that the slogan of the dictatorship of the proletariat shall not be desecrated by the practice of a lily-livered proletarian government.

The Organisation of Competition

Among the absurdities which the bourgeoisie are fond of spreading about socialism is the allegation that socialists deny the importance of competition. In fact, it is only socialism which, by abolishing classes, and, consequently, by abolishing the enslavement of the people, for the first time opens the way for competition on a really mass scale. And it is precisely the Soviet form of organisation, by ensuring transition from the formal democracy of the bourgeois republic to real participation of the mass of working people in *administration*, that for the first time puts competition on a broad basis. It is much easier to organise this in the political field than in the economic field; but for the success of socialism, it is the economic field that matters.

Take, for example, a means of organising competition such as publicity. The bourgeois republic ensures publicity only formally; in practice, it subordinates the press to capital, entertains the 'mob' with sensationalist political trash and conceals what takes place in the workshops, in commercial transactions, contracts, etc, behind a veil of 'trade secrets', which protect 'the sacred right of property'. The Soviet government has abolished trade secrets[7]; it has taken a new path; but we have done hardly anything to utilise publicity for the purpose of encouraging economic competition. While ruthlessly suppressing the thoroughly mendacious and insolently slanderous bourgeois press, we must set to work systematically to create a press that will not entertain and fool the people with political sensation and trivialities, but which will submit the questions of everyday economic life to the people's judgement and assist in the serious study of these questions. Every factory, every village is a producers' and consumers' commune, whose right and duty it is to apply the general Soviet laws in their own way ('in their own way', not in the sense of violating them, but in the sense that they can apply them in various forms) and in their own way to solve the problem of accounting in the production and distribution of goods. Under capitalism, this was the 'private affair' of the individual capitalist, landowner or kulak. Under the Soviet system, it is not a private affair, but a most important affair of state.

We have scarcely yet started on the enormous, difficult but rewarding task of organising competition between communes, of introducing accounting and publicity in the process of the production of grain, clothes and other things, of transforming dry, dead, bureaucratic accounts into living examples, some repulsive, others attractive. Under the capitalist mode of production, the significance of individual example, say the example of a co-operative workshop, was inevitably very much restricted, and only those imbued with petty-bourgeois illusions could dream of 'correcting' capitalism through the example of virtuous institutions. After political power has passed to the proletariat, after the expropriators have been expropriated, the situation radically changes and – as prominent socialists have repeatedly pointed out – force of example for the first time is able to influence the people. Model communes must and will serve as educators, teachers, helping to raise the backward communes. The press must serve as an instrument of socialist construction, give publicity to the successes achieved by the model communes in all their details, must study the causes of these successes, the methods of management these communes employ, and, on the other hand, must put on the 'black list' those communes which persist in the 'traditions of capitalism', i.e. anarchy, laziness, disorder and profiteering. In capitalist society, statistics were entirely a matter for 'government servants', or for narrow specialists; we must carry statistics to the people and make them popular so that the working people themselves may gradually learn to understand and see how long and in what way it is necessary to work, how much time and in what way one may rest, so that *the comparison of the business results* of the various communes may become a matter of general interest and study, and that the most outstanding communes may be rewarded immediately (by reducing the working day, raising remuneration, placing a larger amount of cultural or aesthetic facilities or values at their disposal, etc).

When a new class comes on to the historical scene as the leader and guide of society, a period of violent 'rocking', shocks, struggle and storm, on the one hand, and a period of uncertain steps, experiments, wavering, hesitation in regard to the selection of new methods corresponding to new objective circumstances, on the other, are inevitable. The moribund feudal nobility avenged themselves on the bourgeoisie which vanquished them and took their place, not only by conspiracies and attempts at rebellion and restoration, but also by pouring ridicule over the lack of skill, the clumsiness and the mistakes of the 'upstarts' and the 'insolent' who dared to take over the 'sacred helm' of state without the centuries of training which the princes, barons, nobles and dignitaries had had; in exactly the same way the Kornilovs and Kerenskys, the Gotzes and Martovs, the whole of that fraternity of heroes of bourgeois swindling or bourgeois scepticism, avenge themselves on the working class of Russia for having had the 'audacity' to take power.

Of course, not weeks, but long months and years are required for a new social class, especially a class which up to now has been oppressed and crushed by poverty and ignorance, to get used to its new position, look around, organise its work and promote its *own* organisers. It is understandable that the Party which leads the revolutionary proletariat has not been able to acquire the experience and habits of large organisational undertakings embracing millions and tens of millions of citizens; the remoulding of the old, almost exclusively agitators' habits is a very lengthy process. But there is nothing impossible in this, and as soon as the necessity for a change is clearly appreciated, as soon as there is firm determination to effect the change and perseverance in pursuing a great and difficult aim, we shall achieve it. There is an enormous amount of organising talent among the 'people', i.e. among the workers and the peasants who do not exploit the labour of others. Capital crushed these talented people in thousands; it killed their talent and threw them on to the scrap-heap. We are not yet able to find them, encourage them, put them on their feet, promote them. But we shall learn to do so if we set about it with all-out revolutionary enthusiasm, without which there can be no victorious revolutions.

No profound and mighty popular movement has ever occurred in history without dirty scum rising to the top, without adventurers and rogues, boasters and ranters attaching themselves to the inexperienced innovators, without absurd muddle and fuss, without individual 'leaders' trying to deal with twenty matters at once and not finishing any of them. Let the lap-dogs of bourgeois society, from Belorussov to Martov, squeal and yelp about every extra chip that is sent flying in cutting down the big, old wood. What else are lap-dogs for if not to yelp at the proletarian elephant? Let them yelp. We shall go our way and try as carefully and as patiently as possible to test and discover real organisers, people with sober and practical minds, people who combine loyalty to socialism with ability without fuss (and in spite of muddle and fuss) to get a large number of people working together steadily and concertedly within the framework of Soviet organisation. *Only* such people, after they have been tested a dozen times, by being transferred from the simplest to the more difficult tasks, should be promoted to the responsible posts of leaders of the people's labour, leaders of administration. We have not yet learned to do this, but we shall learn.

'Harmonious Organisation' and Dictatorship

The resolution adopted by the recent Moscow Congress of Soviets advanced as the primary task of the moment the establishment of a 'harmonious organisation', and the tightening of discipline.[8] Everyone now readily 'votes for' and 'subscribes to' resolutions of this kind; but usually people do not think over the fact that the application of such resolutions calls for coercion – coercion precisely in the form of dictatorship. And yet it would be extremely stupid and absurdly utopian to assume that the transition from capitalism to socialism is possible without coercion and without dictatorship. Marx's theory very definitely opposed this petty-bourgeois-democratic and anarchist absurdity long ago. And Russia of 1917-18 confirms the correctness of Marx's theory in this respect so strikingly, palpably and imposingly that only those who are hopelessly dull or who have obstinately decided to turn their backs on the truth can be under any misapprehension concerning this. Either the dictatorship of Kornilov (if we take him as the Russian type of bourgeois Cavaignac), or the dictatorship of the proletariat – any other choice is *out of the question* for a country which is developing at an extremely rapid rate with extremely sharp turns and amidst desperate ruin created by one of the most horrible wars in history. Every solution that offers a middle path is either a deception of the people by the bourgeoisie – for the bourgeoisie dare not tell the truth, dare not say that they need Kornilov – or an expression of the dull-wittedness of the petty-bourgeois democrats, of the Chernovs, Tseretelis and Martovs, who chatter about the unity of democracy, the dictatorship of democracy, the general democratic front, and similar nonsense. Those whom even the progress of the Russian Revolution of 1917-18 has not taught that a middle course is impossible, must be given up for lost.

On the other hand, it is not difficult to see that during every transition from capitalism to socialism, dictatorship is necessary for two main reasons, or along two main channels. Firstly, capitalism cannot be defeated and eradicated without the ruthless suppression of the resistance of the exploiters, who cannot at once be deprived of their wealth, of their advantages of organisation and knowledge, and consequently for a fairly long period will inevitably try to overthrow the hated rule of the poor; secondly, every great revolution, and a socialist revolution in particular, even if there is no external war, is inconceivable without internal war, i.e. civil war, which is even more devastating than external war, and involves thousands and millions of cases of wavering and desertion from one side to another, implies a state of extreme indefiniteness, lack of equilibrium and chaos. And of course, all the elements of disintegration of the old society, which are inevitably very numerous and connected mainly with the petty bourgeoisie (because it is the petty bourgeoisie that every war and every crisis ruins and destroys first), are bound to 'reveal themselves' during such a profound revolution. And these elements of disintegration *cannot* 'reveal themselves' otherwise than in an increase of crime, hooliganism, corruption, profiteering and outrages of every kind. To put these down requires time and *requires an iron hand*.

There has not been a single great revolution in history in which the people did not instinctively realise this and did not show salutary firmness by shooting thieves on the spot. The misfortune of previous revolutions was that the revolutionary enthusiasm of the people, which sustained them in their state of tension and gave them the strength to suppress ruthlessly the elements of disintegration, did not last long. The social, i.e. the class, reason for this instability of the revolutionary enthusiasm of the people was the weakness of the proletariat, which *alone* is able (if it is sufficiently numerous, class-conscious and disciplined) to win over to its side *the majority* of the working and exploited people (the majority of the poor, to speak more simply and popularly) and retain power sufficiently long to suppress completely all the exploiters as well as all the elements of disintegration.

It was this historical experience of all revolutions, it was this world-historic – economic and political – lesson that Marx summed up when he gave his short, sharp, concise and expressive formula: dictatorship of the proletariat. And the fact that the Russian revolution has been correct in its approach to this world-historic task *has been proved* by the victorious progress of the Soviet form of organisation among all the peoples and tongues of Russia. For Soviet power is nothing but an organisational form of the dictatorship of the proletariat, the dictatorship of the advanced class, which raises to a new democracy and to independent participation in the administration of the state tens upon tens of millions of working and exploited people, who by their own experience learn to regard the disciplined and class-conscious vanguard of the proletariat as their most reliable leader.

Dictatorship, however, is a big word, and big words should not be thrown about carelessly. Dictatorship is iron rule, government that is revolutionarily bold, swift and ruthless in suppressing both exploiters and hooligans. But our government is excessively mild, very often it resembles jelly more than iron. We must not forget for a moment that the bourgeois and petty-bourgeois element is fighting against the Soviet system in two ways; on the one hand, it is operating from without, by the methods of the Savinkovs, Gotzes, Gegechkoris and Kornilovs, by conspiracies and rebellions, and by their filthy 'ideological' reflection, the flood of lies and slander in the Constitutional-Democratic, Right Socialist-Revolutionary and Menshevik press; on the other hand, this element operates from within and takes advantage of every manifestation of disintegration, of every weakness, in order to bribe, to increase indiscipline, laxity and chaos. The nearer we approach the complete military suppression of the bourgeoisie, the more dangerous does the element of petty-bourgeois anarchy become. And the fight against this element cannot be waged solely with the aid of propaganda and agitation, solely by organising competition and by selecting organisers. The struggle must also be waged by means of coercion.

As the fundamental task of the government becomes, not military suppression, but administration, the typical manifestation of suppression and compulsion will be, not shooting on the spot, but trial by court. In this respect also the revolutionary people after October 25, 1917 took the right path and demonstrated the viability of the revolution by setting up their own workers' and peasants' courts, even before the decrees dissolving the bourgeois bureaucratic judiciary were passed. But our revolutionary and people's courts are extremely, incredibly weak. One feels that we have not yet done away with the people's attitude towards the courts as towards something official and alien, an attitude inherited from the yoke of the landowners and of the bourgeoisie. It is not yet sufficiently realised that the courts are an organ which enlists precisely the poor, every one of them, in the work of state administration (for the work of the courts is one of the functions of state administration), that the courts are an *organ of the power* of the proletariat and of the poor peasants, that the courts are an instrument *for inculcating discipline*. There is not yet sufficient appreciation of the simple and obvious fact that if the principal misfortunes of Russia at the present time are hunger and unemployment, these misfortunes cannot be overcome by spurts, but only by comprehensive, all-embracing, country-wide organisation and discipline in order to increase the output of bread for the people and bread for industry (fuel), to transport these in good time to the places where they are required, and to distribute them properly; and it is not fully appreciated that, consequently, it is *those* who violate labour discipline at any factory, in any undertaking, in any matter, who are *responsible* for the sufferings caused by the famine and unemployment, that we must know how to find the guilty ones, to bring them to trial and ruthlessly punish them. Where the petty-bourgeois anarchy against which we must now wage a most persistent struggle makes itself felt is in the failure to appreciate the economic and political connection between famine and unemployment, on the one hand, and general laxity in matters of organisation and discipline, on the other – in the tenacity of the *small-proprietor* outlook, namely, I'll grab all I can for myself; the rest can go hang.

In the rail transport service, which perhaps most strikingly embodies the economic ties of an organism created by large-scale capitalism, the struggle between the element of petty-bourgeois laxity and proletarian organisation is particularly evident. The 'administrative' elements provide a host of saboteurs and bribe-takers; the best part of the proletarian elements fight for discipline; but among both elements there are, of course, many waverers and 'weak' characters who are unable to withstand the 'temptation' of profiteering, bribery, personal gain obtained by spoiling the whole apparatus, upon the proper working of which the victory over famine and unemployment depends.

The struggle that has been developing around the recent

decree on the management of the railways, the decree which grants individual executives dictatorial powers (or 'unlimited' powers),[9] is characteristic. The conscious (and to a large extent, probably, unconscious) representatives of petty-bourgeois laxity would like to see in this granting of 'unlimited' (i.e. dictatorial) powers to individuals a departure from the collegiate principle, from democracy and from the principles of Soviet government. Here and there, among Left Socialist-Revolutionaries, a positively hooligan agitation, i.e. agitation appealing to the base instincts and to the small proprietor's urge to 'grab all he can', has been developed against the dictatorship decree. The question has become one of really enormous significance. Firstly, the question of principle, namely, is the appointment of individuals, dictators with unlimited powers, in general compatible with the fundamental principles of Soviet government? Secondly, what relation has this case – this precedent, if you will – to the special tasks of government in the present concrete situation? We must deal very thoroughly with both these questions.

That in the history of revolutionary movements the dictatorship of individuals was very often the expression, the vehicle, the channel of the dictatorship of the revolutionary classes has been shown by the irrefutable experience of history. Undoubtedly, the dictatorship of individuals was compatible with bourgeois democracy. On this point, however, the bourgeois denigrators of the Soviet system, as well as their petty-bourgeois henchmen, always display sleight of hand: on the one hand, they declare the Soviet system to be something absurd, anarchistic and savage, and carefully pass over in silence all our historical examples and theoretical arguments which prove that the Soviets are a higher form of democracy, and what is more, the beginning of a *socialist* form of democracy; on the other hand, they demand of us a higher democracy than bourgeois democracy and say: personal dictatorship is absolutely incompatible with your, Bolshevik (i.e. not bourgeois, but *socialist*), Soviet democracy.

These are exceedingly poor arguments. If we are not anarchists, we must admit that the state, *that is, coercion*, is necessary for the transition from capitalism to socialism. The form of coercion is determined by the degree of development of the given revolutionary class, and also by special circumstances, such as, for example, the legacy of a long and reactionary war and the forms of resistance put up by the bourgeoisie and the petty bourgeoisie. There is, therefore, absolutely *no* contradiction in principle between Soviet (*that is*, socialist) democracy and the exercise of dictatorial powers by individuals. The difference between proletarian dictatorship and bourgeois dictatorship is that the former strikes at the exploiting minority in the interests of the exploited majority, and that it is exercised – *also through individuals* – not only by the working and exploited people, but also by organisations which are built in such a way as to rouse these people to history-making activity. (The Soviet organisations are organisations of this kind.)

In regard to the second question, concerning the significance of individual dictatorial powers from the point of view of the specific tasks of the present moment, it must be said that large-scale machine industry – which is precisely the material source, the productive source, the foundation of socialism – calls for absolute and strict *unity of will*, which directs the joint labours of hundreds, thousands and tens of thousands of people. The technical, economic and historical necessity of this is obvious, and all those who have thought about socialism have always regarded it as one of the conditions of socialism. But how can strict unity of will be ensured? By thousands subordinating their will to the will of one.

Given ideal class-consciousness and discipline on the part of those participating in the common work, this subordination would be something like the mild leadership of a conductor of an orchestra. It may assume the sharp forms of a dictatorship if ideal discipline and class-consciousness are lacking. But be that as it may, *unquestioning subordination* to a single will is absolutely necessary for the success of processes organised on the pattern of large-scale machine industry. On the railways it is twice and three times as necessary. In this transition from one political task to another, which *on the surface* is totally dissimilar to the first, lies the whole originality of the present situation. The revolution has only just smashed the oldest, strongest and heaviest of fetters, to which the people submitted under duress. That was yesterday. Today, however, the same revolution demands – precisely in the interests of its development and consolidation, precisely in the interests of socialism – that the people *unquestioningly obey the single will* of the leaders of labour. Of course, such a transition cannot be made at one step. Clearly, it can be achieved only as a result of tremendous jolts, shocks, reversions to old ways, the enormous exertion of effort on the part of the proletarian vanguard, which is leading the people to the new ways. Those who drop into the philistine hysterics of *Novaya Zhizn* or *Vperyod*, *Dyelo Naroda* or *Nash Vek*[10] do not stop to think about this.

Take the psychology of the average, ordinary representative of the toiling and exploited masses, compare it with the objective, material conditions of his life in society. Before the October Revolution he did *not* see a single instance of the propertied, exploiting classes making any real sacrifice for him, giving up anything for his benefit. He did *not* see them giving him the land and liberty that had been repeatedly promised him, giving him peace, sacrificing 'Great Power' interests and the interests of Great Power secret treaties, sacrificing capital and profits. He saw this only *after* October 25, 1917, when he took it himself by force, and had to defend by force what he had taken, against the Kerenskys, Gotzes, Gegechkoris, Dutovs and Kornilovs. Naturally, for a certain time, all his attention, all his thoughts, all his spiritual strength, were concentrated on taking a breath, on unbending his back, on straightening his shoulders, on taking the blessings of life that were there for the taking, and that had always been denied him by the now overthrown exploiters. Of course, a certain amount of time is required to enable the ordinary working man not only to see for himself, not only to become convinced, but also to feel that he cannot simply 'take', snatch, grab things, that this leads to increased disruption, to ruin, to the return of the Kornilovs. The corresponding change in the conditions of life (and consequently in the psychology) of the ordinary working men is only just beginning. And our whole task, the task of the Communist Party (Bolsheviks), which is the class-conscious spokesman for the strivings of the exploited for emancipation, is to appreciate this change, to understand that it is necessary, to stand at the head of the exhausted people who are wearily seeking a way out and lead them along the path of co-ordinating the task of arguing at mass meetings *about* the conditions of work with the task of unquestioningly obeying the will of the Soviet leader, of the dictator, *during* the work.

The 'mania for meetings' is an object of the ridicule, and still more often of the spiteful hissing of the bourgeoisie, the Mensheviks, the *Novaya Zhizn* people, who see only the chaos, the confusion and the outbursts of small-proprietor egoism. But without the discussions at public meetings the mass of the oppressed could never have changed from the discipline forced upon them by the exploiters to conscious, voluntary discipline. The airing of questions at public meetings is the genuine democracy of the working people, their way of unbending their backs, their awakening to a new life, their first steps along the road which they themselves have cleared of vipers (the exploiters, the imperialists, the landowners and capitalists) and which they want to learn to build themselves, in their own way, for themselves, on the principles of their own *Soviet*, and not alien, not aristocratic, not bourgeois rule. It required precisely the October victory of the working people over the exploiters, it required a whole historical period in which the working people themselves could first of all discuss the new conditions of life and the new tasks, in order to make possible the durable transition to superior forms of labour discipline, to the conscious appreciation of the necessity for the dictatorship of the proletariat, to unquestioning obedience to the orders of individual representatives of the Soviet government during the work.

This transition has now begun.

We have successfully fulfilled the first task of the revolution; we have seen how the mass of working people evolved in themselves the fundamental condition for its success: they united their efforts against the exploiters in order to overthrow them. Stages like that of October 1905, February and October 1917 are of world-historic significance.

We have successfully fulfilled the second task of the

revolution: to awaken, to raise those very 'lower ranks' of society whom the exploiters had pushed down, and who only after October 25, 1917 obtained complete freedom to overthrow the exploiters and to begin to take stock of things and arrange life in their own way. The airing of questions at public meetings by the most oppressed and downtrodden, by the least educated mass of working people, their coming over to the side of the Bolsheviks, their setting up everywhere of their own Soviet organisations – this was the second great stage of the revolution.

The third stage is now beginning. We must consolidate what we ourselves have won, what we ourselves have decreed, made law, discussed, planned – consolidate all this in stable forms of *everyday labour discipline*. This is the most difficult, but the most gratifying task, because only its fulfilment will give us a socialist system. We must learn to combine the 'public meeting' democracy of the working people – turbulent, surging, overflowing its banks like a spring flood – with *iron* discipline while at work, with *unquestioning obedience* to the will of a single person, the Soviet leader, while at work.

We have not yet learned to do this.

We shall learn it.

Yesterday we were menaced by the restoration of bourgeois exploitation, personified by the Kornilovs, Gotzes, Dutovs, Gegechkoris and Bogayevskys. We conquered them. This restoration, this very same restoration menaces us today in another form, in the form of the element of petty-bourgeois laxity and anarchism, or small-proprietor 'it's not my business' psychology, in the form of the daily, petty, but numerous sorties and attacks of this element against proletarian discipline. We must, and we shall, vanquish this element of petty-bourgeois anarchy.

The Development of Soviet Organisation

The socialist character of Soviet, i.e. *proletarian*, democracy, as concretely applied today, lies first in the fact that the electors are the working and exploited people; the bourgeoisie is excluded. Secondly, it lies in the fact that all bureaucratic formalities and restrictions of elections are abolished; the people themselves determine the order and time of elections, and are completely free to recall any elected person. Thirdly, it lies in the creation of the best mass organisation of the vanguard of the working people, i.e. the proletariat engaged in large-scale industry, which enables it to lead the vast mass of the exploited, to draw them into independent political life, to educate them politically by their own experience; therefore for the first time a start is made by the *entire* population in learning the art of administration, and in beginning to administer.

These are the principal distinguishing features of the democracy now applied in Russia, which is a higher *type* of democracy, a break with the bourgeois distortion of democracy, transition to socialist democracy and to the conditions in which the state can begin to wither away.

It goes without saying that the element of petty-bourgeois disorganisation (which must *inevitably* be apparent to some extent in *every* proletarian revolution, and which is especially apparent in our revolution, owing to the petty-bourgeois character of our country, its backwardness and the consequences of a reactionary war) cannot but leave its impress upon the Soviets as well.

We must work unremittingly to develop the organisation of the Soviets and of the Soviet government. There is a petty-bourgeois tendency to transform the members of the Soviets into 'parliamentarians', or else into bureaucrats. We must combat this by drawing *all* the members of the Soviets into the practical work of administration. In many places the departments of the Soviets are gradually merging with the Commissariats. Our aim is to draw *the whole of the poor* into the practical work of administration, and all steps that are taken in this direction – the more varied they are, the better – should be carefully recorded, studied, systematised, tested by wider experience and embodied in law. Our aim is to ensure that *every* toiler, having finished his eight hours' 'task' in productive labour, shall perform state duties *without pay*; the transition to this is particularly difficult, but this transition alone can guarantee the final consolidation of socialism. Naturally, the novelty and difficulty of the change lead to an abundance of steps being taken, as it were, gropingly, to an abundance of mistakes, vacillation –

without this, any marked progress is impossible. The reason why the present position seems peculiar to many of those who would like to be regarded as socialists is that they have been accustomed to contrasting capitalism with socialism abstractly, and that they profoundly put between the two the word 'leap' (some of them, recalling fragments of what they have read of Engels's writings, still more profoundly add the phrase 'leap from the realm of necessity into the realm of freedom')[11]. The majority of these so-called socialists, who have 'read in books' about socialism but who have never seriously thought over the matter, are unable to consider that by 'leap' the teachers of socialism meant turning-points on a world-historical scale, and that leaps of this kind extend over decades and even longer periods. Naturally, in such times, the notorious 'intelligentsia' provides an infinite number of mourners of the dead. Some mourn over the Constituent Assembly, others mourn over bourgeois discipline, others again mourn over the capitalist system, still others mourn over the cultured landowner, and still others again mourn over imperialist Great Power policy, etc, etc.

The real interest of the epoch of great leaps lies in the fact that the abundance of fragments of the old, which sometimes accumulate more rapidly than the rudiments (not always immediately discernible) of the new, calls for the ability to discern what is most important in the line or chain of development. History knows moments when the most important thing for the success of the revolution is to heap up as large a quantity of the fragments as possible, i.e. to blow up as many of the old institutions as possible; moments arise when enough has been blown up and the next task is to perform the 'prosaic' (for the petty-bourgeois revolutionary, the 'boring') task of clearing away the fragments; and moments arise when the careful nursing of the rudiments of the new system, which are growing amidst the wreckage on a soil which as yet has been badly cleared of rubble, is the most important thing.

It is not enough to be a revolutionary and an adherent of socialism or a Communist in general. You must be able at each particular moment to find the particular link in the chain which you must grasp with all your might in order to hold the whole chain and to prepare firmly for the transition to the next link; the order of the links, their form, the manner in which they are linked together, the way they differ from each other in the historical chain of events, are not as simple and not as meaningless as those in an ordinary chain made by a smith.

The fight against the bureaucratic distortion of the Soviet form of organisation is assured by the firmness of the connection between the Soviets and the 'people', meaning by that the working and exploited people, and by the flexibility and elasticity of this connection. Even in the most democratic capitalist republics in the world, the poor never regard the bourgeois parliament as 'their' institution. But the Soviets are 'theirs' and not alien institutions to the mass of workers and peasants. The modern 'Social-Democrats' of the Scheidemann or, what is almost the same thing, of the Martov type are repelled by the Soviets, and they are drawn towards the respectable bourgeois parliament, or to the Constituent Assembly, in the same way as Turgenev, sixty years ago, was drawn towards a moderate monarchist and noblemen's Constitution and was repelled by the peasant democracy of Dobrolyubov and Chernyshevsky.[12]

It is the closeness of the Soviets to the 'people', to the working people, that creates the special forms of recall and other means of control from below which must be most zealously developed now. For example, the Councils of Public Education, as periodical conferences of Soviet electors and their delegates called to discuss and control the activities of the Soviet authorities in this field, deserve full sympathy and support. Nothing could be sillier than to transform the Soviets into something congealed and self-contained. The more resolutely we now have to stand for a ruthlessly firm government, for the dictatorship of individuals *in definite processes of work*, in definite aspects of *purely executive* functions, the more varied must be the forms and methods of control from below in order to counteract every shadow of a possibility of distorting the principles of Soviet government, in order repeatedly and tirelessly to weed out bureaucracy.

Conclusion

An extraordinarily difficult, complex and dangerous situation in international affairs; the necessity of manoeuvring and retreating; a period of waiting for new outbreaks of the revolution which is maturing in the West at a painfully slow pace; within the country a period of slow construction and ruthless 'tightening up', of prolonged and persistent struggle waged by stern, proletarian discipline against the menacing element of petty-bourgeois laxity and anarchy – these in brief are the distinguishing features of the special stage of the socialist revolution in which we are now living. This is the link in the historical chain of events which we must at present grasp with all our might in order to prove equal to the tasks that confront us before passing to the next link to which we are drawn by a special brightness, the brightness of the victories of the international proletarian revolution.

Try to compare with the ordinary everyday concept 'revolutionary' the slogans that follow from the specific conditions of the present stage, namely, manoeuvre, retreat, wait, build slowly, ruthlessly tighten up, rigorously discipline, smash laxity.... Is it surprising that when certain 'revolutionaries' hear this they are seized with noble indignation and begin to 'thunder' abuse at us for forgetting the traditions of the October Revolution, for compromising with the bourgeois experts, for compromising with the bourgeoisie, for being petty bourgeois, reformists, and so on and so forth?

The misfortune of these sorry 'revolutionaries' is that even those of them who are prompted by the best motives in the world and are absolutely loyal to the cause of socialism fail to understand the particular, and particularly 'unpleasant', condition that a backward country, which has been lacerated by a reactionary and disastrous war and which began the socialist revolution long before the more advanced countries, inevitably has to pass through; they lack stamina in the difficult moments of a difficult transition. Naturally, it is the 'Left Socialist-Revolutionaries' who are acting as an 'official' opposition of *this* kind against our Party. Of course, there are and always will be individual exceptions from group and class types. But social types remain. In the land in which the small-proprietor population greatly predominates over the purely proletarian population, the difference between the proletarian revolutionary and petty-bourgeois revolutionary will inevitably make itself felt, and from time to time will make itself felt very sharply. The petty-bourgeois revolutionary wavers and vacillates at every turn of events; he is an ardent revolutionary in March 1917 and praises 'coalition' in May, hates the Bolsheviks (or laments over their 'adventurism') in July and apprehensively turns away from them at the end of October, supports them in December, and, finally, in March and April 1918 such types, more often than not, turn up their noses contemptuously and say: 'I am not one of those who sing hymns to "organic" work, to practicalness and gradualism'.

The social origin of such types is the small proprietor, who has been driven to frenzy by the horrors of war, by sudden ruin, by unprecedented torments of famine and devastation, who hysterically rushes about seeking a way out, seeking salvation, places his confidence in the proletariat and supports it one moment and the next gives way to fits of despair. We must clearly understand and firmly remember the fact that socialism cannot be built on such a social basis. The only class that can lead the working and exploited people is the class that unswervingly follows its path without losing courage and without giving way to despair even at the most difficult, arduous and dangerous stages. Hysterical impulses are of no use to us. What we need is the steady advance of the iron battalions of the proletariat.

Notes

[1] See CW XXVII, p 200 – *ed*.

[2] Bogayevsky was a counter-revolutionary leader in the Don area, who surrendered in spring 1918 – *ed*.

[3] Controls over foreign trade were initiated in the early days of Soviet power, but by December 1917, Lenin was proposing a total state monopoly. This was introduced by a decree of the Council of People's Commissars on 22 April 1918 – *ed*.

[4] In the early months of Soviet power, special taxes and indemnities were a major source of state revenue. Once Soviet power became more

firmly established there was a need for a regular system of taxation. In June 1918 a decree was passed instituting a rigorous income and property tax – *ed*.

[5] After a number of consultations, the Presidium of the Supreme Economic Council of Trade Unions drew up a general statute on labour discipline. The draft drawn up by them, and amended by Lenin, was published in the magazine *Narodnoye Khozyaistvo* in April 1918. The statute called for increased productivity in state-owned enterprises through output quotas, bonuses, and the introduction of piece-work. It also called for strong labour discipline, to be reinforced by stern action against transgressors. The Central Committee of the Metalworkers Union had urged the introduction of the piece-work system into the statute, and was one of the first to introduce the system into industry – *ed*.

[6] After October 1917 piece work had been largely replaced by payment based on the amount of time worked; but this had adversely affected productivity and labour discipline. Hence there was a rethinking and a reintroduction of piece rates, which were officially endorsed in the Soviet Labour Code of December 1918 – *ed*.

[7] Commercial secrecy – the right to keep secret all production, trade and financial operations – was abolished by the Soviet government on November 14 (27), 1917. This was seen as an important measure for making workers' control effective. Lenin outlined the arguments against such secrecy in the *Impending Catastrophe and How to Combat it*. See pp 192-6 in this book – *ed*.

[8] This was the Extraordinary Fourth All-Russian Congress of Soviets which was held from March 14 to 16, 1918. The main purpose of the Congress was to decide the question of the ratification of the treaty of Brest-Litovsk – *ed*.

[9] The decree referred to was 'On the Centralisation of Management, Protection on Roads and The Improvement of their Carrying Capacity', 26 March, 1918. It centralised powers over the railway system under the individual control of a Commissar for Communication. This was opposed by the railway workers executive who were unhappy that control was being taken from them – *ed*.

[10] These were Menshevik and Cadet papers – *ed*.

[11] Lenin is referring to Engels's *Anti-Duhring* (Lawrence and Wishart 1975, p 336) – *ed*.

[12] Turgenev's position was described by Chernyshevsky in an account of a conversation between the two men in the 1860s which appeared in 'An Expression of Gratitude', *Chernyshevsky Collected Works*, Vol 10, Russian edition, Moscow 1951, pp 122-23 – *ed*.

8. Speech at the First Congress of Economic Councils

Comrades, permit me first of all to greet the Congress of Economic Councils in the name of the Council of People's Commissars.[1]

Comrades, the Supreme Economic Council now has a difficult, but a most rewarding task. There is not the slightest doubt that the further the gains of the October Revolution go, the more profound the upheaval it started becomes, the more firmly the socialist revolution's gains become established and the socialist system becomes consolidated, the greater and higher will become the role of the Economic Councils, which alone of all the state institutions are to endure. And their position will become all the more durable the closer we approach the establishment of the socialist system and the less need there will be for a purely administrative apparatus, for an apparatus which is solely engaged in administration. After the resistance of the exploiters has been finally broken, after the working people have learned to organise socialist production, this apparatus of administration in the proper, strict, narrow sense of the word, this apparatus of the old state, is doomed to die; while the apparatus of the type of the Supreme Economic Council is destined to grow, to develop and become strong, performing all the main activities of organised society.

That is why, comrades, when I look at the experience of our Supreme Economic Council and of the local councils, with the activities of which it is closely and inseparably

Newspaper report published in *Izvestia* May 28, 1918.
CW XXVII 408-415.

connected, I think that, in spite of much that is unfinished, incomplete and unorganised, we have not even the slightest grounds for pessimistic conclusions. For the task which the Supreme Economic Council sets itself, and the task which all the regional and local councils set themselves, is so enormous, so all-embracing, that there is absolutely nothing that gives rise to alarm in what we all observe. Very often – of course, from our point of view, perhaps too often – the proverb 'measure thrice and cut once' has not been applied. Unfortunately, things are not so simple in regard to the organisation of the economy on socialist lines as they are expressed in that proverb.

With the transition of all power – this time not only political and not even mainly political, but economic power, that is, power that affects the deepest foundations of everyday human existence – to a new class, and, moreover, to a class which for the first time in the history of humanity is the leader of the overwhelming majority of the population, of the whole mass of the working and exploited people – our tasks become more complicated.

It goes without saying that in view of the supreme importance and the supreme difficulty of the organisational tasks that confront us, when we must organise the deepest foundations of the existence of hundreds of millions of people on entirely new lines, it is impossible to arrange matters as simply as in the proverb 'measure thrice and cut once'. We, indeed, are not in a position to measure a thing innumerable times and then cut out and fix what has been finally measured and fitted. We must build our economic edifice as we go along, trying out various institutions, watching their work, testing them by the collective common experience of the working people, and, above all, by the results of their work. We must do this as we go along, and, moreover, in a situation of desperate struggle and frenzied resistance by the exploiters, whose frenzy grows the nearer we come to the time when we can pull out the last bad teeth of capitalist exploitation. It is understandable that if even within a brief period we have to alter the types, the regulations and the bodies of administration in various branches of the national economy several times, there are not the slightest grounds for pessimism in these conditions, although, of course, this gives considerable grounds for malicious outbursts on the part of the bourgeoisie and the exploiters, whose best feelings are hurt. Of course, those who take too close and too direct a part in this work, say, the Chief Water Board, do not always find it pleasant to alter the regulations, the norms and the laws of administration three times; the pleasure obtained from work of this kind cannot be great. But if we abstract ourselves somewhat from the direct unpleasantness of extremely frequent alteration of decrees, and if we look a little deeper and further into the enormous world-historic task that the Russian proletariat has to carry out with the aid of its own still inadequate forces, it will become immediately understandable that even far more numerous alterations and testing in practice of various systems of administration and various forms of discipline are inevitable; that in such a gigantic task, we could never claim, and no sensible socialist who has ever written on the prospects of the future ever even thought, that we could immediately establish and compose the forms of organisation of the new society according to some predetermined instruction and at one stroke.

All that we knew, all that the best experts on capitalist society, the greatest minds who foresaw its development, exactly indicated to us was that transformation was historically inevitable and must proceed along a certain main line, that private ownership of the means of production was doomed by history, that it would burst, that the exploiters would inevitably be expropriated. This was established with scientific precision, and we knew this when we grasped the banner of socialism, when we declared ourselves socialists, when we founded socialist parties, when we transformed society. We knew this when we took power for the purpose of proceeding with socialist reorganisation; but we could not know the forms of transformation, or the rate of development of the concrete reorganisation. Collective experience, the experience of millions can alone give us decisive guidance in this respect, precisely because, for our task, for the task of building socialism, the experience of the hundreds and hundreds of thousands of those upper sections which have made history up to now in feudal society and in capitalist society is insufficient. We cannot proceed in this way precisely because we rely on joint experience, on the experience of millions of working people.

We know, therefore, that organisation, which is the main and fundamental task of the Soviets, will inevitably entail a vast number of experiments, a vast number of steps, a vast number of alterations, a vast number of difficulties, particularly in regard to the question of how to fit every person into his proper place, because we have no experience of this; here we have to devise every step ourselves, and the more serious the mistakes we make on this path, the more the certainty will grow that with every increase in the membership of the trade unions, with every additional thousand, with every additional hundred thousand that come over from the camp of working people, of exploited, who have hitherto lived according to tradition and habit, into the camp of the builders of Soviet organisations, the number of people who should prove suitable and organise the work on proper lines is increasing.

Take one of the secondary tasks that the Economic Council – the Supreme Economic Council – comes up against with particular frequency, the task of utilising bourgeois experts. We all know, at least those who take their stand on the basis of science and socialism, that this task can be fulfilled only when – that this task can be fulfilled only to the extent that international capitalism has developed the material and technical prerequisites of labour, organised on an enormous scale and based on science, and hence on the training of an enormous number of scientifically educated specialists. We know that without this socialism is impossible. If we reread the works of those socialists who have observed the development of capitalism during the last half-century, and who have again and again come to the conclusion that socialism is inevitable, we shall find that all of them without exception have pointed out that socialism alone will liberate science from its bourgeois fetters, from its enslavement to capital, from its slavery to the interests of dirty capitalist greed. Socialism alone will make possible the wide expansion of social production and distribution on scientific lines and their actual subordination to the aim of easing the lives of the working people and of improving their welfare as much as possible. Socialism alone can achieve this. And we know that it must achieve this, and in the understanding of this truth lies the whole complexity and the whole strength of Marxism.

We must achieve this while relying on elements which are opposed to it, because the bigger capital becomes the more the bourgeoisie suppresses the workers. Now that power is in the hands of the proletariat and the poor peasants and the government is setting itself tasks with the support of the people, we have to achieve these socialist changes with the help of bourgeois experts who have been trained in bourgeois society, who know no other conditions, who cannot conceive of any other social system. Hence, even in cases when these experts are absolutely sincere and loyal to their work they are filled with thousands of bourgeois prejudices, they are connected by thousands of ties, imperceptible to themselves, with bourgeois society, which is dying and decaying and is therefore putting up furious resistance.

We cannot conceal these difficulties of endeavour and achievement from ourselves. Of all the socialists who have written about this, I cannot recall the work of a single socialist or the opinion of a single prominent socialist on future socialist society, which pointed to this concrete, practical difficulty that would confront the working class when it took power, when it set itself the task of turning the sum total of the very rich, historically inevitable and necessary for us store of culture and knowledge and technique accumulated by capitalism from an instrument of capitalism into an instrument of socialism. It is easy to do this in a general formula, in abstract reasoning, but in the struggle against capitalism, which does not die at once but puts up increasingly furious resistance the closer death approaches, this task is one that calls for tremendous effort. If experiments take place in this field, if we make repeated corrections of partial mistakes, this is inevitable because we cannot, in this or that sphere of the national economy, immediately turn specialists from servants of capitalism into servants of the working people, into their advisers. If we cannot do this at once it should not give rise to the slightest pessimism, because the task which we set ourselves is a task of world-historic difficulty and significance. We do not shut our eyes to the fact that in a single country, even if it were a much less backward country than Russian, even if we were living in better conditions than those prevailing after four years of unprecedented, painful, severe and ruinous war, we could not carry out the socialist revolution completely, solely by our own efforts. He who turns away from the socialist revolution now taking place in Russia and points to the obvious disproportion of forces is like the conservative 'man in a muffler' who cannot see further than his nose, who forgets that not a single historical change of any importance takes place without there being several instances of a disproportion of forces. Forces grow in the process of the struggle, as the revolution grows. When a country has taken the path of profound change, it is to the credit of that country and the party of the working class which achieved victory in that country, that they should take up in a practical manner the tasks that were formerly raised abstractedly, theoretically. This experience will never be forgotten. The experience which the workers now united in trade unions and local organisations are acquiring in the practical work of organising the whole of production on a national scale cannot be taken away, no matter how difficult the vicissitudes the Russian revolution and the international socialist revolution may pass through. It has gone down in history as socialism's gain, and on it the future world revolution will erect its socialist edifice.

Permit me to mention another problem, perhaps the most difficult problem, for which the Supreme Economic Council has to find a practical solution. This is the problem of labour discipline. Strictly speaking, in mentioning this problem, we ought to admit and emphasise with satisfaction that it was precisely the trade unions, their largest organisations, namely, the Central Committee of the Metalworkers' Union and the All-Russia Trade Union Council, the supreme trade union organisations uniting millions of working people, that were the first to set to work independently to solve this problem and this problem is of world-historic importance. In order to understand it we must abstract ourselves from those partial, minor failures, from the incredible difficulties which, if taken separately, seem to be insurmountable. We must rise to a higher level and survey the historical change of systems of social economy. Only from this angle will it be possible to appreciate the immensity of the task which we have undertaken. Only then will it be possible to appreciate the enormous significance of the fact that on this occasion, the most advanced representatives of society, the working and exploited people are, on their own initiative, taking on themselves the task which hitherto, in feudal Russia, up to 1861, was solved by a handful of landed proprietors, who regarded it as their own affair. At that time it was their affair to bring about state integration and discipline.

We know how the feudal landowners created this discipline. It was oppression, humiliation and the incredible torments of penal servitude for the majority of the people. Recall the whole of this transition from serfdom to the bourgeois economy. From all that you have witnessed – although the majority of you could not have witnessed it – and from all that you have learned from the older generations, you know how easy, historically, seemed the transition to the new bourgeois economy after 1861, the transition from the old feudal discipline of the stick, from the discipline of starvation, to so-called free hire, which in fact was the discipline of capitalist slavery. This was because mankind passed from one exploiter to another; because one minority of plunderers and exploiters of the people's labour gave way to another minority, who were also plunderers and exploiters of the people's labour; because the feudal landowners gave way to the capitalists, one minority gave way to another minority, while the toiling and exploited classes remained oppressed. And even this change from one exploiter's discipline to another exploiter's discipline took years, if not decades, of effort; it extended over a transition period of years, if not decades. During this period the old feudal landowners quite sincerely believed that everything was going to rack and ruin, that it was impossible to manage the country without serfdom; while the new, capitalist boss encountered practical difficulties at every step and gave up his enterprise as a bad job. The material evidence, one of the substantial proofs of the difficulty of this transition was that Russia at that time imported machinery from abroad, in order to have the best machinery to use, and it turned out that no one was available to handle this machinery, and there were no managers. And all over Russia one could see excellent machinery lying around unused, so difficult was the transition from the old feudal discipline to the new, bourgeois capitalist discipline.

And so, comrades, if you look at the matter from this angle, you will not allow yourselves to be misled by those people, by those classes, by those bourgeoisie and their hangers-on whose sole task is to sow panic, to sow despondency, to cause complete despondency concerning the whole of our work, to make it appear to be hopeless, who point to every single case of indiscipline and corruption, and for that reason give up the revolution as a bad job, as if there has ever been in the world, in history, a single really great revolution in which there was no corruption, no loss of discipline, no painful experimental steps, when the people were creating a new discipline. We must not forget that this is the first time that this preliminary stage in history has been reached, when a new discipline, labour discipline, the discipline of comradely contact, Soviet discipline, is being created in fact by millions of working and exploited people. We do not claim, nor do we expect, quick successes in this field. We know that this task will take an entire historical epoch. We have begun this historical epoch, an epoch in which we are breaking up the discipline of capitalist society in a country which is still bourgeois, and we are proud that all politically conscious workers, absolutely all the toiling peasants are everywhere helping this destruction; an epoch in which the people voluntarily, on their own initiative, are becoming aware that they must – not on instructions from above, but on the instructions of their own living experience – change this discipline based on the exploitation and slavery of the working people into the new discipline of united labour, the discipline of the united, organised workers and working peasants of the whole of Russia, of a country with a population of tens and hundreds of millions. This is a task of enormous difficulty, but it is also a thankful one, because only when we solve it in practice shall we have driven the last nail into the coffin of capitalist society which we are burying.

Notes

[1] This Congress was held from May 26 to June 4, 1918, in Moscow – *ed.*

9. Report on Combating the Famine

Comrades, the subject I am about to speak of today is the great crisis which has overtaken all modern countries and which perhaps weighs most heavily on Russia, or, at any rate, is being felt by her far more severely than by other countries. I must speak of this crisis, the famine which has afflicted us, in conjunction with the problems that confront us as a result of the general situation. And when we speak of the general situation, we cannot of course confine ourselves to Russia, particularly as all countries of modern capitalist civilisation are now bound together more painfully and more distressingly than ever before.

Everywhere, both in the belligerent countries and in the neutral countries, the war, the imperialist war between two groups of gigantic plunderers, has resulted in an utter exhaustion of productive forces. Ruin and impoverishment have reached such a pitch that the most advanced, civilised and cultured countries, which for decades, nay for centuries, had not known what famine means, have been brought by the war to the point of famine in the genuine and literal sense of the term. It is true that in the advanced countries, especially in those in which large-scale capitalism has long since trained the population to the maximum level of economic organisation possible under that system, they have succeeded in properly distributing the famine, in keeping it longer at bay and in rendering it less acute. But Germany and Austria, for example, not to speak of the countries that have been defeated and enslaved, have for a long time been suffering from real starvation. We can now open hardly a

Report made to an emergency meeting in Moscow, 4 June 1918, published in *Pravda* 5 June 1918.
CW XXVII 421-439.

single issue of a newspaper without coming across numerous reports from a number of the advanced and cultured countries – not only belligerent, but also neutral countries, such as Switzerland and certain of the Scandinavian countries – regarding the famine and the terrible hardships that have overtaken humanity as a result of the war.

Comrades, for those who have been following the development of European society it has for long been indisputable that capitalism cannot end peacefully, and that it must lead either to a direct revolt of the broad masses against the yoke of capital or to the same result by the more painful and bloody way of war.

For many years prior to the war the socialists of all countries pointed out, and solemnly declared at their congresses, that not only would a war between advanced countries be an enormous crime, that not only would such a war, a war for the partition of the colonies and the division of the spoils of the capitalists, involve a complete rupture with the latest achievements of civilisation and culture, but that it might, that, in fact, it inevitably would, undermine the very foundations of human society. Because it is the first time in history that the most powerful achievements of technology have been applied on such a scale, so destructively and with such energy, for the annihilation of millions of human lives. When all means of production are being thus devoted to the service of war, we see that the most gloomy prophecies are being fulfilled, and that more and more countries are falling a prey to retrogression, starvation and a complete decline of all the productive forces.

I am therefore led to recall how justified Engels, one of the great founders of scientific socialism, was, when in 1887, thirty years before the Russian revolution, he wrote that a European war would not only result, as he expressed it, in crowns falling from crowned heads by the dozen without anybody to pick them up, but that this war would also lead to the brutalisation, degradation and retrogression of the whole of Europe; and that, on the other hand, war would result either in the domination of the working class or in the creation of the conditions which would render its domination indispensable.[1] On this occasion the co-founder of Marxism expressed himself with extreme caution, for he clearly saw that if history took this course, the result would be the collapse of capitalism and the extension of socialism, and that a more painful and severe transition period, greater want and a severe crisis, disruptive of all productive forces, could not be imagined.

And we now clearly see the significance of the results of the imperialist slaughter of the peoples which has been dragging on for more than three years, when even the most advanced countries feel that the war has reached an impasse, that there is no escape from war under capitalism, and that it will lead to agonising ruin. And if we, comrades, if the Russian revolution – which is not due to any particular merit of the Russian proletariat but to the general course of historical events, which by the will of history has temporarily placed that proletariat in a foremost position and made it for the time being the vanguard of the world revolution – if it has befallen us to suffer particularly severe and acute agony from the famine, which is afflicting us more and more heavily, we must clearly realise that these misfortunes are primarily and chiefly a result of the accursed imperialist war. This war has brought incredible misfortunes on all countries, but these misfortunes are being concealed, with only temporary success, from the masses and from the knowledge of the vast majority of the peoples.

As long as military oppression continues, as long as the war goes on, as long as, on the one hand, it is accompanied by hopes of victory and a belief that this crisis may be resolved by the victory of one of the imperialist groups, and, on the other hand, an unbridled military censorship prevails and the people are intoxicated by the spirit of militarism, as long as this continues the mass of the population of the majority of the countries, will be kept in ignorance of the abyss into which they are about to fall and into which half of them have already fallen. And we are feeling this with particular intensity now, because nowhere but in Russia is there such a glaring contrast to the vastness of the tasks the insurgent proletariat has set itself, realising that it is impossible to end the war, the world war between the world's most powerful imperialist giants, that this war cannot be ended without a mighty proletarian revolution, also embracing the whole world.

And since the march of events has placed us in one of the most prominent positions in this revolution and forced us to remain for a long time, at least since October 1917, an isolated contingent, prevented by events from coming quickly enough to the aid of other contingents of international socialism, the position we find ourselves in is now ten times more severe. Having done all that can be done by the directly insurgent proletariat, and the poor peasantry supporting it, to overthrow our chief enemy and to protect the socialist revolution, we find nevertheless that at every step oppression by the imperialist predatory powers surrounding Russia and the legacy of the war are weighing on us more and more heavily. These consequences of the war have not yet made themselves fully felt. We are now, in the summer of 1918, facing what is perhaps one of the most difficult, one of the most severe and critical transitional stages of our revolution. And the difficulty is not confined to the international arena, where our policy is inevitably bound to be one of retreat as long as our true and only ally, the international proletariat, is only preparing, is only maturing, for revolt, but is not yet in a position to act openly and concertedly, although the whole course of events in Western Europe, the furious savagery of the recent battles on the Western front, the crisis which is growing increasingly acute in the belligerent countries, all go to show that the revolt of the European workers is not far off, and that although it may be delayed it will inevitably come.

It is in a situation like this that we have to experience enormous internal difficulties, owing to which considerable vacillations have been caused mainly by the acute food shortage, by the agonising famine which has overtaken us and which compels us to face a task demanding the maximum exertion of effort and the greatest organisation, and which at the same time cannot be tackled by the old methods. We shall undertake the solution of this problem together with the class that was with us in opposing the imperialist war, the class together with which we overthrew the imperialist monarchy and the imperialist republican bourgeoisie of Russia, the class that must forge its weapons, develop its forces and create its organisation in the midst of increasing difficulties, increasing tasks and the increasing scope of the revolution.

We are now facing the most elementary task of human

society – to vanquish famine, or at least to mitigate at once
the direct famine, the agonising famine which has afflicted
both our two principal cities and numerous districts of
agricultural Russia. And we have to solve this problem in
the midst of a civil war and the furious and desperate
resistance of the exploiters of all ranks and colours and of all
orientations. Naturally, in such a situation those elements in
the political parties which cannot break with the old and
cannot believe in the new find themselves in a state of war,
which is being exploited for only one aim – to restore the
exploiters.

The news we are receiving from every corner of Russia
demands that we shall face this question, the connection
between the famine and the fight against the exploiters,
against the counter-revolution which is raising its head. The
task confronting us is to vanquish the famine, or at least to
mitigate its severities until the new harvest, to defend the
grain monopoly and the rights of the Soviet state, the rights
of the proletarian state. All grain surpluses must be
collected; we must see to it that all stocks are brought to the
places where they are needed and that they are properly
distributed. This fundamental task means the preservation
of human society; at the same time it involves incredible
effort, it is a task which can be performed in only one way –
by general and increased intensification of labour.

In the countries where this problem is being solved by
means of war, it is being solved by military servitude, by
instituting military servitude for the workers and peasants; it
is being solved by granting new and greater advantages to
the exploiters. In Germany, for instance, where public
opinion is stifled, where every attempt to protest against the
war is suppressed, but where a sense of reality, of socialist
hostility to the war nevertheless persists, you will find no
more common method of saving the situation than the rapid
increase in the number of millionaires who have grown rich
on the war. These new millionaires have been enriching
themselves fantastically.

In all the imperialist countries the starvation of the masses
offers a field for the most furious profiteering; incredible
fortunes are being amassed on poverty and starvation.

This is encouraged by the imperialist countries, e.g.

Germany, where starvation is organised best of all. And not without reason it is said that Germany is a centre of organised starvation, where rations and crusts of bread are distributed among the population better than anywhere else. We see there that new millionaires are a common feature of the imperialist state; indeed, they know no other way of combating starvation. They permit twofold, threefold and fourfold profits to be made by those who possess plenty of grain and who know how to profiteer and to turn organisation, rationing, regulation and distribution into profiteering. We do not wish to follow that course, no matter who urges us to do so, whether wittingly or unwittingly. We say that we have stood and shall continue to stand shoulder to shoulder with the class together with which we opposed the war, together with which we overthrew the bourgeoisie and together with which we are suffering the hardships of the present crisis. We must insist on the grain monopoly being observed, not so as to legitimise capitalist profiteering, large or small, but so as to combat deliberate racketeering.

And here we see greater difficulties and greater dangers than those that faced us when we were confronted by tsarism armed to the teeth against the people; or when we were confronted by the Russian bourgeoisie, which was also armed to the teeth, and which in the offensive of last June did not consider it a crime to shed the blood of hundreds of thousands of Russian workers and peasants while it kept in its pocket the secret treaties providing it with a share in the spoils, but which does consider it a crime for the toilers to wage war against the oppressors, the only just and sacred war, the war of which we spoke at the very outset of the imperialist slaughter and which events at every step are now inevitably associating with the famine.

We know that the tsarist autocracy from the very beginning instituted fixed prices for grain and raised those prices. Why not? It remained faithful to its allies, the grain merchants, the profiteers and the banking magnates who made millions out of it.

We know how the compromisers of the Constitutional-Democratic Party – together with the Socialist-Revolutionaries and the Mensheviks – and Kerensky introduced a grain monopoly, because all Europe was saying that without a monopoly they could not hold out any longer. And we know how this same Kerensky in August 1917 evaded the democratic law of the time. That is what democratic laws and artfully interpreted regimes are for – to be evaded. We know that in August Kerensky doubled those prices and that at that time socialists of every shade and colour protested against and resented this measure. There was not a single newspaper at the time that was not outraged by Kerensky's conduct and that did not expose the fact that behind the republican Ministers, behind the Cabinet of Mensheviks and Socialist-Revolutionaries, were the manipulations of the profiteers, that the doubling of grain prices was a concession to the profiteers, that the whole business was nothing but a concession to the profiteers. We know that story.

We can now compare the course of the grain monopoly and of the fight against the famine in European capitalist countries with the course taken in our country. We see what use the counter-revolutionaries are making of these events. They are a lesson from which we must draw definite and rigorous conclusions. The crisis, having reached the pitch of a severe famine, has rendered the civil war still more acute. It has led to the exposure of parties like the Right Socialist-Revolutionaries and the Mensheviks, who differ from that avowed capitalist party, the Constitutional-Democrats, only in that the Constitutional-Democratic Party is an open party of the Black Hundreds.[2] The Constitutional-Democrats have nothing to say, and are not obliged to address themselves to the people, they are not obliged to conceal their aims, whereas these parties, who compromised with Kerensky and shared power and the secret treaties with him, are obliged to address themselves to the people. And so they are from time to time forced to expose themselves, despite their wishes and their plans.

When, as a result of the famine, we see on the one hand an outbreak of uprisings and revolts of starving people and on the other a series of counter-revolutionary rebellions, spreading like fire from one end of Russia to the other, obviously fed with funds from the Anglo-French imperialists, and aided by the efforts of the Right Socialist-Revolutionaries and the Mensheviks, we say to ourselves the picture is clear and we leave it to whoever so desires to dream of united fronts.

And we now see very clearly that after the Russian bourgeoisie was defeated in open military conflict, all the open collisions between the revolutionary and counter-revolutionary forces in the period from October 1917 to February and March 1918 proved to the counter-revolutionaries, even to the leaders of the Don Cossacks, in whom the greatest hopes had been placed, that their cause was lost, lost because everywhere the majority of the people were opposed to them. And every new attempt, even in the most patriarchal districts, where the agriculturists are most wealthy and most socially isolated from the outside world, as, for instance, the Cossacks – every new attempt without exception has resulted in new sections of the oppressed toilers actually rising against them.

The experience of the civil war in the period from October to March has shown that the masses of the working people, the Russian working class and the peasants who live by their own labour and not by exploiting others, are all over Russia, the vast majority of them, in favour of Soviet power. But those who thought that we were already on the path of greater organic development have been obliged to admit that they were mistaken.

The bourgeoisie saw that it was defeated.... Then there came a split among the Russian petty bourgeoisie. Some of them are drawn towards the Germans, others towards the Anglo-French orientation, while both have this in common, that they are united by the famine orientation.

In order that it may be clear to you, comrades, that it is not our Party but its enemies and the enemies of Soviet power who are reconciling the German orientation and the Anglo-French orientation and uniting them on a common programme, viz, to overthrow the Soviet power as the result of famine – in order to make it clear how this is taking place, I will take the liberty of briefly quoting from the report of the recent conference of the Mensheviks.[3] This report appeared in the newspaper *Zhizn*.

From this report, printed in No. 26 of *Zhizn*, we learn that Cherevanin, who made a report on economic policy, criticised the policy of the Soviet government and proposed a compromise solution of the problem – to enlist the services of representatives of merchant capital, as practical businessmen, to act as commission agents on terms which would be very favourable for them. We learn from this report that the chairman of the Northern Food Board, Groman, who was present at the conference, announced the following conclusions, which he had arrived at, so that report states, on the basis of a vast store of personal and of all sorts of other observations – observations, I would add, made entirely in bourgeois circles. 'Two methods,' he said, 'must be adopted: the first is that present prices must be raised; the second, that a special reward must be offered for prompt deliveries of grain,' etc. (*Voice*: 'What is wrong with that?') Yes, you will hear what is wrong with that, although the speaker, who has not been given the floor, but has taken it from that corner over there, thinks he can convince you that there is nothing wrong with it. But he has presumably forgotten the course the Menshevik conference took. This same paper, *Zhizn*, states that Groman was followed by the delegate Kolokolnikov, who said the following: 'We are being invited to participate in the Bolshevik food organisations.' Very wrong, is it not? That is what we have to say, recalling the interjection of the previous speaker. And if this speaker, who refuses to calm down and is taking the floor although he has not been granted it, cries out that it is a lie and that Kolokolnikov did not say that, I take note of the statement and request you to repeat that denial coherently and so that all may hear you. I take the liberty of recalling the resolution proposed at the conference by Martov, who is not unknown to you, and which on the question of the Soviet government literally says the same thing, although in different terms and phrases. Yes, you may laugh, but the fact remains that in connection with a report on the food situation Menshevik representatives say that the Soviet government is not a proletarian organisation, that it is a useless organisation.

And at such a time, when counter-revolutionary uprisings are breaking out owing to the famine, and taking advantage of the famine, no denials and no tricks will avail, for the fact is obvious. We see the policy on this question effectively developed by Cherevanin, Groman and Kolokolnikov. The Civil War is reviving, counter-revolution is raising its head, and I am convinced that ninety-nine per cent of the Russian workers and peasants have drawn – although not everybody yet knows this – are drawing and will draw their conclusions from these events, and that this conclusion will be that only by smashing counter-revolution, only by continuing a socialist policy over the famine, to combat the famine, shall we succeed in vanquishing both the famine and the counter-revolutionaries who are taking advantage of the famine.

Comrades, we are in fact approaching a time when Soviet power, after a long and severe struggle against numerous and formidable counter-revolutionary enemies, has defeated them in open conflict, and, having overcome the military resistance of the exploiters and their sabotage, has come to grips with the task of organisation. This difficult struggle with famine, this tremendous problem is actually explained by the fact that we have now come directly face to face with a task of organisation.

Success in an uprising is infinitely more easy. It is a million times easier to defeat the resistance of counter-revolution than to succeed in the sphere of organisation. This particularly applies to the cases when we dealt with a task in which the insurgent proletarian and the small property-owner, i.e. the broad sections of the petty bourgeoisie, among whom there were many general-democratic and general-labour elements, could to a considerable extent act together. We have now passed from this task to another. Serious famine has driven us to a purely communist task. We are being confronted by a revolutionary socialist task. Incredible difficulties face us here.

We do not fear these difficulties. We were aware of them. We never said that the transition from capitalism to socialism would be easy. It will involve a whole period of violent civil war, it will involve taking painful measures, when the contingent of the insurgent proletariat in one country is joined by the proletariat of another country in order to correct their mistakes by joint efforts. The tasks that face us here are organisational tasks, concerned with articles of general consumption, concerned with the deepest roots of profiteering, which are connected with the upper strata of the bourgeois world and of capitalist exploitation, and which cannot be so easily removed by mere mass pressure. We have to deal here with the roots and runners of bourgeois exploitation, the shallow ones and those that have taken a deep or shallow hold in all countries in the form of the small property-owners, their whole system of life, and in the habits and sentiments of the small property-owner and the small master; we have to deal here with the small profiteer, with his unfamiliarity with the new system of life, his lack of faith in it and his despair.

For it is a fact that when they sensed the tremendous difficulties that confront us in the revolution, many members of the working masses gave way to despair. We do not fear that. There never has been a revolution anywhere in which certain sections of the population were not overcome by despair.

When the masses put up a certain disciplined vanguard, and that vanguard knows that this dictatorship, this firm government, will help to win over all the poor peasants – this is a long process, involving a stern struggle – it is the beginning of the socialist revolution in the true sense of the term. But when we see that the united workers and the mass of poor peasants, who were about to organise against the rich and the profiteers, against the people to whom intellectuals like Groman and Cherevanin are wittingly or unwittingly preaching profiteers' slogans, when these workers, led astray, advocate the free sale of grain and the importing of freight transport, we say that this means helping the kulaks out of a hole! That path we shall never take. We declare that we shall rely on the working elements, with the help of whom we achieved the October victory, and that only together with our own class, and only by establishing proletarian discipline among all sections of the working population, shall we be able to solve the historic task now confronting us.

We have vast difficulties to overcome. We shall have to gather up all surpluses and stocks, properly distribute them and properly organise transportation for tens of millions of people. We shall have to see that the work proceeds with the regularity of clockwork. We shall have to overcome the disruption which is being fostered by the profiteers and by the doubters, who are spreading panic. This task of organisation can be accomplished only by the class-conscious workers, meeting the practical difficulties face to face. It is worth devoting all one's energies to this task; it is worth engaging in this last, decisive fight. And in this fight we shall win.

Comrades, the recent decrees on the measures taken by the Soviet government[4] show us that the path of the proletarian dictatorship, as every socialist who is a real socialist can see, will obviously and undoubtedly involve severe trials.

The recent decrees deal with the fundamental problem of life – bread. They are all inspired by three guiding ideas. First, the idea of centralisation: the uniting of everybody for the performance of the common task under leadership from the centre. We must prove that we are serious and not give way to despondency, we must reject the services of the bag-traders and merge all the forces of the proletariat; for in the struggle against the famine we rely on the oppressed classes and we see the solution only in their energetic resistance to all exploiters, in uniting all their activities.

Yes, we are told that the grain monopoly is being undermined by bag-trading and profiteering on every hand. We frequently hear the intellectuals say that the bag-traders are helping us, are feeding us. Yes, but the bag-traders are feeding us on kulak lines: they are doing just what is needed to establish, strengthen and perpetuate the power of the kulaks, to enable those who have power to extend that power over those around them with the help of their profits and through various individuals. And we assert that if the forces of those whose chief sin at the present moment is their lack of belief were to be united, the fight would be considerably easier. If there ever existed a revolutionary who hoped that we could pass to the socialist system without difficulties, such a revolutionary, such a socialist, would not be worth a brass farthing.

We know that the transition from capitalism to socialism is a struggle of an extremely difficult kind. But we are prepared to overcome a thousand difficulties, we are prepared to make a thousand attempts; and having made a thousand attempts we shall go on to the next attempt. We are now enlisting all the Soviet organisations in this new creative life, we are getting them to display new energies. We count on overcoming the new difficulties with the help of new strata, by organising the poor peasants. And now I shall pass to the second main task.

I have said that the first idea that runs through all these decrees is that of centralisation. Only by collecting all the grain in common bag shall we be able to overcome the famine. And even then grain will barely suffice. Nothing is left of Russia's former abundance, and all minds must be deeply imbued with communism, so that everybody regards surplus grain as the property of the people and is alive to the interests of the working people. And this can be achieved only by the method proposed by the Soviet government.

When they tell us of other methods, we reply as we did at the session of the All-Russia Central Executive Committee. When they talked of other methods, we said: Go to Skoropadsky, to the bourgeoisie. Teach them your methods, such as raising grain prices or forming a bloc with the kulaks. There you will find willing ears. But the Soviet government says only one thing, that the difficulties are immense and you must respond to every difficulty by new efforts of organisation and discipline. Such difficulties cannot be overcome in a single month. There have been cases in the history of nations when decades were devoted to overcoming smaller difficulties, and these decades have gone down in history as great and fruitful decades. You will never cause us to despond by referring to the failures of the first half-year or the first year of a great revolution. We shall continue to utter our old slogan of centralisation, unity and proletarian discipline on an all-Russia scale.

When they say to us, as Groman says in his report, that 'the detachments you have sent to collect grain are taking to drink and are themselves becoming moonshiners and robbers', we reply that we are fully aware how frequently this is the case. We do not conceal such facts, we do not whitewash them, we do not try to avoid them with pseudo-Left phrases and intentions. No, the working class is not separated by a Chinese wall from the old bourgeois society. And when a revolution takes place, it does not happen as in the case of the death of an individual, when the deceased is simply removed. When the old society perishes, its corpse cannot be nailed up in a coffin and lowered into the grave. It disintegrates in our midst; the corpse rots and infects us.

No great revolution has ever proceeded otherwise; no great revolution can proceed otherwise. The very things we have to combat in order to preserve and develop the sprouts of the new order in an atmosphere infested with the miasmas of a decaying corpse, the literary and political atmosphere; the play of political parties, which from the Constitutional-Democrats to the Mensheviks are infested with these miasmas of a decaying corpse, are all going to be used against us to put a spoke in our wheel. A socialist revolution can never be engendered in any other way; and not a single country can pass from capitalism to socialism except in an atmosphere of disintegrating capitalism and of painful struggle against it. And so we say that our first slogan is centralisation and our second slogan is the unity of the workers. Workers, unite and unite again! That is not new, it may not sound sensational or novel. It does not promise the specious successes with which you are being tempted by people like Kerensky, who in August 1917 doubled prices, just as the German bourgeois has raised them to twice and even ten times their level. These people promise you direct and immediate successes, as long as you offer new inducements to the kulaks. Of course that is not the road we shall follow. We say that our second method may be an old method, but it is a permanent method: Unite!

We are in a difficult situation. The Soviet Republic is perhaps passing through one of its most arduous periods. New strata of workers will come to our aid. We have no police, we shall not have a special military caste, we have no other apparatus than the conscious unity of the workers. They will save Russia from her desperate and tremendously difficult situation. The workers must unite, workers' detachments must be organised, the hungry people from the non-agricultural districts must be organised – it is to them we turn for help, it is to them our Commissariat for Food appeals, it is they we call upon to join the crusade for bread, the crusade against the profiteers and the kulaks and for the restoration of order.

A crusade used to be a campaign in which physical force

was supplemented by faith in something which centuries ago people were compelled by torture to regard as sacred. But we desire, we think, we are convinced, we know that the October Revolution has led the advanced workers and the advanced representatives of the poor peasants to regard the preservation of their power over the landowners and capitalists as sacred. They know that physical force is not enough to influence the masses of the population. We need physical force because we are building a dictatorship, we are applying force to the exploiters, and we shall cast aside with contempt all who fail to understand this, so as not to waste words in talking about the form of socialism.

We say that a new historical task is confronting us. We must get the new historical class to understand that we need detachments of agitators from among the workers. We need workers from the various uyezds of the non-producing gubernias. We need them to go thence as conscious advocates of Soviet power; they must sanctify and legitimise our food war, our war against the kulaks, our war against disorders; they must make possible the carrying on of socialist propaganda; they must establish in the countryside the distinction between the poor and the rich, which every peasant can understand and which is a profound source of our strength. It is a source which it is difficult to get to flow at full pressure, because the exploiters are numerous. And these exploiters resort to the most varied methods in order to subjugate the masses, such as bribing the poor peasants by permitting the latter to make money out of illicit distilling or to make a profit of several rubles on every ruble by selling at profiteering prices. Such are the methods to which the kulaks and the rural bourgeoisie resort in order to establish their hold over the masses.

We cannot blame the poor peasants for this, for we know that they have been enslaved for hundreds, thousands of years that they have suffered from serfdom and from the system which was left by serfdom in Russia. Our approach to the poor peasants must consist not only in the guns directed against the kulaks, but also in the propaganda of enlightened workers who bring the strength of their organisation into the countryside. Representatives of the poor, unite! – that is our third slogan. This is not making advances to the kulaks, and it is not the senseless method of raising prices. If we were to double prices, they would say: 'They are raising prices. They are hungry. Wait a bit, they will raise prices still higher.'

It is a well-trodden path, this path of playing up to the kulaks and profiteers. It is easy to take this path and to hold out tempting prospects. Intellectuals, who call themselves socialists, are quite prepared to paint such prospects for us; and the number of such intellectuals is legion. But we say to you: 'You who wish to follow the Soviet government, you who value it and regard it as a government of the working people, as a government of the exploited class, on you we call to follow another path'. This new historical task is a difficult thing. If we accomplish it, we shall raise a new stratum, give a new form of organisation to those sections of the working and exploited people, who are mostly downtrodden and ignorant, who are least united and have still to be united.

All over the world the foremost contingents of the workers of the cities, the industrial workers, have united, and united unanimously. But hardly anywhere in the world have systematic, supreme and self-sacrificing attempts been made to unite those who are engaged in small-scale agricultural production and, because they live in remote out-of-the-way places and in ignorance, have been stunted by their conditions of life. The task that faces us here unites for a single purpose both the fight against the food shortage and the fight for the profound and important system of socialism. The fight for socialism which faces us now is one to which it is worth devoting all our energies, for which it is worth staking everything, because it is a fight for socialism (*applause*) because it is a fight for the state power of the working and exploited people.

In following this path we shall regard the working peasants as our allies. Solid achievements await us along this path, not only solid, but inalienable. That is our third significant slogan!

Such are the three fundamental slogans: centralisation of food work, unity of the proletariat and organisation of the poor peasants. And our appeal, the appeal of our Commissariat for Food, to every trade union, to every factory committee, says: Life is hard for you, comrades;

then help us, join your efforts to ours, punish every breach of the regulations, every evasion of the grain monopoly. It is a difficult task; but fight bag-trading, profiteering and the kulaks, again and again, a hundred times, a thousand times, and we shall win. For this is the path on to which the majority of the workers are being led by the whole course of their lives and by the severity of our failures and trials in the matter of food supply. They know that, whereas when there was still no absolute shortage of grain in Russia the shortcomings of the food supply organisations were corrected by individual and isolated actions, this can no longer be the case now. Only the joint effort and the unity of those who are suffering most in the hungry cities and gubernias can help us. That is the path the Soviet government is calling on you to follow – unity of the workers, of their vanguard, for the purpose of carrying on agitation in the villages and of waging a war for grain against the kulaks.

According to the calculations of the most cautious experts, not far from Moscow, in gubernias quite close by – Kursk, Orel and Tambov – there is still a surplus of up to ten million poods of grain. We are very far from being able to collect this surplus for the common state fund.

Let us set about this task energetically. Let an enlightened worker go to every factory where despair is temporarily in the ascendant, and where, driven by hunger, people are prepared to accept the specious slogans of those who are reverting to the methods of Kerensky, to an increase of the fixed prices, and let him say: 'We see people who are despairing of the Soviet government. Join our detachments of militant agitators. Do not be dismayed by the many cases in which these detachments have disintegrated and turned to drink. We shall use every such example to show not that the working class is not fit, but that the working class has still not rid itself of the shortcomings of the old predatory society and cannot rid itself of them at once. Let us unite our efforts, let us form dozens of detachments, let us combine their activities, and in this way we shall get rid of our shortcomings.'

Comrades, allow me in conclusion to draw your attention to some of the telegrams which are being received by the

Council of People's Commissars and particularly by our Commissariat for Food.

Comrades, in this matter of the food crisis, of the torments of hunger that are afflicting all our cities, we observe that, as the proverb says, ill news hath wings. I should like to read you certain documents which were received by Soviet government bodies and institutions after the issue of the decree of May 13 on the food dictatorship, in which it is stated that we continue to rely only on the proletariat. The telegrams indicate that in the provinces they have already started to organise the crusade against the kulaks and to organise the rural poor, as we proposed. The telegrams we have received are proof of this.

Let the Cherevanins and the Gromans blow their trumpets, let their raucous voices sow panic and demand the destruction and abolition of the Soviet government! Those who are hard at work will be least disturbed by this; they will see the facts, they will see that the work is progressing and that new ranks are forming and uniting.

A new form of struggle against the kulaks is emerging, namely, an alliance of the poor peasants, who need assistance and who need to be united. It is proposed that awards be given for deliveries of grain, and we must help. We are willing to make such awards to the poor peasants, and we have already begun to do so. But against the kulaks, the criminals who are subjecting the population to the torments of hunger, and on account of whom millions of people are suffering, against them we shall use force. We shall give every possible inducement to the rural poor, for they are entitled to it. The poor peasant has for the first time obtained access to the good things of life, and we see that he is living more meagerly than the worker. We shall encourage and give every possible inducement to the poor peasants and shall help them if they help us to organise the collection of grain, to secure grain from the kulaks. We must spare no resources to make that a reality in Russia.

We have already adopted this course, and it will be still further developed by the experience of every enlightened worker and by the new detachments.

Comrades, the work has been started and is progressing. We do not expect dazzling success, but success there certainly will be. We know that we are now entering a period of new destruction, one of the most severe and difficult periods of the revolution. We are not in the least surprised that counter-revolution is raising its head, that the number of waverers and despairers in our ranks is growing. We say: stop your wavering; abandon your despair, of which the bourgeoisie will take advantage, because it is in its interests to sow panic; get to work; with our food decrees and our plan based on the support of the poor peasants we are on the only right road. In the face of the new historical tasks we call upon you to make a new exertion of effort. This task is an infinitely difficult one, but, I repeat, it is an extremely rewarding one. We are here fighting for the basis of communist distribution and for the actual creation of the foundations of a communist society. Let us all set to work. We shall vanquish the famine and achieve socialism.

Notes

[1] Lenin is referring to an argument put forward by Engels in *Einleitung zu Sigismund Borkheims Broschüre zur Erinnerung für die deutschen Mordspatrioten 1806-7* (Marx Engels *Werke*, Volume 21, pp 346-51) – *ed*.

[2] The Black Hundreds was an organisation of thugs formed during Tsarist times to carry out massacres of strikers, revolutionaries and Jews. The name soon became the accepted epithet for ultra-reactionary monarchists and supporters of anti-semitism.

[3] The All-Russia Conference of Mensheviks was held in Moscow from May 21 to 27, 1918. It was highly critical of the Soviet government's response to the food crisis – *ed*.

[4] On 13 May and 27 May 1918, the All-Russia Central Executive Committee passed two decrees giving to the people's commissars powers to organise the complete centralisation of food supply and distribution – *ed*.

10. Theses on the Food Question

For the Commissariats of Food, Agriculture, The
Supreme Economic Council, Finance, Trade and Industry

I propose that these Commissariats hurry to debate and
formulate the following measures no later than today
(August 2) so that they can be put through the Council of
People's Commissars today or tomorrow.

(Some of these measures should be in decrees, others in
unpublished decisions.)

(1) Out of the two schemes – lowering prices on
manufactured and other goods or raising the purchasing
price of grain – we must certainly choose the latter for,
though the two are essentially the same, only the latter can
help us in quickly getting more grain from a number of
grain-growing provinces like Simbirsk, Saratov, Voronezh,
etc, and help us neutralise as many peasants as possible in
the Civil War.

(2) I suggest raising the grain prices to 30 rubles a pood,
and correspondingly (and even more) to raise prices on
manufactured and other goods.

(3) I suggest for discussion: whether to make this a
temporary rise (so that we can sum up the practical
indications as to the correct principle on which our trade
exchange should be organised), say, for a month or month
and a half, promising to *lower prices* afterwards (thereby
offering bonuses for quick collection).

(4) To enact several very urgent measures for *requisitioning all* the products of urban industry for exchange (and put
up their prices after requisitioning to a *greater* extent than
the rise in grain prices).

Written 2 August 1918, first published 1931.
CW XXVIII 45-47.

(5) To preface the decree on grain price rise with a popular elucidation of the measure connected with the trade exchange and the establishment of the correct correlation between the prices of grain, manufactured and other goods.

(6) The decree should immediately compel the co-operatives; a) to set up a grain-collection point in each village shop; b) to give goods *only* according to the customers' ration books; c) *not* to give a *single* item to peasant-farmers except in exchange for grain.

To establish forms and means of control over the implementation of these measures and introduce stern punishment (confiscation of all property) for their violation.

(7) To confirm (or to formulate more precisely) the rules and regulations concerning property confiscation for *not handing over* to the state (*or the co-operatives*) grain surpluses *and all other* food products for registration.

(8) To impose a tax *in kind*, in grain, on the rich peasants. This category should include those whose amount of grain (including the new harvest) is double or more than double their own consumption (taking into account needs for their family, livestock and sowing).

This is to be designated as an *income* and property tax and made progressive.

(9) To establish for *workers* of the hungry regions temporarily, let's say for one month, preferential carriage of 1.5 poods of grain on condition of special certificate and special control.

The certificate must contain the exact address and authority; a) from a factory committee; b) from a house committee; c) from a trade union; and control must establish that it is for *personal* consumption, with a very severe penalty to anyone who cannot prove the impossibility of its reselling.

(10) To make it a rule to issue a receipt, two or three copies, for literally *every* requisition (particularly in the countryside and on the railway). To print forms of the receipt. Shooting to be the penalty for not giving a receipt.

(11) To enforce the same penalty for members of all kinds of requisitioning, food and other teams for any blatantly unjust action towards the working people or any infringement of the rules and regulations or actions liable to

rouse the indignation of the population, as well as for failure to keep a record and to hand over a copy to anyone who has already suffered requisitioning or punishment.

(12) To make it a rule that the workers and poor peasants in the hungry regions should have the right to have a goods train delivered to *their* station directly, under certain conditions: a) authorisation of local organisations (Soviet of Deputies plus the trade union without fail and others); b) making up a *responsible* team; c) inclusion in it of teams from other regions; d) participation of an inspector and Commissar from the Food, War, Transport and other Commissariats; e) their control of the train load and the distribution of grain. They must see that a *compulsory* part (a third to a half or more) goes to the Food Commissariat.

(13) As an exception, in view of the acute hunger among some railway *workers* and the particular importance of railways for grain delivery, to establish temporarily that: requisitioning or anti-profiteering teams, in requisitioning the grain, shall issue receipts to those from whom it has been taken, and put the grain into the goods waggons and dispatch these waggons to the *Central Food Bureau*, while observing the following forms of control: a) sending a telegram to the Food and Transport Commissariats notifying them about each goods waggon; b) summoning officials from both Commissariats to meet the goods waggon and distribute the grain under the Food Commissariat's supervision.

11. Measures Governing the Transition from Bourgeois Co-operative to Proletarian Communist Supply and Distribution

The question of the co-operatives and consumers' communes (see *Izvestia*, February 2) recently discussed in the Council of People's Commissars involves the *most vital* problem of the day, measures of *transition from* the bourgeois co-operatives *to* a communist consumers' and producers' union of the whole population.

Let us imagine co-operatives embrace 98 per cent of the population. This happens in the countryside.

Does this make them communes?

No, *if* the co-operative: (1) gives advantages (dividends on shares, etc) to a group of special shareholders; (2) preserves its own special apparatus which shuts out the population at large, in particular the proletariat and semi-proletariat; (3) does not give preference in produce distribution to the semi-proletariat over the middle peasants, to the middle peasants over the rich; (4) does not confiscate the surplus produce first from the rich, then from the middle peasants, and does not rely on the proletariat and semi-proletariat. And so on and so forth.

The whole difficulty of the task (and the whole *essence* of the present task which confronts us right now) springs from the fact that we have to work out a system of *practical* measures governing the *transition* from the old co-operatives (which are bound to be bourgeois since they have a group of

Written 2 February 1919, first published 1931.
CW XXVIII 443-444.

shareholders who constitute a *minority* of the population, as well as for other reasons) to a new and to a real *commune*. These are measures for the transition from bourgeois-co-operative to proletarian-communist supply and distribution.

It is essential

(1) to discuss this question in the press;

(2) to organise the movement of all the central and local government institutions (particularly of the Supreme Economic Council and the other Economic Councils, the Food Commissariat and food departments, the Central Statistical Board and the People's Commissariat of Agriculture) to tackle this task;

(3) to instruct the Co-operative Department of the Supreme Economic Council and the institutions enumerated in paragraph 2 to work out a *programme* of these measures and a form for collecting information on such measures and facts which enable us to develop these measures;

(4) to award a bonus for the best programme of measures, for the most practicable programme, for the most convenient and effective form and means of collecting information about it.

12. Integrated Economic Plan

What is being said and written on this subject leaves a very painful impression. Take L. Kritsman's articles in *Ekonomicheskaya Zhizn*[1] (I – December 14, 1920; II – December 23; III – February 9; IV – February 16; and V – February 20). There is nothing there but empty talk and word-spinning, a refusal to consider and look into what has been done in this field. Five long articles of reflection on how to approach the study of facts and data, instead of any actual examination of them.

Take Milyutin's theses (*Ekonomicheskaya Zhizn*, February 19), or Larin's (ibid, February 20); listen to the speeches of 'responsible' comrades: they all have the same basic defects as Kritsman's articles. They all reveal the dullest sort of scholasticism, including a lot of twaddle about the law of concatenation, etc. It is a scholasticism that ranges from the literary to the bureaucratic, to the exclusion of all practical effort.

But what is even worse is the highbrow bureaucratic disdain for the vital work that has been done and that needs to be continued. Again and again there is the emptiest 'drawing up of theses' and a concoction of plans and slogans in place of painstaking and thoughtful study of our own practical experience.

The only serious work on the subject is the *Plan for the Electrification of the RSFSR*, the report of GOELRO (the State Commission for the Electrification of Russia) to the Eighth Congress of Soviets, published in December 1920 and distributed at the Congress. It outlines an integrated economic plan which has been worked out – only as a rough approximation, of course – by the best brains in the

Published in *Pravda*, 22 February 1921.
CW XXXII 137-145.

Republic on the instructions of its highest bodies. We have to make a very modest start in fighting the complacency born of the ignorance of the grandees, and the intellectualist conceit of the Communist literati, by telling the story of this book, and describing its content and significance.

More than a year ago – February 2-7, 1920 – the All-Russia Central Executive Committee met in session and adopted a resolution on electrification which says:

> Along with the most immediate vital and urgent tasks in organising transport, coping with the fuel and food crisis, fighting epidemics, and forming disciplined labour armies, Soviet Russia now has, for the first time, an opportunity of starting on more balanced economic development, and working out a nation-wide state economic plan on scientific lines and consistently implementing it. In view of the prime importance of electrification ... mindful of the importance of electrification for industry, agriculture and transport, ... and so on and so forth..., the Committee resolves: to authorise the Supreme Economic Council to work out, in conjunction with the People's Commissariat for Agriculture, a project for the construction of a system of electric power stations ...

This seems to be clear enough, doesn't it? 'A nationwide state economic plan on scientific lines': is it possible to misread these words in the decision adopted by our highest authority? If the literati and the grandees, who boast of their communism before the 'experts', are ignorant of this decision it remains for us to remind them that ignorance of our laws is no argument.

In pursuance of the All-Russia CEC resolution, the Presidium of the Supreme Economic Council, on February 21, 1920, confirmed the Electrification Commission set up under the Electricity Department, after which the Council of Defence endorsed the statute on GOELRO, whose composition the Supreme Economic Council was instructed to determine and confirm by agreement with the People's Commissariat for Agriculture. On April 24, 1920, GOELRO issued its *Bulletin* No. 1, containing a detailed programme of works and a list of the responsible persons, scientists, engineers, agronomists and statisticians on the several subcommissions to direct operations in the various areas, together with the specific assignments each had undertaken. The list of persons and their assignments runs to ten printed pages of *Bulletin* No. 1. The best talent available to the Supreme Economic Council, the People's Commissariat for Agriculture and the People's Commissariat for Communications has been recruited.

The GOELRO effort has produced this voluminous – and first-class – scientific publication. Over 180 specialists worked on it. There are more than 200 items on the list of works they have submitted to GOELRO. We find, first, a summary of these works (the first part of the volume, running to over 200 pages): a) electrification and a state economic plan; followed by b) fuel supply (with a detailed 'fuel budget' for the RSFSR *over the next ten years*, with an estimate of the manpower required); c) water power; d) agriculture; e) transport; and f) industry.

The plan ranges over about ten years and gives an indication of the number of workers and capacities (in 1,000 hp). Of course, it is only a rough draft, with possible errors, and a 'rough approximation', but it is a real scientific plan. We have precise calculations by experts for every major item, and every industry. To give a small example, we have their calculations for the output of leather, footwear at two pairs a head (300 million pairs), etc. As a result, we have a material and a financial (gold rubles) balance-sheet for electrification (about 370 million working days, so many barrels of cement, so many bricks, poods of iron, copper, and other things; turbine generator capacities, etc). It envisages ('at a very rough estimate') an 80 per cent increase in manufacturing, and 80-100 per cent, in extracting industry over the next ten years. The gold balance deficit (+ 11,000 million – 17,000 million leaves a total deficit of about 6,000 million) 'can be covered by means of concessions and credit operations'.

It gives the site of the first 20 steam and 10 water power district electric stations, and a detailed description of the economic importance of each.

The general summary is followed, in the same volume, by a list of works for each area (with a separate paging): Northern, Central Industrial (both of which are especially well set out in precise detail based on a wealth of scientific data), Southern, Volga, Urals, Caucasian (the Caucasus is taken as a whole in anticipation of an economic agreement between its various republics), Western Siberia and Turkestan. For each of the areas, electric power capacities are projected beyond the first units; this is followed by the 'GOELRO Programme A', that is, the plan for the use of *existing* electric power stations on the most rational and economic lines. Here is another small example: it is estimated that a grid of the Petrograd stations (Northern Area) could yield the following economy (p 69): up to one-half of the capacities could be diverted to the logging areas of the North, such as Murmansk and Archangel, etc. The resulting increase in the output and export of timber could yield '*up to 500 million rubles' worth of foreign exchange a year in the immediate period ahead*'.

'Annual receipts from the sale of our northern timber could very well equal our gold reserves over the next few years' (ibid, p 70), provided, of course, we stop talking about plans and start studying and *applying* the plan already worked out by our scientists.

Let me add that we have an embryonic calendar programme for a number of other items (though not for all, of course). This is more than a general plan: it is an estimate for each year, from 1921 to 1930, of the number of stations that can be run in, and the proportions to which the existing ones can be enlarged, provided again we start doing what I have just said, which is not easy in view of the ways of our intellectualist literati and bureaucratic grandees.

A look at Germany will bring out the dimensions and value of GOELRO's effort. Over there, the scientist Ballod produced a similar work: he compiled a scientific plan for the socialist reconstruction of the whole national economy of Germany.[2] But his being a capitalist country, the plan never got off the ground. It remains a lone-wolf effort, and an exercise in literary composition. With us over here it was a state assignment, mobilising hundreds of specialists and producing an integrated economic plan on scientific lines within 10 months (and not two, of course, as we had originally planned). We have every right to be proud of this work, and it remains for us to *understand how* it should be used. What we now have to contend with is failure to understand *this fact*.

The resolution of the Eighth Congress of Soviets says: 'The Congress ... *approves the work of the Supreme Economic Council*, etc, especially that of GOELRO *in drawing up the plan for the electrification of Russia* ... regards this plan *as the first step in a great economic endeavour*, authorises the All-Russian Central Executive Committee, etc, *to put the finishing touches to the plan and to endorse it*, at the very earliest date.... It authorises the adoption of all measures for *the most extensive popularisation* of this plan.... A study of this plan must be an item in the curricula of *all educational establishments of the Republic, without exception*', etc.

The bureaucratic and intellectualist defects of our apparatus, especially of its top drawer, are most glaringly revealed by the attitude to this resolution taken by some people in Moscow and their efforts to twist it, to the extent of ignoring it altogether. Instead of advertising the plan, the literati produce theses and empty disquisitions on how to start working out a plan. The grandees, in purely bureaucratic fashion, lay stress on the need to 'approve' the plan, by which they do not mean concrete assignments (the dates for the construction of the various installations, the purchase of various items abroad, etc) but some muddled idea, such as working out a *new* plan. The misunderstanding this produces is monstrous, and there is talk of partially restoring the old before getting on with the new. Electrification, it is said, is something of an 'electrofiction'. Why not gasification, we are asked; GOELRO, they also say, is full of bourgeois specialists, with only a handful of Communists; GOELRO should provide the cadre of experts, instead of staffing the general planning commission, and so forth.

The danger lies in this discord, for it betrays an inability to work, and the prevalence of intellectualist and bureaucratic complacency, to the exclusion of all real effort. The conceited ignoramus is betrayed by his jibes at the 'fantastic' plan, his questions about gasification, etc. The nerve of their trying, offhand, to pick holes in something it took an army of first-class specialists to produce! Isn't it a shame to try to shrug it off with trite little jokes, and to put on airs about one's right 'to withhold approval'?

It is time we learned to put a value on science and got rid of the 'communist' conceit of the dabbler and the bureaucrat; it is time we learned to work systematically, making use of our own experience and practice.

Of course, 'plans' naturally give rise to endless argument and discussion, but when the task is to get down to the study of the only scientific plan before us, we should not allow ourselves to engage in general statements and debates about underlying 'principles'. We should get down to correcting it on the strength of *practical* experience and a more detailed study. Of course, the grandees always retain the right to 'give or withhold approval'. A sober view of this right, and a reasonable reading of the resolution of the Eighth Congress concerning the approval of the plan, which it endorsed and handed down to us for the broadest popularisation, show that approval must be taken to mean the placing of a series of orders and the issue of a set of instructions, such as the items to be purchased, the building to be started, the materials to be collected and forwarded, etc. Upon the other hand, 'approval' from the bureaucratic standpoint means arbitrary acts on the part of the grandees, the red-tape runaround, the commissions-of-inquiry game, and the strictly bureaucratic foul-up of anything that is going.

Let us look at the matter from yet another angle. There is a special need to tie in the scientific plan for electrification with existing short-term plans and their actual implementation. That this must be done is naturally beyond doubt. But how is it to be done? To find out, the economists, the literati, and the statisticians should stop their twaddle about the plan in general, and get on with a detailed study of the implementation of our plans, our mistakes in this practical business, and ways of correcting them. Otherwise we shall have to grope our way long. Over and above such a study of our practical experience, there remains the very small matter of administrative technique. Of planning commissions we have more than enough. Take two men from the department under Ivan Ivanovich and integrate them with one from the department under Pavel Pavlovich, or vice versa. Link them up with a subcommission of the general planning commission. All of which boils down to administrative technique. Various combinations should be tried out, and the best selected. That is elementary.

The whole point is that we have yet to learn the art of approach, and stop substituting intellectualist and bureaucratic projecteering for vibrant effort. We have, and have had, short-term food and fuel plans, and there are glaring mistakes in both. That is unquestionable. But the efficient economist, instead of penning empty theses, will get down to a study of the facts and figures, and analyse our own practical experience. He will pin-point the mistakes and suggest a remedy. This kind of study will suggest to the efficient administrator the transfers, alterations of records, recasting of the machinery, etc, to be proposed or put through. You don't find us doing anything of the sort.

The main flaw is in the wrong approach to the relationships between the Communists and the specialists, the administrators and the scientists and writers. There is no doubt at all that some aspects of the integrated economic plan, as of any other undertaking, call for the administrative approach or for decisions by Communists alone. Let me add that new aspects of that kind can always come to the fore. That, however, is the purely abstract way of looking at it. Right now, our communist writers and administrators are taking quite the wrong approach, because they have failed to realise that in this case we should be learning all we can from the bourgeois specialists and scientists, and cutting out the administrative game. GOELRO's is the only integrated economic plan we can hope to have just now. It should be amplified, elaborated, corrected and applied in the light of well scrutinised practical experience. The opposite view boils down to the purely 'pseudo-radical conceit, which in actual fact is nothing but ignorance', as our Party Programme puts it.[3] Ignorance and conceit are equally betrayed by the view that we can have another general planning commission in the RSFSR in addition to GOELRO, which, of course, is not to deny that some advantage may be gained from partial and business-like changes in its membership. It is only on this basis – by continuing what has been started – that we can hope to make any serious improvements in the general economic plan; any other course will involve us in an administrative game, or high-handed action, to put it bluntly. The task of the

Communists inside GOELRO is to issue fewer orders, rather, to refrain from issuing any at all, and to be very tactful in their dealings with the scientists and technicians (the RCP Programme says: 'Most of them inevitably have strong bourgeois habits and take the bourgeois view of things'). The task is to learn from them and to help them to broaden their world-view on the basis of achievements in their particular field, always bearing in mind that the engineer's way to communism is *different* from that of the underground propagandist and the writer; he is guided along *by the evidence of his own science*, so that the agronomist, the forestry expert, etc, each have *their own path* to tread towards communism. The Communist who has failed to prove his ability to bring together and guide the work of specialists in a spirit of modesty, going to the heart of the matter and studying it in detail, is a potential menace. We have many such Communists among us, and I would gladly swap dozens of them for one conscientious qualified bourgeois specialist.

There are two ways in which Communists outside GOELRO can help to establish and implement the integrated economic plan. Those of them who are economists, statisticians or writers should start by making a study of our own practical experience, and suggest corrections and improvements only after such a detailed study of the facts. Research is the business of the scientist, and once again, because we are no longer dealing with general principles, but with practical experience, we find that we can obtain much more benefit from a 'specialist in science and technology', even if a bourgeois one, than from the conceited Communist who is prepared, at a moment's notice, to write 'theses', issue 'slogans' and produce meaningless abstractions. What we need is more factual knowledge and fewer debates on ostensible communist principles.

Upon the other hand, the Communist administrator's prime duty is to see that he is not carried away by the issuing of orders. He must learn to start by looking at the achievements of science, insisting on a verification of the facts, and locating and studying the mistakes (through reports, articles in the press, meetings, etc), before proceeding with any corrections. We need more practical studies of our mistakes, in place of the Tit Titych[4] type of tactics ('I might give my approval, if I feel like it').

Men's vices, it has long been known, are for the most part bound up with their virtues. This, in fact, applies to many leading Communists. For decades, we had been working for the great cause, preaching the overthrow of the bourgeoisie, teaching men to mistrust the bourgeois specialists, to expose them, deprive them of power and crush their resistance. That is a historic cause of world-wide significance. But it needs only a slight exaggeration to prove the old adage that there is only one step from the sublime to the ridiculous. Now that we have convinced Russia, now that we have wrested Russia from the exploiters and given her to the working people, now that we have crushed the exploiters, we must learn to run the country. This calls for modesty and respect for the efficient 'specialists in science and technology', and a business-like and careful analysis of our numerous *practical* mistakes, and their gradual but steady correction. Let us have less of this intellectualist and bureaucratic complacency, and a deeper scrutiny of the practical experience being gained in the centre and in the localities, and of the available achievements of science.

Notes

[1] *Ekonomicheskaya Zhizn* (Economic Life) was an official daily published from 1918 to 1937 – *ed*.

[2] Karl Ballod, *Der Zukunftsstaat. Produktion und Konsum im Sozialstaat* (The State of the Future. Production and Consumption in the Socialist State), 1898 – *ed*.

[3] This and subsequent quotes are from the party programme adopted by the Eighth Party Congress in March 1919 – *ed*.

[4] See note 2, chapter 6 – *ed*.

13. The Tax in Kind
(The Significance of the
New Policy and its Conditions)

In Lieu of Introduction

The question of the tax in kind is at present attracting very great attention and is giving rise to much discussion and argument. This is quite natural, because in present conditions it is indeed one of the principal questions of policy.

The discussion is somewhat disordered, a fault to which, for very obvious reasons, we must all plead guilty. All the more useful would it be, therefore, to try to approach the question, not from its 'topical' aspect, but from the aspect of general principle. In other words, to examine the general, fundamental background of the picture on which we are now tracing the pattern of definite practical measures of present-day policy.

In order to make this attempt I will take the liberty of quoting a long passage from my pamphlet, *The Chief Task of Our Day. 'Left-Wing' Childishness and the Petty-Bourgeois Mentality*. It was published by the Petrograd Soviet of Workers' and Soldiers' Deputies in 1918 and contains, first, a newspaper article, dated March 11, 1918, on the Brest Peace, and, second, my polemic against the then existing group of Left Communists, dated May 5, 1918. The polemic is now superfluous and I omit it, leaving what appertains to the discussion on 'state capitalism' and the main elements of

Published as a pamphlet May 1921.
CW XXXII 329-365.

our present-day economy, which is transitional from capitalism to socialism.

Here is what I wrote at the time:

THE PRESENT-DAY ECONOMY OF RUSSIA
(extract from the 1918 pamphlet)

State capitalism would be a step forward as compared with the present state of affairs in our Soviet Republic. If in approximately six months' time state capitalism became established in our Republic, this would be a great success and a sure guarantee that within a year socialism will have gained a permanently firm hold and will have become invincible in this country.

I can imagine with what noble indignation some people will recoil from these words.... What! The transition to state *capitalism* in the Soviet Socialist Republic would be a step forward?... Isn't this the betrayal of socialism?

We must deal with this point in greater detail.

Firstly, we must examine the nature of the *transition* from capitalism to socialism that gives us the right and the grounds to call our country a Socialist Republic of Soviets.

Secondly, we must expose the error of those who fail to see the petty-bourgeois economic conditions and the petty-bourgeois element as the *principal* enemy of socialism in our country.

Thirdly, we must fully understand the economic implications of the distinction between the *Soviet* state and the bourgeois state.

Let us examine these three points.

No one, I think, in studying the question of the economic system of Russia, has denied its transitional character. Nor, I think, has any Communist denied that the term Soviet Socialist Republic implies the determination of the Soviet power to achieve the transition to socialism, and not that the existing economic system is recognised as a socialist order.

But what does the word 'transition' mean? Does it not mean, as applied to an economy, that the present system contains elements, particles, fragments of both capitalism and socialism? Everyone will admit that it does. But not all who admit this take the trouble to consider what elements actually constitute the various socio-economic structures that exist in Russia at the present time. And this is the crux of the question.

Let us enumerate these elements:

(1) patriarchal, i.e. to a considerable extent natural, peasant farming;

(2) small commodity production (this includes the majority of those peasants who sell their grain);

(3) private capitalism;

(4) state capitalism;

(5) socialism.

Russia is so vast and so varied that all these different types of socio-economic structures are intermingled. This is what constitutes the specific feature of the situation.

The question arises: What elements predominate? Clearly, in a small-peasant country, the petty-bourgeois element predominates and it must predominate, for the great majority – those working the land – are small commodity producers. The shell of state capitalism (grain monopoly, state-controlled entrepreneurs and traders, bourgeois co-operators) is pierced now in one place, now in another by *profiteers*, the chief object of profiteering being *grain*.

It is in this field that the main struggle is being waged. Between what elements is this struggle being waged if we are to speak in terms of economic categories such as 'state capitalism'? Between the fourth and fifth in the order in which I have just enumerated them? Of course not. It is not state capitalism that is at war with socialism, but the petty bourgeoisie plus private capitalism fighting together against state capitalism and socialism. The petty bourgeoisie oppose *every kind* of state interference, accounting and control, whether it be state-capitalist or state-socialist. This is an unquestionable fact of reality whose misunderstanding lies at the root of many economic mistakes. The profiteer, the commercial racketeer, the disrupter of monopoly – these are our principal 'internal' enemies, the enemies of the economic measures of the Soviet power. A hundred and twenty-five years ago it might have been excusable for the French petty bourgeoisie, the most ardent and sincere revolutionaries, to try to crush the profiteer by executing a few of the 'chosen' and by making thunderous declarations. Today, however, the purely French approach to the question assumed by some Left Socialist-Revolutionaries can arouse nothing but disgust and revulsion in every politically conscious revolutionary. We know perfectly well that the economic basis of profiteering is both the small proprietors, who are exceptionally widespread in Russia, and private capitalism, of which every petty bourgeois is an agent. We know that the million tentacles of this petty-bourgeois octopus now and again encircle various sections of the workers, that instead of state monopoly, profiteering forces its way into every pore of our social and economic organism.

Those who fail to see this show by their blindness that they are slaves of petty-bourgeois prejudices....

The petty bourgeoisie have money put away, the few thousands that they made during the war by 'honest' and especially by dishonest means. They are the characteristic economic type, that is, the basis of profiteering and private capitalism. Money is a certificate entitling the possessor to receive social wealth; and a vast section of small proprietors, numbering millions, cling to this certificate and conceal it from the 'state'. They do not believe in socialism or communism, and 'mark time' until the proletarian storm blows over. Either we subordinate the petty bourgeoisie to our control and accounting (we can do this if we organise the poor, that is, the majority of the population or semi-proletarians, round the politically conscious proletarian vanguard), or they will overthrow our workers' power as surely and as inevitably as the revolution was overthrown by the Napoleons and the Cavaignacs who sprang from this very soil of petty proprietorship. That is how the question stands. That is the only view we can take of the matter....

The petty bourgeois who hoards his thousands is an enemy of state capitalism. He wants to employ these thousands just for himself, against the poor, in opposition to any kind of state control. And the sum total of these thousands, amounting to many thousands of millions, forms the base for profiteering, which undermines our socialist construction. Let us assume that a certain number of workers produce in a few days values equal to 1,000. Let us then assume that 200 of this total vanishes owing to petty profiteering, various kinds of embezzlement and the evasion by the small proprietors of Soviet decrees and regulations. Every politically conscious worker will say that if better order and organisation could be obtained at the price of 300 out of the 1,000 he would willingly give 300 instead of 200, for it will be quite easy under the Soviet power to reduce this 'tribute' later on to, say, 100 or 50, once order and organisation are established and the petty-bourgeois disruption of state monopoly is completely overcome.

This simple illustration in figures, which I have deliberately simplified to the utmost in order to make it absolutely clear, explains the present correlation of state capitalism and socialism. The workers hold state power and have every legal opportunity of 'taking' the whole thousand, without giving up a single kopek, except for socialist purposes. This legal opportunity, which rests upon the actual transition of power to the workers, is an element of socialism. But in many ways, the small-proprietary and private-capitalist element undermines this legal position, drags in profiteering and hinders the execution of Soviet decrees. State capitalism would be a gigantic step forward *even if* we paid *more* than we are paying at present (I took the numerical example deliberately to bring this out more sharply), because it is worth paying for 'tuition', because it is useful for the workers, because victory over disorder, economic ruin and laxity is the most important thing, because the continuation of the anarchy of small ownership is the greatest, the most serious danger, and it will *certainly* be our ruin (unless we overcome it), whereas not only will the payment of a heavier tribute to state capitalism not ruin us, it will lead us to socialism by the surest road. When the working class has learned how to defend the state system against the anarchy of small ownership, when it has learned to organise large-scale production on a national scale along state-capitalist lines, it will hold, if I may use the expression, all the trump cards, and the consolidation of socialism will be assured.

In the first place *economically* state capitalism is immeasurably superior to our present economic system.

In the second place there is nothing terrible in it for the Soviet power, for the Soviet state is a state in which the power of the workers and the poor is assured....

To make things even clearer, let us first of all take the most concrete example of state capitalism. Everybody knows what this example is. It is Germany. Here we have 'the last word' in modern large-scale capitalist engineering and planned organisation, *subordinated to Junker-bourgeois imperialism*. Cross out the words in italics, and in place of the militarist, Junker, bourgeois, imperialist state put also a state, but of a different social type, of a different class content – a Soviet state, that is, a proletarian state, and you will have the sum total of the conditions necessary for socialism.

Socialism is inconceivable without large-scale capitalist engineering based on the latest discoveries of modern science. It is inconceivable without planned state organisation which keeps tens of millions of people to the strictest observance of a unified standard in production and distribution. We Marxists have always spoken of this, and it is not worth while wasting two seconds talking to people who do not understand even this (anarchists and a good half of the Left Socialist-Revolutionaries).

At the same time socialism is inconceivable unless the proletariat is the ruler of the state. This also is ABC. And history (which nobody, except Menshevik blockheads of the first order, ever expected to bring about 'complete' socialism smoothly, gently, easily and simply) has taken such a peculiar course that it has given birth in 1918 to two unconnected halves of socialism existing side by side like two future chickens in the single shell of international imperialism. In 1918, Germany and Russia had become the most striking embodiment of the material realisation of the economic, the productive and the socio-economic conditions for socialism, on the one hand, and the political conditions, on the other.

A victorious proletarian revolution in Germany would immediately and very easily smash any shell of imperialism (which unfortunately is made of the best steel, and hence cannot be broken by the efforts of any chicken) and would bring about the victory of world socialism for certain, without any difficulty, or with only slight difficulty – if, of course, by 'difficulty' we mean difficulty on a world-historical scale, and not in the parochial philistine sense.

While the revolution in Germany is still slow in 'coming forth', our task is to *study* the state capitalism of the Germans, to *spare no effort* in copying it and not shrink from adopting dictatorial methods to hasten the copying of Western culture by barbarian Russia, without hesitating to use barbarous methods in fighting barbarism. If there are anarchists and Left Socialist-Revolutionaries (I recall offhand the speeches of Karelin and Ghe at the meeting of the Central Executive Committee) who indulge in Karelin-like reflections and say that is unbecoming for us revolutionaries to 'take lessons' from German imperialism, there is only one thing we can say in reply: the revolution that took these people seriously would perish irrevocably (and deservedly).

At present petty-bourgeois capitalism prevails in Russia, and it is *one and the same road* that leads from it to both large-scale state capitalism and to socialism, *through one and the same* intermediary station called 'national accounting and control of production and distribution'. Those who fail to understand this are committing an unpardonable mistake in economics. Either they do not know the facts of life, do not see what actually exists and are unable to look the truth in the face, or they confine themselves to abstractly comparing 'socialism' with 'capitalism' and fail to study the concrete forms and stages of the transition that is taking place in our country.

Let it be said in parenthesis that this is the very theoretical mistake which misled the best people in the *Novaya Zhizn* and *Vperyod* camp. The worst and the mediocre of these, owing to their stupidity and spinelessness, tag along behind the bourgeoisie, of whom they stand in awe; the best of them have failed to understand that it was not without reason that the teachers of socialism spoke of a whole period of transition from capitalism to socialism and emphasised the 'prolonged birth pangs' of the new society.[1] And this new society is again an abstraction which can come into being only by passing through a series of varied, imperfect and concrete attempts to create this or that socialist state.

It is because Russia cannot advance from the economic situation now existing here without traversing the ground *which is common* to state capitalism and to socialism (national accounting and control) that the attempt to frighten others as well as themselves with 'evolution *towards* state capitalism' is utter theoretical nonsense. This is letting one's thoughts wander away from the true road of 'evolution', and failing to understand what this road is. In practice, it is equivalent to *pulling us back* to small-proprietary capitalism.

In order to convince the reader that this is not the first time I have given this 'high' appreciation of state capitalism and that I gave it *before* the Bolsheviks seized power, I take the liberty of quoting the following passage from my pamphlet, *The Impending Catastrophe and How To Combat It*, written in September 1917.

'Try to substitute for the Junker-capitalist state, for the landowner-capitalist state, a revolutionary-democratic state, i.e. a state which in a revolutionary way abolishes all privileges and does not fear to introduce the fullest democracy in a revolutionary way. You will find that, given a really revolutionary-democratic state, state-monopoly capitalism inevitably and unavoidably implies a step ... towards socialism....

'For socialism is merely the next step forward from state-capitalist monopoly....

'State-monopoly capitalism is a complete material preparation for socialism, the threshold of socialism, a rung on the ladder of history between which and the rung called socialism there are no intermediate rungs' (pp 27 and 28).

Please note that this was written when Kerensky was in power, that we are discussing *not* the dictatorship of the proletariat, *not* the socialist state, but the 'revolutionary-democratic' state. Is it not clear that *the higher* we stand on this political ladder, *the more completely* we incorporate the socialist state and the dictatorship of the proletariat in the Soviets, *the less* ought we to fear 'state capitalism'? Is it not clear that from the *material*, economic and productive point of view, we are not yet on the 'threshold' of socialism? Is it not clear that we cannot pass through the door of socialism without crossing the 'threshold' we have not yet reached?...

The following is also extremely instructive.

When we argued with Comrade Bukharin in the Central Executive Committee, he declared, among other things, that on the question of high salaries for specialists 'they' were 'to the right of Lenin', for in this case 'they' saw no deviation from principle, bearing in mind Marx's words that under certain conditions it is more expedient for the working class to 'buy out the whole lot of them'[2] (namely, the whole lot of capitalists, i.e. to *buy* from the bourgeoisie the land, factories, works and other means of production).

That is a very interesting statement....

Let us consider Marx's idea carefully.

Marx was talking about the Britain of the seventies of the last century, about the culminating point in the development of pre-monopoly capitalism. At that time Britain was a country in which militarism and bureaucracy were less pronounced than in any other, a country in which there was the greatest possibility of a 'peaceful' victory for socialism in the sense of the workers 'buying out' the bourgeoisie. And Marx said that under certain conditions the workers would certainly not refuse to buy out the bourgeoisie. Marx did not commit himself, or the future leaders of the socialist revolution, to matters of form, to ways and means of bringing about the revolution. He understood perfectly well that a vast number of new problems would arise, that the whole situation would change in the course of the revolution, and that the situation would change radically and often in the course of the revolution.

Well, and what about Soviet Russia? Is it not clear that *after* the seizure of power by the proletariat and *after* the crushing of the exploiters' armed resistance and sabotage – *certain* conditions prevail which correspond to those which might have existed in Britain half a century ago had a peaceful transition to socialism begun there? The subordination of the capitalists to the workers in Britain would have been assured at that time owing to the following circumstances: (1) the absolute preponderance of workers, of proletarians, in the population owing to the absence of a peasantry (in Britain in the seventies there were signs that gave hope of an extremely rapid spread of socialism among agricultural labourers); (2) the excellent organisation of the proletariat in trade unions (Britain was at that time the leading country in the world in this respect); (3) the comparatively high level of culture of the proletariat, which had been trained by centuries of development of political liberty; (4) the old habit of the well-organised British capitalists of settling political and economic questions by compromise – at that time the British capitalists were better organised than the capitalists of any country in the world (this superiority has now passed to Germany). These were the circumstances which at the time gave rise to the idea that the *peaceful* subjugation of the British capitalists by the workers was possible.

In our country, at the present time, this subjugation is assured by certain premises of fundamental significance (the victory in October and the suppression, from October to February, of the capitalists' armed resistance and sabotage). But *instead of* the absolute preponderance of workers, of proletarians, in the population, and *instead of* a high degree of organisation among them, the important factor of victory in Russia was the support the proletarians received from the poor peasants and those who had experienced sudden ruin. Finally, we have neither a high degree of culture nor the habit of compromise. If these concrete conditions are carefully considered, it will become clear that we now can and ought to employ a *combination* of two methods. On the one hand, we must ruthlessly suppress the uncultured capitalists who refuse to have anything to do with 'state capitalism' or to consider any form of compromise, and who continue by means of profiteering, by bribing the poor peasants, etc, to hinder the realisation of the measures taken by the Soviets. On the other hand, we must use the *method of compromise*, or of buying out the cultured capitalists who agree to 'state capitalism', who are capable of putting it into practice and who are useful to the proletariat as intelligent and experienced organisers of the largest types of enterprises, which actually supply products to tens of millions of people.

Bukharin is an extremely well-read Marxist economist. He therefore remembered that Marx was profoundly right when he taught the workers the importance of preserving the organisation of large-scale production, precisely for the purpose of facilitating the transition to socialism. Marx taught that (as an exception, and Britain was then an exception) the idea was conceivable of *paying the capitalists well*, of buying them out, if the circumstances were such as to compel the capitalists to submit peacefully and to come over to socialism in a cultured and organised fashion, provided they were paid well.

But Bukharin went astray because he did not go deep enough into the specific features of the situation in Russia at the present time – an exceptional situation when we, the Russian proletariat, are *in advance* of any Britain or any Germany as regards political system, as regards the strength of the workers' political system, as regards the strength of the workers' political power, but are *behind* the most backward West-European country as regards organising a good state capitalism, as regards our level of culture and the degree of material and productive preparedness for the 'introduction' of socialism. Is it not clear that the specific nature of the present situation creates the need for a specific type of 'buying out' operation which the workers must offer to the most cultured, the most talented, the most capable organisers among the capitalists who are ready to enter the service of the Soviet power and to help honestly in organising 'state' production on the largest possible scale? Is it not clear that in this specific situation we must make every effort to avoid two mistakes, both of which are of a petty-bourgeois nature? On the one hand, it would be a fatal mistake to declare that since there is a discrepancy between our economic 'forces' and our political strength, it 'follows' that we should not have seized power. Such an argument can be advanced only by a 'man in a muffler', who forgets that there will always be such a 'discrepancy', that it always exists in the development of nature as well as in the development of society, that only by a series of attempts – each of which, taken by itself, will be one-sided and will suffer from certain inconsistencies – will complete socialism be created by the revolutionary co-operation of the proletarians of *all* countries.

On the other hand, it would be an obvious mistake to give free rein to ranters and phrase-mongers who allow themselves to be carried away by the 'dazzling' revolutionary spirit, but who are incapable of sustained, thoughtful and deliberate revolutionary work which takes into account the most difficult stages of transition.

Fortunately, the history of the development of revolutionary parties and of the struggle that Bolshevism waged against them has left us a heritage of sharply defined types, of which the Left Socialist-Revolutionaries and anarchists are striking examples of bad revolutionaries. They are now shouting hysterically, choking and shouting themselves hoarse, against the 'compromise' of the 'Right Bolsheviks'. But they are incapable of understanding *what* is bad in 'compromise', and *why* 'compromise' has been justly condemned by history and the course of the revolution.

Compromise in Kerensky's time meant the surrender of power to the imperialist bourgeoisie, and the question of power is the fundamental question of every revolution. Compromise by a section of the Bolsheviks in October-November 1917 either meant that they feared the proletariat seizing power or wished to *share* power equally, not only with 'unreliable fellow-travellers' like the Left Socialist-Revolutionaries, but also with enemies, with the Chernovists and the Mensheviks. The latter would inevitably have hindered us in fundamental matters, such as the dissolution of the Constituent Assembly, the ruthless suppression of the Bogayevskys, the universal setting up of the Soviet institutions, and in every act of confiscation.

Now power has been seized, retained and consolidated in the hands of a single party, the party of the proletariat, even without the 'unreliable fellow-travellers'. To speak of compromise at the present time when there is no question, and can be none, of sharing *power*, of renouncing the dictatorship of the proletariat over the bourgeoisie, is merely to repeat, parrot-fashion, words which have been learned by heart but not understood. To describe as 'compromise' the fact that, having arrived at a situation when we can and must rule the country, we try to win over to our side, not grudging the cost, the most efficient people capitalism has trained and to take them into our service against small proprietary disintegration, reveals a total incapacity to think about the economic tasks of socialist construction.

Tax in Kind, Freedom to Trade and Concessions

In the arguments of 1918 quoted above there are a number of mistakes as regards the periods of time involved. These turned out to be longer than was anticipated at that time. That is not surprising. But the basic elements of our economy have remained the same. In a very large number of cases the peasant 'poor' (proletarians and semi-proletarians) have become middle peasants. This has caused an increase in the small-proprietor, petty-bourgeois 'element'. The Civil War of 1918-20 aggravated the havoc in the country, retarded the restoration of its productive forces, and bled the proletariat more than any other class. To this was added the 1920 crop failure, the fodder shortage and the loss of cattle, which still further retarded the rehabilitation of transport and industry, because, among other things, it interfered with the employment of peasants' horses for carting wood, our main type of fuel.

As a result, the political situation in the spring of 1921 was such that immediate, very resolute and urgent measures had to be taken to improve the condition of the peasants and to increase their productive forces.

Why the peasants and not the workers?

Because you need grain and fuel to improve the condition of the workers. This is the biggest 'hitch' at the present time, from the standpoint of the economy as a whole. For it is impossible to increase the production and collection of grain and the storage and delivery of fuel except by improving the condition of the peasantry, and raising their productive forces. We must start with the peasantry. Those who fail to understand this, and think this putting the peasantry in the forefront is 'renunciation' of the dictatorship of the proletariat, or something like that, simply do not stop to think, and allow themselves to be swayed by the power of words. The dictatorship of the proletariat is the direction of policy by the proletariat. The proletariat, as the leading and ruling class, must be able to direct policy in such a way as to solve first the most urgent and 'vexed' problem. The most urgent thing at the present time is to take measures that will immediately increase the productive forces of peasant farming. Only *in this way* will it be possible to improve the condition of the workers, strengthen the alliance between the workers and peasants, and consolidate the dictatorship of the proletariat. The proletarian or representative of the proletariat who *refused* to improve the condition of the workers *in this way* would *in fact* prove himself to be an accomplice of the whiteguards and the capitalists; to refuse to do it in this way means putting the craft interests of the workers above their class interests, and sacrificing the interests of the whole of the working class, its dictatorship, its alliance with the peasantry against the landowners and capitalists, and its leading role in the struggle for the emancipation of labour from the yoke of capital, for the sake of an immediate, short-term and partial advantage for the workers.

Thus, the first thing we need is immediate and serious measures to raise the productive forces of the peasantry.

This cannot be done without making important changes in our food policy. One such change was the replacement of the surplus appropriation system by the tax in kind, which implies a free market, at least in local economic exchange, after the tax has been paid.

What is the essence of this change?

Wrong ideas on this point are widespread. They are due mainly to the fact that no attempt is being made to study the meaning of the transition or to determine its implications, it being assumed that the change is from communism in general to the bourgeois system in general. To counteract this mistake, one has to refer to what was said in May 1918.

The tax in kind is one of the forms of transition from that peculiar War Communism, which was forced on us by extreme want, ruin and war, to regular socialist exchange of products. The latter, in its turn, is one of the forms of transition from socialism, with the peculiar features due to the predominantly small-peasant population, to communism.

Under this peculiar War Communism we actually took from the peasant all his surpluses – and sometimes even a part of his necessaries – to meet the requirements of the army and sustain the workers. Most of it we took on loan, for paper money. But for that, we would not have beaten the landowners and capitalists in a ruined small-peasant country. The fact that we did (in spite of the help our exploiters got from the most powerful countries of the world) shows not only the miracles of heroism the workers and peasants can perform in the struggle for their emancipation; it also shows that when the Mensheviks, Socialist-Revolutionaries and Kautsky and Co. *blamed* us for this War Communism they were acting as lackeys of the bourgeoisie. We deserve credit for it.

Just how much credit is a fact of equal importance. It was the war and the ruin that forced us into War Communism. It was not, and could not be, a policy that corresponded to the economic tasks of the proletariat. It was a makeshift. The correct policy of the proletariat exercising its dictatorship in a small-peasant country is to obtain grain in exchange for the manufactured goods and peasant needs. That is the only kind of food policy that corresponds to the tasks of the proletariat, and can strengthen the foundations of socialism and lead to its complete victory.

The tax in kind is a transition to this policy. We are still so ruined and crushed by the burden of war (which was on but yesterday and could break out anew tomorrow, owing to the rapacity and malice of the capitalists) that we cannot give the peasant manufactured goods in return for *all* the grain we need. Being aware of this, we are introducing the tax in kind, that is, we shall take the minimum of grain we require (for the army and the workers) in the form of a tax and obtain the rest in exchange for manufactured goods.

There is something else we must not forget. Our poverty and ruin are so great that we cannot restore large-scale socialist state industry *at one stroke*. This can be done with large stocks of grain and fuel in the big industrial centres, replacement of worn-out machinery, and so on. Experience has convinced us that this cannot be done at one stroke, and we know that after the ruinous imperialist war even the wealthiest and most advanced countries will be able to solve this problem only over a fairly long period of years. Hence, it is necessary, to a certain extent, to help to restore *small* industry, which does not demand of the state machines, large stocks of raw material, fuel and food, and which can immediately render some assistance to peasant farming and increase its productive forces right away.

What is to be the effect of all this?

It is the revival of the petty bourgeoisie and of capitalism on the basis of some freedom of trade (if only local). That much is certain and it is ridiculous to shut our eyes to it.

Is it necessary? Can it be justified? Is it not dangerous?

Many such questions are being asked, and most are merely evidence of simple-mindedness, to put it mildly.

Look at my May 1918 definition of the elements (constituent parts) of the various socio-economic structures in our economy. No one can deny the existence of all these five stages (or constituent parts), of the five forms of economy – from the patriarchal, i.e. semi-barbarian, to the socialist system. That the small-peasant 'structure', partly patriarchal, partly petty bourgeois, predominates in a small-peasant country is self-evident. It is an incontrovertible truth, elementary to political economy, which even the layman's everyday experience will confirm, that once you have exchange the small economy is bound to develop the petty-bourgeois-capitalist way.

What is the policy the socialist proletariat can pursue in the face of this economic reality. Is it to give the small peasant *all* he needs of the goods produced by large-scale socialist industries in exchange for his grain and raw materials? This would be the most desirable and 'correct' policy – and we have started on it. But we cannot supply *all* the goods, very far from it; nor shall we be able to do so very soon – at all events not until we complete the first stage of the electrification of the whole country. What is to be done? One way is to try to prohibit entirely, to put the lock on all development of private, non-state exchange, i.e. trade, i.e. capitalism, which is inevitable with millions of small producers. But such a policy would be foolish and suicidal for the party that tried to apply it. It would be foolish because it is economically impossible. It would be suicidal because the party that tried to apply it would meet with inevitable disaster. Let us admit it: some Communists have sinned 'in thought, word and deed' by adopting just *such* a policy. We shall try to rectify these mistakes, and this must be done without fail, otherwise things will come to a very sorry state.

The alternative (and this is the only sensible and the last *possible* policy) is not to try to prohibit or put the lock on the development of capitalism, but to channel it into *state capitalism*. This is economically possible, for state capitalism exists – in varying form and degree – wherever there are elements of unrestricted trade and capitalism in general.

Can the Soviet state and the dictatorship of the proletariat be combined with state capitalism? Are they compatible?

Of course they are. This is exactly what I argued in May 1918. I hope I had proved it then. I had also proved that state capitalism is a step forward compared with the small-proprietor (both small-patriarchal and petty-bourgeois) element. Those who compare state capitalism only with socialism commit a host of mistakes, for in the present political and economic circumstances it is essential to compare state capitalism also with petty-bourgeois production.

The whole problem – in theoretical and practical terms – is to find the correct methods of directing the development of capitalism (which is to some extent and for some time inevitable) into the channels of state capitalism, and to determine how we are to hedge it about with conditions to ensure its transformation into socialism in the near future.

In order to approach the solution of this problem we must first of all picture to ourselves as distinctly as possible what state capitalism will and can be in practice inside the Soviet system and within the framework of the Soviet state.

Concessions are the simplest example of how the Soviet government directs the development of capitalism into the channels of state capitalism and 'implants' state capitalism. We all agree now that concessions are necessary, but have we all thought about the implications? What are concessions under the Soviet system, viewed in the light of the above-mentioned forms of economy and their inter-relations? They are an agreement, an alliance, a bloc between the Soviet, i.e. proletarian, state power and state capitalism against the small-proprietor (patriarchal and petty-bourgeois) element. The concessionaire is a capitalist.

He conducts his business on capitalist lines, for profit, and is willing to enter into an agreement with the proletarian government in order to obtain superprofits or raw materials which he cannot otherwise obtain, or can obtain only with great difficulty. Soviet power gains by the development of the productive forces, and by securing an increased quantity of goods immediately, or within a very short period. We have, say, a hundred oilfields, mines and forest tracts. We cannot develop all of them for we lack the machines, the food and the transport. This is also why we are doing next to nothing to develop the other territories. Owing to the insufficient development of the large enterprises the small-proprietor element is more pronounced in all its forms, and this is reflected in the deterioration of the surrounding (and later the whole of) peasant farming, the disruption of its productive forces, the decline in its confidence in the Soviet power, pilfering and widespread petty (the most dangerous) profiteering, etc. By 'implanting' state capitalism in the form of concessions, the Soviet government strengthens large-scale production as against petty production, advanced production as against backward production, and machine production as against hand production. It also obtains a larger quantity of the products of large-scale industry (its share of the output), and strengthens state-regulated economic relations as against the anarchy of petty-bourgeois relations. The moderate and cautious application of the concessions policy will undoubtedly help us quickly to improve (to a modest extent) the state of industry and the condition of the workers and peasants. We shall, of course, have all this at the price of certain sacrifices and the surrender to the capitalist of many millions of poods of very valuable products. The scale and the conditions under which concessions cease to be a danger and are turned to our advantage depend on the relation of forces and are decided in the struggle, for concessions are also a form of struggle, and are a continuation of the class struggle in another form, and in no circumstances are they a substitution of class peace for class war. Practice will determine the methods of struggle.

Compared with other forms of state capitalism within the Soviet system, concessions are perhaps the most simple and clear-cut form of state capitalism. It involves a formal written agreement with the most civilised, advanced, West-European capitalism. We know exactly what our gains and our losses, our rights and obligations are. We know exactly the term for which the concession is granted. We know the terms of redemption before the expiry of the agreement if it provides for such redemption. We pay a certain 'tribute' to world capitalism; we 'ransom' ourselves under certain arrangements, thereby immediately stabilising the Soviet power and improving our economic conditions. The whole difficulty with concessions is giving the proper consideration and appraisal of all the circumstances when concluding a concession agreement, and then seeing that it is fulfilled. Difficulties there certainly are, and mistakes will probably be inevitable at the outset. But these are minor difficulties compared with the other problems of the social revolution and, in particular, with the difficulties arising from other forms of developing, permitting and implanting state capitalism.

The most important task that confronts all Party and Soviet workers in connection with the introduction of the tax in kind is to apply the principles of the 'concessions' policy (i.e. a policy that is similar to 'concession' state capitalism) to the other forms of capitalism – unrestricted trade, local exchange, etc.

Take the co-operatives. It is not surprising that the tax in kind decree immediately necessitated a revision of the regulations governing the co-operatives and a certain extension of their 'freedom' and rights. The co-operatives are also a form of state capitalism, but a less simple one; its outline is less distinct, it is more intricate and therefore creates greater practical difficulties for the government. The small commodity producers' co-operatives (and it is these, and not the workers' co-operatives, that we are discussing as the predominant and typical form in a small-peasant country) inevitably give rise to petty-bourgeois, capitalist relations, facilitate their development, push the small capitalists into the foreground and benefit them most. It cannot be otherwise, since the small proprietors predominate, and exchange is necessary and possible. In Russia's present conditions, freedom and rights for the co-operative societies means freedom and rights for capitalism. It would be stupid or criminal to close our eyes to this obvious truth.

But, unlike private capitalism, 'co-operative' capitalism under the Soviet system is a variety of state capitalism, and as such it is advantageous and useful for us at the present time – in certain measure, of course. Since the tax in kind means the free sale of surplus grain (over and above that taken in the form of the tax), we must exert every effort to direct *this* development of capitalism – for a free market *is* development of capitalism – into the channels of co-operative capitalism. It resembles state capitalism in that it facilitates accounting, control, supervision and the establishment of contractual relations between the state (in this case the Soviet state) and the capitalist. Co-operative trade is more advantageous and useful than private trade not only for the above-mentioned reasons, but also because it facilitates the association and organisation of millions of people, and eventually of the entire population, and this in its turn is an enormous gain from the standpoint of the subsequent transition from state capitalism to socialism.

Let us make a comparison of concessions and co-operatives as forms of state capitalism. Concessions are based on large-scale machine industry; co-operatives are based on small, handicraft, and partly even on patriarchal industry. Each concession agreement affects one capitalist, firm, syndicate, cartel or trust. Co-operative societies embrace many thousands and even millions of small proprietors. Concessions allow and even imply a definite agreement for a specified period. Co-operative societies allow of neither. It is much easier to repeal the law on the co-operatives than to annul a concession agreement, but the annulment of an agreement means a sudden rupture of the practical relations of economic alliance, or economic coexistence, with the capitalist, whereas the repeal of the law on the co-operatives, or any law, for that matter, does not immediately break off the practical coexistence of Soviet power and the small capitalists, nor, in general, is it able to break off the actual economic relations. It is easy to 'keep an eye' on a concessionaire but not on the co-operators. The transition from concessions to socialism is a transition from one form of large-scale production to another. The transition from small-proprietor co-operatives to socialism is a transition from small to large-scale production, i.e. it is more complicated, but, if successful, is capable of embracing wider masses of the population, and pulling up the deeper and more tenacious roots of the old, pre-socialist and even pre-capitalist relations, which most stubbornly resist all 'innovations'. The concessions policy, if successful, will give us a few model – compared with our own – large enterprises built on the level of modern advanced capitalism. After a few decades these enterprises will revert to us in their entirety. The co-operative policy, if successful, will result in raising the small economy and in facilitating its transition, within an indefinite period, to large-scale production on the basis of voluntary association.

Take a third form of state capitalism. The state enlists the capitalist as a merchant and pays him a definite commission on the sale of state goods and on the purchase of the produce of the small producer. A fourth form: the state leases to the capitalist entrepreneur an industrial establishment, oilfields, forest tracts, land, etc, which belong to the state, the lease being very similar to a concession agreement. We make no mention of, we give no thought or notice to, these two latter forms of state capitalism, not because we are strong and clever but because we are weak and foolish. We are afraid to look the 'vulgar truth' squarely in the face, and too often yield to 'exalting deception'.[3] We keep repeating that 'we' are passing from capitalism to socialism, but do not bother to obtain a distinct picture of the 'we'. To keep this picture clear we must constantly have in mind the whole list – without any exception – of the constituent parts of our national economy, of all its diverse forms that I gave in my article of May 5, 1918. 'We', the vanguard, the advanced contingent of the proletariat, are passing directly to socialism; but the advanced contingent is only a small part of the whole of the proletariat while the latter, in its turn, is only a small part of the whole population. If 'we' are successfully to solve the problem of our immediate transition to socialism, we must understand what *intermediary* paths, methods, means and instruments are required for the transition from *pre-capitalist* relations to socialism. That is the whole point.

Look at the map of the RSFSR. There is room for dozens of large civilised states in those vast areas which lie to the north of Vologda, the south-east of Rostov-on-Don and Saratov, the south of Orenburg and Omsk, and the north of Tomsk. They are a realm of patriarchalism, and semi- and downright barbarism. And what about the peasant backwoods of the rest of Russia, where scores of versts of country track, or rather of trackless country, lie between the villages and the railways, i.e. the material link with the big cities, large-scale industry, capitalism and culture? Isn't that also an area of wholesale patriarchalism, Oblomovism[4] and semi-barbarism?

Is an immediate transition to socialism from the state of affairs predominating in Russia conceivable? Yes, it is, to a certain degree, but on one condition, the precise nature of which we now know thanks to a great piece of scientific work that has been completed. It is electrification. If we construct scores of district electric power stations (we now know where and how these can and should be constructed), and transmit electric power to every village, if we obtain a sufficient number of electric motors and other machinery, we shall not need, or shall hardly need, any transition stages or intermediary links between patriarchalism and socialism. But we know perfectly well that it will take at least ten years only to complete the first stage of this 'one' condition; this period can be conceivably reduced only if the proletarian revolution is victorious in such countries as Britain, Germany or the USA.

Over the next few years we must learn to think of the intermediary links that can facilitate the transition from patriarchalism and small production to socialism. 'We' continue saying now and again that 'capitalism is a bane and socialism is a boon'. But such an argument is wrong, because it fails to take into account the aggregate of the existing economic forms and singles out only two of them.

Capitalism is a bane compared with socialism. Capitalism is a boon compared with medievalism, small production, and the evils of bureaucracy which spring from the dispersal of the small producers. Inasmuch as we are as yet unable to pass directly from small production to socialism, some capitalism is inevitable as the elemental product of small production and exchange; so that we must utilise capitalism (particularly by directing it into the channels of state capitalism) as the intermediary link between small production and socialism, as a means, a path, and a method of increasing the productive forces.

Look at the economic aspect of the evils of bureaucracy. We see nothing of them on May 5, 1918. Six months after the October Revolution, with the old bureaucratic apparatus smashed from top to bottom, we feel none of its evils.

A year later, the Eighth Congress of the Russian Communist Party (March 18-23, 1919) adopted a new Party Programme in which we spoke forthrightly of '*a partial revival of bureaucracy within the Soviet system*' – not fearing to admit the evil, but desiring to reveal, expose and pillory it and to stimulate thought, will, energy and action to combat it.

Two years later, in the spring of 1921, after the Eighth Congress of Soviets (December 1920), which discussed the evils of bureaucracy, and after the Tenth Congress of the Russian Communist Party (March 1921), which summed up the controversies closely connected with an analysis of these evils, we find *them* even more distinct and sinister. What are their economic roots? They are mostly of a dual character: on the one hand, a developed bourgeoisie needs a bureaucratic apparatus, primarily a military apparatus, and then a judiciary, etc, to use against the revolutionary movement of the workers (and partly of the peasants). That is something we have not got. Ours are class courts directed against the bourgeoisie. Ours is a class army directed against the bourgeoisie. The evils of bureaucracy are not in the army, but in the institutions serving it. In our country bureaucratic practices have different economic roots, namely, the atomised and scattered state of the small producer with his poverty, illiteracy, lack of culture, the absence of roads and *exchange* between agriculture and industry, the absence of connection and interaction between them. This is largely the result of the Civil War. We could not restore industry when we were blockaded, besieged on all sides, cut off from the whole world and later from the grain-bearing South, Siberia, and the coalfields. We could not afford to hesitate in introducing War Communism, or daring to go to the most desperate extremes: to save the workers' and peasants' rule we had to suffer an existence of semi-starvation and worse than semi-starvation, but to hold on at all costs, in spite of unprecedented ruin and the absence of economic intercourse. We did not allow ourselves to be frightened, as the Socialist-Revolutionaries and Mensheviks did (who, in fact, followed the bourgeoisie largely because they were scared). But the factor that was crucial to victory in a blockaded country – a besieged fortress – revealed its negative side by the spring of 1921, just when the last of the whiteguard forces were finally driven from the territory of the RSFSR. In the besieged fortress, it was possible and imperative to 'lock up' all exchange; with the masses displaying extraordinary heroism this could be borne for three years. After that, the ruin of the small producer increased, and the restoration of large-scale industry was further delayed, and postponed. Bureaucratic practices, as a legacy of the 'siege' and the superstructure built over the isolated and downtrodden state of the small producer, fully revealed themselves.

We must learn to admit an evil fearlessly in order to combat it the more firmly, in order to start from scratch again and again; we shall have to do this many a time in every sphere of our activity, finish what was left undone and choose different approaches to the problem. In view of the obvious delay in the restoration of large-scale industry, the 'locking up' of exchange between industry and agriculture has become intolerable. Consequently, we must concentrate on what we can do: restoring small industry, helping things from that end, propping up the side of the structure that has been half-demolished by the war and blockade. We must do everything possible to develop trade at all costs, without being afraid of capitalism, because the limits we have put to it (the expropriation of the land-owners and of the bourgeoisie in the economy, the rule of the workers and peasants in politics) are sufficiently narrow and 'moderate'. This is the fundamental idea and economic significance of the tax in kind.

All Party and Soviet workers must concentrate their efforts and attention on generating the utmost local initiative in economic development – in the gubernias, still more in the uyezds, still more in the volosts and villages – for the special purpose of immediately improving peasant farming, even if by 'small' means, on a small scale, helping it by developing small local industry. The integrated state economic plan demands that this should become the focus of concern and 'priority' effort. Some improvement here, closest to the broadest and deepest 'foundation', will permit of the speediest transition to a more vigorous and successful restoration of large-scale industry.

Hitherto the food supply worker has known only one fundamental instruction: collect 100 per cent of the grain appropriations. Now he has another instruction: collect 100 per cent of the tax in the shortest possible time and then collect another 100 per cent in exchange for the goods of large-scale *and small* industry. Those who collect 75 per cent of the tax and 75 per cent (of the second hundred) in exchange for the goods of large-scale and small industry will be doing more useful work of national importance than those who collect 100 per cent of the tax and 55 per cent (of the second hundred) by means of exchange. The task of the food supply worker now becomes more complicated. On the one hand, it is a fiscal task: collect the tax as quickly and as efficiently as possible. On the other hand, it is a general economic task: try to direct the co-operatives, assist small industry, develop local initiative in such a way as to increase the exchange between agriculture and industry and put it on a sound basis. Our bureaucratic practices prove that we are still doing a very bad job of it. We must not be afraid to admit that in this respect *we still have a great deal to learn from the capitalist*. We shall compare the practical experience of the various gubernias, uyezds, volosts and villages: in one place private capitalists, big and small, have achieved so much; those are their approximate profits. That is the tribute, the fee, we have to pay for the 'schooling'. We shall not mind paying for it if we learn a thing or two. That much has been achieved in a neighbouring locality through co-operation. Those are the profits of the co-operatives. And in a third place, that much has been achieved by purely state and communist methods (for the present, this third case will be a rare exception).

It should be the primary task of every regional economic centre and economic conference of the gubernia executive committees immediately to organise various experiments, or systems of 'exchange' for the surplus stocks remaining after the tax in kind has been paid. In a few months' time practical results must be obtained for comparison and study. Local or imported salt; paraffin oil from the nearest town; the handicraft wood-working industry; handicrafts using local raw materials and producing certain, perhaps not very important, but necessary and useful, articles for the peasants; 'green coal' (the utilisation of small local water power resources for electrification), and so on and so forth – all this must be brought into play in order to stimulate exchange between industry and agriculture at all costs. Those who achieve the best results in this sphere, even by means of private capitalism, even without the co-operatives, or without directly transforming this capitalism into state capitalism, will do more for the cause of socialist construction in Russia than those who 'ponder over' the purity of communism, draw up regulations, rules and instructions for state capitalism and the co-operatives, but do nothing practical to stimulate trade.

Isn't it paradoxical that private capital should be helping socialism?

Not at all. It is, indeed, an irrefutable economic fact. Since this is a small peasant country with transport in an extreme state of dislocation, a country emerging from war and blockade under the political guidance of the proletariat – which controls the transport system and large-scale industry – it inevitably follows, first, that at the present moment local exchange acquires first-class significance, and, second, that there is a possibility of assisting socialism by means of private capitalism (not to speak of state capitalism).

Let's not quibble about words. We still have too much of that sort of thing. We must have more variety in practical experience and make a wider study of it. In certain circumstances, the exemplary organisation of local work, even on the smallest scale, is of far greater national importance than many branches of central state work. These are precisely the circumstances now prevailing in peasant farming in general, and in regard to the exchange of the surplus products of agriculture for industrial goods in particular. Exemplary organisation in this respect, even in a single volost, is of far greater national importance than the 'exemplary' improvement of the central apparatus of any People's Commissariat; over the past three and a half years our central apparatus has been built up to such an extent that it has managed to acquire a certain amount of harmful routine; we cannot improve it quickly to any extent, we do not know how to do it. Assistance in the work of radically improving it, securing an influx of fresh forces, combating bureaucratic practices effectively and overcoming this harmful routine must come from the localities and the lower ranks, with the model organisation of a 'complex', even if on a small scale. I say 'complex', meaning not just one farm, one branch of industry, or one factory, but a *totality* of economic relations, a *totality* of economic exchange, even if only in a small locality.

Those of us who are doomed to remain at work in the centre will continue the task of improving the apparatus and purging it of bureaucratic evils, even if only on a modest and immediately achievable scale. But the greatest assistance in this task is coming, and will come, from the localities. Generally speaking, as far as I can observe, things are better in the localities than at the centre; and this is understandable, for, naturally, the evils of bureaucracy are concentrated at the centre. In this respect, Moscow cannot but be the worst city, and in general the worst 'locality', in the Republic. In the localities we have deviations from the average to the good and the bad sides, the latter being less frequent than the former. The deviations towards the bad side are the abuses committed by former government officials, landowners, bourgeois and other scum who play up to the Communists and who sometimes commit abominable outrages and acts of tyranny against the peasantry. This calls for a terrorist purge, summary trial and the firing squad. Let the Martovs, the Chernovs, and non-Party philistines like them, beat their breasts and exclaim: 'I thank Thee, Lord, that I am not as "these", and have never accepted terrorism'. These simpletons 'do not accept terrorism' because they choose to be servile accomplices of the whiteguards in fooling the workers and peasants. The Socialist-Revolutionaries and Mensheviks 'do not accept terrorism' because under the flag of 'socialism' they are fulfilling their function of *placing* the masses *at the mercy of the whiteguard terrorism*. This was proved by the Kerensky regime and the Kornilov putsch in Russia, by the Kolchak regime in Siberia, and by Menshevism in Georgia. It was proved by the heroes of the Second International and of the 'Two-and-a-Half'[5] International in Finland, Hungary, Austria, Germany, Italy, Britain, etc. Let the flunkey accomplices of whiteguard terrorism wallow in their repudiation of all terrorism. We shall speak the bitter and indubitable truth: in countries beset by an unprecedented crisis, the collapse of old ties, and the intensification of the class struggle after the imperialist war of 1914-18 – and that means all the countries of the world – terrorism cannot be dispensed with, notwithstanding the hypocrites and phrase-mongers. Either the whiteguard, bourgeois terrorism of the American, British (Ireland), Italian (the fascists), German, Hungarian and other types, or Red, proletarian terrorism. There is no middle course, no 'third' course, nor can there be any.

The deviations towards the good side are the success achieved in combating the evils of bureaucracy, the great attention shown for the needs of the workers and peasants, and the great care in developing the economy, raising the productivity of labour and stimulating local exchange between agriculture and industry. Although the good examples are more numerous than the bad ones, they are, nevertheless, rare. Still, they are there. Young, fresh communist forces, steeled by civil war and privation, are coming forward in all localities. We are still doing far too little to promote these forces regularly from lower to higher posts. This can and must be done more persistently, and on a wider scale than at present. Some workers can and should be transferred from work at the centre to local work. As leading men of uyezds, and of *volosts*, where they can organise economic work *as a whole* on *exemplary* lines, they will do far more good, and perform work of far greater *national* importance, than by performing some function at the centre. The exemplary organisation of the work will help to train new workers and provide examples that other districts could follow with relative ease. We at the centre shall be able to do a great deal to encourage the other districts all over the country to 'follow' the good examples, and even make it mandatory for them to do so.

By its very nature, the work of developing 'exchange' between agriculture and industry, the exchange of after-tax surpluses for the output of small, mainly handicraft, industry, calls for independent, competent and intelligent *local initiative*. That is why it is now extremely important from the national standpoint to organise the work in the uyezds and volosts on exemplary lines. In military affairs, during the last Polish war, for example, we were not afraid of departing from the bureaucratic hierarchy, 'downgrading', or transferring members of the Revolutionary Military Council of the Republic to lower posts (while allowing them to retain their higher rank at the centre). Why not now transfer several members of the All-Russia Central Executive Committee, or members of collegiums, or other high-ranking comrades, to uyezd or even volost work? Surely, we have not become so 'bureaucratised' as to 'be ashamed' of that. And we shall find scores of workers in the central bodies who will be glad to accept. The economic development of the whole Republic will gain enormously; and the exemplary volosts, or uyezds, will play not only a great, but a positively crucial and historic role.

Incidentally, we should note as a small but significant circumstance the necessary change in our attitude to the problem of combating profiteering. We must foster 'proper' trade, which is one that does not evade state control; it is to our advantage to develop it. But profiteering, in its politico-economic sense, *cannot* be distinguished from 'proper' trade. Freedom of trade is capitalism; capitalism is profiteering. It would be ridiculous to ignore this.

What then should be done? Shall we declare profiteering to be no longer punishable?

No. We must revise and redraft all the laws on profiteering, and declare all *pilfering* and every direct or indirect, open or concealed *evasion of state control, supervision and accounting* to be a punishable offence (and in fact prosecuted with redoubled severity). It is by presenting the question in this way (the Council of People's Commissars has already started, that is to say, it has ordered that work be started, on the revision of the anti-profiteering laws) that we shall succeed in directing the rather inevitable but necessary development of capitalism into the channels of *state* capitalism.

Political Summary and Deductions

I still have to deal, if briefly, with the political situation, and the way it has taken shape and changed in connection with the economic developments outlined above.

I have already said that the fundamental features of our economy in 1921 are the same as those in 1918. The spring of 1921, mainly as a result of the crop failure and the loss of cattle, brought a sharp deterioration in the condition of the peasantry, which was bad enough because of the war and blockade. This resulted in political vacillations which, generally speaking, express the very 'nature' of the small producer. Their most striking expression was the Kronstadt mutiny.

The vacillation of the petty-bourgeois element was the most characteristic feature of the Kronstadt events.[6] There was very little that was clear, definite and fully shaped. We heard nebulous slogans about 'freedom', 'freedom of trade', 'emancipation', 'Soviets without the Bolsheviks', or new elections to the Soviets, or relief from 'Party dictatorship', and so on and so forth. Both the Mensheviks and the Socialist-Revolutionaries declared the Kronstadt movement to be 'their own'. Victor Chernov sent a messenger to Kronstadt. On the latter's proposal, the Menshevik Valk, one of the Kronstadt leaders, voted for the *Constituent Assembly*. In a flash, with lightning speed, you might say, the whiteguards mobilised all their forces '*for Kronstadt*'. Their military experts in Kronstadt, a number of experts, and not Kozlovsky alone, drew up a plan for a landing at Oranienbaum, which scared the vacillating mass of Mensheviks, Socialist-Revolutionaries and non-party elements. More than fifty Russian whiteguard newspapers published abroad conducted a rabid campaign '*for Kronstadt*'. The big banks, all the forces of finance capital, collected funds to assist Kronstadt. That shrewd leader of the bourgeoisie and the landowners, the Cadet Milyukov, patiently explained to the simpleton Victor Chernov directly (and to the Mensheviks Dan and Rozhkov, who are in jail in Petrograd for their connection with the Kronstadt events, indirectly) that there is no need to hurry with the Constituent Assembly, and that *Soviet power* can and must be supported – *only without the Bolsheviks*.

Of course, it is easy to be cleverer than conceited simpletons like Chernov, the petty-bourgeois phrase-monger, or like Martov, the knight of philistine reformism doctored to pass for Marxism. Properly speaking, the point is not that Milyukov, as an individual, has more brains, but that, because of his class position, the party leader of the big bourgeoisie sees and understands the class essence and political interaction of things more clearly than the leaders of the petty bourgeoisie, the Chernovs and Martovs. For the bourgeoisie is really a class force which, under capitalism, inevitably rules both under a monarchy and in the most democratic republic, and which also inevitably enjoys the support of the world bourgeoisie. But the petty bourgeoisie, i.e. all the heroes of the Second International and of the 'Two-and-a-Half' International, cannot, by the very economic nature of things, be anything else than the expression of class impotence; hence the vacillation, phrase-mongering and helplessness. In 1789, the petty bourgeois could still be great revolutionaries. In 1848, they were ridiculous and pathetic. Their actual role in 1917-21 is that of abominable agents and out-and-out servitors of reaction, be their names Chernov, Martov, Kautsky, MacDonald, or what have you.

Martov showed himself to be nothing but a philistine Narcissus when he declared in his Berlin journal[7] that Kronstadt not only adopted Menshevik slogans but also proved that there could be an anti-Bolshevik movement which did not entirely serve the interests of the whiteguards, the capitalists and the landowners. He says in effect: 'Let us shut our eyes to the fact that all the genuine whiteguards hailed the Kronstadt mutineers and collected funds in aid of Kronstadt through the banks!' Compared with the Chernovs and Martovs, Milyukov is right, for he is revealing the *true* tactics of the *real* whiteguard force, the force of the capitalists and landowners. He declares: 'It does not matter whom we support, be they anarchists or any sort of Soviet government, *as long as* the Bolsheviks are overthrown, *as long as there is a shift in power*; it does not matter whether to the right or to the left, to the Mensheviks or to the anarchists, as long as it is away from the Bolsheviks. As for the rest – 'we', the Milyukovs, 'we', the capitalists and landowners, will do the rest 'ourselves'; we shall slap down the anarchist pygmies, the Chernovs and the Martovs, as we did Chernov and Maisky in Siberia, the Hungarian Chernovs and Martovs in Hungary, Kautsky in Germany and the Friedrich Adlers and Co. in Vienna.' The real, hard-headed bourgeoisie have made fools of hundreds of these philistine Narcissuses – whether Menshevik, Socialist-Revolutionary or non-party – and have driven them out scores of times in all revolutions in all countries. History proves it. The facts bear it out. The Narcissuses will talk; the Milyukovs and whiteguards will act.

Milyukov is absolutely right when he says, 'If only there is a power shift away from the Bolsheviks, no matter whether it is a little to the right or to the left, the rest will take care of itself'. This is class truth, confirmed by the history of revolutions in all countries, and by the centuries of modern history since the Middle Ages. The scattered small producers, the peasants, are economically *and politically* united either by the bourgeoisie (this has always been – and will always be – the case under capitalism in all countries, in all modern revolutions), or by the proletariat (that was the case in a rudimentary form for a very short period at the peak of some of the greatest revolutions in modern history; that has been the case in Russia in a more developed form in 1917-21). Only the Narcissuses will talk and dream about a 'third' path, and a 'third force'.

With enormous difficulty, and in the course of desperate struggles, the Bolsheviks have trained a proletarian vanguard that is capable of governing; they have created and successfully defended the dictatorship of the proletariat. After the test of four years of practical experience, the relation of class forces in Russia has become as clear as day: the steeled and tempered vanguard of the only revolutionary class; the vacillating petty-bourgeois element; and the Milyukovs, the capitalists and landowners, lying in wait abroad and supported by the world bourgeoisie. It is crystal-clear: only the latter are able to take advantage of any 'shift of power', and will certainly do so.

In the 1918 pamphlet I quoted above, this point was put very clearly: 'the principal enemy' is the 'petty-bourgeois element'. 'Either we subordinate it to our control and accounting, or it will overthrow the workers' power as surely and as inevitably as the revolution was overthrown by the Napoleons and the Cavaignacs who sprang from this very soil of petty proprietorship. This is how the question stands. That is the only view we can take of the matter.' (Excerpt from the pamphlet of May 5, 1918, cf. above.)

Our strength lies in complete clarity and the sober consideration of *all* the existing class magnitudes, both Russian and international: and in the inexhaustible energy, iron resolve and devotion in struggle that arise from this. We have many enemies, but they are disunited, or do not know their own minds (like all the petty bourgeoisie, all the Martovs and Chernovs, all the non-party elements and anarchists). But we are united – directly among ourselves and indirectly with the proletarians of all countries; we know just what we want. That is why we are invincible on a world scale, although this does not in the least preclude the possibility of defeat for individual proletarian revolutions for longer or shorter periods.

There is good reason for calling the petty-bourgeois element an element, for it is indeed something that is most amorphous, indefinite and unconscious. The petty-bourgeois Narcissuses imagine that 'universal suffrage' abolishes the nature of the small producer under capitalism. As a matter of fact, it *helps* the bourgeoisie, through the church, the press, the teachers, the police, the militarists and a thousand and one forms of economic oppression, to *subordinate* the scattered small producers. Ruin, want and the hard conditions of life give rise to vacillation: one day for the bourgeoisie, the next, for the proletariat. Only the steeled proletarian vanguard is capable of withstanding and overcoming this vacillation.

The events of the spring of 1921 once again revealed the role of the Socialist-Revolutionaries and Mensheviks: they help the vacillating petty-bourgeois element to recoil from the Bolsheviks, to cause a 'shift of power' in favour of the capitalists and landowners. *The Mensheviks and Socialist-Revolutionaries have now learned to don the 'non-party' disguise.* This has been fully proved. Only fools now fail to see this and understand that we must not allow ourselves to be fooled. Non-Party conferences are not a fetish. They are valuable if they help us to come closer to the impassive masses – the millions of working people still outside politics. They are harmful if they provide a platform for the Mensheviks and Socialist-Revolutionaries masquerading as 'non-party' men. They are helping the mutinies, and the whiteguards. The place for Mensheviks and Socialist-Revolutionaries, avowed or in non-party guise, is not at a non-Party conference but in prison (or on foreign journals, side by side with the white-guards; we were glad to let Martov go abroad). We can and must find other methods of testing the mood of the masses and coming closer to them. We suggest that those who want to play the parliamentary, constituent assembly and non-Party conference game, should go abroad; over there, by Martov's side, they can try the charms of 'democracy' and ask Wrangel's soldiers about them. We have no time for this 'opposition' at 'conferences' game. We are surrounded by the world bourgeoisie, who are watching for every sign of vacillation in order to bring back 'their own men', and restore the landowners and the bourgeoisie. We will keep in prison the Mensheviks and Socialist-Revolutionaries, whether avowed or in 'non-party' guise.

We shall employ every means to establish closer contacts with the masses of working people untouched by politics – except such means as give scope to the Mensheviks and Socialist-Revolutionaries, and the *vacillations that benefit Milyukov*. In particular, we shall zealously draw into Soviet work, primarily economic work, hundreds upon hundreds of non-Party people, real non-Party people from the masses, the rank and file of workers and peasants, and not those who have adopted non-party colours in order to crib Menshevik and Socialist-Revolutionary instructions which are so much to Milyukov's advantage. Hundreds and thousands of non-Party people are working for us, and scores occupy very important and responsible posts. We must pay more attention to the way they work. We must do more to promote and test thousands and thousands of rank-and-file workers, to try them out systematically and persistently, and appoint hundreds of them to higher posts, if experience shows that they can fill them.

Our Communists still do not have a sufficient understanding of their real duties of administration: they should not strive to do 'everything themselves', running themselves down and failing to cope with everything, undertaking twenty jobs and finishing none. They should check up on the work of scores and hundreds of assistants, arrange to have their work checked up from below, i.e. by the real masses. They should *direct* the work and *learn* from those who have the knowledge (the specialists) and the experience in organising large-scale production (the capitalists). The intelligent Communist will not be afraid to learn from the military expert, although nine-tenths of the military experts are capable of treachery at every opportunity. The wise Communist will not be afraid to learn from a capitalist (whether a big capitalist concessionaire, a commission agent, or a petty capitalist co-operator, etc), although the capitalist is no better than the military expert. Did we not learn to catch treacherous military experts in the Red Army, to bring out the honest and conscientious, and, on the whole, to utilise thousands and tens of thousands of military experts? We are learning to do the same thing (in an unconventional way) with engineers and teachers, although we are not doing it as well as we did it in the Red Army (there Denikin and Kolchak spurred us on, compelled us to learn more quickly, diligently and intelligently). We shall also learn to do it (again in an unconventional way) with the commission agents, with the buyers working for the state, the petty capitalist co-operators, the entrepreneur concessionaires, etc.

The condition of the masses of workers and peasants needs to be improved right away. And we shall achieve this by putting new forces, including non-Party forces, to useful work. The tax in kind, and a number of measures connected with it, will facilitate this; we shall thereby cut at the economic root of the small producer's inevitable vacillations. And we shall ruthlessly fight the political vacillations, which benefit no one but Milyukov. The waverers are many, we are few. The waverers are disunited, we are united. The waverers are not economically independent, the proletariat is. The waverers don't know their own minds: they want to do something very badly, but Milyukov won't let them. We know what we want.

And that is why we shall win.

Conclusion

To sum up.

The tax in kind is a transition from War Communism to a regular socialist exchange of products.

The extreme ruin rendered more acute by the crop failure in 1920 has made this transition urgently necessary owing to the fact that it was impossible to restore large-scale industry rapidly.

Hence, the first thing to do is to improve the condition of the peasants. The means are the tax in kind, the development of exchange between agriculture and industry, and the development of small industry.

Exchange is freedom of trade; it is capitalism. It is useful to us inasmuch as it will help us overcome the dispersal of the small producer, and to a certain degree combat the evils of bureaucracy; to what extent this can be done will be determined by practical experience. The proletarian power is in no danger, as long as the proletariat firmly holds power in its hands, and has full control of transport and large-scale industry.

The fight against profiteering must be transformed into a fight against stealing and the evasion of state supervision, accounting and control. By means of this control we shall direct the capitalism that is to a certain extent inevitable and necessary for us into the channels of state capitalism.

The development of local initiative and independent action in encouraging exchange between agriculture and industry must be given the fullest scope at all costs. The practical experience gained must be studied; and this experience must be made as varied as possible.

We must give assistance to small industry servicing peasant farming and helping to improve it. To some extent, this assistance may be given in the form of raw materials from the state stocks. It would be most criminal to leave these raw materials unprocessed.

We must not be afraid of Communists 'learning' from bourgeois experts, including merchants, petty capitalist co-operators and capitalists, in the same way as we learned from the military experts, though in a different form. The results of the 'learning' must be tested only by practical experience and by doing things better than the bourgeois experts at your side; try in every way to secure an improvement in agriculture and industry, and to develop exchange between them. Do not grudge them the 'tuition' fee: none will be too high, provided we learn something.

Do everything to help the masses of working people, to come closer to them, and to promote from their ranks hundreds and thousands of non-Party people for the work of economic administration. As for the 'non-party' people who are only Mensheviks and Socialist-Revolutionaries disguised in fashionable non-party attire *à la* Kronstadt, they should be kept safe in prison, or packed off to Berlin, to join Martov in freely enjoying all the charms of pure democracy and freely exchanging ideas with Chernov, Milyukov and the Georgian Mensheviks.

Notes

[1] The reference is to Marx, *Critique of the Gotha Programme*, Marx and Engels Selected Works in One Volume, Lawrence and Wishart 1968, p 320 – *ed*.

[2] See Engels, *The Peasant Question in France and Germany*, Marx and Engels Selected Works in One Volume, *op cit*, p 639, where he quotes Marx's opinion – *ed*.

[3] A paraphrase of Pushkin's words from his poem *A Hero* in which he says that he prefers the stimulating falsehood to a mass of sordid truths – *ed*.

[4] Oblomov was a Russian landowner in I A Goncharov's novel of the same name; he symbolises sluggishness and stagnation – *ed*.

[5] The 'Two and-a-Half' International was an international association of parties which left the Second International without actually joining the Third International, adopting an 'in-between' position. It was established in 1921 but broke up in 1923 – *ed*.

[6] Kronstadt was a fortress in the Gulf of Findland. Sailors and workers there played a major part in the October revolution. A revolt took place there in 1921, of a 'leftist' character; it was crushed in a few days – *ed*.

[7] The *Sotsialistichevsky Vestnik* (Socialist Herald) – a Menshevik emigré journal set up by Martov in 1921 – *ed*.

14. On Co-operation

It seems to me that not enough attention is being paid to the co-operative movement in our country. Not everyone understands that now, since the time of the October Revolution and quite apart from NEP (on the contrary, in this connection we must say – because of NEP), our co-operative movement has become one of great significance. There is a lot of fantasy in the dreams of the old co-operators. Often they are ridiculously fantastic. But why are they fantastic? Because people do not understand the fundamental, the rock-bottom significance of the working-class political struggle for the overthrow of the rule of the exploiters. We have overthrown the rule of the exploiters, and much that was fantastic, even romantic, even banal in the dreams of the old co-operators is now becoming unvarnished reality.

Indeed, since political power is in the hands of the working class, since this political power owns all the means of production, the only task, indeed, that remains for us is to organise the population in co-operative societies. With most of the population organised in co-operatives, the socialism which in the past was legitimately treated with ridicule, scorn and contempt by those who were rightly convinced that it was necessary to wage the class struggle, the struggle for political power, etc, will achieve its aim automatically. But not all comrades realise how vastly, how infinitely important it is now to organise the population of Russia in co-operative societies. By adopting NEP we made a concession to the peasant as a trader, to the principle of private trade; it is precisely for this reason (contrary to what

Published as two articles in *Pravda* May 26 and 27, 1923.
CW XXXIII 467-475.

some people think) that the co-operative movement is of such immense importance. All we actually need under NEP is to organise the population of Russia in co-operative societies on a sufficiently large scale, for we have now found that degree of combination of private interest, of private commercial interest, with state supervision and control of this interest, that degree of its subordination to the common interests which was formerly the stumbling-block for very many socialists. Indeed, the power of the state over all large-scale means of production, political power in the hands of the proletariat, the alliance of this proletariat with the many millions of small and very small peasants, the assured proletarian leadership of the peasantry, etc – is this not all that is necessary to build a complete socialist society out of co-operatives, out of co-operatives alone, which we formerly ridiculed as huckstering and which from a certain aspect we have the right to treat as such now, under NEP? Is this not all that is necessary to build a complete socialist society? It is still not the building of socialist society, but it is all that is necessary and sufficient for it.

It is this very circumstance that is underestimated by many of our practical workers. They look down upon our co-operative societies, failing to appreciate their exceptional importance, first, from the standpoint of principle (the means of production are owned by the state), and, second, from the standpoint of transition to the new system by means that are the *simplest, easiest and most acceptable to the peasant*.

But this again is of fundamental importance. It is one thing to draw up fantastic plans for building socialism through all sorts of workers' associations, and quite another to learn to build socialism in practice in such a way that *every* small peasant could take part in it. That is the very stage we have now reached. And there is no doubt that, having reached it, we are taking too little advantage of it.

We went too far when we introduced NEP, but not because we attached too much importance to the principle of free enterprise and trade – we went too far because we lost sight of the co-operatives, because we now underrate the co-operatives, because we are already beginning to forget the vast importance of the co-operatives from the above two points of view.

I now propose to discuss with the reader what can and must at once be done practically on the basis of this 'co-operative' principle. By what means can we, and must we, start at once to develop this 'co-operative' principle so that its socialist meaning may be clear to all?

Co-operation must be politically so organised that it will not only generally and always enjoy certain privileges, but that these privileges should be of a purely material nature (a favourable bank-rate, etc). The co-operatives must be granted state loans that are greater, if only by a little, than the loans we grant to private enterprises, even to heavy industry, etc.

A social system emerges only if it has the financial backing of a definite class. There is no need to mention the hundreds of millions of rubles that the birth of 'free' capitalism cost. At present we have to realise that the co-operative system is the social system we must now give more than ordinary assistance, and we must actually give that assistance. But it must be assistance in the real sense of the word, i.e. it will not be enough to interpret it to mean assistance for any kind of co-operative trade; by assistance we must mean aid to co-operative trade in which *really large masses of the population actually take part*. It is certainly a correct form of assistance to give a bonus to peasants who take part in co-operative trade; but the whole point is to verify the nature of this participation, to verify the awareness behind it, and to verify its quality. Strictly speaking, when a co-operator goes to a village and opens a co-operative store, the people take no part in this whatever; but at the same time guided by their own interests they will hasten to try to take part in it.

There is another aspect to this question. From the point of view of the 'enlightened' (primarily, literate) European there is not much left for us to do to induce absolutely everyone to take not a passive, but an active part in co-operative operations. Strictly speaking, there is '*only*' one thing we have left to do and that is to make our people so 'enlightened' that they understand all the advantages of everybody participating in the work of the co-operatives, and organise this participation. '*Only*' that. There are now no other devices needed to advance to socialism. But to achieve this 'only', there must be a veritable revolution – the entire people must go through a period of cultural development. Therefore, our rule must be: as little philosophising and as few acrobatics as possible. In this respect NEP is an advance, because it is adjustable to the level of the most ordinary peasant and does not demand anything higher of him. But it will take a whole historical epoch to get the entire population into the work of the co-operatives through NEP. At best we can achieve this in one or two decades. Nevertheless, it will be a distinct historical epoch, and without this historical epoch, without universal literacy, without a proper degree of efficiency, without training the population sufficiently to acquire the habit of book-reading, and without the material basis for this, without a certain sufficiency to safeguard against, say, bad harvests, famine, etc – without this we shall not achieve our object. The thing now is to learn to combine the wide revolutionary range of action, the revolutionary enthusiasm which we have displayed, and displayed abundantly, and crowned with complete success – to learn to combine this with (I am almost inclined to say) the ability to be an efficient and capable trader, which is quite enough to be a good co-operator. By ability to be a trader I mean the ability to be a cultured trader. Let those Russians, or peasants, who imagine that since they trade they are good traders, get that well into their heads. This does not follow at all. They do trade, but that is far from being cultured traders. They now trade in an Asiatic manner, but to be a good trader one must trade in the European manner. They are a whole epoch behind in that.

In conclusion: a number of economic, financial and banking privileges must be granted to the co-operatives – this is the way our socialist state must promote the new principle on which the population must be organised. But this is only the general outline of the task; it does not define and depict in detail the entire content of the practical task, i.e. we must find what form of 'bonus' to give for joining the co-operatives (and the terms on which we should give it), the form of bonus by which we shall assist the co-operatives sufficiently, the form of bonus that will produce the civilised co-operator. And given social ownership of the means of production, given the class victory of the proletariat over the bourgeoisie, the system of civilised co-operators is the system of socialism.

II

Whenever I wrote about the New Economic Policy I always quoted the article on state capitalism[1] which I wrote in 1918. This has more than once aroused doubts in the minds of certain young comrades. But their doubts were mainly on abstract political points.

It seemed to them that the term 'state capitalism' could not be applied to a system under which the means of production were owned by the working class, a working class that held political power. They did not notice, however, that I used the term 'state capitalism', *firstly*, to connect historically our present position with the position adopted in my controversy with the so-called Left Communists; also, I argued at the time that state capitalism would be superior to our existing economy. It was important for me to show the continuity between ordinary state capitalism and the unusual, even very unusual, state capitalism to which I referred in introducing the reader to the New Economic Policy. *Secondly*, the practical purpose was always important to me. And the practical purpose of our New Economic Policy was to lease out concessions. In the prevailing circumstances, concessions in our country would unquestionably have been a pure type of state capitalism. That is how I argued about state capitalism.

But there is another aspect of the matter for which we may need state capitalism, or at least a comparison with it. It is the question of co-operatives.

In the capitalist state, co-operatives are no doubt collective capitalist institutions. Nor is there any doubt that under our present economic conditions, when we combine private capitalist enterprises – but in no other way than on nationalised land and in no other way than under the control of the working-class state – with enterprises of a consistently socialist type (the means of production, the land on which the enterprises are situated, and the enterprises as a whole belonging to the state), the question arises about a third type of enterprise, the co-operatives, which were not formerly regarded as an independent type differing fundamentally from the others. Under private capitalism, co-operative enterprises differ from capitalist enterprises as collective enterprises differ from private enterprises. Under state capitalism, co-operative enterprises differ from state capitalist enterprises, firstly, because they are private enterprises, and, secondly, because they are collective enterprises. Under our present system, co-operative enterprises differ from private capitalist enterprises because they are collective enterprises, but do not differ from socialist enterprises if the land on which they are situated and the means of production belong to the state, i.e. the working class.

This circumstance is not considered sufficiently when co-operatives are discussed. It is forgotten that owing to the special features of our political system, our co-operatives acquire an altogether exceptional significance. If we exclude concessions, which, incidentally, have not developed on any considerable scale, co-operation under our conditions nearly always coincides fully with socialism.

Let me explain what I mean. Why were the plans of the old co-operators, from Robert Owen onwards, fantastic? Because they dreamed of peacefully remodelling contemporary society into socialism without taking account of such fundamental questions as the class struggle, the capture of political power by the working class, the overthrow of the rule of the exploiting class. That is why we are right in regarding as entirely fantastic this 'co-operative' socialism, and as romantic, and even banal, the dream of transforming class enemies into class collaborators and class war into class peace (so-called class truce) by merely organising the population in co-operative societies.

Undoubtedly we were right from the point of view of the fundamental task of the present day, for socialism cannot be established without a class struggle for political power in the state.

But see how things have changed now that political power is in the hands of the working class, now that the political power of the exploiters is overthrown and all the means of production (except those which the workers' state voluntarily abandons on specified terms and for a certain time to the exploiters in the form of concessions) are owned by the working class.

Now we are entitled to say that for us the mere growth of co-operation (with the 'slight' exception mentioned above) is identical with the growth of socialism, and at the same time we have to admit that there has been a radical modification in our whole outlook on socialism. The radical modification is this; formerly we placed, and had to place, the main emphasis on the political struggle, on revolution, on winning political power, etc. Now the emphasis is changing and shifting to peaceful, organisational, 'cultural' work. I should say that emphasis is shifting to educational work, were it not for our international relations, were it not for the fact that we have to fight for our position on a world scale. If we leave that aside, however, and confine ourselves in internal economic relations, the emphasis in our work is certainly shifting to education.

Two main tasks confront us, which constitute the epoch – to reorganise our machinery of state, which is utterly useless, and which we took over in its entirety from the preceding epoch; during the past five years of struggle we did not, and could not, drastically reorganise it. Our second task is educational work among the peasants. And the economic object of this educational work among the peasants is to organise the latter in co-operative societies. If the whole of the peasantry had been organised in co-operatives, we would by now have been standing with both feet on the soil of socialism. But the organisation of the entire peasantry in co-operative societies presupposes a standard of culture among the peasants (precisely among the peasants as the overwhelming mass) that cannot, in fact, be achieved without a cultural revolution.

Our opponents told us repeatedly that we were rash in undertaking to implant socialism in an insufficiently cultured country. But they were misled by our having started from the opposite end to that prescribed by theory (the theory of pedants of all kinds), because in our country the political and social revolution preceded the cultural revolution, that very cultural revolution which nevertheless now confronts us.

This cultural revolution would now suffice to make our country a completely socialist country; but it presents immense difficulties of a purely cultural (for we are illiterate) and material character (for to be cultured we must achieve a certain development of the material means of production, must have a certain material base).

Notes

[1] See *The Tax in Kind*, p. 301 in this book – *ed.*

A Complete List
of Lenin's Economic Writings

*All References taken from the 45 volume edition of Lenin's Collected Works, Lawrence & Wishart, London. Book Reviews are indicated by (R), Articles (A), Books (B), and Pamphlets (P). Where only a part of a work refers to economic matters, a symbol [☆] is used, Those marked * have been included in this selection.*

(1) *New Economic Developments in Peasant Life* (On V Y Postnikov's Peasant Farming in South Russia) (P) [Agrarian Relations; Against Economic Romanticism of Narodniks and the Russian *mir*] Vol I (pp 11-73) [Large chunks of quotation from Postnikov].

(2) *On the So-called Market Question* (B) [Can Capitalism develop when the people are poor?; Lenin extensively uses Marx's schema for expanded reproduction] Vol I (pp 75-125)*.

(3) *What the 'Friends of the People' Are and How They Fight the Social Democrats* (B) [Polemic against anti-Marxist Narodniks] Vol I (pp 129-322) [☆].

(4) *The Economic Content of Narodism and the Criticism of it in Mr. Struve's Book* (The Reflection of Marxism in Bourgeois Literature) [Anti-Narodnik] Vol I (pp 333-500) [☆].

(5) *Gymnasium Farms and Collective Gymnasia* (A) [On Narodnik plan for 'communal farms'] Vol II (pp 73-80).

(6) *A Characterisation of Economic Romanticism* (Sismondi and Our Native Sismondists) (B) [Once again on the question of the sufficiency of the home market; comparable remarks on Sismondi in Rosa Luxembourg's Accumulation of Capital; against 'sentimental criticism of capitalism' fashionable among Third World radicals today] Vol II (pp 129-252).

(7) *The Handicraft Census of 1894-95 in Perm Gubernia and General Problems of 'Handicraft' Industry* (A) [Small and cottage industries in a less developed economy during growth of capitalist tendencies] Vol II (pp 355-458) [☆].

(8) *The Development of Capitalism in Russia* (B) [Economic Growth in a Less-developed Economy – Lenin's criticism of anti-capitalist Narodniks from a rigorous Marxist point of view – Summarises a lot of the literature in (1) to (7) above] Vol III (pp 1-603) [☆].

(9) *On the Question of Our Factory Statistics* (P) [Polemic about growth/decline of industrialisation in Russia] Vol IV (pp 13-45).

(10) *Review. A. Bogdanov – A Short Course of Economic Science* (R) [Review of a 'Marxist' economics textbook] Vol IV (pp 46-54).

(11) *A Note on the Question of the Market Theory* (Apropos of the Polemic of Messers Tugan-Baranovsky and Bulgakov) (A) [The question of realisation of surplus-value and the home market; Comparable remarks on Tugan-Baranovsky and Bulgakov in Rosa Luxembourg's Accumulation of Capital] Vol IV (pp 55-64).

(12) *Review – Parvus – The World Market and the Agricultural Crisis* (R) [Incidental mention of the problem of ground rent and agricultural prices] Vol IV (pp 65-6).

(13) *Review – R. Gvozdev – Kulak Usury – Its Social and Economic Significance* (R) [The question of agrarian capitalism – Lenin's criticism of Narodnik cry against 'blood-sucking' usurers – comparable to remarks against rural moneylending and the Green Revolution current in Third World radical literature today] Vol IV (pp 67-9).

(14) *Once More on the Theory of Realisation* (A) [A reply to Struve's comments on Lenin's Note on the Question of the Market Theory (11) above] Vol IV (pp 74-93) [☆].

(15) *Review. Karl Kautsky Die Agrarfrage* (R) [On Capitalism in Agriculture] Vol IV (pp 94-9).

(16) *Review. J.A. Hobson The Evolution of Modern Capitalism* (R) Vol IV (pp 100-3).

(17) *Capitalism in Agriculture* (Kautsky's book and Mr. Bulgakov's Article) (A) [Once again on capitalist relations in agriculture; relevant for current discussion on the Green Revolution] Vol IV (pp 109-165) [☆]*.

(18) *Review. S.N. Prokopovich The Working-Class Movement in the West* (R) [Prokopovich a follower of Bernstein – A Marxist polemic against revisionism] Vol IV (pp 183-192).

(19) *Review. Karl Kautsky. Bernstein und das Sozialdemokratische Programm. Eine Antikritik* [Theory of capitalist crises – Lenin's favourable (to Kautsky) polemic] Vol IV (pp 193-203).

(20) *The Workers' Party and the Peasantry* (Casual Notes) [Class structure in agriculture] Vol IV (pp 420-8).

(21) *The Agrarian Question and the 'Critics of Marx'* (B) [On Chernov and Bulgakov's criticism of Kautsky: Relevant for current discussion of agrarian relations in less developed countries as also the question of Agrarianism that Georgeseu-Roegen has raised] Vol V (pp 103-222).

(22) *Concerning the State Budget* (A) [Comments on Witte's budget of 1902 – Marxist critique of budget deficits] Vol V (pp 331-6).

(23) *From the Economic Life of Russia – 1*. The Savings Banks (A) [Article in *Iskra* purported to be first of a series on Russia's economic life in economic development] Vol VI (pp 86-90).

(24) *The Agrarian Programme of Russian Social Democracy* (P) [Socialist policy on land reform etc.] Vol VI (pp 107-150).

(25) *Marxist Views on the Agrarian Question in Europe and in Russia* [Notes on a planned lecture course] Vol VI (pp 341-7).

(26) *To the Rural Poor: An Explanation for the Peasants of What the Social-Democrats Want*1 (P) [Explaining (24) above from a popular angle]

Vol VI (pp 365-432) [✰].

(27) *Marx on the American 'General Redistribution'* (A) [Relating to an article of Marx in 1876 on the agrarian problem in USA] Vol VIII (pp 323-9).

(28) *Revision of the Agrarian Programme of the Workers' Party* (P) [On the agrarian reform programme] Vol X (pp 165-195).

(29) *The Agrarian Question and the 'Critics of Marx'* (P) [On David's book Socialism and Agriculture; is the use of machines in agriculture of a capitalist character? – the viability of small-scale production in agriculture – related to (21) above – relevant to current discussion of Green Revolution] Vol XIII (pp 171-216) [✰].

(30) *The Agrarian Programme of Social-Democracy in the First Russian Revolution 1905-1907* (B) [Agrarian class structure, agrarian reform, capitalism and agriculture] Vol XIII (pp 217-431) [✰].

(31) *The Agrarian Question in Russia towards the close of the Nineteenth Century* (P) [A factual survey; not much discussion of rival political programmes] Vol XV (pp 69-147).

(32) *Autoabstract (summary) of the Agrarian Programme* [(30) above] Vol XV (pp 158-181).

(33) *The Question of Co-operative Societies at the International Socialist Congress in Copenhagen* (A) [Are workers co-operatives socialist? Interesting in light of Lenin's interest after 1917 in co-operatives as an 'intermediate' form of economic organisation] Vol XVI (pp 275-283).

(34) *Strike statistics in Russia* (A) [Analysis of strike data in Marxist terms – especially the relation of type of industry in which workers are employed to political consciousness and the question of economic as against political demands in strikes – related to Gramsci's work and relevant for current efforts at 'controlling' unions] Vol XVI (pp 393-422)*.

(35) *The Capitalist System of Modern Agriculture* (A) [Employment of hired labour and machinery in forms and growth of capitalist relations in agriculture] Vol XVI (pp 423-446) [✰].

(36) *A Questionnaire on the Organisations of Big Capital* (A) [Concentration of capital in Russia; Big Business as a *stratum* rather than a *class*] Vol XVIII (pp 56-72).

(37) *The Essence of 'The Agrarian Problem in Russia'* (A) [Difference between Russian and European agrarian problem in terms of the degree of capitalist development] Vol XVIII (pp 73-7).

(38) *Economic and Political Strikes* (A) [Relationships between economic and political strikes; related to (34) above] Vol XVIII (pp 83-90)*.

(39) *Capitalism and Popular Consumption* (A) [Analysis of international data on margarine consumption to show that 'the diet of the people deteriorates as capitalism develops'] Vol XVIII (pp 224-6).

(40) *Workers' Earnings and Capitalist Profits in Russia* (A) [Analysis of income data in manufacturing industry for 1908 relating the figures to rate of exploitation] Vol XVIII (pp 256-7).

(41) *The Strike Movement and Wages* (A) [Effect of increase in strikes to wages data for 1901-1910] Vol XVIII (pp 258-9).

(42) *The Working Day in the Factories of Moscow Gubernia* and *The Working Day and Working Year in Moscow Gubernia* (A) [Analysis of a book on working day in Russia in 1908] Vol XVIII (pp 260-9).

(43) *Concentration of Production in Russia* (A) [Growth of large scale

industries etc, related to (36) above] Vol XVIII (pp 272-3).

(44) *Impoverishment in Capitalist Society* (A) [Analysis of German data on relative impoverishment in Russia] Vol XVIII (pp 435-6).

(45) Big Landlord and Small Peasant Ownership in Russia (A) [Analysis of land data on anniversary of abolition of serfdom] Vol XVIII (pp 586-7).

(46) *A 'Scientific' System of Sweating* (A) [Length of the working day and Taylor's system; related to (40) and (42) above; also interesting in light of Lenin's discussion of Taylor's contributions after 1917] Vol XVIII (pp 594-5).

(47) *Our 'Achievements'* (A) [Russia's backwardness contrasted with America's growth – Russian capitalism is underdeveloped] Vol XVIII (pp 596-7).

(48) *'Spare Cash'* (A) [Analysis of budget surplus of 1913] Vol XVIII (pp 601-2).

(49) *Is the Condition of the Peasantry Improving or Worsening?* (A) [Analysis of questionnaires for 1907-1912] Vol XIX (pp 96-8).

(50) *Factory Owners on Workers' Strikes* (A) [Data for 1912 on strikes; related to (38) and (41) above] Vol XIX (pp 125-131)*.

(51) *The Question of the (General) Agrarian Policy of the Present Government* (A) [Stolypin's policies analysed] Vol XIX (pp 180-196).

(52) *Capitalism and Taxation* (A) [Incidence of direct and indirect taxes in USA] Vol XIX (pp 197-200).

(53) *Economic Strikes in 1912 and in 1905* (A) [Industrial strike data analysed for 1905, 1911 and 1912; see (50) above] Vol XIX (pp 201-2).

(54) *The Growth of Capitalist Wealth* (A) [Concentration of wealth] Vol XIX (pp 203-5).

(55) *The Peasantry and the Working Class* (A) [Wage labour in capitalist agriculture; international data cited] Vol XIX (pp 206-8).

(56) *Child Labour in Peasant Farming* (A) [See (55) above] Vol XIX (pp 209-212).

(57) *The Results of Strikes in 1912 as Compared with Those in the Past* (A) [More data than in (53) above] Vol XIX (pp 213-5).

(58) *Petty Production in Agriculture* (A) [Proportion of female labour employed in an industry as indicator of advanced capitalist stage of its development] Vol XIX (pp 280-2).

(59) *Mobilisation of Allotment Lands* (A) [Data on growing concentration of land; is abolition of private property in land a socialist measure?] Vol XIX (pp 288-291).

(60) *How Can Per Capita Consumption in Russia be Increased?* (A) [How feudalism retards capitalist development in Russia] Vol XIX (pp 292-4).

(61) *Iron on Peasant Farms* (A) [Feudalism as a cause of backward, unmechanised agriculture; Hungarian and Russian data] Vol XIX (pp 309-310).

(62) *Metal Workers' Strikes in 1912* (A) [Strike data analysed by industry, region and success/failure, see (53) and (57) above] Vol XIX (pp 311-324).

(63) *New Land 'Reform' Measures* (A) ['protection of small farmers' as a reactionary move] Vol XIX (pp 337-9).

(64) *The Language of Figures* (A) [Data on factories, wages etc, higher wages resulting in more advanced capitalist industries] Vol XIX (pp 358-363).

(65) *Bourgeois Gentlemen on 'Family' Farming* (A) [*Does the family farm*

have any future?] Vol XIX (pp 364-5).

(66) *The Land Question and the Rural Poor* (A) [Against the Narodnik solution of voluntary co-operatives for small farms] Vol XIX (pp 376-8).

(67) *The Liberals and the Land Problem in Britain* (A) [On Lloyd George's campaign for a radical land reform in 1913 – the importance of labour movement for radical politics in Britain] Vol XIX (pp 439-442).

(68) *Capitalism and Workers' Immigration* (A) [European immigration to America] Vol XIX (pp 454-7).

(69) *Strikes in Russia* (A) [Data from 1895-1912 by region, industry and scale] Vol XIX (pp 534-8).

(70) *The Purpose of Zemstvo Statistics* (A) [On the purpose and interpretation of economic statistics] Vol XX (pp 82-8).

(71) *The Peasantry and Hired Labour* (A) [On the proportion of hired labour by size classes of farms] Vol XX (pp 111-3).

(72) *The Taylor System – Man's Enslavement by the Machine* (A) [Related to (46) above] Vol XX (pp 152-4).

(73) *Farm Labourers' Wages* (A) [On relative wages in agriculture and industry – backwardness of feudal agriculture] Vol XX (pp 174-6).

(74) *Socialism Demolished Again* (A) [Review of Struve's book on the Russian economy] Vol XX (pp 187-208).

(75) *The Estimates of the Ministry of Agriculture* (A) [On Stolypin's agrarian reforms] Vol XX (pp 313-8).

(76) *Marx's Economic Doctrine* (P) [Part of a pamphlet on Marx] Vol XXI (pp 59-81).

(77) *New Data Governing the Development of Capitalism in Agriculture – Part One Capitalism and Agriculture in the USA* (B) [Regional, size group and intersectoral data on the impact of rapid capitalist development on agriculture when there are no feudal obstacles] Vol XXII (pp 13-102).

(78) *Preface to N. Bukharin's Pamphlet, Imperialism and the World Economy* (a) [A precursor of Lenin's own work on imperialism] Vol XXII (pp 103-7).

(79) *Imperialism, the Highest Stage of Capitalism* (P) [International concentration of capital and division of labour and power] Vol XXII (pp 185-304).

(80) *Resolution on the Agrarian Question* (A) [Resolution at April 1917 conference of the RSDLPCB] Vol XXIV (pp 290-3).

(81) *Draft Resolution and Speech on the Agrarian Question* (A) [Resolution at the All Russia Congress of Peasants' Deputies, May 17] Vol XXIV (pp 483-505).

(82) *The Impending Catastrophe and How to Combat it* (A) [First time Lenin discusses economic policy that he would propose for a Bolshevik Government – nationalisation of Banks etc – written before the October Revolution] Vol XXV (pp 319-365) [✩]*.

(83) *Original Version of the Article 'The Immediate Tasks of the Soviet Government' Verbatim Report* (P) [More on economic policy tasks of the Soviet Government, March 1918] Vol XXVII (pp 203-218).

(84) *Theses on Banking Policy* (Notes) [Bank nationalisation but also accounting and regulation of the socialistically organised economic life of the country as a whole] Vol XXVII (pp 222-3).

(85) *Speech on the Financial Question at the Session of the All-Russia*

C.E.C., April 18, 1918 (A) [Problem of central coordination in taxation policy] Vol XXVII (pp 227-8).

(86) *The Immediate Tasks of the Soviet Government* (P) [Full version of (83) above – problems of accounting and control and of centralisation/decentralisation] Vol XXVII (pp 237-277)*.

(87) *Basic Propositions on Economic and Especially Banking Policy* (A) [Nationalisation/co-operativisation/centralisation] Vol XXVII (pp 318-9).

(88) *Report to the All-Russia Congress of Representatives of Financial Departments of Soviets, May 18 1918* (A) [Finances/taxation/currency problems] Vol XXVII (pp 383-7).

(89) *Letter Addressed to the Conference of Representatives of Enterprises to Be Nationalised, May 18 1918* [Economic management of nationalised industries/labour discipline] Vol XXVII (pp 388-9).

(90) *Speech at the First Congress of Economic Councils* (A) [Problems of Socialist planning – on using bourgeois experts – labour discipline] Vol XXVII (pp 408-415)*.

(91) *Report on Combating the Famine, June 4 1918* (A) [Problems of food procurement/learning from the bourgeoisie in framing socialist economic policy] Vol XXVII (pp 421-439)*.

(92) *Report of the Council of People's Commissars to the Fifth All-Russia Congress of Soviets* (A) [Parts of the speech from p 515 on are concerned with economic problems of planning, workers' control, food procurement] Vol XXVII (pp 507-528)[*].

(93) *Theses on the Food Question* (A) [On food procurement, terms of trade to be fixed between food and manufacturing products, on the tax in kind to which Lenin devotes more space later] Vol XXVIII (pp 45-7)*.

(94) *Speech to the First All-Russia Congress of Land Departments, Poor Peasants' Committees and Communes, December 11 1918* (A) [On Socialist reform in agriculture and the problems of small peasants] Vol XXVIII (pp 338-348).

(95) *Speech to the Second All-Russia Congress of Economic Councils, December 25 1918* (A) [On planning, on the collegiate system of management and individual responsibility, co-operatives etc] Vol XXVIII (pp 375-381).

(96) *Speech at a Joint Session of the All Russia Central Executive Committee, the Moscow Soviet and All-Russia TUC January 7 1919* (A) [On food policy, profiteers and bureaucrats] Vol XXVIII (pp 391-406).

(97) *Measures Governing the Transition from Bourgeois-Co-operative to Proletarian-Communist Supply and Distribution* (A) [Is the co-operative a commune?] Vol XXVIII (pp 443-4)*.

(98) *Draft Programme of the R.C.P.(B)* (P) [Sections on tasks in the economic and agricultural sphere] Vol XXIX (pp 99-140)[*].

(99) *Resolution on the Attitude to the Middle Peasants* (A) [On agrarian policy and class distinctions] Vol XXIX (pp 217-220).

(100) *The Food and War Situation* (A) [On problems of free trade in grain] Vol XXIX (pp 520-531).

(101) *Freedom to Trade in Grain* (A) [See (100) above] Vol XXIX (pp 567-570).

(102) *Economics and Politics in the Era of the Dictatorship of the Proletariat* (P) [Achievements of economic policy of Soviet Union] Vol

XXX (pp 107-117).

(103) *Speech Delivered at the First Congress of Agricultural Communes and Agricultural Artels, December 4 1919* (A) [Assisting communes, agrarian policy under socialism] Vol XXX (pp 195-204).

(104) *A Letter to R.C.P. Organisations on Preparations for the Party Congress* (A) [On economic achievements and tasks] Vol XXX (pp 403-7) [*].

(105) *Speech Delivered at the Third All-Russia Congress of Water Transport Workers* (A) [On corporate management or individual management] Vol XXX (pp 426-432).

(106) *Preliminary Draft Theses on the Agrarian Question – For the Second Congress of the Communist International* (A) [On agrarian relations in different economies] Vol XXXI (pp 152-164).

(107) *Speech Delivered at a Meeting of Activists of the Moscow organisation of R.C.P.(B) Dec 6 1920* (A) [On concessions as a weapon of economic policy] Vol XXXI (pp 438-459).

(108) *The Eighth All-Russia Congress of Soviets* (P) [On concessions, foreign trade, planning and the need for reestablishing large scale industry] vol XXXI (pp 463-533)[*].

(109) *The Trade Unions, the Present Situation and Trotsky's Mistakes* (A) [On role of trade unions in the transition to socialism; refers repeatedly to a pamphlet of Trotsky's] Vol XXXII 19-42).

(110) *Once Again on the Trade Unions, the Current Situation and the Mistakes of Trotsky and Bukharin* (P) [Another chapter in the heated controversy on the role of trade unions in economic management and political decision making referred to above in (109)] Vol XXXII (pp 70-107).

(111) *Rough Draft of Theses Concerning the Peasants* (A) [First mention of the question of tax in kind – role of compulsory procurement versus market purchase of surplus grain; beginning of one aspect of NEP] Vol XXXII (pp 133).

(112) *Letter on Oil Concessions* (A) [Benefits from inviting foreign capital in a less developed country] Vol XXXII (pp 134-6).

(113) *Integrated Economic Plan* (A) [Electrification and planning] Vol XXXII (pp 137-145)*.

(114) *Tenth Congress of R.C.P.(B)* (P) [Many portions of Report on the Political Work of the Central Committee and summing up speech on economic mistakes on food, fuel crisis, concession – all under the presence of Kronstadt – turning point before NEP] Vol XXXII (pp 167-271) [*].

(115) *Report on the Tax in Kind Delivered at a Meeting of Secretaries etc. of R.C.P.(B) Cells of Moscow and Moscow Gubernia April 9 1921* (P) [Further discussion of tax in kind mentioned in (111) and (114) above] Vol XXXII (pp 286-298).

(116) *Report on Concessions at a Meeting of the Communist Group of the All-Russia Central Council of Trade Unions April 11 1921* (P) [Precise conditions for acceptibility of concessions, i.e. foreign private capital] Vol XXXII (pp 300-315).

(117) *Plan of the Pamphlet The Tax in Kind* (A) [Plan of (118) below] Vol XXXII (pp 320-8).

(118) *The Tax in Kind – The Significance of the New Policy and Its*

Conditions (P) [On free trade in grain – an important plank of NEP, on overlapping modes of production in a backward economy and the general importance of trade as an antidote to bureaucracy, on cooperatives] Vol XXXII (pp 329-365)*.

(119) *To Comrade Krzhizhanovsky, The Presidium of the State Planning Commission* (A) [On priorities in planning] Vol XXXII (pp 371-4).

(120) *Instructions of the Council of Labour and Defence to Local Soviet Bodies* (P) [Economic Questions and NEP outlined in great detail – commodity exchange, role of capitalists etc] Vol XXXII (pp 375-398).

(121) *Tenth All-Russia Conference of the R.C.P.(B) May 26-28 1921* (P) [More on NEP and the Tax in Kind] Vol XXXII (pp 401-437).

(122) *The New Economic Policy and the Tasks of the Political Education Departments* (P) [The background and character of NEP – the principle of personal incentive discussed] Vol XXXIII (pp 60-79).

(123) *Seventh Moscow Gubernia Conference of the R.C.P.(B) October 1921 – Report on the N.E.P.* (P) [More on the NEP] Vol XXXIII (pp 83-108).

(124) *The Importance of Gold Now and After the Complete Victory of Socialism* (A) [On foreign trade in a socialist economy – reformism of NEP] Vol XXXIII (pp 109-116).

(125) *The Theses on the Agrarian Question Adopted by the C.P. of France* (A) [On policy in transition regarding confiscation of lands, on Marx on concentration of capital in agriculture etc] Vol XXXIII (pp 131-7).

(126) *Ninth All-Russia Congress of Soviets December 1921* (P) [On the success of NEP, compromises with capitalism, retreat into state capitalism etc] Vol XXXIII (pp 143-181).

(127) *The Role and Functions of the Trade Unions Under the N.E.P.* (A) [Further developments and decisions regarding trade unions controversy referred to above in (109)-(110)] Vol XXXIII (pp 184-196).

(128) *Eleventh Congress of the R.C.P.(B) March-April 1922* (P) [On state-capitalism in the Political Report and in the replies to Preobrazhensky] Vol XXXIII (pp 261-326).

(129) *Letter to Stalin etc Re: The Foreign Trade Monopoly* (A) [Why is the state monopoly of foreign trade not successful – importance of mixed companies, trade etc] Vol XXXIII (pp 375-8).

(130) Interview with Arthur Ransome Manchester Guardian Correspondent (A) [Questions on likely economic and political consequences of NEP] Vol XXXIII (pp 400-9).

(131) *Fourth Congress of the Comintern. November-December 1922* (P) [Report on the economy in 'Five Years of the Russian Revolution and the Prospects of the World Revolution'] vol XXXIII (pp 417-432) [*].

(132) *Re: The Monopoly of Foreign Trade* (A) [On Bukharin's critics of foreign trade monopoly discussed in (129) above] Vol XXXIII (pp 455-9).

(133) *On Co-operation* (A) [Can co-operatives form intermediate organisations in an economy in transition?] Vol XXXIII (pp 467-475)*.

Biographical Notes

Lenin's writings often contain references to people who are now forgotten. These notes cover every name I came across of any significance which was not totally familiar to me. Well known names (eg. Kerensky) are not included on the assumption that they are well-known and are included in any history of the revolution. In each case I have tried to locate dates of birth and death but in some cases the date of death has been difficult to find.

BOGAYEVSKY, Afrikan Petrovich (1872-1934)   General, prominent leader of the Don Cossacks. President of the White 'Don government' set up by General Kaledin in 1917. After Kaledin's defeat led the White Don Cossacks (kulak) contingent under Denikin (1918-1919) and Wrangel. Emigrated 1920.

BUBLIKOV, A (born 1875)   Russian manufacturer. Organised 'Progressist' group in the Duma, 1912-1917. In March 1917 occupied Ministry of Communications on behalf of the Provisional Government. In August 1917 attended the conference called by Kerensky and the Petrograd Soviets to oppose the Kornilov rising. Emigrated after the October Revolution.

BULGAKOV, Sergei Nikolayevich (1871-1927)   Economist and philosopher. In the 1890s a 'Legal Marxist', criticising Marx's views about the effect of capitalism on agriculture. Member of the 2nd Duma (1906-7). Later developed neo-Kantian views against materialist philosophy. After the October Revolution became a priest and emigrated, joining actively in anti-Soviet propaganda.

BULYGIN, Alexander Grigorievich (1851-1919)   Large landowner, governor of several provinces under Tsardom. Appointed Minister of the Interior after Bloody Sunday (January 1905), leaving active control of repressions to police chief Trepov. Issued regulations for so-called 'Bulygin Duma' (August 1905) under which peasants would have had 51 seats out of 412 (workers none). Idea was dropped after October General Strike. Dismissed and took no further part in politics.

CHERNOV, Victor Mihailovich (1873-1952)   Socialist Revolutionary Party leader from its beginning, took part in the anti-war conferences at Zimmerwald (1915) and Kienthal (1916), opposing Lenin and the Left. Minister of Agriculture in the May 1917 Coalition Government. Actively opposed the October Revolution, took part in the 'Constituent Assembly' counter-revolutionary government in 1918. Emigrated after it was overthrown by Kolchak.

CHERNYSHEVSKY, Nikolai Gavrilovich (1828-1889)   Revolutionary democrat, outstanding opponent of Tsardom, journalist and philosopher. His critical writings on literature and art, in the years of growing peasant revolt (1850-1860s) in the only legal progressive journals, *Otechestvennye Zapiski* and *Sovremennik*, had a profound influence on the educated classes in Russia, and on other contemporary progressive thinkers, through their courageous challenging of reaction. At the same time he took part in illegal propaganda work among the peasants and youth. Arrested in 1862, he spent two years in a fortress, untried, and then was sentenced to seven years hard labour followed by exile for life to Siberia. While still in the Peter and Paul Fortress he wrote a revolutionary novel *What Is To Be Done?* In Siberia he wrote another novel *Prologue* about the political struggle of the 1850s. Both were published legally only after his death. Allowed to retire to his native Saratov (Volga) in 1889, he died the same year. For many years it was officially forbidden to mention his name in print. A volume of his essays appeared in English in 1952.

DAN, Fyodor Illyich (1871-1947)   Originally (1896) member of the 'League of Struggle for the Emancipation of the Working Class' in St Petersburg. From 1903 one of the Mènshevik leaders, becoming a 'liquidator' (of the illegal party organisation) in the years after 1906. In 1914 led the pro-war ('social-patriot') Mensheviks. In March 1917 became one of the leaders of the then Menshevik and SR majority controlling the Petrograd Soviet and the All-Russian Central Executive Committee of Soviets. Opposed the October Revolution, but was allowed to speak for the Mensheviks in Soviet Congresses until he became involved in counter-revolutionary plots and was expelled (1922). Emigrated to Germany, later to the USA. In his book, *The Origins of Bolshevism* (USA, 1946) he made some concessions to the Bolshevik case.

DANIELSON, Nikolai Frantsevich (1844-1918)   Liberal economist, chief theoretical writer of the Narodniks. In 1860s took part in revolutionary youth groups, arrested in 1870. Completed Lopatin's translation into Russian of *Capital* Volume 1, when Lopatin was arrested, and between 1886 and 1896 translated Volume II and III. Wrote under the pen-name of Nik.-on. In his correspondence with Engels, he showed a grasp of capitalist developments in Russia, but developed Narodnik views on its future (after Marx's death). His main work (1893) was *Outlines of Our Social Economy Since the Reform*.

DENIKIN, Anton Ivanovich (1872-1947)   Tsarist general. Took an active part in Kornilov's rebellion. Commanded the White 'Volunteer Army' in Southern Russia 1918-1920. On his defeat handed over to Wrangel and emigrated (1920). His memoirs appeared in Berlin in 1925.

GEGECHKORI, Yevgeni Petrovich (1881-1934)   Georgian Menshevik leader. After the October Revolution negotiated with the US consul in Tiflis about financial aid for an anti-Soviet Transcaucasian government, in which he was Foreign and Labour Minister. Later a member of the Georgian Menshevik government, emigrated when it was overthrown.

GOTZ, Abram Rafailovich (1882-1937)   SR delegate to the Petrograd Soviet in 1917. Later member of the All-Russian Central Executive Committee of Soviets up to the October Revolution. Joined the 'Committee of Salvation', which united several anti-Bolshevik organisations immediately after November 7, and tried to stimulate armed attacks on the Soviet government, first by Krasnov's troops in the Petrograd region, then by those of the Army GHQ at Mogilev. Worked for the State Bank thereafter, but in 1922 was tried with a number of others for conspiracy to organise terrorist acts against Soviet leaders, and White risings in various parts of Russia. Sentenced to death, but execution deferred on condition SRs ceased terrorist campaign. Later, after release, emigrated.

KAUTSKY, Karl (1854-1938)   Leading theoretician of the German Social-Democrats. Founded and edited (1883-1917) their Marxist journal *Neue Zeit*. Opposed the revisionist campaign launched in the SDP by Eduard Bernstein (1899), but did little to prevent its later successes, and in 1914 refused to attack the pro-war Socialists, either in Germany or elsewhere. After the October Revolution virulently attacked the Bolsheviks. His better-known earlier works were *Economic Doctrines of Karl Marx* (1887), *The Agrarian Question* (1899), *Bernstein and the Social-Democratic Programme* (1899), *Ethics and the Materialist Conception of History* (1906) and *Foundations of Christianity* (1908).

KISHKIN, Nikolai Mihailovich (1864-1930)   Doctor by profession, politically a Liberal (Cadet). Commissioner of the Provisional Government. Opposed the October Revolution, but was soon released. In 1919 became a member of the secret 'Tactical Centre', which sought to unite several terrorist organisations without success. In 1920 he and other members of the 'Centre' were put on trial, and he was sentenced to five years imprisonment – a sentence he did not serve out. In 1921, during the Famine, he was allowed to form, with other liberals, an unofficial 'Famine Relief Committee', distinct from the State Committee; but this was dissolved. However Kishkin and others were found to be using their contacts for counter-revolutionary propaganda. Worked until his death in People's Commissariat for Health of RSFSR.

KOLCHAK, Alexander Vasilievich (1870-1920)   Tsarist Admiral (had served in the navy in the Russo-Japanese war and in the 1914 war). In 1917 was in Japan on a mission, sent by Kerensky, when the October Revolution took place. Returning to Siberia, he became War Minister in the 'Constituent Assembly' government at Omsk, but almost immediately seized power (November 1918), with the approval of the British military mission (Colonel Ward) and the leaders of the Czechoslovak Legions which had revolted in the summer against the Soviet government. Financial and arms help from Great Britain enabled him to raise an army of about 100,000 men. At first he advanced across the Urals, and was recognised by the Allies as a 'Supreme Ruler' of Russia, but was almost immediately defeated by the Red Army (January 1919), and began a long retreat which ended in his capture, court-martial and execution (February 1920).

KORNILOV, Lavr Georgievich (1890-1918)   Siberian Cossack general, appointed army commander, Petrograd region, by the Provisional Government (March 1917) and later Commander-in-Chief (July 1917). Attempted a military coup against Kerensky in September, but was defeated, both armed workers and soldiers resisting him. Fled to Ukraine, where he began organising a White Army, but was killed in action in April 1918.

KOZLOVSKY, A R   Former general, given command of artillery in Kronstadt fortress by Soviet authorities after October Revolution. Joined in the revolt there in March 1921. On March 2 he was proclaimed as an outlaw, and on suppression of the revolt escaped to Finland.

KRASNOV, Pietr Nikolayevich (1869-1947)   Tsarist general. Took part in Kornilov's rebellion. After the October Revolution attempted to march on Petrograd in response to Kerensky's appeal, but was defeated. Released on his undertaking to cease fighting the Soviet Government, but immediately fled to the North Causasus, where he secured help from the German occupying forces in Ukraine in organising a counter-revolutionary army. Defeated in 1919, he fled to Germany, where he published memoirs. In 1939-41 cooperated with the Nazis. Captured by the Soviet Army, he was tried by the Soviet Supreme Court and sentenced to death.

LARIN, Yuri (Mihail Zalmanovich Lurye) (1882-1932)   Trade unionist and economist. An internationalist in 1914. Joined Bolsheviks in July 1917. During the negotiations with the Mensheviks and Left Socialist Revolutionaries, immediately after the October Revolution, was one of the Bolsheviks who resigned from the Soviet Government, in which he had been appointed secretary to a committee for drafting new laws. In after years he was prominent in the economic planning bodies, and spoke frequently at Soviet Congresses and Party meetings.

LUXEMBOURG, Rosa (1870-1919)   Born in Poland. Founder-member of the Social Democratic Party of Poland and Lithuania, after working in early years in the historic Marxist 'Proletariat' party. After graduating in Switzerland, settled in Germany (1898), where for the rest of her life she actively supported the left wing in the German working class movement, first in the SDP and then in leading the formation of the Spartacus League (January 1916) and then the Communist Party of Germany (1918). Opposing revisionism in peacetime, she fought 'socialist' chauvinism in the war of 1914-18. Her views on the nature of imperialism, expressed particularly in her work *The Accumulation of Capital* (1913) were criticised by Lenin. She was murdered by German officers in 1919.

MAISKY, Ivan Mihailovich (1883-1975)   Born in Siberia. One of the Menshevik leaders, specialising on trade union questions. Emigrated to London 1912-1917, where he became acquainted with the policies and practices of the labour movement. Returned after the overthrow of Tsardom. Opposed the October Revolution and took part in 1918 in the work of the 'Constituent Assembly' government at Samara and Omsk, but went into hiding after Kolchak's coup, and made his way into Soviet-held territory, where he wrote to Lenin recognising that the Bolsheviks had been right and the Mensheviks wrong. Admitted to the Communist Party, he held several diplomatic posts before working in London as Soviet Ambassador in 1932-1943. After the war he was a senior advisor at the Soviet Foreign Ministry.

MARTOV (Tsederbaum), Yuri Osipovich (1873-1923)   Leader of the Mensheviks after 1903, and of the internationalist wing of the Mensheviks during the 1914-18 war. Supported the Provisional Government in 1917 and opposed the October Revolution. During the Civil War refrained from counter-revolutionary activity, but emigrated with Soviet permission in 1921 to Germany. Until his death he edited the Menshevik anti-Soviet journal *Sotsialisticheski Vestnik* there.

MILYUKOV, Pavel Nikolayevich (1859-1943)   Liberal. Professor of history, Moscow. Led the Cadet Party in the Duma 1910-17. Appointed Foreign Minister in the first Provisional Government of 1917, but had to resign in May owing to his pro-war policy. Actively supported counter-revolution in Southern Russia from 1918, at first advocating cooperation with the Germans. After the Civil War emigrated to Paris, where he edited a 'Liberal' anti-Soviet journal *Poslednie Novosti*, until the Nazi occupation in 1940.

NEKRASOV, Nikolai Vissarionovich (1879-1940)   Cadet. Member of the Duma 1910-17. Minister of Communications in the Provisional Government March-July 1917, and Finance Minister August-September. From 1921 working in Central Union of Cooperative Societies (Centrosoyuz).

PALCHINSKY, P I   Engineer, with industrial and financial connections. Was Deputy Minister for Trade and Industry in the Kerensky government from mid-1917. After the October Revolution worked in Soviet business organisation.

PESHEKHONOV, Alexander Vasuievich (1867-1933)   Populist-Socialist. Member of the Duma, 1912-1917. Food Minister in the first Provisional Government (1917). Expelled from Russia in 1922 for counter-revolutionary activity.

PLEKHANOV, Georgi Valentinovich (1856-1918)   First outstanding theoretician of Marxism in Russia. Organised the Marxist 'Group for the Emancipation of Labour' abroad, which published and smuggled into Russia much Marxist literature. From 1903 supported the Mensheviks, but opposed the liquidationists in the years of reaction (1907-1910). In 1914 became actively pro-war and on return to Russia in 1917 violently opposed to Bolsheviks. Before his death condemned Savinkov's commitment to counter-revolution, saying that after 40 years fighting for the workers he would not help to shoot them down. Lenin called his works 'the best exposition of the philosophy of Marxism and of historical materialism'.

RYABUSHINSKY, Pavel Pavlovich (1871-1924)   Millionaire Moscow manufacturer. In 1914 helped to form the 'Progressist' party and published a reactionary newspaper *Utro Rossii* (suppressed 1918). In 1917 earned notoriety by prophesying that the Revolution would be strangled by 'the bony hand of hunger'. In Paris became leader of an anti-Soviet group of Russian ex-manufacturers.

SAVINKOV, Boris Victorovich (1879-1925)   Pre-1914 organiser of Socialist Revolutionary terrorist 'fighting groups'. Active supporter of 1914-18 war. Deputy Minister of War under Kerensky. After the October Revolution involved in many terrorist anti-Soviet activities, first inside Russia and then from abroad. Arrested when crossing the frontier illegally in 1924, and sentenced to 10 years imprisonment on renouncing his activities; committed suicide in 1925 when his request for immediate release was refused.

SCHEIDEMANN, Philipp (1865-1939)   Leader of opportunist wing in German SDP. Supported war in 1914-18. When Kaiser fled, became head of the German Government which suppressed revolutionary activities of the workers and sailors. Ousted in June 1919. Emigrated when Nazis came to power in 1933.

SKOROPADSKY, Pavel Petrovich (1873-1945)   Large landowner in Ukraine. Head ('Hetman') of a puppet government set up there in 1918 by the Germans. Fled with them to Germany when the Kaiser's government collapsed.

STOLYPIN, Pyotr Arkadievich (1862-1911)   Tsarist official, appointed Premier in July 1906 with mandate to crush the revolution (the gallows became known as 'Stolypin's necktie'). Author of agrarian laws of 1910-11 which promoted the break-up of the village community by encouraging richer peasants (kulaks) to set up separate farms, employing hired labour, in exchange for their strips in common land; thereby creating a new social basis of 'strong' peasantry for Tsardom. Assassinated in 1911 by the Secret Police agent Bagnev.

STRUVE, Pyotr Bernhardovich (1870-1944)   Baltic German (i.e. Russian subject). In the 1890s a 'legal Marxist', on the grounds that Marxism supported the capitalist development of Russia as against the landowning autocracy. In 1905 joined the Cadet party supporting a 'constitutional' monarchy against revolution. From 1917 onwards active in counter-revolution (abroad).

TERESHCHENKO, Mihail Ivanovich (1881-1950)   Millionaire sugar-manufacturer. Finance Minister in the first Provisional Government (March-May 1917), then Foreign Minister succeeding Milyukov. Emigrated after October Revolution.

TSERETELI, Iraklii Georgievich (1881-1958)   Georgian Menshevik leader, and Menshevik deputy in the 2nd Duma (1906-7). Represented Mensheviks in the Petrograd Soviet in 1917. Minister of Posts and Telegraphs in the Kerensky Government, then Minister of the Interior. After the October Revolution went to Georgia, where he became a leader of the Georgian Menshevik Government. Emigrated after its overthrow in 1921.

VORONTSOV, Vasili Pavlovich (1847-1918)   Ideologist of the Narodniks, writing under the pen-name V V.

WRANGEL, Pyotr Nikolayevich (1878-1928)   Member of old-established Baltic-German baronial family. Served in the Tsarist army. Took part in Kornilov's rebellion (August 1917). Served with Denikin 1918-1920, and took over from him when their 'Volunteer Army' was driven back into the Crimea. Defeated in his turn later that year. In France set up an emigrant 'Russian Military Union' in 1924.

Index